# Conversations with James Joyce

Arthur Power

# CONVERSATIONS
# WITH JAMES JOYCE

*edited by Clive Hart*

BARNES & NOBLE
BOOKS
10 East 53d St  New York 10022
(a division of Harper & Row Publishers, Inc.)

Published in the U.S.A. 1974 by
HARPER & ROW PUBLISHERS, INC.
BARNES & NOBLE IMPORT DIVISION

ISBN-06-495672-5

First published 1974 by millington ltd., 109 Southampton Row,
London WC1B 4HH

Printed in the Republic of Ireland by
Cahill & Co. Limited, Dublin.

# Foreword

While patient research has clarified many of the more recondite sources on which Joyce drew for the composition of his books, it has always been far from easy to determine how much of the main stream of European literature he had absorbed or what his literary tastes and opinions were. After his earliest adult years he wrote virtually no criticism, nor was he inclined to speak openly to the journalists and casual acquaintances who repeatedly sought to discover his views. Only a few friends were privileged to know anything of the real personality behind the courteous façade, friends who, with rare exceptions (like Hemingway), were not themselves literary men. Stuart Gilbert had been a judge; Frank Budgen was a painter; Arthur Power, a man of general culture and an art critic more or less by accident, was one of the even smaller number who succeeded in engaging Joyce in repeated and sustained conversation about literature and literary values.

Except for his sporadic and always highly specialized research into works of reference and comparatively rare books (much of it, in any case, carried out for him by willing amanuenses) Joyce was not often a great reader, and it is wise to be guarded in one's assumptions about the depth of his literary background. Arthur Power's conversations with Joyce reveal facets of that background which were previously either veiled or almost unknown. Joyce's interest in, and knowledge of, the great tradition of Russian prose writing can be seen to be more profound than one might have suspected, while his high opinion of Eliot (sometimes disputed) is now shown to be beyond question. Joyce's comments on literary theory are less than exciting, and as always he seems to have avoided prolonged discussion of his own books. Special interest is nevertheless to be found in one or two remarks about *Ulysses* and ' Work in Progress ', such as his response to Power's question about what happened between Bloom and Gerty MacDowell : ' Nothing happened between them. . . . It all took place in Bloom's imagination ', a remark which may help, by slightly altering the status of the first half of the ' Nausikaa ' chapter, to explain the rather different roles played by the girls three hours later, in the nighttown scenes.

Joyce and Power had a number of things in common. Both had left the Church at an early age; both escaped from Ireland, in which they found much to dislike. In the first chapter of this book, Arthur Power presents a refreshingly honest portrait of himself as a young man of direct and open character, eager, like Joyce, to immerse himself in a culture more exciting than anything his native country seemed able to offer. Although less disturbed by his own developing personality than Joyce had been, Power was vividly aware of comparable tensions, and his account of the important moment of his First Communion, in which waning religious conviction confronted a growing sexual interest, presents some analogies with the adolescent experience of Stephen Dedalus. There were nevertheless strong temperamental differences which, as Power reports, occasionally led Joyce to mild displays of courteous exasperation at his young friend's insistence on the worth of the literature which he had undertaken to defend. After a slightly insecure start (an experience shared by many of Joyce's acquaintances) the friendship between Power and the Joyce family flourished in the twenties, for, apart from his personal attractiveness, Power had the important virtue, in Joyce's eyes, of being not only Irish but also loquacious. The days of the composition of *Ulysses* were over, and Joyce no longer needed Irish friends to confirm or modify his recollection of the topography of Dublin, but during the period of ' Work in Progress ' he took every opportunity to listen to users of his native speech rhythms. In this Power served him well, and it seems that Joyce offered oblique thanks for his frequent friendly conversation by allowing him to double, in *Finnegans Wake*, with Frank le Poer ('Ghazi') Power, under the pseudonym 'gaspower'.

It is not only about literary topics that Power has something of value to say. He offers us many small insights into Joyce's daily habits and tastes in more mundane matters. Joyce's intense interest in the notorious Bywaters and Thompson case of 1922 provides hints for the possibility of further meanings in parts of *Finnegans Wake,* while the small vignettes which Power provides of Joyce and his family both at work and in more convivial circumstances are among the freshest to have been recorded. Very few of Joyce's Irish friends have been content to give us any extended account of the Joyce they knew; we are most fortunate that Arthur Power has now chosen to join their company.

CLIVE HART

# Preface

In these conversations I have tried to reconstruct some of the talks I had with Joyce at different times from notes taken when I returned home after spending an evening with him.

I realize how inadequate much of it is, for much that was said has been forgotten or is inadequately expressed, while to give an impression of a man of such talent one would have to have talent equal to his own, as deep a consciousness of the social and psychological changes of his time as he had, and the same almost agonized gift for expressing it.

Also I see that being of a different temperament and opinion I have been too occupied with expressing my own point of view. All I can say is that that is how it was, since I was very talkative, while Joyce was naturally silent.

At the time these conversations took place I was a romantically inclined young man. My point of view has changed and coincides more with his, but such was it then, and as such I have left it. In order to give the reader a clearer notion of my youthful personality and interests, I have prefaced the book with a brief account of my early life in Ireland, London and Paris.

A.P.

# I

## PRELUDE

An early love of France must have been instinctive, for when I was only fourteen I remember I persuaded my mother that we should spend our Christmas holidays at Boulogne, arguing that it would be a great opportunity to improve our French. Crossing the Channel in a paddle steamer, we stayed at a grumbling old hotel full of long passages, half-way up a wide cobbled street on a steep hill. Opposite was the huge gothic pile of the church where we went for Mass on Sundays, and where I was immediately fascinated by the difference between the ceremony I had known in England and Ireland, and that in France. Inside the church a woman in a black knitted shawl and a scarf on her head hired out wooden chairs to the congregation, high backed, narrow and very uncomfortable, which made kneeling a penance, and which scraped noisily on the stone floor when turned around to be sat on for the sermon. Then there were the small pieces of bread which were handed around in a basket before the Communion; and that round black silk bag on the end of the long stick, pushed along in front of the worshippers to collect the sous; and finally the magnificent beadle in his three-cornered hat and gold-tipped staff, breeches and silk stockings, who strode with such an authoritative air in contrast to the shuffling old man in his ordinary black suit who used to function in the church in Hampstead to which my school had been taken on Sundays.

In my afternoons I used to wander about this foreign town

delighted to sit in the cafés listening to the babble of a foreign tongue of which I already understood something, and enjoying the different smells and tastes—much better smells and tastes than I had ever known before. I used to murmur to myself contentedly: 'This is what pleases me.' For I felt more at home here than I did in my own country, or in London.

At school in Hampstead I had only known the brutality of a horde of rough boys herded together, a violent and cruel world which I hated and in which I in turn was hated, so that my life was a wilderness from which there seemed to be no escape. I must have been unusually sensitive, which is a matter of regret since it gave others a great opportunity to prey on me, but some of my unhappiness was relieved one day when a young and attractive French mistress arrived. I immediately recognized her difference from the other prim-faced, raw-boned women who generally taught us. During the school walks I used to be allowed to walk beside her, while on her other side—and it seems to have been my fate all my life—was a tall blond boy called Rusborne who was the one she was really interested in, a silent and self-possessed youth who, in contrast to my ardent feelings, appeared to be quite indifferent to the affection she showed him.

Time has blurred my impressions, and now I only see my youth in a dim haze in which certain things stand out in cameo, while others have been lost. But my memory of Mademoiselle is one of the clearest, and she must have been attractive for I remember that young men, as we approached on our walks, used to lean against a brick wall as we passed, and say to her, ' Miss, can we join your school? '

On these walks she would talk about Paris, and I remember her descriptions of that gay and what seemed to me entrancing world. ' Ah, Paris ', she used to exclaim, ' that is something! Here it is nothing but fog and rain ', and she would go on to describe the Opéra where her father was a member of the orchestra—' *une scène superbe—les loges . . .* ' filled with ' *des gens chics* ' for an opera by Verdi, or by Rossini. Then she would go on to describe the boulevards outside, a blaze of lights, the cafés crowded with people. She told me once, in a moment of bubbling youth and confidence, how when her young admirer came to the house she used to amuse herself curling his moustaches.

Her descriptions of Parisian life haunted my youthful imagination, stemming from a source I did not know, though it has since occurred to me that she must have stirred up some latent atavism since I am a Power, the Irish corruption of Poer—or Poher—the name of a family of Norman extraction who came over to Ireland centuries ago with Strongbow to settle around Waterford. Our family arms are of French origin—a stag bearing a cross between its antlers, taken from the legend of St Hubert, with the device underneath: *Per Crucem ad Coronam*.

Also the French origin of my family had been accentuated by my grandmother, a Miss Kane, who had been brought up in France and married my grandfather at the British Embassy in Paris. When she came to Waterford as a bride, the first thing she did was to break up the massive square Georgian front of the family mansion with a hexagonal two-tiered balcony of granite which jutted out in the semblance of a French château. She filled the hall and library with tapestries from Lyons and Courtray, 'The Descent of Persephone into Hades' being one, 'The Meeting of King Solomon and the Queen of Sheba' another. In the library she placed a very large tapestry of Neptune driving his sea-horses through a torrent of foam. The drawing-room she furnished with gilt-and-marble consul tables and a suite of Louis XVI chairs and settees upholstered with bergère prints of elegant shepherdesses in amorous conversation with equally amorous and well-dressed shepherds, all belonging to a world which is now much past, the aristocratic one.

My visit there when very young must have imprinted itself on my imagination in that period of life when all is surmise and dream: that old Georgian house with its tapestries, gilt furniture, mirrors, and the powder-blue bergère drawing-room suite, surrounded by lawns and shrubs, the river sparkling through the trees at the bottom of the field in front, trees which my grandmother had planted to hide the turbulent and ever-restless river Suir which, being tidal, was always in violent flood either up to Waterford city or racing down between its widely-spread mud banks as it foamed around the shipping buoys. I, who never knew her, was told that she had tried to shut it out.

It was to the French Mademoiselle that I gave my youthful and ardent affection. Twice in the week we used to be sent to the small Roman Catholic Church in Hampstead for instruction by an Irish priest, a handsome and saintly old man with a skin like parchment. We boys used to sit on a bench in the sacristy surrounded by the odour of incense, flowers and vestments. Even then I remember that I was not much impressed by his religious arguments, a fact which he noticed, sensing, as he must have done, a future rebel. I remember his stopping in the middle of his instruction, looking at me and saying, ' I know what is going to happen to you ', words which I still remember even though I did not then understand their meaning. I think he must have meant that I would not remain a believing member of the Roman Catholic community. I nevertheless looked forward to the great day with some excitement, hoping that, in the manner of a miracle, a sudden and mystical event would change my world, and bring me happiness.

At the ceremony Mademoiselle, the daughter of a musician, was to play the organ, and I remember my delight when she told me that she had chosen me to work the organ pump, offering the gallant excuse that I was a strong boy! My anticipated pleasure at being alone with her in the music loft before my First Communion was much reduced when I found I had to stand in a dark cobwebbed hole working an old-fashioned wooden handle up and down. Indeed, I was so bored and tired by it that I stopped several times so that the organ produced only a faint squeak, when she cried out, ' *Qu'est-ce qui se passe, alors?* ' More from love than from duty, I started to pump again, but this was certainly not my idea of preparation for the reception of the Holy Sacrament.

When the supreme moment arrived she called me out and we knelt together against the railing of the choir-loft looking down into the church, and then—a moment which I have remembered with great clarity over the years—as I rose to go down she kissed me on the mouth. I descended those narrow twisting stairs into the church to receive divine love with the imprint of human love on my lips—something which I have tried to repeat all my life.

I do not believe that any Englishwoman, or Irishwoman either (though that is more possible), would have acted as she did. But with the Latins, love is given a mystical quality. It is the outcome of generations of Roman Catholicism. When I was in Spain I used to be fascinated by the photographs of the young Spanish bridal couples I saw in the glass cases outside the photographers' shops: those dark-skinned, smooth-cheeked, serious-looking brides in their white lace mantillas surmounted with a tortoise-shell comb, and the bridegroom equally serious in his white shirt front and dress suit, so that one felt that there should be something sacramental in the consummation.

French marriages are more material, perhaps, but one feels nevertheless something of the same sanctity, and no doubt it was that which made Mademoiselle arrange for me to be with her in the music loft, and which led her to kiss me before I went down to communion—a finesse and intrigue which were particularly French.

Needless to say, I passed a day of supreme happiness for my hope that my world would be transformed had come true, although in a way which was more surprising than I had foreseen. I took care to remain alone as much as possible for the rest of that day in case some rough contact should disturb my feeling of sanctity. All this now seems a long way off, but these memories occur to me in retrospection to explain why I always had a vision of France, and above all of Paris, in the back of my mind.

It was not until the end of the First World War when, after innumerable medical boards, I was released from the Army, that I was able to realize my ambition. First I went to Italy, stopping in Florence, where I enjoyed the parties in the old palaces, the turbulent Arno flowing past their walls, and that famous house-bearing Jeweller's Bridge some hundred yards further down. The modern Florentines seemed as gay and amusing as their lively forebears.

Then I went on to Rome, where I visited museum after museum, but in the end these massive collections from the past depressed me, I, who wanted art to be a living thing, and to visit the studios where it was being created and meet the men who were creating it, with the paint still wet on their canvases, or in the case of a writer, to see his written corrections on the page. In other words, Paris was my objective.

So it was after this journey through Italy to Pisa, Florence and Rome, that at last I arrived in the French capital, worn out by the troublesome journey, for at that time everything in Italy was on strike. I had taken one of the rare overfilled trains in which officials spent their time going up and down the corridors abusing the passengers and kicking their luggage out of the way, piled as it was in the corridors. At last I tumbled out, thankful to have reached journey's end, and entered the Hôtel Terminus attached to the Gare St Lazare, a noisy bustling place rather like the station itself with its continual comings and goings, and the masses of luggage piled in the hall.

After exploring the city for a couple of days I decided to move out to the Latin Quarter where the students and, as I believed, the artists, lived. I was delighted to find an hotel in the Place de la Sorbonne facing the brilliantly lit Café d'Harcourt. The Hôtel Moderne, as it was called, was nothing much in itself except that in contrast to its name it was very old, with walls over a yard thick and small low-ceilinged rooms.

Not knowing a soul in the city, I used to wander about, walking everywhere, for Paris is too interesting to be hurried through in a bus or in the Métro. My evenings I spent on the Boulevard St Michel sauntering past the students' cafés. I looked around for artists, and though I saw an occasional black hat and flowing tie, they were few and scattered, and so eventually tiring of the brash energy of the students I would go for long walks up to the heights of Montmartre, where I knew that many great Impressionists had lived and had their studios. But the district of Montmartre had undergone great changes since their day, and the Boulevard Clichy was now full of sleazy joints, and expensive night clubs, where all America and Europe came to debauch themselves. It was only up on the heights around the Church of the Sacré Coeur that it was quieter, and from that height, leaning over a time-blackened wall, I could see all Paris lying below me bathed in light.

For some ill-defined reason I felt that the present-day artists had migrated elsewhere, for the people one saw sitting on the café terraces were obviously everyday folk or foreign and provincial pleasure seekers. I set off in search again, when one evening, travelling by chance past the tree-enclosed darkness at the top end of the Luxembourg Gardens, I entered a boulevard. Half-way along it I came on a café with lively-looking young men sitting on the terrace. As I sat down I overheard them, to my delight, discussing art, invoking the names of Degas, Renoir, and other artists. After a while I got into conversation with a lively and witty young man sitting at the next table who, as it turned out, was the sculptor Zadkine.

Perhaps because he had been brought up in England he was more sympathetic to the casual Englishman or Irishman than were the others, and one day he invited me around to his studio to see his work.

It was in an alley-way off the rue de Sèvres, and one entered through a wicket-gate across a vine-trellised courtyard. To the right was the entrance, and going up some steps one was enclosed for a moment in complete darkness before emerging on a landing to be faced with the door of his studio. A very large room, one corner of it was filled with a big window made up of innumerable panes, which always reminded me of the window in Rembrandt's picture of 'The Philosopher'. The wide floor was covered with Zadkine's sculptures. At the entrance stood a life-sized figure in wood, 'St John the Baptist'—hollow-cheeked and spare-ribbed, the man of locusts and honey; beside it was the figure of a nude girl in white marble enveloped in a shimmering wing—'Leda and the Swan'; in a corner against the right wall he showed me a

17

group of insect-like figures on a wood base bowed down in tribulation around a single recumbent figure—'Job and his Comforters'.

At the far end was a partition curtained off around a stove, its black pipe winding in snake-like contortions up the wall and finally disappearing out of the window. Set in this alcove were a table, some chairs, and a book-case filled with books.

Zadkine was an amusing and voluble conversationalist, who when he mentioned the word 'sculpture' gave it a peculiarly sensual inflection. Imprisoned in every piece of wood or stone, so he explained, he saw a recumbent form waiting to be released. In the neglected trunk of a tree he had seen this 'John the Baptist', and had released him; in that piece of white marble had been imprisoned his 'Leda and the Swan'. And, showing me the heavy chunk of wood he was then working on: 'In that', he declared, 'lives the most exciting deer you ever imagined, all the way from the Steppes of Russia, now to be released by me in my Paris studio.' Taking me to the window, he pointed into the courtyard where I could see two tall trunks of yellow wood carved into archaic figures, which had been stacked there because they were too large to fit into the studio. 'Gog and Magog', he declared, 'taken from the forest of Vincennes, and now enjoying the amenities of my beautiful courtyard. Sculpture should be a living thing. In the early morning it lies in sleep, then as the light strengthens it awakes, changing hour by hour until at mid-day it reaches its zenith like a rose, or like a woman in the moment of love. And then in the evening it closes up again like a flower, to be reborn in the first light.' While he talked he made me coffee in a Bedouin coffee-pot with a hammered brass base and a decorated spout.

I suppose that in spite of my desire to consort with artists and bohemians I had, perhaps owing to my army training, remained conventionally dressed, even carrying an umbrella at times.

'You are too heavily dressed', Zadkine told me with disapproval. 'Remember Nina', he continued, referring to a mutual friend of ours, an Englishwoman, 'every time I go out I see her wagging that nasty tail of hers up and down the boulevard. When we come to Paris we should lose our tails. They only get in the way.'

As I sat at the table beside the stove listening to him I noticed that he had a number of English books on his shelves: Swift's *Gulliver's Travels* and his brilliant, personal *Instructions to Servants*.

'I brought them from London', he told me, 'for my books are my conscience; they must go where I go. It is all of my English life which is left for I am a Parisian now, or rather an international. We must lose our nationality, like our tails.'

Some days later, meeting me on the boulevard, he told me that he was going down to Savoy for a holiday where, he said, there were some old men 'who do marvellous things with snakes, and whom I wish to sculpt.' He asked me if I would like to rent his studio while he was away. Living as I was then in that hotel room in the Place de la Sorbonne I much preferred the attractions of his studio, one of the most bizarre and original in Paris. Shortly afterwards I moved in to take my place among that wooden population, a silent and fantastic company which in my imagination seemed always to be awaiting my return from the café at night. I used to spend my mornings in the curtained alcove reading Zadkine's books and experimenting with my own writing, while in the evening I used to frequent the Café Rotonde, and the Dôme, at the corner of the Boulevard Raspail and the Boulevard Montparnasse.

At that time there was a great stir in the artistic world, with the young men who had returned from the war showing their determination to create a new art to express modern life, for already Marinetti's famous Futuristic Manifesto was having considerable influence. He had declared that artists must create an art never conceived before, in which all truths learned in classes and studios must be abolished. 'The classical does not concern us. We are at the beginning of a new epoch'—a manifesto which in fact had a greater influence on the Left Bank intellectuals in Paris than it had in his own museum-cluttered Rome where it was first issued. There was considerable confusion, as at the beginning of all adventures, with innumerable false starts led by false leaders. Everybody was experimenting wildly, with novelty at a premium; every avenue and device was explored for ideas. One musician, a friend of Joyce's, composed a piece to be played by a hundred mechanical pianos as well as numerous other mechanical noise-making devices.

At that time the two chief artistic cafés were the Rotonde and the Dôme. The Rotonde was where the Latins and other Continentals used to congregate, Frenchmen, Spaniards, Russians and other Slavs. It consisted chiefly of a long, low-ceilinged room with the usual square marble-topped tables, and the walls hung with innumerable pictures. Through a passage was the traditional zinc-topped *comptoir* where one drank one's morning coffee and ate a *brioche* standing before the row of aluminium geysers in the din and clatter as the waiters called out their orders. Outside, the café terrace faced the Boulevard Montparnasse with the entrance to the Nord-Sud Underground station exactly opposite. The travellers who passed used to gaze curiously and cynically at the arguing intellectuals sitting on the terrace.

In winter the terrace was enclosed in a glass screen and charcoal stoves were placed at intervals, but in spite of this protection one was soon glad enough to go inside and sit in the main café. Here a continual stream of people entered and left: artists, models, viveurs and political revolutionaries. Trotsky frequented the districts before the 1914 war, and even at the time I speak of one would see groups of Spaniards huddled in a corner planning their future Civil War.

Immediately opposite, on the other side of the boulevard, was the Café du Dôme, the chief haunt of the English-speaking element: English, Irish, Americans, with a sprinkling of Danes, Swedes and Norwegians. Inside, the Dôme was more restricted than the Rotonde, for a large semi-circular *comptoir* took up most of its left side. The rooms at the back were dull and unimaginative, with high windows looking out on to the gloomy non-committal houses of the rue de Lambre, a street as depressing as the famous rue Morgue, consisting of a long line of dull houses which ended with the wall of the Montparnasse cemetery. The Dôme's wide and well-appointed terrace made up for its rather depressing interior, and here, as well as on the terrace of the Rotonde, the intellectuals used to collect in their crowds in the evening, so that as one approached this café from the distance at night, under the haze of lights, it looked as though it were a huge hive with innumerable swarming bees. Even in the afternoon there were always a number seated there, recognizable by their coloured shirts, sandals, and variegated head-gear when, apparently detached, they would remain for hours contemplating the busy boulevard before them. Indeed, in the hot and temperamental Paris afternoon their apparent indolence and detachment would sometimes so annoy passing van drivers and others, their nerves already frayed by the city traffic, that I have seen them pull up on the curb and pour abuse upon the half-conscious and immobile intellectuals. There was one man who used to drive up every evening and park his van with relish in front of the café terrace. On it was written, ' Extermination of Rats Undertaken '—that was evidently his business—for if the intellectual hates and despises the bourgeois, the latter in turn hates and despises the intellectual.

I cannot say that when I originally went to France I intended to get a job, in fact such an idea was repugnant to me. But although I preferred to frequent the cafés, *flâner* the boulevards, meet my friends and generally improve my mind, I suddenly found myself a sort of freelance art critic on the *New York Herald*.

In London, during the war, I had met the American sculptor, Jo Davidson. During the war, he and I used to frequent the Café Royal in Piccadilly which had a kind of fevered brilliance. Having lived my life with soldiers I knew nothing about artists, but now I decided that if I survived I would become one of them, for it was the only life, and they were the only people who interested me.

Jo Davidson was the first international artist I had met. I was fascinated by his wit, his vitality, and his freedom from all the shibboleths I had been brought up to revere but which in secret I used to make fun of, a thing which the conventionally minded sensed and made me pay for in their surreptitious way.

Calling for him in the evening at the book shop of Dan Rider, another jovial and pleasant person, I would walk with him to the Café Royal, and from there to some restaurant, often finishing up at a night club in the early hours of the morning, surrounded by a covey of belles attracted by Davidson's personality.

Now, the war over, he had established himself in Paris, where he was engaged in sculpting a huge 'Doughboy' to be erected in the American Cemetery. It was then that he suggested that he could get me a job on the *New York Herald,* for which I was to write a weekly article entitled, 'Around the Studios'. As he said, there was tremendous activity going on about which the public knew nothing.

—Exhibitions are all right, he pointed out, they are well advertised and people know about them, but there is no account of the daily work taking place in the numerous studios all around Paris.

So, undertaking this mission—for so I regarded it—I used to make visits to the different artists' studios, which in itself was an adventure, since they often lived in strange and inaccessible places, up crazy broken stairways and along perilous creaking balconies. If I thought a man had talent I would arrange to pay him a visit, and it was in this way that I first met Sola, the Spanish artist, who was later to be my friend, and it was from him I acquired my first Modigliani, a piece of sculpture.

One day, Davidson, who knew him, showed me some of Sola's drawings. Interested, I decided to make a call. He lived beside the Gare Montparnasse in a plain-faced red brick rambling building with a long, straight, narrow stair running like a ladder up to his studio, a big and bare high-walled room which was always plunged in obscurity. Indeed, with its stark walls and perpetual gloom, it reminded me of the cathedrals of Spain with their creeping lights, their stillness, and their detachment from the outside world.

Sola himself had that mixture of fire and melancholy which seems to be characteristic of his race. He was married to a French girl, a quiet and gentle creature who spent most of her day sitting by the iron stove knitting and taking an occasional drink of cabbage water to relieve her delicate digestion, the cure for all such ills according to her, and I still have a drawing of them sitting opposite one another portraying that grave and intimate austerity which seems to be an essential part of the Spanish character. The occasional exuberances of their famous fiestas and ferias have always seemed to me but temporary flashes of high tension bursting through their cast-iron conventionalism.

When I called on him it was already late in the evening, and as I sat talking to him my eye continually wandered to the far end of the studio where there was an old fashioned and massively built Breton cupboard, the kind that has been passed on through several generations of respectability. It had a lot of things piled in confusion on top of it, but what emerged from this penumbra of shadow and light, and constantly attracted my attention, was a stone head. Egyptian in style, the face was oval in shape and set on a long neck with a straight nose and a very small and full-lipped mouth. The eyes were elongated and smooth like pebbles, and full, soft cheeks had evidently been cut with a sequence of single hammer strokes which gave them a jewel-like quality. I asked Sola if he had done it.

—No, he said, that is by Modigliani. During the war I used to stand him meals. We were both hard up at the time but my parents used to send me money from Spain and so I had a little; enough, that is, for us both to eat, anyway. So one day he climbed up here carrying this head, and gave it to me as a present in return, I suppose.

For days afterwards that piece of sculpture haunted me, as the passion for a particular woman can haunt one, a constant obsession from which it is difficult to rid oneself. No doubt the casualness of its setting on top of the cupboard in the penumbra had originally stirred my imagination. Whatever the reason, I was determined to possess it.

At first Sola refused. It was a present from a friend and as such had sentimental associations. But as his financial circumstances were rather difficult he finally agreed, with reluctance, and after considerable bargaining the head was mine. When I came to carry it away I found it so heavy that I wondered how Modigliani had ever managed to carry it up those stairs by himself. Between us it took all our strength to carry it down and into a taxi, when I took it back to Zadkine's studio.

Some days later Sola called round to see me, and began to regret his sale, so that I had to soothe him as best I could. Forgetting his regrets, he walked around the studio looking at Zadkine's work and talking about Modigliani's theories on sculpture, telling me how Modigliani had hated Rodin's work —*un mouleur en plâtre* he had called him—for in Modigliani's opinion the essence of sculpture was that it should be hard, like a precious stone, ' emotion crystallized ', as he had said.

—Was it not Brancusi who first persuaded him to take up sculpture? I asked him.

—That is so, he replied, though actually he did not care for Brancusi's own work. He thought that though he had a feeling for textures, for wood, stone and metal, he had no real creative power. Indeed, his abstractions, for which he was best known, often touched on the absurd, as for example his ' Torso ', which consisted of two short cylinders serving as two cut-off legs fitted into a larger cylinder. He also disliked the tombstone Brancusi carved in the Montparnasse cemetery, ' The Kiss ', those two seated figures with their arms wrapped around each other ' like ropes ', as Modigliani expressed it.

In Sola's opinion Brancusi's success was chiefly due to the fact that he was a good-looking man with an attractive personality which had helped him to become fashionable.

As he walked around the studio among Zadkine's forest-like figures, with that peculiar flat and square Spanish walk of his—a walk which was not unlike that of Picasso—he turned as if some sudden resentment had struck him, and said to me:

—You are a critic, aren't you? But, after all, a critic's point

of view is a personal one like anybody else's; the only difference is that you have the means of expressing it through the
press. But that does not make it more valid than anybody
else's opinion.

—It is a fate, I told him, like another fate. I have always been
very interested in art, but I did not particularly want to be a
critic. I have found out since that it is not satisfactory to
translate into words what is fundamentally an expression of
line, colour, and form.

Then, as we were talking, he stopped before some Goya
reproductions that I had pinned up on the wall by the door,
among which were the famous 'La Maja Vestida' and 'La
Maja Nuda'.

—I do not admire those as you do, he said. To me they
represent all that is most vile in man and woman. As we say
in Spain, 'all men are on the point of entering a bawdy
house', and I cannot look on them as works of art—that
woman lying on a couch with her arms behind her head the
better to show off her body.

—That she is sensual I admit, in the direct Spanish sense, I
said. She does not belong, as the French women do, to the
daughters of light; nor is she as the Italian women are, a
daughter of the moon. She is the daughter of darkness. But
as a nude you must admit that she is superb. Some nudes
have been painted too hard, and some again too fleshy, as
Rubens', but she is neither, for Goya laid stress on the texture
of her skin, which is fine, uniform, and delicate. Also on that
of her hair. The Egyptians believed that love lay in the hair,
and in the eyes. In 'La Maja Nuda' they are in both.

—It is her eyes I object to, said Sola. They are the eyes of a
houri.

Then, seeing that I was boring him,

—What do you think of Modigliani's nudes? I asked.

He shrugged his shoulders.

—They are very sensual. I came into his studio one evening
as he was finishing what is now known as 'The Great Nude',
and he asked me what I thought of it. 'It is a map of a naked
woman', I told him. 'That's what it is for', he replied

moodily, ' to enable me to find my way around ': and, disappointed at my criticism, he picked it up and turned it to
the wall. But really, that model stretched out for love, or
copulation rather, did not seem to me a work of art.
—I think you were wrong, I said, for she is very beautiful,
and that is all that matters. Only if she were ugly, in my
opinion, would it have been wrong to paint her like that.

# II

The first time I met James Joyce was at the Bal Bullier. I had gone there one Saturday evening to meet Annette, the young blanchisseuse who used to call for my washing every week, a handsome self-willed girl who later became a model, and whose life ended in tragedy.

It was the fact, I think, that I lived in a studio that interested her in my lonely bachelordom, for while I talked with her she used to amuse herself by kicking the odd pieces of coal which lay in front of the stove across the floor, a subtle intimation that she did not think much of my domestic arrangements. She told me she used to go dancing every Saturday so I asked her to meet me at the Bal Bullier, a popular dancehall of the Montparnasse district which, like much of old Paris, has since disappeared, but then it stood at the top of the Boulevard St Michel in the Avenue de L'Observatoire opposite the Luxembourg Gardens.

The Bal itself was a large building and one entered down a flight of stairs, for the foundations were below street level. Inside it consisted of a wide dance-floor surrounded by a balcony supported on iron pillars, and underneath this balcony were placed rows of marble-topped tables and iron chairs. It had two orchestras, a brass one and a string one which played alternately at opposite ends of the floor, neither, as can be imagined, of a very high order, for it was chiefly frequented by the local shop-boys and girls, with a sprinkling of intellectuals who, tiring of the cafés, entered to find distraction and were pleased by its old-fashioned atmosphere and low prices. In its day it had been a fashionable resort, but being outmoded it had gradually declined except for one or two occasions during the winter when the big artistic balls organized by the different studios were held there. On these occasions it used to be completely transformed when the students from the studios erected small stages on the floor and gave burlesque performances during the intervals of the dance. The now deserted balcony was then crowded with supper tables, with all bohemian Paris packed on to its floor. But this night was one of its ordinary nights with only about thirty couples dancing.

As I entered I saw a party seated at one of the tables, one of whom I knew, a lady who was a friend of Jo Davidson. I took care to avoid them, for I had come there to meet Annette and not to pass my evening with intellectuals (my constant and recurring fate). I was excited at the idea of an evening with this handsome girl with whom, as a lonely man, I was already half in love, and would, if fates were kind, be fully in love with before the night was out. As time went on Annette did not appear, though I searched and re-searched that vast hall for her, so that in the end I despaired that she would keep her rendezvous. Anxious for some company to help me forget my disappointment, towards the end of the evening I passed by the table where the party was seated. A lady called me over and introduced me to a slightly built, finely featured man with a small pointed beard who wore thick lensed glasses—' Mr James Joyce ', she said. The introduction came as a surprise for I did not know that he was in Paris. The last time I had heard about him he was living in Switzerland.

While living in Dublin I had read *Dubliners*, and later I had read *A Portrait of the Artist as a Young Man*, but being at that time chiefly interested in romantic literature I had not been greatly impressed by his books. I was nevertheless intrigued to meet one of our most important authors, and I liked the man himself, his quiet sensitive manner and his old-fashioned courtliness, and I soon found myself sitting next to him. He asked if I came from Dublin, seemed pleased when I told him that I did, and asked how long had I left it and whom I had known there. These questions did not altogether please me, for I had gone to Paris to forget Ireland as a whole, and my native Dublin in particular.

Our conversation was interrupted by a young American woman at the table, Miss Sylvia Beach, who proposed that we should all fill our glasses and drink a toast to the success of James Joyce's new book, *Ulysses*. Towards midnight the party broke up, but as we stood on the boulevard outside, Joyce suggested that I should cross over with him to the Closerie des Lilas opposite for a final drink before we parted, when he told me of the difficulty he had had in finding a publisher for this new book, which had taken him eight years to write.

After that night I did not see him again for some time until I received a message through a mutual friend suggesting that I should call on him at an address in the rue de Rennes. So a couple of evenings later as I happened to be passing his flat on my way to a studio party in the Montrouge district I called in to see if he would accompany me. I believed then that an artist should be something of a bohemian, especially in the exciting circumstances which a city like Paris offered, and it had seemed to me, in the short time that I had met Joyce, that he led a very restricted and bourgeois life. I wanted to persuade him to come to this party, which was to be held in the studio of a Russian painter called Feder, whose place was out in the Montrouge district in a garden behind a block of flats. It looked more like a booth in a fair than an artist's studio, and had about five different entrances which in turn had been blocked up by each new tenant in an effort to keep out the draughts. One side of it had been torn badly, and the story was that a painter of animal subjects who had lived in it had had a lioness brought in. She had torn it down, it was said, in protest against ' having to pose in her skin '. In this studio Feder had a magnificent assembly of negro sculpture, one piece of which, a representation of the sun in yellow wood, displayed its pointed rays running down the whole length of the wall. He had also collected numerous dance-masks, exotic and macabre, and some musical instruments. A Russian Jew, he had escaped from the pogroms in Odessa to become a painter in Paris. A kindly and urbane soul with a gentle, cynical wit, he was an excellent host.

I thought that in such an atmosphere Joyce would relax,

have a drink, and talk with the girls, but I was badly received by the family, as I had arrived at his flat with my pockets full of bottles. Since Joyce's eyes were very weak at that time, he had been forbidden to drink, and they looked on me as the proverbial drunken Irishman inviting him out on a Celtic bash. Georgio, his son, stood over my chair with his legs apart as much as to say, ' When are you going to leave?' It was an awkward situation, and I decided to make out as best I could. Joyce, bending to the storm with a rueful smile, refused my invitation, while I, feeling the atmosphere so charged, was glad to make my escape. As I went down the passage Joyce accompanied me to the door and, as I passed out, standing with his back against the wall he said to me in a plaintive, but amused voice:

—You know I am an intelligent man, but I have to put up with this sort of thing—however, he commented with a smile, we will meet again soon.

At the time I thought he was a much bullied man, but when I got to know him and the family better, and to understand the serious threat to his sight, I changed my point of view. Shortly afterwards I met him again in the rue du Bac when he invited me back to his gloomy, iron-shuttered flat. I immediately became great friends with his family, and particularly with Nora, who realized that I had no wish to lead her husband into drinking bouts, that in fact I disliked drinking to excess.

Joyce, a restless man, was continually changing his abode, partly through circumstances no doubt, but also on account of his nature, and shortly afterwards he moved to a pleasant, airy apartment opposite the Eiffel Tower, where I used to visit him frequently.

I always took care not to call at his flat until the late afternoon, when he used to come into the room from his study wearing that short white working-coat of his, not unlike a dentist's, and collapse into the armchair with his usual long, heart-felt sigh. As often as not Mrs Joyce would say to him, —For God's sake, Jim, take that coat off you!

But the only answer she got was his Gioconda smile, and he

would gaze back humorously at me through his thick glasses. Later in the evening it was his normal habit to dine at 'Les Trianons', a smart restaurant opposite the Gare Montparnasse. Once I met Marie Laurencin there when she stopped on her way out to speak to Joyce. A great admirer of her work, I was fascinated by those delicate and supersensitive young girls of hers. But to my surprise, I, who had imagined her to be like them, found her heavily built and rather masculine-looking— a woman who, according to gossip, preferred *hommes de sport* for her companions, footballers and racing cyclists.

—Monsieur Joyce, she told him, I want to do a portrait of your daughter. Tell her to come on Thursday next, at eleven o'clock.

I believe that when Lucia did turn up, Marie Laurencin was lying in a darkened room complaining of a headache from the previous night's *bombe*. She put off the meeting to a later date, and so I never saw the portrait, which is a pity, since Lucia, with her sensitive bearing and that squint of hers, would have been Marie Laurencin's typical subject.

After returning to his flat in the Square Robiac, Joyce would settle down in a sympathetic and social mood. Here in the evening, with his favourite bottle of white wine, 'St Patrice', at his elbow, a wine he discovered while on holiday in the south of France, we used to discuss many things, but the main subject of our conversation was naturally our common interest in literature. In the ordinary sense Joyce was not a conversationalist. In fact he was remarkably taciturn, 'silence, exile and cunning' being his three vaunted weapons, though I must say I never saw any evidence of the third quality, for he was singularly open-hearted and devoid of guile, except perhaps that all silent men seem more cunning than do talkative ones. In our discussions I spoke much more than he, and I think it was my argumentativeness which strangely enough cemented the friendship between us.

Joyce had lent me the manuscript of *Ulysses,* which I carried in a bulky parcel tied up in brown paper, across the taxi-ridden streets back to my studio in constant fear that I should be run over and the manuscript lost. But when I sat down to read it I found myself confused by its novelty and lost in the fantasia of its complicated prose, not knowing if a thing had really happened or was just a Celtic whorl. In fact I later irritated Joyce by enquiring into the details of what actually occurred during Bloom's encounter with Gerty MacDowell on the beach.

—Nothing happened between them, he replied. It all took place in Bloom's imagination.

It is said that when H. G. Wells put down the loosely bound first edition, with pages falling all over the place, he felt that he had suppressed a revolution; but I knew that one had been launched. Taking for his subject his native city, which once he had evidently hated, but which now he had re-found to cherish, Joyce had created a new realism, in an atmosphere that was at the same time half factual and half dream.

In regard to its well-known analogy with Homer's *Odyssey,* an analogy which at the time I questioned, I remember Joyce choosing as an example the 'Sirens' episode which takes place in the Ormond Bar on the quays. He compared the barmaids with Homer's Sirens, pointing out that the barmaids, with careful hair-do, make-up, and smart blouses, looked well only to the waist, and that below the waist they wore old stained skirts, broken and comfortable shoes, and mended stockings. Again, when I once admired the phrase '*Thalatta! Thalatta!* She is our great sweet mother', he looked across at me and said 'Read what I have written above: "The snotgreen sea. The scrotumtightening sea."'

Whereas Homer's *Odyssey* describes prancing horses, handsome men and fair women, gods and goddesses, Joyce's *Ulysses,* as we know, is laid in tattered streets among blowsy women and in jostling bars, culminating in the episode of 'Nighttown'. I remember the brothel area faintly from my youth, a very fly-blown district including a number of thatched cottages in which every trick was practised, with a number of oldish women in black shifts running about. If you got up to talk to somebody, by means of some miracle only known to them you found, when you returned to your seat, that your whiskey had been changed back to water—

while in a back room there lay a peasant Venus with a religious lamp burning over the nuptial bed. Despite these sordid memories, it meant something to me that an Irishman from Zürich had arrived in Paris with a huge masterpiece, in the modern idiom, based on my native city. Indeed, it was perhaps pride in this achievement, rather than a reaction against Joyce's bourgeois life, that had really prompted me to try and bring him to studio parties, in order to show him off to my friends.

One evening we had an argument about the merits of Synge. Joyce knew him when he was living in the rue d'Assas but found him very difficult to get on with.

—He was so excitable, Joyce told me. I remember once going around to him and suggesting that we should spend the 14th July in the Parc de St Cloud. But Synge objected violently to the idea of spending the holiday, as he expressed it, 'like any bourgeois picnicking on the grass', and he refused to go. In fact there were such heated arguments between us that in the end I had to give up seeing him.

—And what do you think of his work? I asked.

—I do not care for it, he told me, for I think that he wrote a kind of fabricated language as unreal as his characters were unreal. Also in my experience the peasants in Ireland are a very different people from what he made them to be, a hard, crafty and matter-of-fact lot, and I never heard any of them using the language which Synge puts into their mouths.

—But he must have got it from somewhere, I said. I know that in the west of Ireland I used to hear marvellous phrases. I remember once asking a peasant on Costelloe Bay if there were many seals in it. 'Seals', he exclaimed, 'sure they do be lying out there as thick as the fingers of my hand, and they sunning themselves on the rocks'—a phrase which seemed to me to be pure Synge. And do you remember the speeches of Mary Byrne in *The Tinker's Wedding* when she talks about the great queens and they making matches from the start to the end, 'and they with shiny silks on them the length of the day, and white shifts for the night'?

33

—Now who ever heard talk like that? protested Joyce.

—The question is, I said, is literature to be fact or is it to be an art?

—It should be life, Joyce replied, and one of the things I could never get accustomed to in my youth was the difference I found between life and literature. I remember a friend of mine going down to stay in the west, who, when he came back, was bitterly disappointed—' I did not hear one phrase of Synge all the time I was down there ', he told me. Those characters only exist on the Abbey stage. But take a man like Ibsen—there is a fine playwright for you. He wrote serious plays about the problems which concern our generation.

—Ibsen, I exclaimed in surprise. I would not compare Ibsen with Synge, for to me there is something essentially ugly about those suburban dramas of his, about those boring people who live in mean surroundings, while Synge's are magnificent creatures in my opinion, living in communion with Nature, ' with the Spring coming up into the trees '; and ' a dry moon in the sky '; and ' a drink-house on the way to the fair ', grand and devil-may-care bodies in contrast to Ibsen's who pass their lives in consulting rooms, or attending board meetings; those frustrated bores who are the official and professional strata in any town.

—What about Dr Stockman in *An Enemy of Society*? Surely you admit that he was a fine character, remarked Joyce.

—He was brave, I suppose, in his own fashion, I admitted, a fine man even, but what a lamentable lack of poetry in the whole play; all that business about infected drains, leaking water-pipes, and the ' Hygienic Baths ' and ' lots of invalids '.

—You have not understood the play, Joyce objected, for the infected water supply and the leaking pipes you mention are all symbolical of what Dr Stockman was protesting against, ' that all our spiritual sources are poisoned '. Surely you must agree that Dr Stockman is a far finer character than any of Synge's and that a man fighting against the corrupt politics of his town is a finer theme than brawling tinkers, and half crazy ' play-boys '.

—I wonder, and wonder very much, I replied. Indeed if I

remember rightly Synge disliked the plays of Ibsen. He dealt with what Synge calls 'seedy problems' in joyless and pallid words but, as Synge says: 'in a good play every speech tastes of nuts or apples'.

Joyce shook his head.

—You have not understood him, he said, neither his purpose nor his psychological depth, as opposed to Synge's romantic fantasy; his brilliant research into modern life when he plumbed new psychological depths which have influenced a whole generation of writers. But whom has Synge influenced? Nobody but a few playwrights also trying to work for the Abbey, writing about provincial comics, characters from whom they hope to raise a laugh.

—Is it so wrong to be humorous? I said. In fact it is Ibsen's deadly seriousness which repels me and the fact that he saw life only as a battlefield for those dreary ideas of his.

—As I say, repeated Joyce, you do not understand him. You ignore the spirit which animated him. The purpose of *The Doll's House*, for instance, was the emancipation of women, which has caused the greatest revolution in our time in the most important relationship there is—that between men and women; the revolt of women against the idea that they are the mere instruments of men.

—And the more the pity, I replied, for the relationship between the sexes has now been ruined; an intellectualism has been allowed to supersede a biological fact, and the result is that neither is happy.

—The relationship between the two sexes is now on a different basis, but I do not know whether they are happier or unhappier than they were before; I suppose it depends on the individuals. But I do know that Ibsen has been the greatest influence on the present generation; in fact you can say that he formed it to a great extent. His ideas have become part of our lives even though we may not be aware of it.

—You are probably right, I said, in fact you are right. But I still dislike his dried up personality so much and the plays he wrote, that I cannot agree with you about him. For me language is all important, and that is why I admire Synge: for his splendid language.

—It is his language that I object to, replied Joyce, those long overweighted sentences, through which the actors have to stumble painfully, wondering, as they seem to do, if they will ever get to the end of them—long flowery speeches which hold up the action. It is a misuse of the stage. Take a dramatist like Sheridan. Look at his quick short sentences, primed and witty. There is no drooling about him.

—That is the actors' fault, I said, if they cannot manage them. In the case of Synge, they seem to me to run naturally if they are taken in the accent and mood of the people they are supposed to represent. They have dignity, passion, colour and personality. I hate the back-chat type of play. It can be very wearisome indeed.

—Drama is the art of significant action and except you are a Shakespeare you should not attempt to smother it in language as Synge does. In contrast, Ibsen's dialogue is always slim and purposeful. It must be Synge's romanticism which appeals to you.

—Maybe you are right, I replied, for the question is, has there ever been any worthwhile art produced which is not romantic?

—It depends what you call art, doesn't it? For in my opinion there are as many forms of art as there are forms of life.

—It is intoxication in one form or another, I said, to be always drunk, as Rimbaud puts it, drunk with life—is not that what an artist should be?

—That is the emotional aspect, said Joyce, but there is also the intellectual outlook which dissects life, and that is now what interests me most, to get down to the residuum of truth about life, instead of puffing it up with romanticism, which is a fundamentally false attitude. In *Ulysses* I have tried to forge literature out of my own experience, and not out of a conceived idea, or a temporary emotion.

—I think you wrote better when you were romantic, I said, as for example in *A Portrait of the Artist*.

—It was the book of my youth, said Joyce, but *Ulysses* is the book of my maturity, and I prefer my maturity to my youth.

*Ulysses* is more satisfying and better resolved; for youth is a time of torment in which you can see nothing clearly. But in *Ulysses* I have tried to see life clearly, I think, and as a whole; for Ulysses was always my hero. Yes, even in my tormented youth, but it has taken me half a lifetime to reach the necessary equilibrium to express it, for my youth was exceptionally violent; painful and violent.

—All one's life is painful and violent as far as I can see, I said. I was looking at an Italian clock in the window of an antique shop the other day, and written across the dial were the words *Every one hurts and the last one kills.*

—Every one hurts and the last one kills. That is good, Joyce remarked, I must remember that.

# III

Joyce hated to go to any restaurant other than those few which he habitually frequented, and nothing would induce him to enter the well-known bohemian cafés of Montparnasse. When he did not go to the 'Trianons', he sometimes dined *en famille* at the Café Francis in the Place Francis which faces the Seine and the Eiffel Tower, and after a visit to the theatre he would call in there before returning home. Once I tried to break his normal habits by taking him to a restaurant near the Madeleine which specialized in Alsatian food and wine. Although it was exceptional, it put him into a difficult mood. On another occasion we went to a famous restaurant in Montmartre where as we waited for a table some Frenchman recognized Joyce and exclaimed in a loud voice that here was a genius. But since it was not his favourite 'Trianons' he was ill-at-ease. By the door I noticed a woman before whom all the men stopped and spoke in a particularly friendly manner, so that one wondered who she was, perhaps a famous actress or a singer. In the end we found that she was the manageress of a well-known *maison close* around the corner, and was thus a person of considerable importance in the neighbourhood, with information about the capabilities of the latest beauty on the market. As Joyce remarked, ' a reigning duchess would not have received more deference and attention.'

He hated anything to do with bohemians, and always showed contempt for their way of life. Once, when I asked where he liked to go for his holidays, he answered abruptly : ' To some place where honest people earn an honest living.'

He seemed to have a passion for an ordered life, and I thought it a reaction from his former life in Dublin, from the poverty and bohemianism of his youth, of which one heard various accounts from people who had known him at that time. One day, meeting his friends in the street, he told each of them that they must meet him again on the following Saturday at midday at the bottom of Grafton Street with a pound note in their pockets—a matter, he intimated to them, of the utmost urgency. On the following Saturday a number of them turned up.

—Have you all got your pound notes? he asked, and when they produced the promised money he said, now let us all go and dine at Jammet's.

(Jammet's being at that time Dublin's best known and most expensive restaurant, a few yards from their meeting place.) Such and other stories are told of Joyce's bohemian youth, but in Paris he lived the most ordinary life imaginable, remaining shut up in his flat during most of the day.

Once I wanted him to meet Jo Davidson, but the meeting was not easy to arrange for Joyce first made innumerable enquiries about him before he would agree to the meeting. I wanted to fix the Deux Magots on the corner of Boulevard St Germain as the meeting place, a café frequented by a few American writers such as Hemingway and some others, and by some of the local French bourgeoisie. But Joyce refused to go there, and made the appointment at a small café or bistro at the juncture of the rue du Bac and the Boulevard St Germain. There he sat waiting for us, a solitary and lonely figure on its deserted terrace, about three minutes' walk from the popular cafés where all his friends met.

Indeed, famous man though he was, the life he lived was, socially speaking, hermetically sealed. On one of those rare occasions when we were sitting in a wellknown café on the Left Bank, some American writers sitting at another table, one of whom I think he knew, sent over a message asking him to join them. He sent back a reply saying that he was with his wife and friends and regretfully refused. Everywhere he went he acted in the same detached manner. If, for instance, anyone he knew came up to greet him in a restaurant, or at a theatre, or in any public place, he would quickly disengage himself and resume his isolation.

While one talked to him one could not but feel, at times, that he was using the conversation as a sort of counterpoint to his own thoughts, which ran in an altogether different vein as he mentally composed 'Work in Progress'. One evening, in a temporary moment of exasperation, I exclaimed as he was serving me a drink at one of his parties:

—You are a cold man!

I will never forget his astonishment.

—I, a cold man? he repeated.

At the constant parties in his flat I admit that to some extent a different man showed himself when, with his open-handed Irish hospitality, friendly and relaxed, he moved among his guests. These, incidentally, were at that time nearly always the same people. They included Miss Beach, the vivacious New Englander whose one absorbing interest was Joyce and his works, and who gave the impression that she was willing to be crucified for him on the sole condition that it was done in a public place; Mlle Monnier, her friend; and an American pair, the Nuttings. The first time I had met Mlle Monnier was in one of those smart restaurants on the Champs Elysées which stand among the trees near the Boissy d'Anglas. A large, impressive woman, she was dressed that evening in a black nun-like garment which completely mystified me until I was told it was the official Communist attire. I must say that it seemed to me strangely out of place in those surroundings. But when she came to Joyce's parties she wore an ordinary black dress, and always appeared to be one of those impassive French who are frequent enough but who always seem out of character. She had her wellknown book shop, 'Le Navire d'argent', in the rue de l'Odéon opposite Miss Beach's. Although we often met at Joyce's parties I do not believe there was the smallest degree of understanding between us.

Towards midnight Joyce would go over to the piano and try running his fingers in a ripple over the keys. He would sing in a light and pleasant tenor voice many Irish ballads in which romance and lament and satire were combined, and which were the secret source of his inspiration.

Curiously enough one was aware of the reverberations of his fame even in these homely surroundings, for one was constantly reading critiques of his work in the numerous literary magazines, and also meeting writers and other intellectuals outside in the cafés with whom his work became a topic of conversation. Even Sola, the Spaniard, who had not one word of English, had heard that *Ulysses* was a masterpiece, and used to ply me with numerous questions about it—was it true that a character called Mrs Bloom had allowed her breast to be milked into the tea?

On principle Joyce refused to give any journalist a personal interview, and when I asked him the reason for this he murmured something about their always being anxious to misrepresent you. But I feel that his real reason was that he wished to remain mysterious and inaccessible. Whereas most artists are anxious for publicity, Joyce took great pains to avoid it. Yet in spite of the stiff barrier which he put against the outside world, he sometimes did unpredictable things. Once as I was entering his flat, I met a strange and very bohemian couple on the landing outside, just about to leave him, a shock-headed young man and a girl of the very type he professed to dislike. I asked him who they were since strangers with him were such an unusual occurrence. But he seemed uncertain of their names.

—What did they want? I asked him, piqued by my curiosity.
—They wanted to translate *Ulysses*.
—And you gave them permission?
—Yes.
—But you don't know anything about them. You don't know who they are, or what they are, I protested. Why did you give them your permission?
—Quite a number of people come to me and ask for my permission to translate *Ulysses*, he remarked, and I always give it to them.
—Always! I repeated, dumbfounded.

—Yes, he replied with a smile, because I know that none of them will ever do it.

And it was this remark more than any other which revealed to me his contempt for people whom he did not regard as serious artists able to undertake the sustained labour of an artistic work, ' people who sleep all day and amuse themselves all night ', as Hemingway put it.

Another reason why he so carefully avoided social contacts was that they might sap his capacity to work in that room of his which was full of books and old newspapers, and which no one was allowed to enter. Indeed in all the years I knew Joyce, I only saw him engaged in writing when one evening I walked in unexpectedly at tea-time to find him working in the dining-room behind the glass partition, the table spread out with manuscripts, each of them in a different coloured ink—the manuscript of ' Work in Progress '.

I sat in the Café Francis with him one evening, close to the glass doors swinging on their hubs, as a train of smart women entered in their furs and jewels, wafting a wave of perfume over us as they passed, presences of which he seemed almost unaware, and I began to wonder not so much what manner of man he was then, but rather what kind of man he had been. For when I consider Joyce's character I have always two different men in mind—the earlier Joyce, the Joyce of *A Portrait,* and the later Joyce of *Ulysses.* As I ponder over this, there comes to my mind the Joyce whom I had seen revealed to me in the small but significant article on James Clarence Mangan, published in 1902.

I have always known that he admired the strange and tragic personality of Mangan, not so much on account of his literary work, much of which is erratic and ill-written, and an acquaintance with which is not to be found far beyond his native island, but for his personality, his almost morbid singleness of purpose. Indeed it was while reading this article that I had first become aware of Joyce's duality of character, for though the article was written in a romantic vein and in a prose which shows the influence of Pater, he makes in it his first attacks on the very romantic mood which he himself was then expressing. So that I think even then his mind was conceiving the new realism which resulted from his experience of battling for a living in Trieste. As a very ambitious young man he must have suffered impatiently at the time he had to waste teaching English there. I remember that he once recounted to me, with some bitterness, an incident which occurred when he was giving an English lesson to a young Italian girl. Having finished the lesson Joyce was collecting his papers and was about to leave when the girl tapped him on the shoulder and pointed to the clock above his head—it wanted five minutes to the hour. Such incidents of daily occurrence irritated his haughty spirit and brooding on them turned him to cynicism.

But though he lived in Europe for most of his life, it did not interest him; his imagination was always centred in Dublin. He nevertheless had the fixed idea that if he returned there someone would shoot him. Indeed after all those years he would probably have passed through it unnoticed. But the idea of persecution seemed constantly to haunt him, and when I suggested that he should make a surreptitious return visit to see what it was like, he stared at me, grinning sardonically as though I were inviting him to commit suicide. He had been told that some man once called into a bookshop in Nassau Street and asked if they had a copy of *Ulysses*. On learning that they had not he remarked: ' Well, the author of that book had better not set his foot in this country again ', the momentary remark of some religious or nationalistic eccentric, as I pointed out. But as Joyce replied,
—It is just such an eccentric who does these things.

And Mrs Joyce backed him up in the decision, which confirmed him in his attitude.

# IV

One evening we were talking about Russian literature and I was busy praising the Russians: Tolstoy, Turgeniev and Gorki, when Joyce said to me, with some irritation I thought, —Is there no English novelist you admire?

For the moment I could not think of any for my mind was too taken with the Russians and with my arguments in their favour.

—What about George Meredith? Joyce asked.

The stream of my thought was checked for the moment, then I said to him,

—No! Meredith is one of those authors I cannot read. I remember I came across a copy of *The Egoist* in the trenches and mad for something to read I was delighted with my find, but after a while, being continually reminded that ' he had a leg', I became so irritated with it that I got some string and tying a stone on it I threw it over to the Germans. But there is a very fine English novelist to my mind.

—And who is that? he asked me.

—Thomas Hardy, I said. *Tess of the D'Urbervilles* and *Jude the Obscure*.

—But is not Hardy also something of a poseur, remarked Joyce, with his big butter-up of a dairymaid; the wicked squire with his curled moustaches and his dog-cart; her easy rape, and the sequence of the illegitimate baby; and then the biblical Angel Clare; their contrived misunderstandings, and that final drama of the murder; and Angel and Tess's sister standing outside the jail to see the black flag go up. To me the whole story is reminiscent of *The Murder in the Red Barn* or *The Woman Pays*. Also some of the writing is as clumsy

44

as the plot, you must admit that. I always remember a sentence of his when he is describing Tess's feelings towards D'Urberville: 'and there was renewed in her the wretched sentiment which had often come to her before, that in inhabiting the fleshly tabernacle with which nature had endowed her she was doing wrong.' And again she says to Angel somewhere: 'the idea is unworthy of you beyond description.' Beyond description! I ask you! Then there is all that silly business about her supposed ancestral knights sleeping in their jewelled armour in their sculptured tombs. What a clutter of Victorian snobbery. And does it ring true, the whole story I mean?

—To me it does, I said, though I admit its clumsiness. But it is only a superficial clumsiness, for the underlying structure of *Tess* is sound enough, and Tess herself, in my opinion, is as fine as any woman in Shakespeare—in some ways she is finer and more human.

—It is more by a device than anything else, he replied, that she is made seem so fine, as you call it, for it is done by making the other characters seem venal: the seducing landowner, the weak Angel, the drunken old father, and so forth. It is the same device as the theatrical manager uses when he surrounds the leading lady on the stage with a plain chorus.

—Maybe, I said, but it works, which is all that matters, and there is always the richness of his language to support her and the originality of his detail which impresses because of the effort he makes to relate what did actually happen instead of polishing it off with a handy phrase: a persistence to say, or to try to say, what he intended to say, instead of fobbing you off with a happy phrase as so many authors do.

—But the murder! protested Joyce. It is contrary to Tess's whole character, for there is nothing in her make-up which leads you to think that she is a murderess. It was a gross psychological blunder on his part.

—She was an emotional type, poor, and a beauty, and the combination is a strong one, I argued.

Joyce shook his head.

45

—If you analyse his plots you will see that they contain all the tricks and subterfuges of melodrama, that ancient and creaking paraphernalia of undelivered messages, misunderstandings and eavesdroppings, in which the simple are over-simple, and the wicked are devilish.

—Maybe, I said, but those old-fashioned tricks, as you call them, are still effective.

—And then what about *The Dynasts?* he asked me.

He rose from his chair and went over to the reproduction *bois chêne* Breton bookshelf and took out a large green volume.

—Here it is, he said and, sitting down again in the chair, he opened it at the first page, and read it out to me.

—What does all that mean? he asked me, putting down the book, for if you can tell me you are a better man than I am. If ever there was a case of an author over-blowing himself this is surely it.

Then picking it up again he turned over some more pages at random.

—This is from a battle scene, he said, and he read out—


### FIRST AIDE

*The Archduke Charles retreats, your Majesty;*
*And the issue wears a dirty look just now.*


—' The issue wears a dirty look just now '. Really, he exclaimed, it is just bad prose.

—I wouldn't try to defend it, I said, and I don't think anyone would try to. It is just one of those things. Hardy made up his mind to write an epic drama, for which he did not have even the ghost of a talent, or more important, the inspiration. That he was no poet we are agreed, but that does not prevent him from being a great novelist: the most serious of the English novelists, for he was not afraid to grapple life with both hands, different from most of the others who being commercially minded were over-anxious to entertain their readers and so became trivial.

—There was Kipling, said Joyce. There was something of the

46

artist in him in such a story as ' The Butterfly who Stamped '. Also the *Just So Stories* have delightful touches of fantasy in them, and it is that quality which seems to appeal to you.

—Yes, I agreed, but there was another side to Kipling which I do not like.

—You mean that vein of crude practicability which runs through him, like that of the suburban subaltern. I agree, and then there is that jingling jingoism of his which must be very offensive to foreigners.

—Yes, I said. Writers like Dostoevski and Turgeniev and Gorki never presumed on their nationality. Surely that is the mark of a great artist.

—I agree with you, he said, it is a damning trait, and it is to be safe from the rabid and soul-destroying political atmosphere in Ireland that I live here, for in such an atmosphere it is very difficult to create good work, while in the atmosphere which ' Father Murphy ' creates it is impossible. At a very early stage I came to the conclusion that to stay in Ireland would be to rot, and I never had any intention of rotting, or at least if I had to, I intended to rot in my own way, and I think most people will agree that I have done that.

# V

Joyce seemed very interested in the religious aspects of Tutankhamen's tomb, which we discussed shortly after its discovery on 26 November 1922.

—Whenever I walked through the British Museum, he told me, I was always impressed by the Assyrian and Egyptian monuments; those winged monsters with their cloven hoofs, mitred heads, priest-like faces, and long curled beards; and those Egyptian figures of birds and cats. It always occurred to me that both the Assyrians and the Egyptians understood better than we do the mystery of animal life, a mystery which Christianity has almost ignored, preoccupied as it is with man, and only regarding animals as the servants of man. I cannot remember at the moment a sympathetic mention of a dog or a cat in the New Testament, and I have always objected that the devils were transferred into the Gadarene swine. It is true that the parable of the lilies of the field touches on a deeper note, but one wonders why that parable was not taken further, and why the great subconscious life of Nature was ignored, a life which without effort reaches to such great perfection. Indeed since the advent of Christianity we seem to have lost our sense of proportion, for too great stress is laid on man, 'man made in the image of God', and I think that the Babylonian star-worshipper had a greater sense of religious awe than we have. But nowadays the churches regard the worship of God through Nature as a sin.

As I listened I was surprised to hear Joyce commit himself on religion, even as far as this, because in general he carefully avoided the subject. Indeed, I remember one evening meeting an Irish painter who had turned into a bitter anti-Catholic, and sitting in Joyce's room he had scoffed at what he had called this Italian conspiracy in which one of their number was appointed to represent God on earth. He had ridiculed the idea of man's creating God and enclosing Him in a tabernacle under lock and key to give Him only to those who were of the same sect as themselves. He had also attacked Confession as taking away God's power of forgiveness, and many other Roman Catholic practices, the details of which I have forgotten. Joyce was said to be anti-Catholic and I waited for him to express his opinion, but he retained his character-istic silence, his thin lips tightly compressed, uttering no word of approval or disapproval in the argument that raged between us.

The only comment I ever heard him make on these matters was his once telling me that when the new pope was being elected the conclave of cardinals were fed with less food each day so that in the end they were forced to overcome their personal jealousies and elect a pope, which, whether true or not, seemed to amuse him greatly.

His determined silence on the subject of religion and on man's survival after death, a subject which I often confronted him with, so intrigued, and even annoyed me, that one day, the subject having arisen between us as we were walking past the Odéon Theatre, I pushed him into a corner of the street, and I asked him the straight question,
—Do you believe in a next life?
Embarrassed by my sudden seriousness he quickly dis-engaged himself and with a shrug of his slim shoulders he answered,
—I don't think much of this life,
and closed the conversation, so that I realized that I would never get a direct answer on this subject from him.

Indeed, one of his marked characteristics was his avoidance of giving a direct opinion about anyone or about anything, and I attributed some of his reticence to his early life in the provincial atmosphere of Dublin, where everything one said was echoed back and forth with considerable distortion among

49

one's associates, until in the end it could assume the fantastic proportions of a Celtic myth, so that one was inclined to disbelieve all one heard. He so rarely expressed his opinion that his fundamental beliefs were very hard to gauge. In fact his mind appeared to be occupied to the exclusion of everything else with two main problems—that of human behaviour and that of human environment—and then only as related to Dublin. The surrounding French life with all its brilliance and attraction seemed to pass over him, and fed his talent only so far as he appreciated its intellectual freedom and its 'convenience', as he termed it. All he would say about Paris, when any one asked his opinion about it, was that 'it is a very convenient city', though what he meant by this phrase I was never able to discover.

# VI

Joyce seemed restless and ill-at-ease one evening, and I decided that he wanted to do some work or that he was bored with my company. I had already got up to leave when some remark of his about Russian writers set off an argument between us. I had told him earlier that the two literatures which I admired most were the Chinese, about which we know very little, and the Russian; and if I had to choose two favourite authors, one would be Lady Murasaki who, though she was Japanese, wrote in the Chinese tradition, and the other would be Pushkin, who of all the European writers is the one I would like to model myself on.

—Lady Murasaki I don't know, he replied, so I cannot give an opinion on her, but Pushkin! and he looked at me with a puzzled expression on his face. I cannot understand how you can be entertained by such simple fare—tales which might have amused one's boyhood, of soldiers, and camps, villains, gallant heroes, and horses galloping over the wide open spaces, and tucked away in a suitable corner a beautiful maiden of about seventeen years of age to be rescued at a suitable moment. I know that the Russians admire Pushkin, but, as I understand it, it is chiefly for his poetry which since I do not know Russian I cannot read. But I remember once reading a translation of Pushkin's prose, *The Captain's Daughter*—a bustling affair that might interest the Upper Fourth. As I say there was not a pin's worth of intellect in it, and I do not understand how you prefer him to the other Russians such as Tolstoy, who did much the same thing but on a grander scale; or Chekhov.

—Turgeniev looked on Pushkin as the greatest Russian writer, I remarked by way of an argument.

—You think that he was greater than Turgeniev then? Joyce asked.

—Yes, I do, I replied, for he was simpler, he was purer, and he was braver, and I think that all art, all writing, comes back to the man himself. I think that Pushkin was a finer specimen of humanity than Turgeniev. It is said that the Czar admired his wife and secretly wore her miniature, and that Pushkin's enemies, out of jealousy for his talent, or because of a personal slight, or mere impishness perhaps, sent him that infamous ill-scribbled note saying that he had joined 'The Honourable Company of Royal Cocu's'. And the over-gallant, over-impetuous, and over-proud Pushkin sent them a challenge, and they chose their deadliest shot to face him, his own brother-in-law I think it was, and three hours later the most brilliant literary genius in Europe lay dead.

—Yes, I always thought that he lived like a boy, wrote like a boy, and died like a boy, Joyce remarked.

I could not help smiling at his quip, even though it was essentially untrue.

—We have to remember the code of duelling that existed at that time, I argued, when men were very hot about their honour, or that of their wives. Still, I suppose Pushkin could have ignored the letter in the circumstances, or found excuses; but that would have been against his temperament for his chief quality was his eternal youth, in which the oldest things were reborn in wonder; bandits, maidens-in-distress, and his personal honour, all of which were the themes in *The Captain's Daughter*.

—I suppose it was good for its period, remarked Joyce, but I certainly would not take him for my model, for people have become more complicated nowadays and demand more than such simple excitements as bandits, gallant young officers, and maidens-in-distress. The modern writer has other problems facing him, problems which are more intimate and unusual. We prefer to search in the corners for what has been hidden; and moods, atmospheres and intimate relationships are the modern writers' theme. Also, when you say that Pushkin was a finer writer than Turgeniev I am not sure what you mean. If you had said that he was simpler, then I might agree with you. —Yes, simpler and finer, I said, it is much the same thing. Take Turgeniev's long short story 'Roudine'—it is one of his best stories, yet it has not the quality of *The Captain's Daughter* for, compared with Pyotr, Roudine is corrupt and weak. He even doubts himself. Natalia the heroine is not the ideal heroine that Masha is, because she changes in her affection after Roudine has failed to run away with her, though all things considered, he being poor and a wanderer, it was an honourable act on his part, rather than cowardice. Turgeniev's story, I admit, is more realistic and its psychology deeper perhaps; but Pushkin's conception is more ideal, more abstract as the painters would say, and it is the ideal which humanity loves. For instead of being immersed in psychological doubts, Pushkin's characters face circumstances with a youthful audacity which wins over everything, and that is why he is to be preferred to Turgeniev, in spite of the latter's subtlety.

Joyce sighed and poured himself out another glass of 'St Patrice'.

—Here we are, he said, back into a discussion as to what is 'poetry' as distinct from 'literature', to what is life, and what is a lie trumped up by the imagination: the difference between the perpetual adolescent and *homo sapiens*. And for anyone to try and write in the style of a Pushkin as you said you wanted to do just now, or even Turgeniev, seems to me to be like trying to paint a picture in the style of Greuze, or Watteau: a piece of historical plagiarism perhaps, but not contemporary literature. For you must be caught up in the spirit of your time, and you admit that the best authors of any period have always been the prophets: the Tolstoys, the Dostoevskis, the Ibsens—those who brought something new into literature. As for the romantic classicism you admire so much, *Ulysses* has changed all that; for in it I have opened the new way, and you will find that it will be followed more and more. In fact, from it you may date a new orientation in literature—the new realism; for though you criticize *Ulysses,* yet the one thing you must admit that I have done is to liberate literature from its age-old shackles. You are evidently a die-hard traditionalist, but you should realize that a new way of thinking and writing has been started, and those who don't fall in with it are going to be left behind. Previously, writers were interested in externals and, like Pushkin and Tolstoy even, they thought only on one plane; but the modern theme is the subterranean forces, those hidden tides which govern everything and run humanity counter to the apparent flood: those poisonous subtleties which envelop the soul, the ascending fumes of sex.

—Maybe, I replied, for I do not deny your influence on present-day literature, and that of all the other psychologists, even though at times I may regret it; but also I believe the *beau sabreur* still has his place in the world. He may not be very adult and he may not produce masterpieces, or attempt modern masterpieces, though when I come to think of it, even Hamlet was a *beau sabreur manqué*. In fact in that very trait lies his greatness, for his tragedy is that he is a hero hampered by thought. And much modern literature is Hamlet-like in character in that action is overcome by thought which leads to pessimism.

But Joyce seemed to tire of the argument and, turning the conversation, he asked me:

—What literary personalities would you like to have known?

—You mean within recent years? I asked him.

—Yes, in recent years.

—The great Russians, I said, Pushkin, Turgeniev, and Chekhov.

—And Tolstoy? he enquired.

—Yes, I would have been anxious to know him, I admitted, though I don't think that I would have liked him. He was too fierce a man. Also at the end he became too socially minded, but I have to recognize the great artist in him, the writer of some of the best short stories ever written. I could not have loved him, but I could have admired him, for we do not love people who overwhelm us; and to me he is the 'Ivan the Terrible' of literature, brilliant, kingly, and cruel, for no matter how charming he seems to be, underneath we feel that he is hiding something unpleasant and ruthless; and though one cannot but admire his talent yet he does not touch us the way Turgeniev does. Indeed, whenever I think of Russian literature, I think of Turgeniev's *Collection of Gentlemen,* and there comes into my mind that beautiful girl, Liza: her pride, her seriousness, and her inward conflict. The story flows on as inevitably as life itself, and as imperceptibly. ' Une jeune fille grande, svelte avec de beaux cheveux noirs ', that is the only description he gives of her. He lets you fashion her according to your desire and imagination, and her emotions become your emotions.

—You have odd tastes, remarked Joyce, for I think that it is his weakest work, with the indecisive ' cocu ' Lavretzky, and the anaemic cloistered Liza; and all that eccentric collection of aunts, uncles and cousins, who hedge her in in a novel which tasted to me like a literary seidlitz-powder, in which if I remember rightly they are always shutting themselves up in their rooms for knitting and devotions; and their one relaxation is an occasional carriage drive through the country when they sit around a lake and sigh, and then hurry home in case someone should catch a cold: the ineffectual life of farmers who refuse to work on their land. And again, the novel ends in the smoke it began in, when she decides to go into a convent . . .

—That is hardly a fair summary, I protested. Liza may not have the *élan* of some of the French heroines, or the brilliance of the Duchess Sanseverina in *La Chartreuse de Parme,* for instance, for the Duchess is more beautifully and exceptionally passionate; but we feel that Liza is animated with an inner spiritual radiance which is the fundamental difference between the Slav and the Latin races. It is only towards the end of the book and in that scene in Martha Timofeevna's room when she kneels down in the blaze of candlelight before the icons that we begin to understand the real Liza—do you remember it?

—Yes, I remember it, exclaimed Joyce, and a fine piece of treachery it was, staged there for the benefit of that unfortunate 'cocu' she had kept waiting all that time. To me she has always seemed to be the quintessence of religious selfishness, of cowardice even, for she cannot face the scandal of running away with Lavretzky, nor can she leave the cotton-wool comfort of her home and live abroad with Lavretzky in exile. So she goes into a convent—' away with her to a nunnery '. Indeed, the only merit of that book that I could see was that it is one of the first attempts at psychology in the novel. But the whole story is written in such an old-fashioned style that it creaks. Her secret thoughts remain hidden, as does the real movement of her inner being; for he is like all the classical writers who show you a pleasant exterior but ignore the inner construction, the pathological and psychological body which our behaviour and thought depend on. Comprehension is the purpose of literature, but how can we know human beings if we continue to ignore their most vital functions? Turgeniev was a sentimentalist who wished to remain enamoured of his own sensualism. He saw life in an ordered fashion, in spite of his proclaimed admiration for revolutionaries; in fact, he seems to have taken a special pleasure in taming and defeating them, as he tames and defeats Bazarov in *Fathers and Sons* and, in contrast to Dostoevski for example, he was a nicely mannered Russian gentleman playing occasionally with fire but taking care never to get burnt. Tolstoy was a more sincere man in my opinion, for Turgeniev preferred his slippered ease and his literary circles to anything else, and the only people who are convincing in his novels are his anaemic gentlefolk. His interest was in isolation and not in action, and his world is a faded world of water colours. I admit that he was an amiable person, and you cannot help liking him as you like a weak but pleasant personality, but I cannot admire him as a great writer. I think his best work was those early *Sportsman's Sketches* of his, for in those he went into life deeper than in his novels, and reading them I get the impression of the confused and simmering cauldron that Russia was in the 1840s, before the great boil-over. And I always remember the answer a peasant gave to Turgeniev to explain why he was not married: 'Have you got a family? Are you married?' 'No, sir, impossible,

Tatyana Vassilyevna, our last mistress—God rest her soul—allowed no one to marry. She even went so far as to say before the priest, " God keep me from having to put up with that—I, I am a spinster and as long as I live I will stay one. And what is all this to-do about? They are spoilt, that's what they are; what will they be asking next? " '

And Joyce gave one of those sudden explosions of laughter which were so rare with him.

—And *Spring Waters*?, I asked him after a while, when his burst of humour had subsided.

But he shook his head in negation.

—It did not make much impression on me, so my memory of it is rather hazy, but I remember the young Russian, Sanine, and his love affair with that little sugar-sweet Italian girl, Gemma, a long and tiresome episode which even an artificially induced duel fails to bring to life. That ride into the forest and the consummation of their passion in the thunderstorm, that I thought as dated as an opera by Bellini.

—He was a classical writer, I said, and, in contrast to a man like Dostoevski, his sane and balanced qualities are out of favour these days. Nevertheless, they are the lasting ones. Dostoevski passes over us like a storm, and like a storm he will be remembered, occasionally—but there is a quality in Turgeniev which is as polished and firm as Maupassant was.

—No, said Joyce, sentimentalism is never firm, nor can it be; it is a trend of warm comfortable fog. The present generation cannot stand him, and do you wonder? Passion creates and destroys, but sentimentalism is only a backwash into which every kind of rubbish has been cluttered, and I cannot think of a single sentimental work which has survived more than a couple of generations. Crude force is better; at least you are dealing with something primary. His short work was best.

—No! he went on, after a while; the writer of that period I admire most is Chekhov. For he brought something new into literature, a sense of drama in opposition to the classical idea which was for a play to have a definite beginning, a definite middle, a definite end, and for the author to work up to a climax in the second act and resolve it in the last. But in a

Chekhov play there is no beginning, no middle, and no end, nor does he work up to a climax; his plays are a continuous action in which life flows on to the stage and flows off again, and in which nothing is resolved, for with all his characters we feel that they have lived before they came on to the stage and will go on living just as dramatically after they have left it. His drama is not so much a drama of individuals as it is the drama of life and that is his essence, in contrast, say, to Shakespeare whose drama is of conflicting passions and ambitions. And whereas in other plays the contact between personalities is close to the point of violence, Chekhov's characters are never able to make any contacts. Each lives within his own world, and even in love they are unable to become part of the others' lives and their loneliness frightens them. Other plays you feel are contrived and stagy; abnormal people do abnormal things; but with Chekhov all is muffled and subdued as it is in life, with innumerable currents and cross-currents flowing in and out, confusing the sharp outlines, those sharp outlines so loved by other dramatists. He is the first dramatist who relegated the external to its proper significance: and yet with the most casual touch he can reveal tragedy, comedy, character and passion. As the play ends, for a moment you think that his characters have awakened from their illusions, but as the curtain comes down you realize that they will soon be building new ones to forget the old.

—I agree, I said, he was unique; his humanity was unique and it is in a play like *The Three Sisters* that you feel it most. But since we are talking about Russian literature, what do you think of Dostoevski? Does he appeal to you?

—Of course, replied Joyce, for he is the man more than any other who has created modern prose, and intensified it to its present-day pitch. It was his explosive power which shattered the Victorian novel with its simpering maidens and ordered commonplaces; books which were without imagination or violence. I know that some people think that he was fantastic, mad even, but the motives he employed in his work, violence and desire, are the very breath of literature. Much as we know has been made of his sentence to execution, which was com-

58

muted as he was waiting for his turn to be shot, and of his subsequent four years' imprisonment in Siberia. But those events did not form his temperament though they may have intensified it, for he was always enamoured of violence, which makes him so modern. Also it made him distasteful to many of his contemporaries, Turgeniev for instance, who hated violence. Tolstoy admired him but he thought that he had little artistic accomplishment or mind. Yet, as he said, ' he admired his heart', a criticism which contains a great deal of truth, for though his characters do act extravagantly, madly, almost, still their basis is firm enough underneath.

—'Vapour and tumult', is how George Moore described him. ' His farrago is wonderful but I am not won . . .', and neither am I, I said.

—Yes, replied Joyce, but how could a man like George Moore, the Parisian, admire a writer like Dostoevski—Moore whose literary heroes were Balzac and Turgeniev, traditionalists like Moore himself with all the inherited weariness of the traditionalists. But there are people, and many people, who think that *The Brothers Karamazov* is one of the greatest novels ever written. Certainly it made a deep impression on me.

—Nevertheless, he is chaos, I said, the first of the great incomprehensibles who tried to illuminate chaos, but only made it more obscure.

—In some ways, perhaps, agreed Joyce, but as I say he created some unforgettable scenes. Do you remember when Alyosha goes to see his father after Dmitri has attacked him; his father's head is still wrapped up in a red silk scarf, and he gets up every now and then to examine his wounds in the mirror while he declares he will go on living as he has always lived, passionately, evilly; his pride, his boasting; his desire for the young Grouschengka, the strumpet and virgin in one.

—I remember, I said, being asked by a friend, a writer, his eyes burning with enthusiasm, what I thought of Grouschengka. But I did not know what to answer him, and it was then that I realized that Grouschengka and in fact all of Dostoevski's characters were unreal, so while I am reading him, I am asking myself all the time would any reasonable beings act and speak as they do; exaggerations larger than life; or to speak plain useful language, they are mad, all of them. —Madness you may call it, said Joyce, but therein may be the secret of his genius. Hamlet was mad, hence the great drama; some of the characters in the Greek plays were mad; Gogol was mad; Van Gogh was mad; but I prefer the word exaltation, exaltation which can merge into madness, perhaps. In fact all great men have had that vein in them; it was the source of their greatness; the reasonable man achieves nothing.

# VII

Like everybody else Joyce was very interested in the Bywaters
and Thompson case of which the English papers were full in
December 1922, even the *Times* giving it a detailed report.
Bywaters, a young ship's steward, had known a Mrs Thompson
for seven years and was always writing letters to her when he
was away on his voyages, letters which she destroyed. But he
kept hers in which she suggested ways of poisoning her
husband, letters which were produced at the trial, and which
damned her.

Tragic though the whole affair was, it was not without its
humorous side. Mrs Thompson used to get her husband up in
the night to drink his ground-up electric light bulb. In one
of her letters to Bywaters, read at the trial, she said: ' I was
buoyed up with hope of the light bulb and used a lot of big
pieces. . . . Would not the stuff make some small pills coated
with soap, and dipped in liquorice, like Beecham . . . I know
I feel I shall never get him to take a sufficient quantity of
anything bitter.' In another letter she said: ' I used the light
bulb three times. At the third time he found a piece so I have
given it up until you come home.'

Bywaters was a fine clean-looking young man of whom I
saw a photograph in the paper as he was being led into the
Old Bailey, the detectives ushering him in with the exaggerated
care of a mother for her only child, to judgment and death. I do
not know why one has such pity for them, but I suppose it is
because it is the age-old battle between youth and love against
convention; though why they did not decide to run away
together is hard to understand. It seems that she had a good
job, and was afraid that if she ran away with Bywaters she

would have had to live on his small pay, a fear which seems rather exaggerated, for in the first place she might not have lost her job; and in the second place, since she was such an efficient businesswoman she would probably have got another one without much difficulty. But evidently she made up her mind that in order to remain respectable she must have her husband die. Bywaters seems to have been a simple sort of boy, gallant and chivalrous, according to his behaviour at the trial, when he seemed anxious to take the blame and did all he could to protect her: an over-sexed and unbalanced young man completely under her influence, who during his voyage brooded over what she had written to him. Something of his state of mind can be gathered from his collection of newspaper cuttings, some of which she sent him and others of which he had collected himself, cuttings such as: 'The Poisoned Curate', 'Women who Hate Men', 'The Battle of the Calves and Ankles', 'Chicken Broth Death', 'The Shadow Marriages', and so forth. No doubt he would have been willing to run away with her, but she insisted on murder. Indeed it seemed to have been an obsession with her, for she wrote in one of her letters to him: 'Yesterday I met a woman who had lost three husbands in eleven years and not through war. Two were drowned and one committed suicide; and some people I know cannot lose one. How unfair everything is. . . .' The ideal solution for her was for Thompson to commit suicide, but he seems to have been an unusually unimaginative sort of man who drank his electric light bulb with equanimity until he found large pieces in the mixture. He seems to have known that Bywaters was in love with his wife and that they were plotting against him, but I suppose he did not believe that things would come to such a pass. Undoubtedly he was fond of her, though she secretly hated him, but at times, with her woman's wiles, she managed to hide her hatred from him, for in another of her letters to Bywaters she wrote: 'I told him I did not love him and he seemed astounded' . . . and when Bywaters asked him to divorce her he placidly ignored him. It is suggested that Thompson used to beat her occasionally which drove Bywaters into a frenzy.

—The mystery man in the case is the husband, remarked Joyce, the immovable mass before the irresistible force so deeply bedded in his habits that anything outside seemed to him unreal; and of him we have no clear picture. But one thing I am certain of is that if all this had happened in France they would not have been executed, and I think that English justice was at fault in trying them side-by-side in the same dock, for if one was found guilty the other was guilty also, yet evidence against one of them was not necessarily evidence against the other. There was a certain vindictiveness shown there. After all she did not murder him: indeed she may, for all we know, have objected to his assassination and have been powerless to prevent it. It is true she had incited Bywaters, and had incited him for years, but that is not quite the same as actually doing it. It was a difficult case I admit, but I think it was gruesome and inhuman for the judge to try them the way he did.

—There is no doubt that he stabbed her husband to death, I said.

—I know, and like the mills of God, English justice grinds slowly but exceeding small, and yet I think everyone has been shocked by it; and what a terrible thing the law can be sometimes. Like everything else, it should be subjected to evolution as the French have done, even over-done as some think, and some of its implacability removed. I see that she once wrote him a letter in which she said that ' He [the husband] has the right by Law of all that you have the right to by nature and love', on which the judge commented in his summing up: ' If that nonsense meant anything, it meant that the love of a husband for his wife meant nothing, because marriage was acknowledged by law', while he remarked that ' Bywaters' letters only breathed silly, insensate, silly affection '. In other words, humanity meant nothing, and the law meant everything: right, I suppose, to a point, but there should be some tempering of the law to suit the difference between a brutal murder, and the act, for instance, of a woman killing her child in desperation, and then trying to kill herself—a double crime in the eyes of the law.

—I saw some photographs in the newspaper of the personalities of the trial, I told him, and the husband looked like a typical young Englishman, good-looking and not unlike Bywaters himself—in fact they might have been brothers—a type which seems to have attracted her. She was pretty, and quite an unusual character, the self-confident manageress of a dressmaking department in the city. From a photograph taken of them on their holiday together, all three of them, her husband seemed very fond of her, for he is lying with his head resting on her lap.

—There was no real evidence against her, said Joyce, in spite of all her letters saying she had given her husband this, and there was not a trace of any poison, glass, etc., found in his body, and it took Bywaters' six-shilling knife to finish him off. Also at the trial she swore she had given her husband nothing, and it was all fantasy written by Bywaters, for her mind was evidently full of the stuff she had been reading, while she wrote those letters to make her seem romantic in his eyes because in turn he used to taunt her with descriptions of his life while on his voyages. As a picture I can see it all clearly, exclaimed Joyce, Ilford—the dark streets with dim lights showing behind the yellow window-blinds, and from the distance a soft wind coming up with the raw smell of fish and chips on it, the Thompsons walking arm in arm under the trees when this young man suddenly dashes out and stabs him, her crying and wailing, and her search, or pretended search, for help. I can smell the English effluvia here—and it reminds me . . . yes . . . of the Strand, say, on a Saturday night, the huddles of people in the passage outside the pubs; the sudden fights; the traffic-weary streets; the arc-lights shining down on the muddy tramped pavements. I remember how I disliked it all and I decided that I could never have become part of English life, or even have worked there, for somehow I would have felt that in that atmosphere of power, politics, and money, writing was not sufficiently important. Also though there is plenty of legal liberty in England, in spite of all that may be said, there is not much individual liberty, for in England every man acts as a censor to his neighbour, while in Paris here you have the only real freedom in Europe, where no one gives a damn what his neighbour thinks or does, provided he does not make himself obnoxious. But in England everybody is busy about everybody else, which, except for an Englishman, is intolerable. In the Dublin of my day there was the kind of desperate freedom which comes from a lack of responsibility, for the English were in governance then, so everyone said what he liked. Now I hear since the Free State came in there is less freedom. The Church has made inroads everywhere, so that we are in fact becoming a bourgeois nation, with the Church supplying our aristocracy . . . and I do not see much hope for us intellectually. Once the Church is in command she will devour everything . . . what she will leave will be a few old rags not worth the having: and we may degenerate to the position of a second Spain.

# VIII

I gave a party in my studio in the rue de la Grande Chaumière, to which I invited the Jo Davidsons and some American journalist who was staying with them, my friend Barlow, a Miss Vail, Lady Orde and the Joyces.

In the morning I went out on the Boulevard and bought some cakes, trying to get them at those shops where they are most eatable. I thought of going down to Rumplemeyer's in the rue de Rivoli and getting some of their famous pastries, but I decided it was too far to go. Also they were expensive. I had to buy some cups and saucers, and the rest of the morning I spent giving my studio a cleaning, which it badly needed.

It was a fine old place with a big window facing down on to a tree-covered courtyard, on the other side of which were the Carlarossi Studios. It had a big wide floor and a *soupent* above it where I slept, and it was heated, as all these studios were, with a stove, the round barrel type, with a long pipe crossing over the *soupent* and out through the wall. By filling it sufficiently I could at times get it red hot, for the heat spread up the pipe also, which went a dull red, and so in spite of its big window the studio could be got very warm even in the dreadful cold of a Paris winter.

The first to arrive was Lady Orde, who was married to a painter, and then came Jo Davidson, his wife Yvonne, and the American journalist, a busy little man whose attitude seemed to be that there was a take-in somewhere in all this Paris artistic life and his mission was to expose it.

Then came Rudolph, an old friend of mine whom I knew in London during the war, and who, having acted as a courier for a travel agency, had been stranded in Paris. Some French-woman whom he had met at a party thought he had talent, and very nobly gave him a small allowance so that he could remain there and write.

Next arrived Anita, a girl of Irish and Polish extraction who was trying to dry the Irish rain out of her system; and with her that splendid-looking American girl I had asked at the last moment, who was half Red-Indian and half American, a cross between Venus and Adonis though gossip said that it was the Adonis in her which predominated.

Finally Joyce, the guest of honour, arrived with Mrs Joyce, and as Jo Davidson knew him and I was busy looking after the kettles boiling, I let him introduce Joyce to everybody, which was an up-hill task, for Joyce, having painfully gone through the formalities of an introduction, retired a couple of steps backwards and made no further effort. Though he was the essence of politeness, he appeared either to be bored by my guests or to be too shy to make an effort to overcome the initial strangeness.

Mrs Joyce on the other hand was much more sociable, but when he was there she remained glued to his side and her natural sociability seemed to desert her. Jo Davidson, who had more social personality than any man I have ever met, did most of the talking and kept things going, while I went about desperately, backwards and forwards to the gas-stove in the far corner fetching the boiling water etc., with all the worries of a host on my shoulders. While I was bent over the stove a knock sounded on the door and who should enter but the handsome blanchisseuse, who had called to explain about her earlier failure to arrive at the Bal Bullier. She was in her rough work-ing clothes, but seemed to want to come in, so I murmured something about helping me with the kettles. There was a pause in the conversation among my guests as the girl entered, and everyone concluded that I had an intrigue with her, which unfortunately was not true, and I returned more confused than ever to my party, offering and re-offering the cakes with a desperate bravado to people I had already offered them to. When I returned to get some more hot water, she had disappeared as unexpectedly and as mysteriously as she had arrived; this concourse of well-dressed foreigners was not to her liking.

Slipping past my guests I went over to Joyce to see if I could bring him into the company, for I was always expecting from him a sudden ebullience of the high spirits, wit, and violence which fill his books. But he remained impassive, polite but impassive, answering a query when he was asked one, but no more. In fact where he stood against the wall, behind the stove, he might not have been in the room at all. While I was with him the bespectacled American journalist came over in a business-like manner to talk to him, or really to interview him, and I drew aside so as not to interfere, since no doubt it was an important occasion for him, a much-read journalist covering Paris, to meet one of its most famous characters at a studio party. He moved to the assault, but Joyce stood before him in the same limp, apathetic attitude, plainly refusing to respond in any way, while the journalist made every effort to prize open this literary oyster, wondering perhaps if this was the same James Joyce who had penned *Ulysses* or had some other man been fobbed off on to him.

At last he had to give up, a defeated man, or what is worse, a defeated journalist. He returned to Davidson, shrugging his shoulders, and I overheard him say:
—There is nothing left in him. It has all gone into his book.

I could not help but be amused, remembering as I did how, one afternoon a little while before, I had been with Joyce in his flat and was about to leave when he suddenly asked me to stay, for he said that two editors of the *Little Review* were arriving and would I help him to meet them. I must say that the suggestion came as a surprise to me, for these two women, having crossed the Atlantic to meet their literary hero for whom they had already compassed so much, had no wish to meet him through a go-between. One would think that Joyce would have welcomed them with enthusiasm—but no, when they arrived he remained standing at the far end of the table, only answering them in monosyllables, trying to turn the conversation on to me. In fact, being used in this manner as a buffer between them and their enthusiasm irritated them and in the end I fled. I am certain that a similar situation occurred many times over, for Joyce's shyness, or his extreme sensitivity, prevented him from behaving naturally to strangers.

It was now getting late and the studio was almost in darkness except for the glimmer from the huge window and the red glow of the stove, when I heard Joyce cry out my name as a soul might cry out in its pain in purgatory—and he came forward in the obscurity, putting out his hands in his semi-blindness to feel his way. I was just in time to prevent him from putting his hand on to the red-hot pipe. Certainly parties did not amuse him and he had come there no doubt because I was the host. Now he was anxious to go, his debt of loyalty paid. As I escorted him to the top of the perilous stairs, trebly perilous for him on account of his bad sight, I wondered—as was natural, even as the American journalist must have done—' is this the man who has written the book which has shocked the whole world—the man who in *Ulysses* has described Bob Doran weeping in the pub about Paddy Dignam's death: " The finest man, says he, snivelling, the finest purest character "...'?

Truly, appearances are deceptive, for who would think that this slight and delicately built man with his smooth clerkly face, small pointed beard, with those strong spectacles glassing his weak eyes, was the most revolutionary character in this age of artistic revolutions? Indeed I realized that there was much of the Fenian about him—his dark suiting, his wide hat, his light carriage, and his intense expression—a literary conspirator, who was determined to destroy the oppressive and respectable cultural structures under which we had been reared, and which were then crumbling. Indeed, I remember his saying to me once:

—You know that there are people who would refuse to sit in the same room as me.

And, sensitive man as he was, it may have been the fear of suddenly meeting with such people who would cause an explosion that gave him that restless shyness.

Mrs Joyce did not seem to be quite so conscious of his difficult position. Indeed the only time she ever mentioned the subject to me was one day when I met her in the rue du Bac. She had been to see a priest about something—maybe it was to go to confession—and she told me the priest had said to her:

—Mrs Joyce, cannot you stop your husband from writing those terrible books?

But she replied:

—What can I do?

Indeed it was the only answer she could give, for what rebel worth his salt is going to be persuaded out of his course either by his wife or by a priest?

In all, she was more philosophical than he was, and was always ready to accept the worst with the best in the ordinary sense, a down-and-out lodging house or the table of honour in a restaurant-de-luxe. About people she was more difficult, though she managed to hide her true feelings, but in private she would let an odd phrase drop to show how deep her resentment lay. She could not bear deception or insincerity in any form, and just as one of Joyce's main defences was silence, she, too, had learned the value of silence from him, when the occasion arose. I know at times she used to revolt secretly against the artificiality of Parisian life, and once at a party, when the dancing had started in a very uncertain and self-conscious way, she exclaimed to me:

—If this was happening in Galway we'd all be out in a minute on the road kicking up our heels in the dust.

Her natural spontaneity never deserted her, except after Joyce's death, when, it seemed to me, she deliberately suppressed it.

His sister Eva disapproved of the marriage and believed that her brother, having got himself into a false position, could not get out of it. She told me of an occasion in Trieste when they were re-arranging a room in a new flat they had taken. Satisfied at last, they all relaxed, when Mrs Joyce picked up a pee-pot and placed it triumphantly on the highest piece of furniture in the room. Eva quoted this incident as an example of her sister-in-law's common origin, though I could not regard it as other than a Ulyssian touch. For my part I never experienced anything from Mrs Joyce but a natural refinement. Indeed, in the Joyces' home there were never any dirty stories told; even risky ones were taboo, and if anyone started telling them they did not last long as a friend. Again, one could expect a very cold reception from both Joyce and Mrs Joyce if one brought to their flat a casual girl friend one had met in a café as, indeed, I was often tempted to do. Your *belle amie,* yes!—provided it was always she—but a casual piece, no. Joyce's sensitivity was such that during the composition of ' Oxen of the Sun ', which takes place in the lying-in hospital, he was put off his food because his imagination was filled with half-born foetuses, swabs, and the smell of disinfectants.

# IX

One day, in a state of excitement, I went to see Joyce. I had come across a volume of *Plutarch's Lives* and had been reading it, and all the time I had been wondering how it was I had not read or heard much about it before.

The volume I picked up starts with an account of Phocion which I did not read, and then of Cato the Younger, only part of which I read, since I was not particularly interested in either lawyers or politicians. Then turning over some pages I read about Antony, and it was he who captured my imagination for he seemed to me to be the outstanding figure of the ancient world.

—The history of Antony and Cleopatra, I remarked, is one of the greatest love stories in which passion dominates wealth and power; and finally there is their brave contempt for death.

—Yes, agreed Joyce, it is Christianity which has made us afraid of death, for men, nowadays, live in two halves in which their desire to live is tempered by their fear of death so that we no longer know which way to turn, and as a result both our public and private lives are smothered in hypocrisy. The pagans faced death as bravely as they faced life; 'one life one death' was their philosophy. But I don't know why you have chosen Antony as your hero. Surely there were many better Romans than he.

—It is because Antony is my idea of a full man, I told him. I believe that he could turn straight away from a life of luxury and debauch as only the Romans understood it to the utmost hardship, eating animals and things which no other men ever had eaten, as he did, for instance, during his retreat over the

Alps. In fact the greater the adversity the greater the man he became, and in his lifetime there was no hardship and no luxury which he did not experience. And in Plutarch he found an author who was worthy of him. I admire Plutarch's account, it is concise, imaginative and clear. I have tried to read Shakespeare's *Antony and Cleopatra* since, but I got lost in its sea of words. There is a dramatic tension in Plutarch's account which I find missing in Shakespeare, for words can drain so much away. Life is clean, spare, and hard —or can be; and I can understand why men of action fling books aside as I have often seen them do, as something second-rate, something that they cannot be bothered with: just as I understand why they look with contempt on intellectuals and literary folk, and other life-tasters.

—You're just being emotional, said Joyce, and carried away by the exotic background of their lives which appeals to your romantic nature. You are talking like a philistine.

—Maybe, I said, but even a good writer must have a good deal of the philistine in him.

—Yes, to a certain extent that is true, he agreed, for an author must not write for the arty. There must be a sound basis of fact in his work. You said that the man of action pretends a contempt for the artist and writer. But that is a very superficial point of view, for if it were not for the writer their actions would be lost and forgotten in the dust that they created. It is an artist such as Plutarch who makes them live again: the men of action and men of imagination are the complement of each other. Nobody was more aware of it than the ancient Romans whose emperors, generals and statesmen were the friends of men of letters. Indeed, if they conquered a city they always sought to enter it with the leading philosopher or intellectual of that city, holding him by the hand to show their good intentions towards the people. Today we are less civilized. But I am still not clear about the original point you intended to make, said Joyce.

—What I have wanted to say was that the classical style still seems to me to be the best form of writing.

—Perhaps, but to my mind it is a form of writing which contains little or no mystery, commented Joyce, and since we are surrounded by mystery it has always seemed to me inadequate. It can deal with facts very well, but when it has to deal with motives, the secret currents of life which govern everything, it has not the orchestra, for life is a complicated problem. It is no doubt flattering and pleasant to have it presented in an uncomplicated fashion, as the classicists pretend to do, but it is an intellectual approach which no longer satisfies the modern mind, which is interested above all in subtleties, equivocations and the subterranean complexities which dominate the average man and compose his life. I would say that the difference between classical literature and modern literature is the difference between the objective and the subjective: classical literature represents the daylight of human personality while modern literature is concerned with the twilight, the passive rather than the active mind. We feel that the classicists explored the physical world to its limit, and we are now anxious to explore the hidden world, those undercurrents which flow beneath the apparently firm surface. But as our education was based on the classical, most of us have a fixed idea of what literature should be, and not only literature but also of what life should be. And so we moderns are accused of distortion; but our literature is no more distorted than classical literature is. All art in a sense is distorted in that it must exaggerate certain aspects to obtain its effect and in time people will accept this so-called modern distortion, and regard it as the truth. Our object is to create a new fusion between the exterior world and our contemporary selves, and also to enlarge our vocabulary of the subconscious as Proust has done. We believe that it is in the abnormal that we approach closer to reality. When we are living a normal life we are living a conventional one, following a pattern which has been laid out by other people in another generation, an objective pattern imposed on us by the church and state. But a writer must maintain a continual struggle against the objective: that is his function. The eternal qualities are the imagination and the sexual instinct, and the formal life tries to suppress both. Out of this present conflict arise the phenomena of modern life.

74

—In my Mabbot Street scene I approached reality closer in my opinion than anywhere else in the book except perhaps for moments in the last chapter. Sensation is our object, heightened even to the point of hallucination. You described Plutarch's account of Antony as concise, imaginative and clear. In my opinion it is more concise than clear or imaginative; what is really imaginative is the contrary to what is concise and clear.
—Also in regard to environment, or 'background' to use a literary term, the background of the classicists and romantics is unreal for the majority of men. It has no relation to the lives that most of us live and to the surroundings which enclose them:

> Ordure amons, ordure nous assuit;
> Nous deffuyons onneur, il nous deffuit,
> En ce bordeau ou tenons nostre estat.

as Villon puts it. If we are to paint the twilight of the human personality we must darken the landscape also. Idealism is a pleasant bauble, but in these days of overwhelming reality it no longer interests us, or even amuses. We regard it as a sort of theatrical drop-scene. Most lives are made up like the modern painter's themes, of jugs, and pots and plates, back-streets and blowsy living-rooms inhabited by blowsy women, and of a thousand daily sordid incidents which seep into our minds no matter how we strive to keep them out. These are the furniture of our life, which you want to reject for some romantic and flimsy drop-scene.
—I admit I prefer my illusion, I said.
—There you are mistaken, said Joyce, for the fact of things as they are is far more exciting. Eliot has a mind which can appreciate and express both and by placing one in contrast to the other he has obtained striking effects. It is true that one cannot shed the past completely and one must take both worlds into consideration, but the hidden or subconscious world is the most exciting and the modern writer is far more interested in the potential than in the actual—in the unexplored and hallucinatory even—than in the well-trodden romantic or classical world.

# X

We talked about André Gide's *Voyage au Congo,* an account of his experiences when he accompanied the Citroën advertising expedition into Africa. Joyce had a great admiration for Gide; in fact he was the only French writer, or indeed the only modern writer, whom I ever heard him admire with any real enthusiasm.

I myself had looked forward to Gide's book very much, for I thought the combination of Gide and darkest Africa would be splendid, but I was greatly disappointed in spite of the widespread interest which was shown in it. *Voyage au Congo—carnets de route* is its title, so I suppose I should not have expected so much. Still, think what Pierre Loti would have made of it, for in a sense *Fleurs d'Ennui* was started as notes in something of the same style, but how much evocation and art is in the subjects inspiring him. In Gide's *carnets* there is a complete absence of art. They are journalism, and rather crude journalism at that; notes, one supposes, which were taken down from day to day and thrown into book form, an unsatisfactory and lazy way of composing.

Leaving aside the searchlight he throws on the social conditions of Africa, which were a matter for the French Government, I could not understand what literary merit Joyce saw in this book, or indeed in Gide's writing at all.

I have another book by him, the first copy of the first edition of *La Symphonie pastorale* which Joyce gave me as a Christmas present.

—Read that, he said to me, and let it be your model.

But I cannot read it: or at least to speak the truth I have

man-handled myself through it, that tiresome over-written faded story. It is, I admit, subtle and even poetic in intention, but it is written in such a wandering and indeterminate way that one feels one is dragging a dead weight after one, it saps one's vitality, and one is irritated by the same faded literary personality who wrote *Voyage au Congo*. So I protested to Joyce about him as an example of a writer who had a big reputation but who was of no value.

Joyce sighed.

Then he said after a while:

—I suppose there are people who think the same about me.

—Ah, no, I replied. You have salt, much salt, whereas Gide had to scrape the bottom of the 1890s with its faded classicisms and drawing-room psychology to cover a page.

—He has a beautiful style, protested Joyce. What about *La Porte étroite*?

—It is his best book, I admitted. His only book.

—It is a little masterpiece, he said. It is as fine as a spire on Notre Dame.

—I admit that it has merit, I said, some merit, but otherwise I can see nothing in him but a literary *vieux marcheur,* not so big a figure as Anatole France, but just as deceptive.

Joyce sighed again, his habitual sigh of weariness at my contradiction. Our points of view were too far apart to continue the conversation, so turning to me he said:

—Then whom do you admire in modern French literature?

It was a difficult question to answer for I did not read much contemporary literature. Only one name came to me, an author whom I had so liked that I had taken the trouble to collect some first editions of his work in the belief that one day they might be valuable.

—Max Jacob, I said.

—Who? asked Joyce.

—Max Jacob, I repeated. I was reading a book of his only the other day, *Cinématoma,* lively and witty sketches of French life.

But I could see by his expression that he did not think much of Max Jacob.

—How did you come to admire him? he asked.

—Somebody told me about him and I found his book original and personal, with individual and interesting literary cameos, very lively and original.

—He has not much significance, replied Joyce, putting Max Jacob aside. But what about Proust? he asked. There is somebody, surely. He is the most important French author of our day.

I had only read the first two volumes of *À l'ombre des jeunes filles en fleurs* in the translation by Scott-Moncrieff. I had tried to read *Du côté de chez Swann* in the original, but I had found it too difficult and had got lost in the tangle of his sentences.

—They seemed to me to be much over-written, I said, and those long sentences of his. . . . He wore me out with his refinements.

—You should have given him more patience, said Joyce, for he is the best of the modern French writers, and certainly no one has taken modern psychology so far, or to such a fine point. I myself think, however, that he would have done better if he had continued to write in his earlier style, for I remember reading once some early sketches in a book of his entitled *Les plaisirs et les jours,* studies of Parisian society in the '90s, and there was one in it, ' Mélancolique Villégiature de Mme de Breyves ' which impressed me greatly. If he had continued in that early style, in my opinion he would have written the best novels of our generation. But instead he launched into *À la recherche du temps perdu*, which suffers from over-elaboration.

—Yes, I agreed, for I like him and yet I don't like him—and I remember him, and yet I don't remember him, for he sees everything through a veil, and his characters get lost in a sea of words. There is no sharpness about him; no noise even. His mind is one of the most noiseless in literature. And his snobism irritates me.

—He is a special writer, I admit, yet in spite of the fact that he writes about decaying aristocrats, I rank him with Balzac and Thackeray.

—I am sorry, but all those well-fed leisured people irritate me, I said, people isolated out of life to whom love seems more like a disease than a passion. Though you say that his purpose was to give as full an impression as he could, I feel that he lacks the necessary restraint that every artist should have and, as a pampered and over-delicate man himself, he luxuriated in his hobby and could not decide when to stop. What did he gain by this experimentation in style?

—It was not experimentation, said Joyce, his innovations were necessary to express modern life as he saw it. As life changes, the style to express it must change also. Take the theatre: no one would think of writing a modern play in the style the Greeks used, or in the style of the Morality plays of the Middle Ages. A living style should be like a river which takes the colour and texture of the different regions through which it flows. The so-called classical style has a fixed rhythm and a fixed mood which make it to my mind an almost mechanical device. Proust's style conveys that almost imperceptible but relentless erosion of time which, as I say, is the motive of his work.

—I believe he was an extraordinary man, as eccentric as his style was, I said, who no matter what the time of year was, always wore a heavy overcoat and dark spectacles and was muffled up to the chin.

—Yes, said Joyce, I met him once at a literary dinner and when we were introduced all he said to me was: ' Do you like truffles?' ' Yes', I replied, ' I am very fond of truffles.' And that was the only conversation which took place between the two most famous writers of their time, remarked Joyce—who seemed to be highly amused at the incident.

—What about Barrès, Anatole France? I asked, but Joyce waved them aside with his hand without making a single comment on their work. Indeed I have been told that the nearest man to compare with Proust is Saint Simon.

—I cannot see the analogy, Joyce said, except that they both had this admiration—and in Proust's case one might say it was an adoration—for ' blood '. But in Saint Simon's case it was entirely political. He believed that the ' nobles ' or the higher aristocracy should govern the France of his day, and he was always intriguing for that purpose. Otherwise he had a totally different personality. Saint Simon was a realist if ever there was one, and his account of the intrigues, political and otherwise, of the Court of Louis XIV is written in a hard, dry, incisive manner without imagination or psychology even, but I suppose psychology was hardly of his time, for in those days they saw everything with a clear eye. Nevertheless he could give a masterly description, as, for instance, of the death of Louis XIV. I remember feeling very unhappy while I was reading those memoirs, that court atmosphere with all its unpleasant and spoilt personalities impinging themselves on me, and all those greedy harpies of women, and those arrogant and false men: the Duc d'Orléans, Saint Simon's patron, and his terrible duchesse, and that fat over-eating 'Monsieur', Louis XIV's brother. There is a description I remember of him coming to dine with the king, and he was so apoplectic looking that the king threatened to have him carried into the next room and bled by force. But that very evening on his return home he had a stroke, and there is a description of how he lies dying on the floor with only one unwilling valet present. ... It was all very macabre, I thought.

—No man was less of an artist than Saint Simon, I said. Think of that court with its handsome women in their powdered hair and their jewels, their fêtes and their gallantries. Saint Simon seems to have been insensitive to it all or took it for granted, and his continued political hatred of the king's illegitimate children seems to have blinded him to everything else. Indeed in the whole book he has scarcely a good word for anyone except for the young Prince de Bourbon who died young from an accident out hunting when his horse stumbled and the pummel ruptured his stomach. It is one of his few genuine notes of regret.

—Yes, and there is a doctor Faquet, I remember, the Court physician, said Joyce, who used to hold long consultations whether he would bleed his patient from the foot or the elbow, a sort of *deus ex machina,* who killed off one member of the royal family after the other, though I daresay he prolonged their lives in some cases, since most of them suffered from over-eating. But I cannot see any relationship between Proust and Saint Simon, no—not even on the question of ' blood '; for with Proust, as I say, it had an almost mystic significance. Do you remember his description of the first time he met a duchess: an Irish prelate meeting the Pope could not have made a greater occasion of it, a wizened old dame, if I remember rightly, but whose tread sanctified the ground.

—It is a cult I cannot understand, I argued. As Bacon remarked: ' old gold is old family '. It all seems to me to be on such a material basis; while with genius on the other hand one feels it is a gift of the gods.

—I would not altogether agree with you there, he said. There must be some quality in ' blood ' for it to maintain its position generation after generation: some strength and some wisdom. Also how often do we find that some nobleman was the patron of an artist, or a musician, even when the rest of the world did not take notice of him. Indeed some people think that the decline of the patron has caused a decline in art.

—It was only art of a certain kind, art which flattered them or their sensibilities: a Boucher, a Watteau, or a Fragonard, or a Velasquez with his royal portraits.

—That is not altogether true, he objected. Louis XIV patronized Racine, whose art was of an aristocratic type I admit, but he also befriended Molière. And the royal court of Spain favoured Goya until he disgraced himself by making friends with the French invader, even helping them to choose the pictures from the Prado to be sent to France, I believe. You must admit that patrons have played an important part in the arts. Indeed in many cases they would not have been created but for their help.

Indeed what was the constant tragedy of the *Quartier* but lack of money? One is constantly hearing of the desperate circumstances of artists. Take the case of Modigliani, for instance, who died on 25 January 1920. He lived in continual poverty, a poverty which in the end, you may say, killed him. I remember being in the café the evening the news came in that he had died in hospital, and only a little later we heard

F

that his poor wife had jumped off the roof of her parents' house. When I asked, rather stupidly, why she had done it, they all shrugged their shoulders and answered: *Elle était dans la misère.* For that seemed to everybody to be the complete and explanatory answer, *la misère,* a word for which there seems to be no adequate equivalent in English.

I had been introduced to Modigliani by my friend Sola. He was standing at the *comptoir* of the Dôme drinking a rum when, for something to say, I asked him why the artists had deserted Montmartre for Montparnasse, which was an ugly bourgeois quarter in comparison.

—Studios have become hard to get in Montmartre, he told me, for ordinary people who are not artists at all have found them cheap and easy lodgings. And then perhaps a new art requires a new district. The art of Montmartre is *vieux jeu.* Also there are the two big Academies around the corner where one can draw a model for a few francs. . . . *Enfin,* the change has taken place, and anyway it is easier to sell a modern picture in Montparnasse than in Montmartre.

A singularly handsome fellow with stout deep chest, Modigliani was already ravaged-looking, for poverty, drink and drugs had done their work. Nevertheless, in spite of his debauched appearance he still retained an air of distinction and of singular nobility, and even as I talked with him I remembered some of those fine drawings of his which I had admired in the windows of the various *marchands de tableaux*: a fusion of the Italian primitive and Negro sculpture, those girls of his with their slender necks, sightless eyes, and delicately etched mouths. Of the many there is one in particular which always stands out in my memory. It is of Madame Hastings, done in 1915 at the beginning of the love affair which was to become a legend in the *Quartier.* Drawn in pencil and crayon, it is just a head: her hair divided down the centre, the eyes blank and almond-shaped, the mouth small and full-lipped, the neck long and slender, with the black tags of hair hanging down from behind the ears on either side—the impression of a young woman in love. It was a drawing originally done for a sculpture perhaps, and one of the many he did of her at that time in which he recorded his numerous and changing reactions from love to hate, so that one can almost tell what were his daily, or even hourly feelings towards her.

It was by chance that I met her some time later after Modigliani's death, one afternoon on the terrace of the Café Rotonde: a small compact brunette, *bien roulée* as the French say, who spoke in a quiet voice tempered with disillusion. After I had told her how interested I was in Modigliani, I was delighted to be asked up to tea for the following Saturday at her apartment near the Lion de Belfort. She promised to lend me the diary which she had kept at that time.

As she poured out the tea and handed me the cups she complained about the failure of her literary ambitions. When she had first come to Paris she used to write a weekly article for a well-known English magazine, an episode in which a mythical young lady used to lose her clothes, with the subsequent adventures during the course of the evening to recover them. I naturally asked what she thought of Modigliani's work, and to my surprise she told me that she did not think much of it.

—Paris, she said, has many such fads and they quickly pass. He will soon be forgotten like the rest. He was a fashion in the *Quartier* because of the life he lived, but his work was too sentimental to have any value. It is the one thing we cannot stand, today—those sickly-looking women of his.

I was too dumbfounded and disappointed to make an adequate answer. Indeed, she seemed to treat the whole affair of her relationship with Modigliani as an episode of slight importance, she, who had been at the very core of Parisian artistic life, consorting with such remarkable personalities as Picasso and Utrillo. It had been an affair, she intimated to me, in which she had wasted her affection and her energy, and which had evidently brought her only disillusionment. The conversation veered around to literature, when for some reason, perhaps because Modigliani used constantly to quote him, the subject of Dante came up, and she remarked with bitterness:

—How could Dante, knowing as he did what life was like, have written that stuff about Beatrice and the Paradiso? All of which she evidently regarded as a bitter joke.

It was nevertheless with some excitement that I took back her diary to where I was living at the time, a studio overlooking the Parc Montsouris. Seating myself at the window in the fading light, I was prepared for a revelation as I opened the leaves of her manuscript, an account of their exalted if strained relationship, of Modigliani's doings and sayings, his dicta on art, and also of those sudden and unaccountable moods which seemed to pass over him like a storm changing the aspect of everything. But as I read on I was disappointed, for she seemed chiefly to be interested in Max Jacob's sexual abnormality, saying little about Modigliani except for a brief description of their first meeting: 'A complex character: a cross between a pig and a pearl: hashish and brandy: he looked ugly, ferocious and greedy. Met again at the Café Rotonde, he was shaved and charming . . .'. All very feminine and literary no doubt, but I did not feel the breath of passion stirring through the leaves. Indeed, even as a diary it would have been better if it had been written in a plain factual manner instead of in its rather artificial literary style. It might then have been an invaluable record of Modigliani's life during his most creative and emotional period, when she had lived with him and Max Jacob in *Le Bateau-Lavoir,* the famous 'Floating Laundry', as it was nicknamed, in the rue Ravignan close to the Butte de Montmartre. This unique experience had made little or no impact on her. Either she had not understood its significance or—which is probably the truth—she had had neither the sympathy nor the talent to describe it. Now she seemed only to remember her lover's difficult character, the violence and drunkenness, which had submerged his finer qualities. Her general tone indicated that she had looked on him as another foreign *voyou* with whom she, an English lady, had got mixed up.

Shortly after Modigliani died I was taken up to his studio. It was a small single narrow room at the top of the house next to mine in the rue de la Grande Chaumière with a bare floor and bare walls and a single window with a small balcony. The artist then living in it was an Algerian, and very poor himself, so that there was practically no furniture in it, not even a bed, but a mattress laid on the floor, around which he told me he used to pour a little water to keep the bugs off. On the wall was hung the death-mask of Modigliani which some friends had taken in the hospital, with its sunken cheeks and indrawn lips, a very different face from the fine, robust-looking young man he had been. I asked who owned the mask. But the Algerian shrugged his shoulders.

—I found it when I came in here with the rest of the stuff. No one owns it. It is there.

But the thought came to my mind as I examined it, this shrunken image, how lucky was the man, a man like Joyce, who had a patron and so had been spared this calvary for if with increasing years Joyce had decided to abandon everything for his writing it might have happened to him. Though Modigliani had some artistic success, the appreciation had not been sufficiently general to save him financially. *Moi—moi—j'ai brulé la vie*, as he had exclaimed to me once . . . and what else in his hard circumstances could the poor fellow do? The demon of creation had entered him, and after that few men think of their personal safety.

# XI

I had been thinking over our conversation about Proust, and it seemed to me that the nearest approach to him was the Japanese writer, Lady Murasaki, whose work Joyce did not know. I had recently come upon Arthur Waley's translation and found *The Tale of Genji* the most feminine book I had read, a meandering satire written in a steady monotone which never rises to a crescendo but at the same time distils an intangible essence, just as Proust does.

Lady Murasaki was, like Proust, a complete snob. To her, rank and position at Court were all important, and everything and everybody outside it was awkward and uncivilized, while the country she looked on as a barbarous place where youth and beauty waste their lives. She had no interest in achievement, for when the governors of the different provinces come to Court, all she notes about them is that they are rough and ignorant, and though Prince Genji himself is the principal Officer of the State she barely remarks on it, for it is his handsome appearance and masculine charm that interest her, and, perhaps more than anything else, his royal blood, for he was the illegitimate son of the emperor.

Her book is a question of style, and the pictures she gives us of the Court of Japan a thousand years ago do not differ so much in tone from the section of Parisian society which Proust describes. I had been wondering whether I should send the book to Joyce, and I talked to him about it at some length but my description was so confused that he evidently had no wish to read it. When I suggested lending it to him he almost ignored the suggestion.

—If you like, he replied in the most off-hand manner.

So I did not feel like bringing it. Pleasure hangs on such a fine balance that I did not want mine upset. Lady Murasaki's conception of life is so different from his that I am sure it would have bored him with its numerous complications and cross motives in which desire defeats itself, for in spite of his many successes Prince Genji is drawn in too many directions to be happy. Not that Joyce would have expected a happy hero, he was too tortured a man himself, but its aesthetic and romantic association would have irritated the realist in him.

I returned instead to the subject of Pierre Loti, in an effort to convince Joyce of his merit, but he could not understand my admiration for him. In fact my insistence seemed rather to irritate him and he said to me :

—If you must admire a French romantic writer why not admire a man like Stendhal with his *Le rouge et le noir* and his *La Chartreuse de Parme*. Passion was his *raison d'être,* and that surely is the religion of all romantics—exaltation through the passions.

—Maybe, I answered, but to be a romantic does not mean necessarily that you are cruel and ruthless, or even absurd as Fabrice often is. Loti was a romantic, a romantic impressionist if you will, but there is no ruthlessness, or cruelty, or absurdity about him.

—Maybe, but Stendhal was a product of the Napoleonic age, when the French saw themselves as world conquerors, and his attitude was such. But putting that aside one must admit that *La Chartreuse* is a good book in the romantic tradition.

—In a sense, yes, but it is not satisfying. It is too highly coloured for my taste even, and that long episode about Fabrice's incarceration in the Farnese Tower with the jailor's daughter Celia, a latin mixture of prayer and passion, throwing messages into his cell from her window.

—But you must admit to his merit, insisted Joyce, for few men have conveyed passion with such intensity as he has, as for instance in that scene in *Le rouge et le noir* when Julien hides in Madame de Rênal's bedroom : or again later in the book when he climbs up the ladder at night into the bedroom of Mathilde de La Mole. His description of their emotional frenzy is magnificent. And he wrote some excellent scenes, he continued, his unexpected praise of a romantic writer more and more surprising me,—like the one of the ball in *Le rouge et le noir* at which Mathilde becomes interested in Count Altamira for the singular reason that he was once condemned to death. Compare for instance Thackeray's social scenes in *Vanity Fair* with Stendhal's, how flat they are, yet their books were written about the same period and deal with much the same kind of people. Stendhal never became sentimental and soft the way Thackeray did, especially over women; in his greatest extravagance he remains hard and glittering.

—Agreed, but nevertheless, I said, perversely taking up the cudgels for *Vanity Fair,* it is a well-written book, and the characters are well sustained, and if they themselves do not develop much, their history develops in that subtle atmosphere of social assassination which you get in England. Thackeray has described the social life of his time in a broad and clear manner, but without pride, flair or brilliance.

—Yes, I admit that, said Joyce, but Thackeray has something which Stendhal did not have: humour.

—Humour, I exclaimed, it is that which has always prevented the English novel from rising to its full height.

—Do you think so?, interposed Joyce. What about Swift: and what about Bernard Shaw?

—They were not novelists, I said.

—Novelists or not, I think that there is something very inhuman about an author who has no sense of humour, and it is a thing which Stendhal lacked—and which some Frenchmen lack, their very emotional pitch prevents it, for they cannot but take life seriously, and no Frenchman will admit his inferiority before life. His vanity prevents it. But an Englishman is better balanced, and he will admit his powerlessness before fate by means of his humour.

—True, I said, but I nevertheless prefer Stendhal to Thackeray in spite of his confusion and obscurity for the reason that I prefer most things for their beauty. That is the quality we all admire in a work of art, not intellect and description of character, but beauty—beauty as you get it in Pierre Loti, in Turgeniev, in Mérimée. Indeed, to refer to your own work, I prefer your *Portrait* to *Ulysses* for the same reason—for its lambent beauty, its softly flowing phrases full of ascending lights, incandescent forms, and veiled images. It is the best description there is of adolescence, for the first of everything is the best. We are inclined to value experience too highly, but in all it is an ugly thing.

—It is the descent into hell, and *Ulysses* is that descent, for one cannot always remain an adolescent. Ulysses is the man of experience. Out of this marriage, this forced marriage of the spirit and matter, humour is created, for *Ulysses* is fundamentally a humorous work, and when all this present critical confusion about it has died down, people will see it for what it is.

—Then in your opinion, I said, the critics and the intellectuals have boggled the issue, have not seen your intention clearly, and have put meanings into it which did not exist, which they have invented for themselves.

—Yes and no, replied Joyce shrugging his shoulders evasively, for who knows but it is they who are right. What do we know about what we put into anything? Though people may read more into *Ulysses* than I ever intended, who is to say that they are wrong: do any of us know what we are creating? Did Shakespeare know what he was creating when he wrote *Hamlet;* or Leonardo when he painted ' The Last Supper '? After all, the original genius of a man lies in his scribblings: in his casual actions lies his basic talent. Later he may develop that talent until he produces a *Hamlet* or a ' Last Supper ', but if the minute scribblings which compose the big work are not significant, the big work goes for nothing no matter how grandly conceived. Which of us can control our scribblings? They are the script of one's personality like your voice or your walk. And as for this beauty you talk about, an idea which seems to haunt you, one may say, in the terms of the new aesthetic of today, that ' only that which is ugly is beautiful '.

# XII

One afternoon Joyce asked me to go with him to Larbaud's flat as he wanted to collect some books he had left there. Larbaud had lent Joyce his flat when he first arrived in Paris. It was a flat containing, according to Joyce, a room specially designed for writing which I was very anxious to see.

We crossed the Luxembourg Gardens and passed by the Round Pond in front of the Senate where there always seems to be a collection of small boys and girls sailing their boats, boats which seem to suffer the same fate as real boats, being wrecked around the base of the fountain, in the centre, or in collision with other boats, or entangled with rivals. Yet the French children never seem to show their annoyance openly or start those rough-and-tumbles that you see among English and Irish boys, and even among the girls sometimes. They treat each other with a cynical politeness which must date from the Grand Epoch and which, as Joyce remarked, is amusing to watch.

Mounting the balustrade steps we approached those big golden-topped gates opposite the Panthéon. Crossing the Boulevard St Michel we went towards the Church of St Etienne-du-Mont, and turning down a narrow street we stopped before one of those tall grey houses which you find in that quarter. Joyce took out a key and opened the door into Larbaud's flat. I have seen rooms designed for many purposes but never as yet had I seen a room specially designed for writing. It was shaped like the cabin of a ship, had a low, rounded ceiling with a light in the middle and a long table running down the centre with shelves like small bunks along the wall on either side at an arm's length. Situated where it was it would be cool in summer, and as it was small it should be easy to heat in winter. It was also sound-proof and draught-proof in contrast to the average room in a flat in which most writers have to work. But to my surprise Joyce told me that he did not like working in it.

—I don't like being shut up, he said. When I am working I like to hear noise going on around me—the noise of life; there it was like writing in a tomb. I suppose I would have got used to it, but I didn't want to because then I might have lost my ability to work wherever I happen to be, in a lodging-house, or in a hotel room, and silence might have become a necessity to me as it was, for example, to Proust.

Having collected his books and also some manuscripts, he put them into an attaché case and deposited the key with the concierge. Returning by the Panthéon, we re-entered the Boulevard St Michel and started to saunter down towards the river.

To my mind the Boulevard St Michel is one of the most attractive in Paris. Indeed in no other part of Paris were you aware of the distinctive spirit of the Middle Ages, and as we walked down towards the river our conversation turned on such men as Raymond Lulle, Duns Scotus, and Albertus Magnus, and the strange world they had created.

—Yes, it was the true spirit of western Europe, Joyce remarked, and if it had continued, think what a splendid civilization we might have had today. After all, the Renaissance was an intellectual return to boyhood. Compare a Gothic building with a Greek or Roman one: Notre Dame, for instance, with the Madeleine. I remember once standing in the gardens beside Notre Dame and looking up at its roofs, at their amazing complication—plane overlapping plane, angle countering angle, the numerous traversing gutters and runnels, flying buttresses and erupting gargoyles. In comparison, classical buildings always seem to me to be over-simple and lacking in mystery. Indeed one of the most interesting things about present-day thought in my opinion is its return to mediaevalism.

—A return to mediaevalism, I exclaimed in surprise.

—Yes, replied Joyce. The old classical Europe which we knew in our youth is fast disappearing; the cycle has returned upon its tracks, and with it will come a new consciousness which will create new values returning to the mediaeval. There is an old church I know of down near Les Halles, a black foliated building with flying buttresses spread out like the legs of a spider, and as you walk past it you see the huge cobwebs hanging in its crevices, and more than anything else I know of it reminds me of my own writings, so that I feel that if I had lived in the fourteenth or fifteenth century I should have been much more appreciated. Men realized then that evil was a necessary complement to our lives and had its own spiritual value. I see that note constantly recurring among the younger poets today.

—There is nothing new in diabolism, I objected, it has always existed. You get it in Goya, and in Spanish literature, and it exists even in their gypsy music, while in France it re-emerged in the last century in Baudelaire and Rimbaud.

And halting in his step Joyce quoted to me out loud some lines from Baudelaire:

> *Loin des peuples vivants, errantes condamnées,*
> *A travers les déserts courez comme les loups;*
> *Faites votre destin, âmes désordonnées . . .*

—That, he exclaimed, is the new order of the day, and it is the constant strife between the two opposing types which creates the drama of the world. It was the intense consciousness of this battle which gave the mediaeval world its colour —the windows in Chartres Cathedral, the *Imitation of Christ*

He hesitated a moment and then said:

—And in my opinion one of the most interesting things about Ireland is that we are still fundamentally a mediaeval people, and that Dublin is still a mediaeval city. I know that when I used to frequent the pubs around Christ Church I was always reminded of those mediaeval taverns in which the sacred and the obscene jostle shoulders, and one of the reasons is that we were never subjected to the Lex Romana as other nations were. I have always noticed, for instance, that if you show a

Renaissance work to an Irish peasant he will gape at it in a kind of cold wonder, for in a dim way he realizes that it does not belong to his world. His symbolism is still mediaeval, and it is that which separates us from the Englishman, or the Frenchman, or the Italian, all of whom are Renaissance men. Take Yeats, for example, he is a true mediaevalist with his love of magic, his incantations and his belief in signs and symbols, and his later bawdiness. *Ulysses* also is mediaeval but in a more realistic way, and so you will find that the whole trend of modern thought is going in that direction, for as it is I can see there is going to be another age of extremes, of ideologies, of persecutions, of excesses which will be political perhaps instead of religious, though the religious may reappear as part of the political, and in this new atmosphere you will find the old way of writing and thinking will disappear, is fast disappearing in fact, and *Ulysses* is one of the books which has hastened that change.

—But America, I protested, there is nothing mediaeval about her, and her influence is going to be greater and greater as time goes on. She is going to produce a lot of literature in the next fifty years, in fact she is producing it at the moment.

—Political influence, yes, he agreed, but not cultural. I do not think that she is going to produce much literature of importance as yet, for to produce literature a country must first be vintaged, have an odour in other words. What is the first thing you notice about a country when you arrive in it? Its odour, which is the gauge of its civilization, and it is that odour which percolates into its literature. Just as Rabelais smells of France in the Middle Ages and *Don Quixote* smells of the Spain of his time, so *Ulysses* smells of the Dublin of my day.

—It certainly has an effluvium, I agreed.

—Yes, it smells of the Anna Liffey, smiled Joyce, not always a very sweet smell perhaps, but distinctive all the same.

—What about Walt Whitman? I asked.

—Yes, agreed Joyce, he has a certain flavour it is true, the smell of virgin forest is in him, and of the wooden shack, a kind of primitive colonialism, but that is a long way from being civilized.

—Then what about Thoreau?

—No, he said. I look on Thoreau as an American Frenchman, a disciple of Bernadin de St Pierre, Chateaubriand, and others of that school. He is not a real American in my opinion, he just carried the European *fin-de-siècle* passivism into the new world, that is all. Certainly he does not reflect the American mind as I understand it, the real American writers so far have all been minor writers, such as Jack London, Bret Harte, Robert Service in Canada and such like, and it will take a long time before they produce any art which is worthwhile. What they want in my opinion is a few more wars. Nothing matures a nation like war, for in war men are suddenly and violently brought down to fundamentals. Indeed some of the best art in the world was produced in conditions of war and by men who were also soldiers. Shakespeare, so they say, trailed a pike in Flanders, Cervantes was for years a prisoner-of-war in Algiers, and when he was not making fortifications for his patrons, Leonardo painted a picture for them.

—In Ireland we have had a lot of war, I argued, but it does not seem to have produced much art, in fact it stifled it altogether.

—Maybe—but you must remember that Ireland was never a highly civilized nation in the sense that Italy and France were. We are too far removed from the main stream of European civilization to be really affected by it, and as a result the ordinary Irishman never seems intellectually to have got beyond religion and politics. As a result we have never produced a large body of art in the wide sense—painting, architecture, sculpture. What talent we have seems to have gone into literature, and in that you must admit we have not done badly, especially in drama. The best English plays have been written by Irishmen, while in prose we have Sterne, Wilde, Swift (if you can count him as an Irishman), and then there is George Moore, according to you, and a few others.

—And now there is *Ulysses*.

—Yes—that is my contribution, and in it I have tried to lift Irish prose to the level of the international masterpieces and to give a full representation of the Irish genius, and my hope is that it will rank among the important books of the world, for it was conceived and written in an original style. If we have a merit it is that we are uninhibited. An Irishman will seldom behave as convention demands; restraint is irksome to him. And so I have tried to write naturally, on an emotional basis as against an intellectual basis. Emotion has dictated the course and detail of my book, and in emotional writing one arrives at the unpredictable which can be of more value, since its sources are deeper, than the products of the intellectual method. In the intellectual method you plan everything beforehand. When you arrive at the description, say, of a house you try and remember that house exactly, which after all is journalism. But the emotionally creative writer refashions that house and creates a significant image in the only significant world, the world of our emotions. The more we are tied to fact and try to give a correct impression, the further we are from what is significant. In writing one must create an endlessly changing surface, dictated by the mood and current impulse in contrast to the fixed mood of the classical style. This is ' Work in Progress '. The important thing is not what we write, but how we write, and in my opinion the modern writer must be an adventurer above all, willing to take every risk, and be prepared to founder in his effort if need be. In other words we must write dangerously : everything is inclined to flux and change nowadays and modern literature, to be valid, must express that flux. In *Ulysses* I tried to express the multiple variations which make up the social life of a city—its degradations and its exaltations. In other words what we want to avoid is the classical, with its rigid structure and its emotional limitations. The mediaeval, in my opinion, had greater emotional fecundity than classicism, which is the art of the gentleman, and is now as out-of-date as gentlemen are, classicism in which the scents are only sweet, he added, but I have preferred other smells. A book, in my opinion, should not be planned out beforehand, but as one writes it will form itself, subject, as I say, to the constant emotional promptings of one's personality.

# XIII

One evening the conversation turned on reputations, when I remarked how strange and varied they were.

—For example, I said, there are those men who have had a reputation for one thing when it was something else which they did well: for being a poet, when in fact they were good prose writers, as in the case of Lamartine.

—He was also a bad prose writer, remarked Joyce.

—Yes, I replied, except for one book.

—I cannot say that I know him very well, said Joyce, for he was not a writer who appealed to me much, with his exaggerated romanticism, his conventional mysticism, and his plethora of description, but I remember liking 'Le Lac'.

*Aimons donc, aimons donc! de l'heure fugitive*
   *Hâtons-nous, jouissons!*
*L'homme n'a point de port, le temps n'a point de rive;*
   *Il coule, et nous passons!*

I said, quoting a stanza.

—There is nothing original and sincere in that. It may be his best poem; at least it is considered so. Indeed the *Méditations* is, of all, the best volume of poetry he wrote. I read a good deal of his work because I am interested in him and because in my opinion he wrote one of the prose masterpieces of French literature: 'Graziella'.

—I remember, said Joyce, reading it a long time ago, a story about his affair with an Italian fisher-girl. My recollection of it is that it was a well-sugared piece of sentimentalism in which they continually *fondent en larmes*. Indeed what I have always objected to about Lamartine is his fundamental insincerity.

—Maybe, I agreed, but talent is talent wherever it is found, and the strange thing about it is that a man can be the essence of sincerity but it avails nothing if he has not the gift, otherwise his work tastes like last year's fruit. But in the case of 'Graziella' he was really stirred. And there is great music in Lamartine's prose: he was a lyrical writer, in contrast to what I would call an intellectual writer.

—I suppose you would call me an intellectual writer, interposed Joyce.

—No, not altogether, I said. Your early works were lyrical—parts of *Dubliners* are lyrical, *A Portrait* is lyrical, but *Ulysses* is not, and perhaps that is the reason why it does not appeal to me. Much of it seems to me to be over-conscious, and inspiration is what I admire.

—Depends on what you call inspiration, doesn't it? remarked Joyce, and it seems to me that you mistake romantic flair for inspiration. The inspiration I admire is not the temperamental one, but the steady sequence of built-up thought, such as you get in *Gulliver's Travels,* in Defoe and in Rabelais even. But Lamartine's writing was just a flood of sentimentality.

—And of poetry, I added.

—Of false poetry, he replied.

—That 'Graziella' is not a great work I agree. It may be considered sentimental but it describes life as many understand it: the open air life on the shores of the Mediterranean. And it is in pleasant contrast to the modern books which are mostly urban, about the artificial life that is lived in towns and cities.

—That is because cities are of primary interest nowadays, said Joyce. This is the period of urban domination. The modern advance in techniques has made them so.

—It is degeneration, I said.

Joyce shrugged his delicate shoulders.

—A writer's purpose is to describe the life of his day, he said, and I chose Dublin because it is the focal point of the Ireland of today, its heart-beat you may say, and to ignore that would be affectation.

G

—But let us return to 'Graziella', I said, for I do not see it as you do, as a sweet piece of sentimentality. For Lamartine's picture of Graziella is in all a straightforward one and yet in reading it one is acutely conscious of the mystery of her being. Indeed I think that the essence of a personality is more truly given by a straightforward account than by the modern pretentious effort to deal in mystery. In life we often sense the mystery of a personality in a casual gesture rather than in hours of careful observation. It is Graziella's unawareness which reveals her to you. It is through the colour and tone of his words rather than by any intellectual analysis that a writer conveys his impression.

—About the use of words I agree, said Joyce. I know when I was writing *Ulysses* I tried to give the colour and tone of Dublin with my words; the drab, yet glistening atmosphere of Dublin, its hallucinatory vapours, its tattered confusion, the atmosphere of its bars, its social immobility—they could only be conveyed by the texture of my words. Thought and plot are not so important as some would make them out to be. The object of any work of art is the transference of emotion; talent is the gift of conveying that emotion. But I cannot understand your admiration for the romantic. If ever there was an exploded myth that is one.

—It persists, I replied, and will always persist.

—Maybe, but in realism you are down to facts on which the world is based: that sudden reality which smashes romanticism into a pulp. What makes most people's lives unhappy is some disappointed romanticism, some unrealizable or misconceived ideal. In fact you may say that idealism is the ruin of man, and if we lived down to fact, as primitive man had to do, we would be better off. That is what we were made for. Nature is quite unromantic. It is we who put romance into her, which is a false attitude, an egotism, absurd like all egotisms. In *Ulysses* I tried to keep close to fact. There is humour of course, for though man's position in this world is fundamentally tragic it can also be seen as humorous. The disparity between what he wants to be and what he is, is no doubt laughable, so much so that a comedian has only to come on to the stage and trip and everyone roars with laughter. Imagine how much more humorous it would be if it happened accidentally to some ardent romantic in pursuit of his romanticism. That is why we admire the primitives nowadays. They were down to reality —reality which always triumphs in the end.

# XIV

I met Joyce by chance one evening in the Champs Elysées and we sat down for a drink in 'Le Béri', with its scarlet canopy and the straw-coloured chairs spread out over the pavement. It was getting on towards six and the cars were racing up towards the Arc de Triomphe. The sky was pale over the roofs of the houses opposite and in front of us the boulevard trees were shimmering in that dark enamelled green which is a combination of artificial light and daylight. As we sat there on the terrace drinking our cinzano Joyce repeated some lines from *The Waste Land,* which had evidently caught his fancy :

*O O O O that Shakespeherian Rag—*
*It's so elegant*
*So intelligent*
*' What shall I do now? What shall I do? '*
*' I shall rush out as I am, and walk the street*
*' With my hair down, so. What shall we do tomorrow?*
*' What shall we ever do? '*

And as he repeated the lines I found them irritating. Sensing my mood he turned to look at me.

—I see that you do not care for Eliot, he remarked.

—I do not care for those particular lines, I said, though I admit that he has written some excellent verse, light verse such as 'Sweeney among the Nightingales'. But for me a poet must be serious, I said, and remembering some lines out of *Sordello* I quoted them to him :

*Not any strollings now at even-close*
*Down the field path, Sordello! by thorn-rows*
*Alive with lamp-flies, swimming spots of fire*
*And dew, outlining the black cypress' spire*
*She waits you at, Elys, who heard you first*
*Woo her, the snow-month through, but ere she durst*
*Answer 't was April. Linden-flower-time-long*
*Her eyes were on the ground; 't is July, strong*
*Now; and because white dust-clouds overwhelm*
*The woodside, here or by the village elm*
*That holds the moon, she meets you, somewhat pale . . .*

—Look at the seriousness of it, the weight of the emotion, the richness of the imagery.

But Joyce criticized it strongly.

—It is full of clichés, he exclaimed, which have been used by literary men ad nauseam—' strolling down the field-path '—' the lamp-flies '—' the cypress' spire '—and the girl waiting for him in the wood, and refusing to give her answer in April —oh dear! Haven't we had enough of all that. It was written in a tradition that is dying—is already dead, one may say.

—But does tradition ever die? I asked him. What is art but the same formula used over and over again in a different way?

—Browning of the many words, replied Joyce, whose characters, no matter who they are, all talk like intellectuals: a mind that creeps along repeating itself endlessly until eventually he is lost in the maze of words. But did you ever hear anyone talk like Browning's characters? Or if you did, didn't you feel you were going crazy, or getting drunk? *The Waste Land* is the expression of our time in which we are trying to lift off the accumulated weight of the ages which was stifling original thought: formulas which may have meant something in the past but which mean nothing today. Eliot searches for images of emotion rather than for an ordered sequence, and in this he is related to all the other modern poets. Is it because he is not traditional that you do not care for him?

—There is something in that, I said, for I wonder if one can work outside tradition. What, after all, is tradition but the accumulated wisdom of the ages? Eliot has some good lines, I admit, and even whole verses. But the total man does not satisfy me.

—Does any total man satisfy us? asked Joyce. Certainly not the total Browning, if anyone could digest him. At least Eliot has not over-written himself as Browning did.

After a pause I asked him what he thought of Browning's great rival, Tennyson.

—Lawn Tennyson, he said, repeating the quip in *Ulysses,* the rectory prude, a poet deficient in intellect.

—At least he was not urban, like Eliot, I countered.

—No, he was suburban. It is not the wild countryside he writes about, but gardens. No, I do not care for Tennyson. Compare him with a poet like Donne, whose verse is a rich contrapuntal music which makes Tennyson seem as though he played with one stop. And Donne's love poems are more intricate, deeper than any others I know. To me he is very English, far more so than Tennyson, for the English mind, in spite of all that has been said about it, is intricate, and with Donne you enter a maze of thought and feeling. A poem of his is an adventure in which you do not know where you will end, which is what a piece of writing should be. In life you don't know where an experience will lead, and a work of literature should be the same. It is that which gives it the excitement. Donne is Shakespearian in his richness, and in comparison the famous French love poets sound trivial. He was a typical mediaevalist before classicism straightened out the English genius, for Donne and Chaucer were the two splendid geniuses in love with life before the puritans put out their ice-cold hands. Classicism was all right when it was paganism, but when it came to the Renaissance it had lost its purpose, and so it has continued miserably until this day, getting weaker and weaker until it has petered out in Tennyson, and in the stultified nudes of Alma-Tadema.

I was particularly interested to hear Joyce mention Alma-Tadema. It was the first time to my knowledge he had mentioned the work of an artist, for his attitude was like that of some other literary men who regard painting as an inferior art. Music interested him but not the plastic arts, and the only picture that I had ever seen in his flat, apart from his family portraits in which he had a sentimental interest, was Vermeer's picture of Delft. It hung over his mantelpiece, and he considered it a very fine work of art. I think one of the reasons, if not *the* reason, why he admired it so much was that it is the portrait of a city.

But in general he was not interested in modern art which was the rage in Paris. Picasso, Matisse, Braque, were names which never seemed to occupy his mind. I was, as it happens, more interested in painting than in literature and as a critic on the *New York Herald* I was constantly in touch with the art of the day. Often as we passed an art gallery in the rue de Seine, of which there are a great number, I stopped in front of them and asked his opinion of the latest Picasso, or Braque, but he would stare blankly at them, his face registering no interest or emotion, and would ask, after a time:

—How much are they worth?

I could not understand how he, a leader in modern literature, could ignore the efforts in another art which I regard as the most vital and exciting of our time.

The Russian ballet was also the rage, and I remember one of the early performances of ' Sacre du Printemps ' during which an uproar broke out in the audience. As I stood at the buffet afterwards I saw a girl pass through the foyer with her evening dress half ripped off, and remember thinking to myself that this was truly a civilized nation where their passion for the arts would take them to such lengths. When I asked Joyce how he liked the ballet he shrugged his shoulders and told me he did not care for it. He went once but never again. He thought the merit of the ballet exaggerated, an opinion so strange, and to me incomprehensible, that I doubted if I had heard him correctly.

In fact, he had a contempt for the multiple artistic activities of Paris. Either he did not understand them, or it was his bourgeois caution, a prejudice one might say, against anything new and fashionable which he looked on as a 'racket', a novelty which would subside as quickly as it had arisen.

His attitude to painting had a curious consequence, for one day he told me that he wanted someone to do a portrait of his father, to be painted in Dublin, and asked if I knew of anyone who could do it. I suggested Orpen, Paul Henry, and others, but he did not respond. Then I thought of Patrick Tuohy whom I knew slightly, a competent realist, but in truth nothing more. Joyce immediately decided on him because, as far as I could make out, he had known his father in Dublin, and so Tuohy was duly commissioned to paint the portrait which, when it arrived, turned out to be surprisingly good. Tuohy then proposed to come over to Paris himself and paint the rest of the family. I had been away over in Ireland but when I returned I found Tuohy installed, and every time I entered the flat I found him seated on the floor with a mirror in his hand touching up one of the portraits. But the situation was not a happy one, for he and Joyce jarred on one another, and no doubt Joyce resented Tuohy's continual presence. Tuohy could be very irritating, for he was nervously unbalanced. I remember his describing to me how he believed he had some abscess on the roof of his mouth which was poisoning his brain. I suggested that he should consult a doctor, but he replied that they could find nothing—They never can, he added hopelessly.

I do not know whether it was jealousy, that acid which eats into so many Irishmen, but he got the habit of constantly attacking Joyce. An unattractive, ordinary-looking man, provincial even to the point of being boorish, Tuohy may have envied this brilliant, international character. I know that I once invited him and Joyce to a tea-party at which there were some American friends. Tuohy had come up the stairs before Joyce and sat on a bench by the door, and when Joyce entered the room he started clapping in mock applause, which annoyed Joyce intensely. When some conversation arose about Joyce's work, Tuohy kept on interrupting from his corner saying: —Write a best-seller, that is what you have to do—write a best-seller.

Whether it was Tuohy's way of conveying that he did not like Joyce's work, or was a rude intimation that he thought that Joyce's work was written for sensation and money, I do not know, but the atmosphere he created was very unpleasant.

At that party Tuohy made friends with an American lady, and later, when he went to America, he stayed with her family as he had done with Joyce's. She wrote to me complaining that the beautiful Southern States girls had completely gone to his head, and that he had behaved in such an eccentric manner that, as she put it, 'no other Irishman need come down here for fifty years'. After that I did not hear from her for a year or more, when one day I received a telegram: 'Tuohy committed suicide in New York. Can you do anything?' But what could I do? I did not even know he was in New York. It seems that the poor fellow had pasted up his studio with newspapers, and then had turned on the gas. He was a fortnight dead before he was found.

When I told Joyce the news he showed no emotion.

—I am not surprised, he said. He nearly made me commit suicide too.

# XV

Joyce once said to me, more or less in relation to his work: 'To fault a writer because his work is not logically conceived seems to me poor criticism, for the object of a work of art is not to relate facts but to convey an emotion. Some of the best books ever written are absurd. Take for instance *La Chartreuse de Parme,* about which you were complaining, the facts of which no one could take seriously, any more than one could take those of *Gulliver's Travels* seriously. Indeed, judging from modern trends it seems that all the arts are tending towards the abstraction of music; and what I am writing at present is entirely governed by that purpose, for the more you tie yourself down to facts the more you limit yourself. It is the spirit which governs facts, not facts the spirit.'

I did not say anything at the time but thinking it over since I realize how completely I differ from him, for facts to my mind are far more wonderful and varied than any man's imagination. Indeed it would seem to me that a writer's purpose should be to follow the amazing sequence of reality rather than to scorn it. A writer who ignores it, as Joyce has done in *Finnegans Wake,* may startle us at first, but we do not forgive him in the end, for he has ignored the hard core of truth with which we are constantly faced. After all, the universal man is not the intellectual man but the sensual man, the man who gets his emotions, his very life from his contact with fact.

—I do not think I know exactly what you mean when you say 'sensual man', Joyce said.

—I mean the ordinary everyday 'Tom-noddy', the man who

appears to be without purpose or ambition, who does a job to keep his body and soul together, whose pleasures and desires are those of his body, and whose chief interest is in his love-affairs, his personal comforts, and the pleasures he obtains from his emotional contact with everyday life.

—I do not attach the importance to him that you do, replied Joyce, for to my mind he is the putty which is moulded by men of greater intelligence and character than he has and he has no judgements except derived ones.

—Perhaps he has not immediate ones, I agreed, but in time he forms them and then they are irrevocable, and if a work of art has not that sensual element which is the substance of his life he will reject it. Take Hemingway. He seems on the way to the top because he is original. But his originality is a venal one, and what he writes about smells in life, and in time it will smell in literature too: stories about alcoholics and nymphomaniacs and people who live in a waste land of violence and who have no emotional depth. I admit to his merit, of course, that he is very much of our time. But in my opinion he is too much of our time, in fact his writing is now more the work of a journalist than that of a literary man.

—He has reduced the veil between literature and life, said Joyce, which is what every writer strives to do. Have you read ' A Clean Well Lighted Place '?

—Yes, I said, and it is one of his best, and I wish that they were all up to that standard.

—It is masterly, replied Joyce, in a glow of enthusiasm. Indeed, I think it is one of the best short stories ever written; there is bite there.

—But did you ever read Maupassant's *Bel Ami*?

—Yes, I read it a long time ago. It was an amusing and lively book, I admit, and I suppose it gave a good picture of the Paris of the 1880s among a certain section of society, but I could not call it a great work. Like everything Maupassant wrote it is in miniature. In fact I thought it read like a series of excellent short stories, but I could not take the principal character, Duroy, seriously—a sort of French studbull.

—He entertained me more than Hemingway's arena bulls, I

could not help replying. Also I dislike the climate of Hemingway's stories, that hard, crude, boozy world he writes about. And it may or may not be a personal prejudice, but I dislike a man swimming in liquor. Drunkenness is a subtle form of insult to everyone and to everything. It dirties the world more than anything else, and I get that dirtying in Hemingway's stories.

—Copulation doesn't affect you in the same way?

—No, I said, there you are dealing with a mystery which can become anything and transform everything. Love-making can end in love, it often does, and so its possibilities can be limitless.

—You do not agree with Aquinas then, that the act of copulation is the death of the soul?

—I suppose in the Christian sense every material contact is death to the soul, but since I am not a religious man I am not too certain what the word ' soul ' means. It can have so many meanings that I cannot decide which is the true one.

Joyce shrugged his shoulders, and turning away, picking up his glass, drank from it without answering, indicating, it seemed to me, that in his opinion it was useless to discuss such abstract matters, a waste of time even. So I decided to return to our original theme, the short story, and I said to him:

—It would not be hard to name some better short story writers than Hemingway: Mérimée, for instance. ' Carmen ' is a real *conte* in the French sense: concentrated, colourful.

—I agree that it is entertaining, said Joyce, but like so much that is French it is miniature in comparison with, say, Tolstoy's short stories. He was an unimportant writer, but at least I am grateful to Mérimée for one thing: he provided the story for the libretto of the best opera ever written.

That *Carmen* was the best opera ever written was hardly an issue worth fighting for and, having been snubbed over my hero, Mérimée, I decided to remain silent. On the whole Joyce was a very reasonable man, and it was only about three things that he was quite fanatical: the first was the merit of Ibsen; the second, strangely enough, the merit of *Carmen;* the third was the relative merits of restaurants, for a bad meal could sour his temper.

Indeed, it was over this last matter that a serious break occurred between us. It was in 1931 when he was staying in London arranging for his marriage, hoping no doubt that in the vast sea of human activity it would pass unnoticed. Living in a flat in a red brick built road off Kensington High Street he hated the whole atmosphere, accustomed as he had been to the continent, and above all Paris, and never did he seem so unhappy and lost as he did in what to him was now an alien atmosphere.

One evening I decided to call and take him in a new car, of which I was quite proud, to dine at a roadhouse on the Portsmouth Road, a place of some repute which still retained an old-fashioned character and where one dined in an oak-panelled room lit by candlelight, a place where tradition said Lord Nelson used to dine with Lady Hamilton. The meal was a bad one, I admit, and as the evening went on Joyce got into a smouldering ill-humour. In fact, I who had known him for so many years had never seen him in such a humour before.

When we got into the car to return to London I hoped that his anger, and also mine by this time, would have simmered down. But no, we only seemed to aggravate each other.

A heavily charged silence fell between us as I drove along the tree-shadowed Portsmouth Road, the mauve-coloured tarmac spreading like a ribbon before us, while I tried to remain as cool as possible, for I felt that this was a real break, which would not be easily healed.

As we had not seen each other for some time, for I was then living in Waterford, I suppose each of us had become reinforced in his own ego: Joyce a world-famous figure, and myself an unknown nonentity—in an obscure clash on the Portsmouth Road.

However, I did not feel like giving way to his ill-humour in spite of the fact that I was grateful to him for his constant kindness and interest all the time I had been living in Paris, much of the time on my own. I tried once or twice to re-start a conversation, but it died stillborn.

Then I suppose in an effort to be friendly again Joyce said in a low, intimate voice:

—I have just received very important news.

—What is it? I asked, thinking it must be something of literary importance.

—A son has been born to Georgio and Helen in Paris.

In truth I am not a family man who dotes on children. Also I was feeling very bitter at that time about the world in general. I had agreed with the remark Sam Beckett made to me that ' It had gone on long enough.'

—Is that all? I replied.

—It is the most important thing there is, said Joyce firmly, his voice charged with meaning.

A sudden suspicion crossed my mind; ' the most important thing there is ' meant that another Joyce had been born into the world. Even to this day I am still in doubt, for Joyce's estimation of his merit would on occasion suddenly flare up to a point of madness.

Anyway, at the mere suspicion of it—for egotism has its limit—my bad temper rose up again and I said:

—I cannot see that it is so important. It is something which happens all the time, everywhere, and with everyone.

A tense silence fell between us as I drove to Kensington High Street. When leaving him back at his flat our ' goodbye ' was a very distant one.

However, in the years that followed when I was in Paris I called on him. But our relationship was never the same again.

The last time I saw him was when I called at his flat off the Champs Elysées, when we discussed the different reactions there had been to his work. As I was leaving he sank down on to a chair in the narrow hallway in that peculiar exhausted manner he had at times, and said with a sigh:

—I suppose my work is middleclass.

His remark surprised me, for what has art to do with class? In my mind I tried to trace back the origin of this remark, and the only one I could think of was a criticism of Joyce which had appeared lately in a book by Wyndham Lewis, an irritating piece of work with a strong political flavour to it, rabid and superficial.

—I cannot see what class has to do with it, I replied, for it occurred to me that few writers were less subject to class prejudice than Joyce was.

As I stood for a moment on the top of the stairs we both raised our hands in salute—a final farewell it was, though I did not know it. Then one morning in the early days of the war, the *Irish Times* rang up and asked me to write a short account of Joyce as he was dead. The news came as a thunderbolt to me and I turned away from the telephone with remorse and dismay. So much of my life in Paris had been bound up with him and Mrs Joyce, both of whom had given me a steady friendship as close as if I had been a member of the family. It had not ended, but had lessened as so many friendships lessen when distance puts its cold hand between them, damped as they are by circumstances and time, and by differences of personality. A personality can fuse with another personality for a time, but when that time is over we gradually re-enter the solitude of ourselves. Then all that remains is the memory of the fire which once warmed us both, and it is fragments of that memory which I have tried to reconstruct in this short book.

# MY GRANDFATHER'S HOUSE

ALSO BY ROBERT CLARK

NOVELS

*Mr. White's Confession*
*In the Deep Midwinter*

NONFICTION

*River of the West*
*The Solace of Food*

# MY GRANDFATHER'S HOUSE

## A GENEALOGY OF DOUBT AND FAITH

# ROBERT CLARK

PICADOR USA

NEW YORK

Picador® is a U.S. registered trademark and is used by St. Martin's Press
under license from Pan Books Limited.

Endpaper illustrations are both by Winslow Homer. *Portrait of Helena
de Kay,* © Museo Thyssen-Bornemisza, Madrid. *Fox Hunt,* 1893.
Courtesy of the Pennsylvania Academy of the Fine Arts, Philadelphia.
Joseph E. Temple Fund.

*Book Design by Ellen R. Sasahara*

ISBN 0-312-20932-0

First Picador USA Edition: November 1999

10 9 8 7 6 5 4 3 2 1

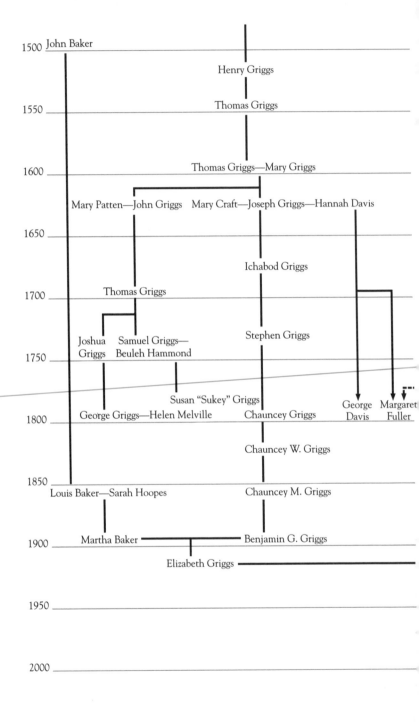

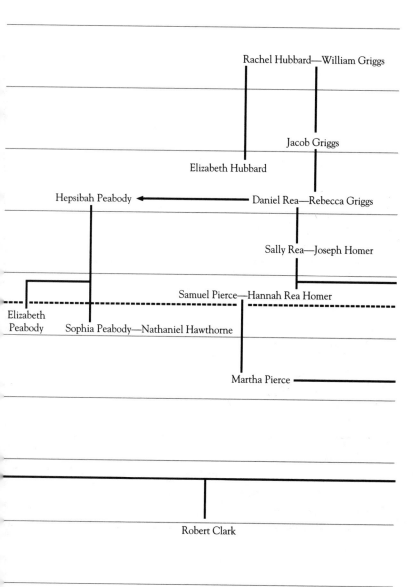

Rachel Hubbard—William Griggs

Jacob Griggs

Elizabeth Hubbard

Hepsibah Peabody ◄—— Daniel Rea—Rebecca Griggs

Sally Rea—Joseph Homer

Samuel Pierce—Hannah Rea Homer

Elizabeth
Peabody    Sophia Peabody—Nathaniel Hawthorne

Martha Pierce ——

Robert Clark

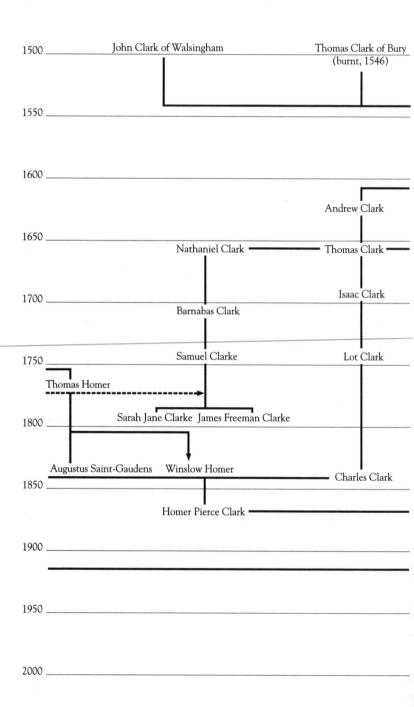

1450

1500        John Clark of Walsingham        Thomas Clark of Bury
                                                (burnt, 1546)

1550

1600

                                            Andrew Clark

1650        Nathaniel Clark ——————— Thomas Clark ——

                                            Isaac Clark
1700
        Barnabas Clark

1750        Samuel Clarke                   Lot Clark

Thomas Homer

        Sarah Jane Clarke  James Freeman Clarke
1800

Augustus Saint-Gaudens    Winslow Homer
                                            Charles Clark
1850
            Homer Pierce Clark ——————

1900

1950

2000

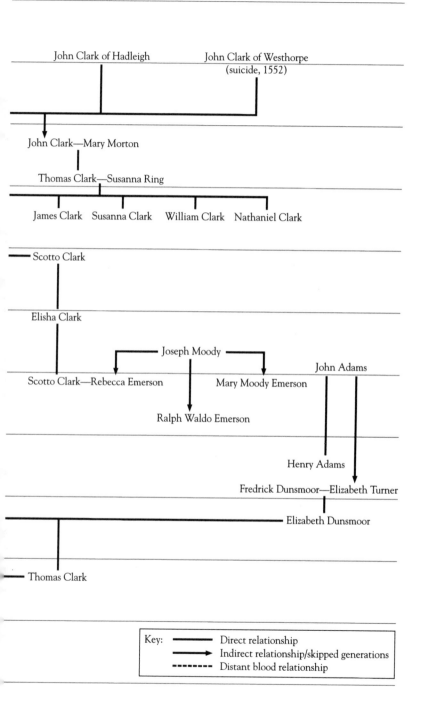

John Clark of Hadleigh    John Clark of Westhorpe
(suicide, 1552)

John Clark—Mary Morton

Thomas Clark—Susanna Ring

James Clark   Susanna Clark   William Clark   Nathaniel Clark

Scotto Clark

Elisha Clark

Joseph Moody

John Adams

Scotto Clark—Rebecca Emerson    Mary Moody Emerson

Ralph Waldo Emerson

Henry Adams

Fredrick Dunsmoor—Elizabeth Turner

Elizabeth Dunsmoor

Thomas Clark

Key:  ——————  Direct relationship
      ——————▶  Indirect relationship/skipped generations
      --------  Distant blood relationship

# PROLOGUE

Five hundred years ago, all my ancestors, like most Europeans, were Roman Catholics. Thirty years later Henry VIII needed a divorce and they became Protestants by the king's volition; and seventy-five years after that, they became Puritans by their own. Three hundred and fifty years ago they voyaged to America and became variously Congregationalists, Presbyterians, Episcopalians, Unitarians, agnostics, and atheists.

Last year, my son Andrew, aged eighteen months, was baptized in the Roman Catholic church, the first member of his family in nearly half a millennium to be so christened. I cannot say what he will make of that, because it was a choice I made on his behalf. Two weeks before, at Easter, I was myself received—I want to say not "received" but "taken back"—into the Catholic faith. The book that follows is a record of how Andrew and I arrived at this most recent of many turnings to and lapses from religious faith over the generations of my family. It is a history of belief and disbelief, of faith and doubt in one American family.

This book is specifically *not* an account of how I was converted—of how my life has been transformed by this change, of how "I once was lost and now am found," as though my transit of that experience marked the beginning and the end of the journey. For I have learned that the work of faith, its risings and ebbings, has been the work of my life—perhaps of anyone's life—and is on that account without end. Once I also thought what was essential to my being, to myself, was myself, my individuality. But now I see that I can know anything only in relation to other things, and myself only in connection to other persons, to communities of memory. Like my forebears, I have been variously, and sometimes simultaneously, a Catholic, a Protestant, a Puritan, a Transcendentalist, an agnostic, and an atheist; and I now know no way to read the text of my life except alongside—in parallel with—their lives. I can only make sense of what I have become through an examination of what I once was, and, moreover, of what those who made me were. I can comprehend life and the living only through, as it were, death and the dead.

Similarly, I can see my faith only through my doubt and unknowing. This book is as concerned with disbelief as it is with belief, with how we lose faith as much as with how we acquire it. For it seems to me that disbelief is no more the opposite or negation of faith than longing is that of love. Committed atheists—those who with perfect and untroubled assurance neither believe nor want to believe in something beyond quotidian reality—are rare as hen's teeth. For most people, disbelief is neither an idea nor a conviction, but an unresolved question, an unmet aspiration, the fulfillment of which we feel unable to bring about or even to imagine. It seems that not just God, but even faith for most of us cannot be seen head-on, but only indirectly by signs and in relation to other things, as in a mirror.

The book that follows, then, is less a family history or even a memoir of myself than something akin to what St. Augustine and his medieval readers called a *confessio,* which we today translate as "confession" with all its implications of sordid truths revealed. But the word's earlier, original sense is a little different. For Augustine, his "confessio"—the title of the book he is most famous for—was an extended meditation, a rumination on and among his memories with the simple end of praising his god and comprehending himself. His aim was not so very different from what the Old Testament poet sought in the Psalms, or, for that matter, what anyone might do in prayer.

Our encounters with the spiritual, and the convictions and ideas that follow from them, are, I think, particularly hard to track, being shadows and traces of things at best hoped for yet unseen. So I have been able to locate my own path through religion only in relation to and through those of other people, among them Augustine and others, but mostly my own forebears and kin. My *confessio,* such as it is, is but a sequel to theirs.

My medieval ancestors of half a millennium ago might have translated the word *"confessio"* as "beknowing." It is a good and useful term that we have lost, a little like our "knowing" but with a reflexive twist: a knowing of one's knowing, in which we set what we think we know in front of us and step back from it. In our time, it is a mode of knowledge that has been almost entirely displaced by irony, which has to do with the position and posture of the self rather than with understanding, with "knowingness" rather than "knowing." Five hundred years ago it seemed the world was as real as the self, perhaps more real than the self, or at the very least coextensive with it. So my ancestors might have used the term "beknowing" to describe what they did when they confessed their sins to the priest; and they might as easily have used it when they went back out into the hills of Suffolk to locate their sheep, to see where the sheep had been and gone since yesterday, or in the hour the village had been at church—to locate themselves in relation to their flock even as I will try to locate myself through and among them. And on the boat that carried them westward to America, I suppose they might have used the word "beknowing" in looking back at the shore vanishing behind them, in considering the past that was closing around and falling away from the stern of the ship. The ship was beating its way toward a new life in a new world, but even more than that, toward the end of the world they knew and into some species—who ever knows which?—of eternity.

# PART I

# THE GREAT DIVORCE

# ONE

he oldest ancestor of whom I have any knowledge was named John Griggs. He was born and lived in a village called Somerton in the county of Suffolk in England, and married a woman named Rose, also of Somerton. He died in April 1497.

Five hundred years and four months later, in August 1997, I brought my wife and my children to Somerton, to the church in which John Griggs was baptized, in which he married Rose, and in whose graveyard what dust is left of him somewhere remains. The church is called All Saints. There is a rectory across the road, and the rest of the village consists of three or four pretty cottages strung along a ridge top. It is sheep-farming country, soft and rolling, green and aglow as though burnished.

The church was locked and I had to fetch the key from the verger's cottage next door. The key was nearly a foot long and must have weighed at least a pound, and it fascinated the children. Tessa, aged thirteen, tried to shift it in the lock, but to no avail. I had no more success, until Carrie, my wife, suggested turning it in the opposite direction. She was right. The lock snapped open, and I returned the key to Tessa. Andrew, not quite two years old, was eager to get his hands on it, and Tessa held it over her head while Andrew danced around, circling her.

I went inside. The main part of the church was Norman, in the vicinity of eight or nine hundred years old, and like most English churches, it has a relatively austere interior, its medieval ornamentation stripped during the Reformation or removed during Victorian restorations. The walls were white and largely bare, but the hexagonal stone font where John Griggs was baptized remained, as did the "squint" in the chancel wall through which the lepers and the sick were allowed to watch the mass at a safe distance from the rest of the parish.

I had hoped there might be some sign of John Griggs or his family inside the church, a monument or an inscription. We had already visited four other churches that day with no sign of kin apparent in any of them. At All Saints there was, of course, nothing: Most of the funereal monuments and stones would also have been removed—along with shrines, stations of the cross, holy water stoups, and the like—and in any case the Griggses were not a prominent enough family to warrant commemoration inside the church. Outside, among the headstones, there was no sign of them either. The oldest markers dated from the early 1600s, and those, weathered and cloaked in moss, were scarcely legible; and by that date my family, in any case, had moved on.

I felt I ought to know better, but I was disappointed that there was no palpable trace of my ancestors, no sign that might make my presence here into a homecoming. My connection to Somerton would be based on a few church and civic documents, on words alone and my belief in them. It was a bright, warm day and from the top of Somerton I could see the hills all around me where my family must have farmed and herded. The land was empty and verdant and brilliant, and I saw it in a still, perfect clarity, as though not through air but through water or a sheet of sparkling glass. I might say that the scene seemed timeless, but at the same time I felt expectant, as if awaiting something. Out there, on the hills, were the people I had come looking for: John and Rose and their parents and their children, and also perhaps myself, by some way down the years, their child too. I might have been waiting for them, for all of us, to return from hills, to come in from our labors; I might have been standing on shore, waiting for them to come back across the sea.

The church they were born into and to which I have returned says that we ought to pray for the dead, and that in turn we ought to ask them to pray for us. This is one of the doctrines whose rejection by the Protestant reformers led to the stripping of All Saints Church, and eventually, to the Griggses leaving Somerton and then England entirely. But here, now, such prayer seemed utterly true and utterly right; it seemed the only thing I could do here, the only thing that was not futile. So in Somerton churchyard, a little way from the porch and the doorway at which the priest would have married John and Rose, I prayed for them and for my whole family and for myself: that we might all have mercy.

I felt a little lost—confounded where I had expected to find something, and I did not know what else to do. The dead teach us, if nothing else, that we are incomplete. Our losses, our lacks, our privations are nowhere so manifest as in the bare and unalterable fact of the absence in our lives of the dead. It is a lack that perhaps necessarily points to our ultimate privation, to that longing that St. Augustine voiced to his God: "You have made us for yourself and our heart is ever unquiet until it rests in you."

When I had finished, Carrie and Tessa and Andrew were waiting for me. Tessa had given the key to Andrew at last, and Andrew, overcome by the heft of it, had dropped it. They were some way down the path from me, but I thought I heard Tessa say, "Pick it up, Andrew. Pick it up."

# TWO

I t is impossible to speak about the Christian religion in general or conversion in particular without reference to St. Augustine. At the time of his birth in A.D. 354, Christianity had been legally tolerated in the then-disintegrating Roman Empire for a mere forty years and contended for adherents in a sort of New Age bazaar of pagan and gnostic sects and cults. Augustine's mother, Monica, was herself a Christian and prayed that her son might also become one. But Augustine, sophisticated, cosmopolitan, and gifted with a knack for philosophy and rhetoric, was drawn elsewhere. He took up with the Manicheans, who saw creation divided in a great bipolar conflict between good and evil, between the physical, fleshly world and that of the intellect and spirit. Later, he studied Neoplatonism, which held that the dualism that really mattered was not between good and evil but between being and nonbeing, the ideal and the real. By the time he was thirty and a professor of rhetoric in Milan, he had come under the influence of Ambrose, Milan's bishop and a compelling homilist and teacher of views not unsympathetic to Neoplatonism.

This brought Augustine—now a veteran of most of the pleasures the Roman Empire could afford in its decadent phase (as well as the father of a son by one of his several mistresses)—to the verge of conversion, if *only* the verge. Among all his many writings, Augustine is perhaps best known for the plea, recorded in the *Confessions*: "Lord, make me good, but just not yet." The work from which the words come is less an account of his conversion than it is of the mul-

6

tiplicity of ways he for so long evaded or perhaps eluded conversion, even once it had become what he chiefly desired in his life. It is as if, wanting it, he was in no better position to effect it—to make himself believe and live according to that belief—than he had been when he did not want it at all.

When belief at last came, after every sort of agony and relapse imaginable, it came simply, slyly, like something small, forgotten, and unremarkable he had found lying at his feet. He is sitting in the garden of a friend's house. Children are playing next door and he can hear their voices, ebbing and rising in volume and pitch, over the garden wall. Then one of them, with perfect and terrible clarity, says, "Pick it up," as though to him alone. "Pick it up."

\*          \*          \*

My own first conversion was different from Augustine's, and occurred when I was fairly young. My parents had divorced when I was two and my father died three years later, after being afflicted with polio. I hardly knew him, save as a paralyzed body lashed to a respirator. In the wake of my parents' divorce, my mother became estranged from my father's family, the Clarks, and so we were not close to them; in any case, my grandfather Clark was eighty-four years old when I was born, and therefore not well equipped to play much of a part in my raising. My grandfather Griggs thus found himself, somewhat unwillingly, in the role of proxy father. He was an extremely kind, generous, but ultimately reserved man, uncomfortable with too much noise or disturbance, as I am myself. I cannot say we were close, but what he gave me—the family outings, visits to his house in the woods on the lake, the stories, the sentimental regard for the past and its inhabitants—is all I have, is everything I came from; the world he made for me without perhaps even knowing it.

My grandfather Griggs had been raised a Presbyterian, but became an Episcopalian when he married my grandmother, who came from Philadelphia and was born Martha Baker. We went to church with them occasionally, but my mother herself was a Unitarian, at least nominally, although I don't recall us attending the local Unitarian church with any frequency. My grandfather Clark had been a member there, although his wife and daughters were staunchly Calvinist Presbyterians. My father, I gathered, had been neither. So my first encounters with religion were occasional and diffuse, which is not to say I was without feelings on the subject. I was acquainted with the Christmas story (if not, in any detail, with the rest of Jesus' life) both explicitly from Unitarian and Episcopalian accounts of it, and implicitly from its centrality to our family's communal life, and it seemed to me the most moving and wonderful thing I had ever heard. I knew nothing of its place in what theologians call "the economy of salvation," nor would I have wanted to. The story was complete and perfect, redemptive in itself, by itself.

When I was eleven I was sent to an Episcopalian boarding school. In retrospect, it seems to me crazy and cruel to send a child away from home at such an early age, but it was not considered unusual at the time; indeed there were nine- and ten-year-olds among the boarders. In the previous year and a half, my grades had declined and I had become something of a "problem" at school, less malevolent than impetuous, but disruptive enough to attract notice. It was decided that a more "masculine influence" was what I lacked, and that a strictly run boys' school would supply it. My Clark grandparents, who were wealthy, agreed to pay the tuition. The fact that it was a church school had nothing to do with the decision, which was based more on Freud by way of Baden-Powell.

The school, located in southern Minnesota and called St. James, does not now seem to have much to recommend it. Most of the instruction was mediocre and the students were as undistinguished as the faculty. It was organized along military lines, with daily afternoon drills, corporal punishment (meted out with belts or slender oak sticks), ranks and rifle practice, stiff woolen uniforms, and parades overseen by thirteen- and fourteen-year-old "senior officers." But the fact was, I thrived. The schoolwork was undemanding and it was absolutely clear what was required to succeed: to do as one was told. It was easy to be good at St. James and I found I loved being good; here, I was "good" at being good.

The religious component of St. James was as desultory as the rest of its curriculum: Bible instruction of which I can recall absolutely nothing, plus weekly attendance at the local Episcopal church or the chapel of the affiliated school for older boys, Shattuck. But religion gave me yet another way to be good, and indeed an overriding context and justification for all my efforts in that direction. There was

nothing calculated about it: I was moved and comforted by the stories, the liturgy, and the language of Thomas Cranmer's Tudor Book
of Common Prayer. After my disillusionments of the past few years
and the confusing arrival of sexual desire, I had found something
that not only made me feel good, but that seemed to offer a way
back to the awe, mystery, and wonder that I had lost. Within three
months of my arrival at St. James, I announced I wanted to be baptized and formally to join the Episcopal church.

It's not clear what my family made of this. My mother had lost
her faith in Christian dogma at college, but she retained a sentimental attachment to the church she was raised in; moreover, she saw
that my own Episcopalianism would gain her the approval of her
parents, approval that she had doubtless jeopardized through her
own lapse from the church and her subsequent divorce. It would be,
in short, an opportunity for her to be good as well as me.

I was baptized at my grandparents' church in St. Paul, St. John
the Evangelist, on December 27, 1963, which was in fact St. John
the Evangelist's feast day. Not that there was anything evangelical
about the church of St. John the Evangelist. The Episcopal church,
and Anglicanism as a whole, are customarily seen as divided into
"high" and "low" church congregations, with the high church contingent being closer to Rome in its liturgy and doctrinal emphases
and the low closer to mainstream Protestantism. St. John's was right
in the middle. It was a beautiful church, full of carved wood and vi-
brantly tinted stained glass. The baptismal font stood near the front
of the church, inside a gated enclosure a few steps from the pew my
grandparents habitually occupied. The font itself consisted of a life-
sized statue in what I suppose was alabaster of an angel who held a
seashell in which the baptismal water was contained. I remember
very little about the ceremony, except for the angel, who seemed an
almost translucent white, and the smell of pine and spruce, with
which the church was still decorated from the Christmas ceremonies
two days earlier. My godparents were my grandfather Griggs and the
St. James School chaplain, a smart and engaging young priest named
Karl Bell. His example made me think for a while I might want to
be a priest myself.

I still have the weekly letters I wrote home to my mother during
this period, but they do not reveal what was going through my

mind. There's no mention at all of my conversion or impending baptism. The only references to religion are oblique, a mention of having attended church and a request that my mother send me a copy of a *Life* magazine book called *The World's Great Religions*. The highlight of my week was the school's Saturday night outing to the movies downtown, usually a showing of something from the beach party genre of Annette Funicello and Frankie Avalon or a romantic comedy starring Doris Day opposite Rock Hudson or James Garner. Thus, a month before my baptism, I wrote, "On Saturday we saw a movie called 'The Thrill of It All.' On Sunday I went to church. Both the sermon and the lesson were about 'the burning fiery furnace.'"

During the next two years, during seventh and eighth grade, I took my religion seriously. A month after my baptism I report that, after coming home from the Saturday night movie, "I talked about Saints with Mr. Bell."

> Today we went to church. It was Holy Communion and lots of boys got in trouble for goofing off in church. We came back from church and then we ate, had rest hour, and went to dancing class. I think I now have a girlfriend.

My life was certainly full. I don't recall anything about the "girl-friend," doubtless one of the girls from town freighted in for us to study the foxtrot with every Sunday afternoon. I suppose nothing came of it. Perhaps she thought I was a prig: What sort of boy, after all, comes home from *That Touch of Mink* to suck up to the school chaplain, and reproves the other boys' behavior in church in letters to his mother?

The following year, 1965, I was confirmed, served as an acolyte, and won a Bible essay contest on the topic "My Favorite Bible Character." I still have a copy of my entry, on Dismas, the good thief who was crucified along with Jesus. The style has more in common with the "muscular Christianity," team-spirit idealism of *Boy's Life* magazine and the Hardy Boys than with, say, St. John of the Cross:

> When I found out this was the topic of the Bible Essay, I realized I had never stopped to think who my favorite bible character was. After thinking over the matter, however, I

decided he should be a worthwhile character and someone who had meaning for me and for others—someone who had a message to get across for the world's benefit.

After recounting the story of the good thief I got to the point:

> Now let's compare ourselves with Dismas. We don't run off with our neighbor's property but yet we are thieves in a way. We steal our fellow man's time, his friendship, his love, and his respect. We are pickpockets of anything that our neighbor has that might benefit us and if we don't like his reaction we "bump him off" with a few words of hate.

I had a poster of John Dillinger in my room at home, which perhaps had some effect on my train of thought:

> I have now pointed out that most of us are really criminals as far as living righteously is concerned. . . . Dismas's message is one of the ever-living love of God for man. When we are hanging on our "crosses" in times of sorrow God is always willing to remember us. That good thief who was crucified many years ago has a message for us to cherish and live by forever.

I'm conscious now of some calculation in my rhetoric; of an effort to dazzle and persuade in the pep-talk style and the "unexpected" choice of subject. Scarcely knowing it, I pursued religion with the same ambition I brought to the pursuit of rewards and acclaim elsewhere at St. James: I wanted to carry off all the prizes.

After a time I began to feel as though I had exhausted the possibilities of the Episcopal church and wondered if there might be something more elsewhere. For Anglicans of the high and middle persuasion, that elsewhere is perennially Roman Catholicism, which in many ways resembles Anglicanism as much as or more than any of the Protestant denominations. Moreover, it is the mother church, the church that—save for Henry VIII's divorce—Anglicans might still be part of, and thus its attractions rest not only on authority and antiquity but on deep, almost familial emotions.

I experienced that pull, but I still had the prejudices of a Midwestern WASP and the ignorance of a twelve-year-old. So, while Catholicism was at once ethereal and profound in its ancient mysteries, it was also arcane, dark, and somewhat spooky. My friends and I all knew Catholics—sometimes as close friends—and their religion often seemed as weird and hermetic to them as it did to us. We knew from them that they had strange dietary customs, that they had to go tell their secrets to a priest in a darkened box, that their teachers at school were nuns who scowled and pinched and lived locked up in hospital-like buildings together. And if that much was acknowledged fact, imagine what we did not know: There were rumors about strange, presumably surgical procedures nuns underwent when they took their vows, and it was said that Catholic girls were sexually insatiable and that Catholic boys had outsized sex organs; at any rate, we'd seen that some of them weren't circumcised. Altogether, with its incense and holy water and holy oil and fish eating, its boisterous Irish and Italian congregations, the Catholic church was, for all its lofty mystery, palpably sensual, swarthy, even carnal.

Despite those misgivings, during vacations I paid a number of visits to our nearest Catholic church at home, the Cathedral of St. Paul. Funded by James J. Hill's railroad fortune, it is a huge and impressive church for a city the size of St. Paul, perched on a hilltop above downtown with a Vatican-sized dome that renders the State Capitol a bit puny. I went in several times just before Easter in 1965, with the statues and shrines shrouded in purple, but never stayed more than a few minutes; I felt a little like a burglar who might be noticed, caught, subjected to some exotic Roman rite of forced conversion or penance. It seemed safer to do my research at the library. I checked out a book called *This Is the Mass,* by Fulton J. Sheen, the celebrity television bishop of 1950s television. The book consisted of a text, describing each part of the Catholic mass, illustrated by a color photo of Sheen enacting it in his private chapel, assisted by a fresh-faced altar boy who might have been me. I pored over it and renewed it from the library countless times.

I served as a real altar boy in the low-church communions in the school chapel and sometimes at home at St. John the Evangelist. And in the eighth grade, when I was thirteen, I did at least one decent thing with respect to religion—or rather, almost in opposition to it.

Although St. James was officially an Episcopal school, only a minority of the boys were Episcopalian, the bulk being variously Protestant of other denominations or Roman Catholic. Probably a tenth were Jewish. One Sunday before church, it was announced that hereafter all boys, regardless of their faith, who did not kneel during the prescribed parts of the service would be punished. Moreover, such kneeling was to be in an upright posture, with no slouching of butts against the pew.

I thought this was an outrageous demand, especially for the Jewish boys, although I'm not sure anyone besides me much cared; most objected to kneeling not on religious principle but on grounds of the interminable, paralysis-inducing sections of the liturgy that required it. But it was 1966, and I had among other things been imbued with the protest politics of the times. After church that day, I drew up a petition objecting to this abridgment of religious freedom. I got about ten other boys to sign it, mostly, I think, as a kind of lark—as a piece of playacting of the civil rights dramas going on around us in the larger adult world. By Sunday afternoon, the petition had been seized by one of the teachers, and by Monday morning it was clear I was in very big trouble.

It never occurred to me that the school authorities would have any objection to my petition: It was just a piece of paper proposing a reasonable accommodation of religious difference. The gravest crime at St. James was probably smoking cigarettes, which could get you expelled, or leaving campus without permission, offenses that I quaked even to think about. My petition was, by contrast, not much different from the mild, pep-fraught editorials I wrote in the school newspaper. I was stunned, then, to hear the headmaster announce that all the signers of the petition were to be punished. As for me, the "instigator," I would be stripped of all privileges and military rank, confined to the dormitory, and given a good beating.

I would like to say that there was something heroic and self-sacrificing in this episode, that I added Boy Martyr to the other laurels I wore, but the truth was, I had no idea that I had risked anything until after the fact. I took my punishment in the humble spirit that the school administration required of me, but I also believed I was right. That moment constituted one of my first experiences of belief in a principle, in holding to a conviction, which is not so very

different from faith; and it was purer or at least clearer and more absolute than anything I had felt about my religion. I had momentarily
found in politics—whose simpler polarities were much more grasp-
able than theology's and whose victories seemed easier to attain—
another sphere in which to be good; to be good by being, in
conventional terms, "bad," by being rebellious in a good cause.

In this, at the age of fourteen, I had stumbled across morality,
which is not the same thing as religion, but often seems to be. For if
we are saved, by what reason are we saved? By something in ourselves—good conduct, faith, or destiny—or in God—his goodness,
justice, or whim—or perhaps both. It seems intuitive that morality
and justice have something to do with it. My conversion did not survive my encounter with these questions. Augustine's, of course, did,
and although he found agonizing difficulties in them, he did not shy
away from trying to grapple with them.

# THREE

At the moment of his conversion, what Augustine picked up was a book, a text of St. Paul. The words his eyes fell upon said, "Clothe yourself with the Lord Jesus Christ, and make no provision for the flesh, to gratify its desires." Thereafter, Augustine was a Christian. It was not that he read these words and resolved to follow them—that he now achieved something he had heretofore failed at—or even that he submitted to something he had been resisting. Rather, his conversion simply befell him. It seemed to Augustine that it was no more or less than a gift, neither earned nor achieved; even his ability to say yes to it was beyond any ordinary kind of willing.

That was how it had felt, and when he considered the matter with his intellect that sense of it seemed all the more reasonable. For if God is above all else unimaginably good and great, how could any mere persons come to Him under their own power or volition? Clearly, only God could bring people to God, no matter how hard they tried, no matter how good they were. And Augustine also saw that God—whose foreknowledge of everything is, in any case, perfect—would of course know in advance which persons He would effect conversion in: God would, it went without saying, know His own intentions.

Augustine's understanding of his own conversion and its underlying logic led to this conclusion; so did his later experiences as a bishop and, perhaps, his temperament. As a bishop, he had to deal with the rise of two influential heresies among his flock. The first, called Donatism, maintained that the sacraments were only as holy as those who administered them; that a Eucharist or ordination performed by a minister in a state of sin was invalid. Augustine countered this proposition with the same logic he had brought to his experience of his conversion: that the efficacy of the sacraments lay in God's power, not in the worthiness of those who administered them. The second heresy, Pelagianism, was in many senses the mirror image of the first. The English monk Pelagius and his followers turned up in Augustine's North African diocese after the sack of Rome in A.D. 410 and caused a stir by proclaiming that people were, in fact, capable of attaining sinlessness and doing good under their own power; that God's grace was not the sole cause of the capacity, but a kind of aid or catalyst to a potential already present in humans.

Both these notions undermined what was at that time a still unformed and shaky Christian orthodoxy, and contradicted everything Augustine felt and knew about human sin and God's goodness. Arguing against and establishing that these views were heresies became what would be perceived as Augustine's central contribution to Christian theology and doctrine; and in a sense the heresies returned him to the intellectual ground of his youth, the unrelenting dualism of the Manicheans. For however much Augustine might insist that God was above all else a loving being, the emphases of his polemics suggested otherwise. For if man was so essentially depraved as Augustine seemed to maintain, how could his creator be so good? And if God alone effected and foreknew salvation, where was his mercy for those who went, despite all their efforts and desires, unredeemed? Unwittingly, perhaps, Augustine's theology tended toward a view of humankind as helplessly mired in sin created and overseen by an indifferent, perhaps even callous God.

This was scarcely Augustine's intent—the *Confessions* make his belief in God's infinite mercy and love more than clear—but his responses to these heresies nonetheless engendered a perennial phenomenon in Christian thought that might be called Augustinian pessimism. The questions raised—of human goodness and the working of God's grace—are real enough and, as in all matters of faith, ultimately unanswerable, but their very presence is troubling. Is it worth trying to live a life that may be fundamentally without value, perhaps even inherently evil? Is there any point in believing in a God who may be indifferent to us?

How we live with these questions (for there is no answering them in this life) is finally a matter of how we are inclined to view the world, to picture for ourselves God's creation and purposes. Faith may have more to do with the imagination, with how we see and what we can envision, than with reason or the will, and from it follows our disposition toward God and our sense of God's disposition toward us. Is the cup half-empty or half-full? The margin between optimism and pessimism is a fine one, perhaps fifty-one percent in one direction versus forty-nine in the other; and we must decide, without any apparent help, what sort of people, on average, we are and whether God loves us for or in spite of ourselves, or at all.

Certainly, Augustine himself believed that God loved him, and loved all humankind, albeit in a way we cannot always comprehend. Augustine was stunned by the depth and power and majesty of God's love, and, in contrast, by the paltriness of human charity: "The good that I do has its source in You and is Your gift," Augustine confessed to his God, "the evil that I do is my own offense and Yours to judge." It is this perception, rather than misanthropy, that may be the source of Augustinian "pessimism." To apprehend the gulf that mercy must bridge to reach us is heartrending, and we might say that God's love broke Augustine's heart in revealing itself to him—that it left him bereft of almost everything he had or had valued before. Perhaps it breaks our hearts as well, for what He asked Augustine to pick up, and what Augustine passed on to us, is not a concrete assurance of our redemption but an unfinished labor of the imagination, which we can never complete and which so often feels unbearable.

*          *          *

The centuries after Augustine are commonly called the Dark Ages. The term reflects a great deal of historical ignorance and misunderstanding, but it does seem that for four hundred or so years, Christianity and Western culture sealed themselves inside a cave, averting their eyes from the wreckage of the Roman epoch. There was a sense that not much good could come of this world, and that Christians had best bide their time waiting out its end in a monastery, copying out texts from an earlier era that, whether pagan or Christian, seemed to say, "We told you it would come to this."

But it is only a sense, a temporary disposition (if four or five hundred years can be called temporary). For by the turn of the millennium, something else emerges: not, as we might expect, a cool and rational appraisal of the human condition, but an intellectual, aesthetic, and spiritual wave of high feeling—of general optimism and even ecstasy, but also, at times, of despair—that will run its course over the next five hundred years, until about the time of the death of John Griggs. It can be said to begin at least in part in England with an archbishop of Canterbury named Anselm. Anselm would be noteworthy if only for his scrap with William the Conqueror's son William II, who felt it ought to be within his power rather than the pope's to control Anselm as archbishop. Over the next four centuries, English kings would prove infinitely perturbable in regard to this subject (witness the fate of another archbishop, Becket, a hundred years later), and it would ultimately precipitate the Reformation.

But Anselm is equally significant as the first great theologian of the High Middle Ages. He coined what might be called the era's mission statement: the phrase "faith seeking understanding." Anselm did not mean by this that humans could in any complete way comprehend God, but that by granting us reason, God meant us to try, however imperfectly; that our awareness of our ignorance implies a kind of knowledge, just as modern physicists can with some confidence posit by mathematical proof what they cannot actually observe. Anselm's most celebrated example of this kind of thinking was his "ontological proof" for the existence of God: that God is "that being than which nothing greater can be conceived." This is exquisitely clever, but one immediately senses that it works by a kind of circularity, that the argument is always swallowing its own tail, for whatever you conceive of as God is instantly not God, by virtue of you being able to conceive it. Logically speaking, Anselm's proof always trumps any objection that can be made to it, and it does so by trumping logic with imagination; by insisting that you cannot rationally apprehend God but only picture what he might be like by inference or analogy, by the traces He leaves in his creation, just as unseeable particles leave tracks in a cloud chamber.

Anselm uses reason, we might say, to go beyond reason—or,

rather, beyond what humans can reason. And having proved that God is incomprehensibly greater than we are, Anselm then uses that very majesty to connect Him to us. In *Why God Became Man,* Anselm showed that God's redemption of human beings through Christ was not simply an act of divine mercy but a kind of logical imperative. The dishonor done to God by original sin could, he argued, be amended only by the incarnation. In a sense, God had no choice but to become man.

Anselm, then, had accomplished two things: He turned the rational apprehension of God into an effectively imaginative act without diminishing the utility of reason; and he showed the essential humanity of God in Christ—his necessary connection to us—without depriving God of his ultimate greatness and mystery. And these, we might say, are the two great themes of medieval spirituality: that God is both wonderful beyond comprehension and yet is like us, a being of whom we can grasp something in our imaginations by a combination of faith and understanding.

This is as much a paradox as the one underlying Augustinian pessimism, but it is one that Anselm and his successors embraced with a kind of joy, as though the multiplicity of truths, contraries, and incomprehensibilities was not troubling but itself evidence of God's immanence in our world. Consider, for example, St. Bernard, writing a generation after Anselm (about 1140) of Mary and the incarnation:

> Perhaps if I direct my attention to this virginal birth, this holy birth, I shall discover the many new and marvelous things to be seen by one who searches diligently. . . . In it one recognizes short length, narrow breadth, lowly height, level depth. There one perceives an unshining light, an unspeaking word, parched water, famished bread. And, if you look carefully, you will see power being ruled, wisdom being taught, strength being borne up; God suckling but giving bread to angels; God crying but comforting the unhappy. If you look carefully you will see sad joy, timorous trust, ailing health, inanimate life, frail strength. But you will also see, which is just as amazing, sadness giving joy, fear giving comfort, pain healing, death vivifying, weakness fortifying. Surely, then, I shall also discover that very marvel for which I am looking.

There is an exaltation in chaos and contradiction here, a determination to find beauty in every aspect of creation, and yet we know these words were written in the ugliest of worlds, one beset by plagues, famines, wars, and incessant suffering, oppression, and death. It is a world that would make optimism, never mind belief in a benevolent God, extremely difficult. Moreover, it arrives at its joy not by averting its eyes from the human condition but by engaging it entire. This is the great age of devotion to the humanity and person of Christ, his suffering in our flesh; to his presence in the Eucharist, not as a symbol but as a corporeal fact; and, not least, to his mother, the very humblest of human beings in whom was engendered the divine.

It is therefore not surprising that a man like St. Francis emerges at this time, a man who embraces this world in all its leprous, impoverished affliction and sees the face of Christ in even the worst of its human inhabitants, and hears the utterance of God in the song of a bird. Nor did Francis do this as gesture or symbol, to point out some other greater thing by reference to some smaller example, but in a most literal fashion. G. K. Chesterton said that for Francis, nothing was "background"; everything was "foreground," the thing entirely in itself, taken at "face" value.

My son Andrew, about two years old as I write this, is at that age when he doesn't distinguish between proper names and generic ones. He calls his stuffed rabbit "Rabbit," and every dog he encounters is named "Dog" rather than "Spot" or "Raggles." It is not that he doesn't understand that there is more than one such creature in the world, but that he has no use for categories or universals. He confronts everything not as an instance but as an essence. The dog he meets in the park this afternoon will be both that particular dog and every dog in its "dogness," its quintessence, and so will the dog he meets on the way home, each wholly and essentially dog yet completely individual.

In this, Andrew and, I think, St. Francis are just the opposite of idealists, not in the sense of being well-intentioned, but as Augustine in his Neoplatonist youth was an idealist; for whom this world, in its imperfection and distance from the divine, and the genuinely "real" was a place in which we could never truly know the essence of things in their being.

By contrast, the High Middle Ages came to the view that we could in fact know things in themselves, both as particular beings and as "quiddities," from the term derived from medieval Latin for a thing's "whatness." Moreover, Francis and his cohorts maintained that we could know at least *something* of God Himself, if not directly then through the medium of the signs through which He manifests Himself in the world; and not only that, but we could communicate with God both through prayer but also through the mediation and intercession of Mary, the saints, and the dead.

This view was first perhaps more felt in the vibrancy of the medieval imagination—in its art and in its obsession with color and light—but soon enough it was being laid down in words and logical structures. An English theologian and philosopher, Robert Grosseteste, living not far from Somerton at around the time of Francis, wrote:

> Wherever we look, we find vestiges of God, not only as a necessary first cause, but as a Trinity of power, wisdom, and love. If we had nothing else to contemplate but a speck of dust, it would display in its essence the nature of God. Similarly, if we had any part of the universe, or the whole of the universe, or just the human mind, the same characteristics of the divine nature could be found. God, nature, and the human mind all lead to the same conclusion.

Nor did Grosseteste—whose name rather unfortunately translates as "Big Head"—confine this notion to the realm of knowledge, "for God is called good because he confers beauty." Nature and art, then, too, are instances of grace, intimations of the inexhaustible "being-in-itself" that is God. A few years later, around 1250, the age's preeminent mind, Thomas Aquinas, summed it up in the remark, "Deus est in omnibus rebus, et intime": God is in all things, and intimately so. This is the crux of the medieval view of creation, and perhaps explains the age's most central expression, its devotion to Mary. For in what or whom did God ever dwell more intimately than in her? St. Bernard had written, "She is our mediatrix, she is the one through whom we have received your mercy, O God, she is the one through whom we, too, have welcomed the Lord

Jesus into our homes." Thomas Aquinas would cast her as the very wellspring of divine immanence in the world:

> She was so full of grace that it overflows on to all mankind. It is indeed a great thing that any one saint has so much grace that it conduces the salvation of many; but most wondrous is it to have so much to suffice for the salvation of all mankind; and thus it is in Christ and in the Blessed Virgin.

It is unsurprising that Mary prompted a great outpouring of art and poetry. The Annunciation is the premier subject of medieval painting, followed closely by Mary at the foot of the cross, an image that also produced the age's most representative poems, the "Stabat Mater" of Jacopone da Todi, and "Salve Regina." And in perhaps the Middle Ages' greatest masterpiece, Dante's *Divine Comedy,* Mary is nothing less than "the face that is most like the face of Christ," so much so that "only through its brightness can you prepare your vision to see him."

In the High Middle Ages, Augustinian pessimism was countered by what might be called Thomist optimism, by the view, given its highest expression in the philosophy and theology of Thomas Aquinas, that a good God must necessarily have fashioned a good creation, and one toward which He is essentially well-disposed. People are therefore made for both this life and the afterlife, and ought to rejoice in both, as Dante put it in his *De Monarchia*":

> Man is a mean between the corruptible and the incorruptible. Just as every mean partakes of both extremes, so Man has a dual nature. And since every nature is ordained for a definite end, it follows that Man has two ends: On the one hand the happiness of this life, and on the other, the happiness of eternal life. The former consists in the exercise of Man's human power and is symbolized by the terrestrial paradise we attain through the teachings of philosophy and the practice of the moral and intellectual virtues. The latter consists in the enjoyment of God, to which Man cannot attain except by God's help.

# FOUR

This, then, is something of the world into which John Griggs and his descendants were born. That is not to say that they read Aquinas or Dante, assuming they could read at all. I do know that in the fifteenth century they were busy acquiring land and wealth and had pretensions toward learning: John's son William owned property not only in Somerton but also in the adjoining villages of Stansfield, Boxted, and Poslingford; his son Robert added land in Brockley and Hartest; and Robert's son Henry directed that his son Thomas be allowed to attend school "as long as he would goe to school or his friends would drive him to schoole." Thomas apparently did well from his schooling: He left his eldest son and heir, William, forty-seven acres and two houses. His will also asked that his sons "be broughte up to perfectly reade and understand their English tounge." More crucially perhaps, he also specified that they learn to "readily and cunningly write and cast an account."

Of their religious life and practices there is no record, although I assume it was ordinary, which is to say up until 1530, orthodox medieval Roman Catholic. But there was nothing simple or perfunctory about it. The stark interior of All Saints Somerton today would be almost unrecognizable to them if in their time it was anything like that of Holy Trinity Long Melford, four miles down the road. According to an inventory taken in 1529, Holy Trinity held no less than twenty-three shrines to various saints, plus rings, coats, and other accoutrements for the statue of the Blessed Virgin; there were thirteen chalices, and, among the priest's many vestments, fifteen copes; there were thirty-eight mass and service books of various sorts, and innumerable banners, crosses, monstrances, bells, and other sundries for processions and feast days.

Thomas Griggs's forty-seven acres abutted Long Melford, and he had a neighbor in that village named Roger Martyn. Martyn, too, was a prosperous man and also a pious one who left behind a unique document, an account of what parish life was like for a layman on the very eve of the Reformation. In it, he records the round of feasts, fasts, and saints days that formed the medieval calendar, that defined and framed every aspect of life in the Suffolk of Thomas Griggs. There were candlelit parades, bell ringings, and processions bearing the consecrated host under a canopy borne by four yeomen; bonfires on the eves of saints' days and, on the day itself, tubs of ale for the whole village; ceremonies for the blessing of herds and springs and the provision of rain. Rents were paid on either Lady Day, Lammas, or Michaelmas, and birthdays, weddings, and anniversaries were regulated by the liturgical calendar. Everyone fasted during Lent and Advent and everyone feasted on Christmas, Easter, and Corpus Christi. Churchgoing and church-related activities were not an aspect of public and civic life; they were, for all intents and purposes, the focus of the entire existence of the community. And while religion in villages like Long Melford and Somerton had a highly visible, even boisterous, public face, its deepest expression occurred within the individual soul at confession, mass, and the dozens of private devotions made at Trinity and All Souls. At the heart of these was, inevitably, Mary. Martyn described her image at Trinity as "having the afflicted body of her dear Son, as he was taken down off the Cross lying along on her lap, the tears as it were running down pitifully upon her beautiful cheeks, as it seemed bedewing the sweet body of her Son. . . ."

This was the world into which Roger Martyn had been born. Like Thomas Griggs, he had seen King Henry's Reformation ebb and flow during the 1530s and 1540s, watched it apparently triumph during the reign of Henry's son Edward, and then saw it undone entirely as the old faith returned under Mary. When Queen Elizabeth took the throne in 1559 and Protestantism was restored, Martyn watched as once more the relics, images, and shrines were removed from his church; and, as he had before, he salvaged what he could of

them and hid them in his house, confident that at some time in what
remained of his life or in the lives of his children, they would return
home to their old places in Trinity church. His last testament in-
structed, "I will that my heirs, when time serve, shall repair, place
there, and maintain all these things again."

*         *         *

That instruction was not to be carried out, for the old faith was
never again restored. When, four centuries after the deaths of Roger
Martyn and Thomas Griggs, I visited the churches the Griggses had
been baptized, married, and buried in, it was hard to imagine that
they had once been decorated as Martyn had described or that they
had been host to the kind of feasts and rites that marked his and
Thomas's passage through life. Even the best-preserved of them, St.
Nicholas Denston, with its great beamed ceiling and carved pews, is
stark by medieval standards. The font at which any number of my
ancestors were baptized is of special interest. As was common, its
eight sides were decorated with carvings of the crucifixion and the
seven sacraments. It would have been difficult to remove these images without destroying the entire font. Therefore, at the time of the
Reformation but mostly likely during the Puritan ascendancy of the
1630s and 1640s, the carvings were merely defaced: Each head of
each figure—Christ, Mary, the Apostles, and saints—was roughly
knocked off. Looking at the font while Andrew and Tessa sat in a
pew surmounted by a carved figure of a rabbit—the medieval emblem of desire—I was struck by the thought that to bother to have
done this at all required either great spite or great conviction. It was
not enough for the old faith to fade away; it had to be literally de-
capitated and effaced.

When I was in high school, the Reformation was presented as a
kind of precursor to the American Revolution, a step toward liberty,
reason, and freedom of conscience in which the pope with his su-
perstitions and strictures stood in for George III with his aristocracy
and dictatorial taxes. In college, a more sophisticated interpretation
was put on these events: The rise of a mercantile, capitalist economy,
coupled with widespread literacy and the availability of printed
books, not least of which was the vernacular Bible, necessitated a religion based on individualism and economic self-interest rather than

on hierarchy, tradition, and community. The lives of my own ancestors seemed to bear this out: Thomas Griggs, for example, was accumulating property and ensuring that his sons would learn to read and write at precisely this time, and those sons would be not only Protestants but Puritans.

But the most recent scholarship attempts to overturn many aspects of these two views. Far from being either a popular uprising against the Roman church or a historical inevitability, the Reformation is seen as an imposition by the rulers of the time of a new spiritual order on a largely content populace. Germany's princes and England's king were, in fact, simply trying to free themselves from what they felt was excessive papal authority over their own national and local political affairs. In England, the rapid, almost seamless return to the old faith under Mary suggests that, with the exception of a radical minority, most of the English people were happy with their traditional religion and the life centered around it.

This, too, is probably an oversimplification. For one thing, the triumph of the high-medieval Thomist optimism I described a few pages ago proved to be but a temporary peace, and its central conviction—that humankind and God were more alike than unalike, that God dwelt intimately in his creation—soon prompted spiritual excesses that the church felt it could not tolerate. As early as 1329, the pope felt compelled to condemn the teaching of Meister Eckhart, who had gone so far as to say, "I am converted *into* God, for God is present to effect his very being in me." Optimism apparently had its limits.

More seriously for the future of the unity of the church, the Thomist theological synthesis was also under attack. The German Martin Luther is usually regarded as the intellectual father of the Reformation, but that distinction may more properly belong to an Englishman, William of Ockham, who lived almost two hundred years before Luther. William was a controversialist—he accused the pope himself of heresy—and a logician of the first rank, still known today for the principle of "Ockham's razor," the notion that a simple argument is always preferable to a complex one. But above all else he was the Middle Ages' greatest "nominalist," which is to say a proponent of the view that, contrary to Thomism, we cannot know the essences and universals of things in themselves but only "name" them as mere words or concepts. Moreover, neither the world around us nor the contents of our own minds can tell us anything about the nature or being of God, since God's creation is utterly contingent on what God willed, a product of the divine intellect, not necessarily its unique mirror image. He might just as easily have willed something else, or indeed, nothing at all. We simply cannot know.

Nominalism and its permutations were more debilitating than devastating to the Church of Anselm, Bernard, Francis, and Thomas Aquinas—the church as the people of Somerton and Long Melford understood it—over the next two centuries, a small but steadily corrosive presence. The church of the High Middle Ages maintained that God was present as love in the world He had made and that faith was the gift or by-product of that love, as were the sacraments and saving work of His church. Nominalism turned that proposition on its head: Since we could know nothing directly of God in or out of this world, the only spiritual reality was faith and nothing but faith, which God might or might not choose to bestow on us. It was as though human beings were suddenly alone and unredeemed in the world, or might as well be, for all they could know of their maker and putative redeemer. And with this the most disturbing aspects of Augustine's views on the economy of salvation reemerged, since under nominalism God and God alone foreknew and predestined the fate of every soul, saved or damned.

Nominalism also served to undermine the church as an institution, an institution whose own predictably human shortcomings and corruptions could not bear too much scrutiny. The church based its authority on its establishment by Christ and the Apostles, its possession of "the deposit of faith"—the accrued traditions and teachings of the church fathers and of the Scriptures—and its sole right to inculcate and judge Christian doctrine through the "magisterium," the church's teaching office. These, together with the papacy instituted by Christ and St. Peter, were the foundation on which the church had presented itself as the bridge and mediator between the coextensive worlds of God and his creation. But in a nominalist world, devoid of comprehensible signs of God, where his grace was a hope rather than a fact, the church's myriad sacraments, saints, and devotions were rather beside the point. God would call us, if He chose to call at all, and there was nothing any human person or institution could do about it.

Nominalism did not take the medieval world by storm. Rather, it played the role of an opposition party waiting patiently for its chance at government, representing the Augustinian pessimist minority. When, after nearly two hundred years, political, ecclesiastical, and social forces had at last prepared the ground for a new church order, nominalism provided, or at least underpinned, the necessary theological justifications.

These things came to a head in the person of Martin Luther. On its face, nominalism is an exceedingly uncomforting view of the world. According to the rigorous logic of William of Ockham and his intellectual descendants, it may be true, but who would want to believe it, never mind base a theology of redemption upon it? Luther, however, was able to salvage something from the wreck nominalism had made of human aspirations to know and comprehend the divine. Specifically, in the course of meditating on the Psalms, Luther hit on the notion that while it was undoubtedly true that he could know nothing of God, he could nevertheless know himself; more specifically, he could know what God meant to him even if he had no idea what he meant to God.

A man, in short, could know his own mind as an individual, as a private and particular person. And while the church as mediator was almost entirely discredited in Luther's view, there was one element of the old faith that retained its authority: the Bible. *Sola scriptura,* Scripture alone, was the core of Luther's faith: A man alone with his Bible, the Word no longer incarnate in the world as Christ among us, but as mere literal words, on which a man might hang his hope that God would be merciful, if only to him alone.

These are some of the reasons advanced for the Reformation, perhaps the most critical event in Western history since the fall of Rome. Some of them, in some combination, may even be true. But I suspect that in Suffolk, the Griggses in Somerton and Boxted and Denston or the Clarks in Westthorpe (who here enter the story) would be a little chagrined at talk of the rise of capitalism and literacy or Thomism and nominalism or Luther off in Germany. They would likely tell you that the fate of the old religion had everything to do with King Henry's divorce, and then with the men who ran things in the name of the young Prince of Wales, Edward, and then Queen Catherine's daughter, Mary, and thereafter Queen Anne's daughter, Elizabeth; that it all had to do with family, with bloodlines and love, as does the better part of man-made misery. And since they are my kin and they were there and I was not, who am I to say otherwise?

# FIVE

I n 1497, the year that my eldest known forebear, John Griggs, died, John Cabot returned home to Bristol from the first English expedition to North America. He had stumbled across Newfoundland and then Nova Scotia, the upper limit of what my ancestors would know one hundred and twenty-five years later as New England. What Cabot did in 1497 had, perhaps, something to do with their eventual passage to America, but another event under way in 1497 had a greater influence: the negotiations for what was called the Spanish Marriage, between Catherine of Aragon and Prince Arthur of England, which were then in their sixth year.

Arthur was heir apparent to his father, Henry VII, head of the upstart Tudor dynasty, which was anxious both to legitimate itself by intermarrying with continental royalty and to secure an alliance with Spain against France. Four years later, in 1501, Arthur and Catherine did indeed marry, but five months later Arthur had died and his younger brother, Henry, became heir to the throne. Henry's father and his counselors saw no reason to waste an opportunity so hard won, and proposed that Henry marry his brother's widow, thus re-cementing the Spanish alliance.

But Henry was a well-read, thoughtful, and even pious young man and he was not keen to marry Catherine. Privately, he may not have cared much for her; publicly he cited the biblical prohibition against a brother marrying his brother's widow. It took six years—by which time Henry's father was dead and Henry himself was about to be crowned king—for the Tudor family advisers and its theologians and jurists to bring him around. A papal dispensation had been obtained on the grounds that the sickly Arthur had never consummated his marriage to Catherine. And so, two weeks before his coronation on June 24, 1509, Henry reluctantly married Catherine. The Tudor succession was assured and France was at bay. England could rest easy.

Catherine bore Henry a stillborn daughter seven months after their wedding; a year later she bore him a son, christened Henry. The king was so moved and overjoyed at this event that he went on pilgrimage to England's greatest shrine, Our Lady of Walsingham in East Anglia. Henry had first been brought there as a boy by his father, who had himself made three pilgrimages to the shrine and had had erected a statue of himself at prayer in front of the great image of Mary. Now his son Henry VIII remained at Walsingham for a week, praying and giving thanks, outdoing his father's piety by walking the mile and a half from his lodgings in his bare feet in the cold. About ten days after Henry returned from Walsingham, his son the infant prince died. This event does not seem to have affected Henry's devotion to Our Lady of Walsingham—later that year, he donated a collar of rubies for her statue and paid for the reglazing of her chapel's windows—but it eroded his faith in something else. Henry, never wholly persuaded of the validity and rightness of the marriage he had contracted, began to have doubts about its legitimacy. Catherine did not conceive again, and Henry wondered if the dead children and his queen's barrenness were a scourge, a punishment being leveled on him for having lain with his brother's widow. It was an age that understood that scourges are real, that accidents are not accidental; that a creation so charged with its creator is necessarily charged with meaning.

Finally, in 1516, Catherine became pregnant again and was successfully delivered of a daughter, who was baptized Mary. By the time she was two, the child had been formally betrothed to the French dauphin, himself also only two. Perhaps there was no scourge after all: Henry had an heir, albeit a female one, and a triangulated peace among England, Spain, and France into the bargain. Then Henry fathered another son, but this one by his mistress. He named him Henry Fitzroy, and later made him duke of Richmond.

By 1521, the works of Martin Luther had reached England.

Henry, as orthodox as he was pious, took strong measures. He made a point of acquainting himself with Luther's ideas, and in particular a book called *The Babylonian Captivity,* in which Luther sought to prove the illegitimacy of the papacy. Henry had Cardinal Wolsey conduct a public burning of this and Luther's other writings in St. Paul's churchyard before an enormous crowd and then went on the offensive himself, composing and publishing a reply to Luther called *An Assertion of the Seven Sacraments.*

Historians argue about the true nature of Henry's intentions regarding this book and the extent of his actual participation in its writing. Most agree that he certainly received help—perhaps from Wolsey, Thomas More, or John Longland, the king's confessor—and that he was not unaware that such a gesture would scarcely hurt him with the pope, who was just then a crucial figure in several important diplomatic and political matters. But they would also agree that it is a genuinely pious and learned work, if not a brilliant one, and that Henry wrote much of it and was the impetus behind it. In any case, the book became a best-seller across Europe, running to twenty editions and translations, and the pope was so impressed that he gave Henry the title "Defender of the Faith," a title his successors to the British throne bear, without apparent irony, to this day.

All this might have made Henry more sanguine about his lack of a male heir, but then in 1525 the French repudiated Mary's betrothal to the dauphin. Catherine had, since Mary's birth, produced two more stillbirths and was now menopausal. Lacking the dynastic alliance with France, having a daughter succeed him as sole occupant of the throne—an unprecedented thing in England—seemed no more workable than having no heir at all. Henry needed a son, yet all his patience with Catherine and his service to the church had been to no avail. He had flouted the prohibition in the book of Leviticus on marrying his brother's bride, and the curse of the book, as it were, was upon him.

It was then, around 1526, that Anne Boleyn caught Henry's eye—or rather, was thrust before it by her powerful and influential relations. The following year, grounds for a possible divorce from Catherine were being explored. Initially, the matter concerned Henry's conscience—his conviction that he had been living in sin for eighteen years—and his heart—he was utterly in love with Anne

Boleyn. For Henry's court and the nation's feuding aristocratic factions, the question was one of power, of who would control the king and his dynasty. The stakes were sufficiently high that the heretofore invulnerable Wolsey was toppled when his negotiations with the papacy failed to yield a church-sanctioned divorce. The reasons had more to do with politics than with faith: From the point of view of Rome, Henry might be a figure to be reckoned with in maintaining the papal power base, but so, too, were Catherine's Spanish relatives and continental supporters.

In 1530, Wolsey evaded the noose or the ax by dying of natural causes as he was being transported to the Tower. A Cambridge divine named Thomas Cranmer soon rose to prominence in the ecclesiastical business of the court. He had nothing of Wolsey's dynamism, and was by every account a serious, cautious, even shy man with a good mind and a knack for finding the essential and unoccupied middle in any situation. Cambridge, unlike Oxford, in Cranmer's time there, had been open to Lutheran ideas, if scarcely Protestant (the term was not yet current); and East Anglia (consisting of Norfolk, Suffolk, and Cambridgeshire itself) was both the part of England closest to Holland and Germany, where Lutheranism had its home, but was also historically a center for England's own heterodox and dissenting religious movements. Cranmer was no radical, but he had been exposed to such ideas and privately approved of many of them; moreover, he found himself at the right time and place to bring a few of them to bear on the king's situation in a most helpful and advantageous way.

Specifically, Thomas Cranmer came up with the strategy of submitting Henry's case to the faculties of both Oxford and Cambridge for consideration by their experts in theology and canon law. Naturally enough, they found that the king did indeed have grounds for divorcing Queen Catherine. Cranmer then followed up by submitting the same matter to the great universities of the Continent, which by and large also found for the king. It seemed apparent by 1532 that the pope must defer to the nearly unanimous opinion of Europe's most brilliant divines. Even Catherine's cousin Francis, the king of France, who normally never forsook an opportunity to discomfit the English, agreed to lobby the pope on Henry's behalf.

The pope might well have yielded to this onslaught. But in January 1533, Anne Boleyn discovered she was pregnant, and Henry took matters into his own hands. With Cranmer's intellectual assistance, he had by now satisfied himself that history and doctrine proved that God and the founders of Christianity intended each local ruler to be the ultimate authority in each local church. As a bishop, the pope was first among equals, but his authority did not extend into the affairs of empires and nations. This idea was not much different from Luther's argument in *The Babylonian Captivity,* which Henry himself had so fervently opposed in *An Assertion of the Seven Sacraments.* But love, as much as politics, finds a way, and sometimes makes hypocrites of us all. It had already made one of Thomas Cranmer, whom Henry made archbishop of Canterbury in mid-January 1533 and who secretly married Henry and Anne Boleyn a few days later.

Cranmer was himself married, not once but twice. His first marriage, contracted when he was still a student at Cambridge—and therefore before he had made a vow of celibacy at his ordination—was brief and heartbreaking: His wife died in the birth of their first child, and the child perished as well. His second marriage had taken place in 1532, only a year before he married Henry and Anne. During his campaign to marshal theological opinion on the king's behalf, Cranmer had visited Nuremberg, a hotbed of Lutheranism, where many of the clergy had renounced their vows of celibacy and had taken wives. Sometime during his visit, in an uncharacteristically impulsive act, he married Margarete, a niece of Andreas Osiander, a leading Lutheran theologian with whom Cranmer had formed a close friendship. Cranmer returned with his new wife to England, where, needless to say, clerical celibacy was still the rule. Somehow the marriage remained a secret.

So did the marriage of Henry and Anne. The king's plan called for Cranmer to be securely in place as archbishop of Canterbury before Henry took any unilateral actions publicly, and for that purpose he needed papal confirmation of Cranmer's appointment. Legates were sent to Rome (bearing payments of ecclesiastical taxes owed Rome, which Henry had been withholding), and despite Cranmer's obvious lack of experience as a bishop in any see anywhere, the pope saw nothing amiss—perhaps he wished to placate Henry in at least some small matter—and approved Henry's application to make Cranmer the most powerful ecclesiastic in England.

Having received the necessary permissions at the end of February, the king and Cranmer went forward. In March, Cranmer was installed as archbishop; in April, Catherine was told that she was no longer queen and Henry formally petitioned his new archbishop to make a finding once and for all on the divorce question. On May 23, after all the necessary hearings had been staged, Cranmer declared Henry's marriage to Catherine null and void. A week later he crowned Anne Boleyn queen.

The speed and calculation of these actions, combined with his treatment of his later wives, contribute to Henry's image in the popular imagination as a cynical lecher, a reputation that alternates with the picture of him as a doddering, infatuated fool, easily manipulated by the power players who surrounded him at court. Cranmer, too, does not emerge with much credit; at best, he seems a man with both a hidden Lutheran agenda on his mind and a hidden marriage of his own on his conscience; at worst, he is Henry's ambitious, spineless episcopal lapdog.

All these things are, at various times and in various situations, undoubtedly true. But we tend to judge these matters with the view of history, as though the people involved could see, looking forward into the unknown future, the same chain of cause and effect that we can see looking backward; and thus that they ought to have been able to foresee what we can see by benefit of hindsight. Yet people do not foresee—or prefer to ignore—the consequences of their actions, and nowhere is this more true than in the realm of love and family.

I am divorced myself, my parents were divorced, and something on the order of fifty or sixty percent of the people I know are divorced. I live in a society where divorces are as common and of not much more complexity or moment than real estate transactions (no small number of which are themselves impelled by divorce). In this I have some connection to—if not sympathy for—Henry, who, if we Americans bothered to give it a thought, was surely the very Babe Ruth of divorce, a great haystack of a man whose record may have been broken but whose legend has never been eclipsed.

More seriously, I recall the way my divorce felt, particularly during the time between the decision to undertake it and its granting: the urgency, the longing, the constant itch I felt for it to be accomplished and over with, a craving beside which any addiction I can imagine must pale. My own experience tells me that the imperatives of divorce are powerful indeed; coupled with new love, as Henry's were, they must be overwhelming, like an enchantment or demonic possession that—whatever the reality of its effects—feels like a holy crusade based on the best intentions imaginable. Imagine what this feels like when you are, by universal acclamation, one of the most powerful men in the world, whose desires and intentions have the force not just of law but of divine right.

Intention is the crucial word, at least for us, looking back. Did Henry set out to divorce two wives and execute two more; did he intend to inaugurate a dynastic and political crisis that lasted almost one hundred and fifty years; and did he intend to be one of the two or three leading figures in breaking apart a church that had endured for one and a half millennia? Probably not, but that does not make it much easier to think well of him; that he may have been as much a fool as a scoundrel, is little comfort.

It seems to me that we today are not much good at thinking about the morality of unintended effects. In my own divorce—a slight thing, to be sure, in comparison to Henry's—I believe my ex-wife and I did everything in our power to minimize the harm that was done to ourselves and to others, but great harm was nonetheless done: to ourselves; to the families and communities in whose context our marriage existed (for surely every divorce diminishes marriage itself to some extent); and especially to our daughter, who like most eight-year-olds wished only for a common and uneventful childhood. It is cruel and wicked to break the heart of a child, and this is something I did, the worst thing I have ever done. That it was the last thing in the world I *intended* to do does not change the fact that something evil happened; that something evil was done, and that I did it.

Of course, I tell myself I would happily undo the hurt done to my daughter, I would do anything to undo it, but I would not undo the divorce. So I would not choose to remove the harm done at its source even if it were now within my power to do it. So much for my good intentions and fundamental decency. They might as well be poses; the evil things that I do—without even knowing it—are facts. And the good things I could do, that I know I ought to do, and yet forgo, I could not even begin to imagine.

The pervasive, perennial, and inescapable nature of this dilemma is perhaps the realest thing we face as moral beings, and it is natural that we shy away from it. Even putting aside questions of guilt and responsibility—the wake of suffering our passage through life inevitably, necessarily leaves—the harm we do makes liars and hypocrites of us all. It reminds us that we are not the people we believe ourselves to be and that we want other people to see us as. We may seem generous and kind, and even at times genuinely be so, but we are also this other unspeakable thing.

Our system for dealing with evil—at least now, at least in North America—is based on two propositions. The first is individualism: the notion that at the source of every action, as opposed to what we call accidents, is an individual agent, an actor to whom the action and its consequences can be traced. The second is legalism, by which I mean the idea that once we have identified the action and its agent, the nature of the action—whether it was "wrongdoing"—and the culpability of the agent can be established by a rational examination of the evidence and the agent's intentions.

Reason is paramount in this system. It depends on the kind of physical, individual facts William of Ockham maintained were the only realities we could know. Yet when it comes around to judging the agent, everything hangs on the altogether more amorphous realm of psychology and belief. The phrase "the defendant's state of mind" is a constant in criminal trials, and in the political scandals of the last twenty-five years. "What did they know and when did they know it?" has been the watchword of every congressional investigation. Despite the process's devotion to reason, it does not often occur to us that in attempting to divine the motives and intentions contained in another mind we are trying to know the unknowable, and thus are proceeding not by reason, but by faith; by what we are inclined, perhaps reasonably, to believe about someone else's mind. Thus, when an act of wrongdoing takes place that was neither unintentional or accidental, the only basis on which the agent can be excused is by a finding of insanity, the finding, that is, of a mind un-amenable to reason or to comprehension by reasonable people.

We might, by the by, say that this system owes its individualist, rationalist component to William of Ockham and its psychological one at least in part to Luther. For it is from Luther that we acquired the notion that, if nothing else, the state of an individual soul can be known, and since God is no longer apparent in our world—may, in-deed, for all we know, be utterly absent from it—the soul and psy-che need to be scrutinized, policed, and judged if we are to have any chance of knowing anything about the likelihood of our redemp-tion. In its refusal to offer any assurances about the remission of our sins, it is an altogether harsher and bleaker moral system than the sacramental rite of penance Luther condemned in the old faith.

Today, in the larger world, it produces strange justice: Which evil, for example, is more profound? The holdup of a convenience store for which I might serve ten years in prison or the breaking of my daughter's heart, for which, in legal terms at least, I get off scot free? The point is not to suggest that every kind of evil can be ad-dressed through the judicial system, but rather to note law's limita-tions as an approach to morality. It deals in wrongdoing rather than evil, in culpability rather than the failure to do good. Its rationalist, individualist premise always locates fault in the discrete acts and thoughts of individual persons rather than in anything larger. Thus evil is made alien, aberrant, something done by a person who is not one of us; it cannot make much sense of the kind of suffering in-flicted by the likes of Henry or me. It can take no account of the pervasive evils and privations that are, in fact, the very air we breathe as human beings; that constitute, in part, what we essentially *are*.

What I did through my divorce—I will not speak for Henry, who was, after all, a king—was what used to be called sin. The term these days is not much in use among educated and sophisticated people. It has an aura of fussy, fastidious scrupulosity, of the finger bowls, each resting on a doily, in which my Victorian (born in 1884) grandmother Clark had us dip our hands to no apparent hygienic purpose. More seriously, it is viewed as a concept designed to repress what is in fact healthy, natural, and fulfilling to the individual and re-place it with shame and self-loathing. We do rather like the idea of at least some wrongdoers having a guilty conscience, of this breed apart from us feeling the weight of their "sin." But that is a misapplication of the term, at least as my forebears in medieval Suffolk would have understood it. Instead, sin is simply the state all humans are in because they are not God but *are* human: not perfect, and therefore not wholly good. Like blood or thought, sin pervades us, not as a pathology or an insult or a curse, but as an existential fact, the imperfection of our being, its lack of absolute goodness. It is who we are, if not all we are. Thus understood, it ought to move us not toward repression or condemnation, but toward compassion, because it is our lot and we are all in it together. It makes it easier to judge myself, knowing that I am not alone in my faults, and harder to judge others. It leads me to sympathize even with Henry, for I might have done what he did; and if I am honest with myself, I have already done it.

I also have sympathy for and a feeling of connection to Thomas Cranmer. It was surely Cranmer, although I did not know his name until many years later, who helped bring me to my first encounter with religion. After the pope excommunicated Henry in 1538 and an independent English church was a fact—possibilities the king had never given a thought to—Cranmer became its chief architect, devising its canons, catechism, and, most notably, its prayer book, which is commonly numbered among the greatest prose works in the English language.

Cranmer had an exquisite gift for words. When, in 1536, Anne Boleyn was condemned for adultery, Cranmer worried that Henry would turn his back on the work of the Reformation that had been promoted by Anne's supporters, and instead favor the conservative, pro-Roman tendencies of the partisans of Jane Seymour, Anne's apparent successor in the king's affections. Cranmer wrote Henry a delicate, almost tender letter, urging him to stay the course and to remember he had not begun reforming the church merely on Anne's account: "Wherefore I trust that your Grace will bear no less entire favour unto the truth of the gospel than you did before; forsomuch as your Grace's favour to the gospel was not led by affection unto her, but by zeal unto the truth." That truth, as Cranmer saw it, would exist only in an English church closer to the one he had discovered in Nuremberg, a church unburdened by doctrines, practices, and institutions incompatible with either biblical authority or individual conscience; one in which he would no longer have to keep Margarete hidden away.

At age twelve, I knew nothing of either Cranmer or Margarete, but I was hungry for comfort and love joined to the aestheticism and hypertrophied emotion that are the stock-in-trade of adolescence. Cranmer's prayer book, then still in use in the Episcopal church, did not disappoint me:

> Hear what comfortable words our Saviour Christ saith unto all who truly turn to him: Come unto me, all ye that travail and are heavy laden, and I will refresh you. So God loved the world, that he gave his only begotten son, to the end that all that believe in him should not perish, but have everlasting life.

I loved these words then, and I love them now; they make love and beauty into one indivisible thing. In that, they seem to have more in common with the medieval church than with the reformed church Cranmer was busy creating. I loved, too, the prayer that followed the consecration in the communion service:

> And we most humbly beseech thee, O merciful Father, to hear us; and, of thy almighty goodness, vouchsafe to bless and sanctify, with thy Word and Holy Spirit, these thy gifts and creatures of bread and wine.

This, too, has that same quality of palpable grace, as though the "gifts and creatures" of the communion might be sheep grazing on the hills of Somerton. Even at its most Augustinian, Cranmer's communion rite is presided over by a gentle God:

> We do not presume to come to this thy table, O merciful Lord, trusting in our own righteousness, but in thy manifold and great mercies. We are not worthy so much as to gather up the crumbs under thy table. But thou art the same Lord, whose property is always to have mercy.

But perhaps the words I loved most were those that the priest said over my head as he laid the communion wafer in the cup of my palms:

> The body of our Lord Jesus Christ, which was given for thee, preserve thy body and soul unto everlasting life. Take and eat this in remembrance that Christ died for thee, and feed on him in thy heart by faith, with thanksgiving.

I could go on at some length about how English prose rhythm doesn't get any more accomplished than this, or about the way the various clauses pile up like symmetrical strata, or about the sheer, mere beauty of the thing. But I want to look at it as I have been looking at everything in this chapter, from the view of theology and the kind of world we construct from and with it. It is not surprising that the earlier passages of Cranmer's communion service replace aspects of the old faith's mass that were unacceptable to him: The "comfortable words" stand in for the blessing of the incense in the Latin Sarum missal: the invocation over the "gifts and creatures" occurs in place of prayers for the dead; and the assertion of our unworthiness to "gather up the crumbs under thy table" sits where a prayer to Mary and the saints was originally said. But the prayer accompanying the offering of the bread to the communicant, the words I loved most, are of a different order, and they reveal a great deal about Cranmer and the English Reformation.

They expand rather than replace the original words, "Corpus Christi," "the body of Christ." But this is Cranmer writing at his smartest and, perhaps, most slippery. Cranmer was at no point free to re-create the church according to his own liking; he had to persuade and mediate among bishops, court, and Parliament and accommodate opinions that ranged from Roman absolutist to hard-core Lutheran. Apart from the issue of papal authority—in itself reason why Cranmer dared not appear too autocratic, lest he be branded a pretender to papal-style power—the greatest point of contention revolved around the "real presence." This was the question of whether the Eucharist—the word "mass" was soon beyond the pale in reformist circles—was a memorial of the Last Supper or, in fact, reenacted Christ's sacrifice and truly transformed bread and wine into his body and blood, which Thomists and the church called transubstantiation.

Cranmer seems to have believed that the Eucharist was essentially symbolic rather than transformative in and of itself, but that position was one minority view among several. At first glance, the opening words of Cranmer's prayer, "The body of our Lord Jesus Christ," suggest that it is indeed the literal body of Christ that the priest is presenting to the communicant in order to preserve his or her "body and soul unto everlasting life." But in fact the words do not make clear whether the body being spoken of is what is being offered to the communicant or is a general statement about Christ's body on the cross at Calvary. It can be taken either way. The following line is less vague in referring to the bread as "this," which is to be taken and eaten "in remembrance that Christ died for thee"—in other words as a memorial. The final exhortation to "feed on him in thy heart by faith"—"faith" being the battle cry of the reformers—clinches it as a statement Luther himself could live with.

It's a brilliant piece of rhetorical diplomacy, or connivance, put together in its final form by others after Cranmer's death, when Queen Elizabeth ascended the throne. Believers in the real presence can seize on the first line, and will find nothing objectionable in the second. Their opponents are free to find the referent of the first sentence in the cross rather than the bread, and focus their attention on the undeniable truth of the second.

All this was lost to me, as Cranmer intended, when I was twelve, when the beauty and comfort of the words blanketed me as I knelt at the altar rail. Now, in retrospect, I feel a little cheated, or at least foolish. And in that, perhaps Cranmer proves his Ockhamist, Lutheran point: What seemed to me to be beautiful was not of necessity true or something in which God dwelt intimately. I have told people that perhaps it was Cranmer who taught me how to write, if only by providing a steady infusion of exquisite prose Sunday after Sunday when I was at an impressionable age. But now I am a little angry with Cranmer on account of his deviousness, of which we will hear more. And then I recall how often I as a writer have manipulated words in the same kinds of ways as Cranmer did in order to manipulate people. So once again the sin of another is my sin, too.

Perhaps we need the view Cranmer was stealthily propounding with his words to make sense of those words, and of our words too. But we also seem to need another view to make sense of Cranmer's life—with its inevitable and inseparable mix of goodness and sin—and of Henry's, too. But that conception of the world—the catholic (in the sense of universal, or what we might call holistic) view that was the ultimate achievement of the Middle Ages and its religion—is the very thing Cranmer and Henry were busy dismantling.

# SIX

I do not know what my forebears thought of Thomas Cranmer, or, for that matter, of King Henry, although I know that they were obliged to pray for both of them whenever they went to church. Their lives were touched by religious conflict as early as 1531, when Henry was declared "supreme head" of the English church and moved into Nonesuch Palace with Anne as his mistress. In that year, the Stour Valley, the river valley in which the Griggses lived, was the site of an outbreak of iconoclasm mounted by supporters of Thomas Bilney, a Cambridge divine and itinerant preacher, who had been executed on order of the conservative bishop of Norwich for spreading Lutheran heresies around East Anglia. Shrines dedicated to the local saint, Petronilla, were vandalized down the road from Somerton in Sudbury and Stoke, as were another shrine to St. Christopher and several other crosses and images located on property owned by the conservative duke of Norfolk, Thomas Howard.

I doubt the Griggses, who were at this time amassing the lands Thomas Griggs would pass on to his son William, had much to say about the surreptitious actions of their neighbors, at least publicly, theirs being an age in which holding the wrong opinion could end in death at the stake. In any case, within three years, what the iconoclasts had accomplished under cover of darkness, Thomas Cranmer would begin to do through the law by royal and parliamentary assent: Popular holy days were banned, the catechism revised, and "superstitious" devotions to the saints officially discouraged. Powerful monasteries and religious houses, such as that at Bury, just north of Somerton, were inspected by government officials with a view to reining them in and eventually closing them down altogether. All this must have been felt at All Saints and other churches around Suffolk. Life as it had been lived for as long as anyone could remember was being transformed.

In the beginning people tended not to believe what was happening. A Franciscan priest told those who came to him for confession (the sacrament of penance itself was soon to be a casualty of Reformation), "These things will not last long, I warrant you. You shall see the world change shortly." But the changes were all too real, and sharp enough to begin to divide families against themselves. In 1536, an uncle warned his reformist nephew that nothing good could come of his Lutheran opinions:

> Remember that this world will not continue long. For although the king hath now conceived a little malice against the bishop of Rome because he would not agree to this marriage, yet I trust that the blessed king will wear the harness on his own back to fight against heretics such as thou art.

But things did not go this way. That very year Henry and Cranmer began a campaign of demolition whose destructiveness exceeded that ever wrought by any of England's foreign invaders. Hundreds of shrines, monuments, chantries, abbeys, monasteries, and other religious buildings were pulled down; thousands of religious objects—statues, images, vestments, plate, embroidery, and the like—were destroyed or junked unless they were hidden by people like Thomas Griggs's neighbor Roger Martyn.

In the midst of this destruction, in 1538, Henry's new queen, Jane Seymour, gave birth to a male heir, Prince Edward, but herself survived his delivery by less than two weeks. On the previous occasion when one of Henry's queens had borne him a son he had gone to give thanks at the shrine of Our Lady of Walsingham in East Anglia, the object of so much devotion by Henry and his father. But now Walsingham was the subject of another kind of attention. The shrine and the priory that oversaw it were to be condemned and the lands sold off. Some of the monks of Walsingham protested, and eleven of them were sentenced to be "drawn, hung, beheaded and quartered for high treason." Those who went along were treated more kindly: The canons who agreed to sign the order surrendering the shrine and abbey were given pensions, some of them generous. In this incident, I first encounter a possible ancestor from my father's side of my family: For his silence John Clarke, a canon of Walsingham Priory, received £4 per annum for life. As for the rest of it:

> It was in the moneth of July, the images of Our Lady of Walsingham and Ipswich were broughte up to London with alle the jewelles that honge about them, at the Kinges commaundement, and divers other images, both in England and Wales, that were used for common pilgrimages, because the people should use noe more idolatrye unto them, and they were burnt at Chelsey by my Lord Privie Seal.

For my purposes, one good thing came out of these years of violence and destruction, this holocaust of objects and images. Among the orders for the removal of shrines, the proscription of devotions, and the lighting of candles for the dead and the saints, was one that mandated that every parish acquire a copy of the Bible in English, and moreover record the baptisms, weddings, and funerals carried out in its churches. Thanks to this, thanks to Henry and Cranmer, I know much more about my forebears after 1538 than before; the only trace of those earlier is contained in the sporadic recordings of wills left, when and if someone left one at all.

In all this, there is a replacement or substitution being worked; of words for things, or of the names of things for the things themselves. The Bible replaces the statues and images of the shrines and the rites and symbols of the liturgy; the parish record book stands in the place of the saints and the dead. Under Protestantism, preaching would be the principal sacrament; words would fill the disenchanted, disembodied, now merely symbolic shell of the Eucharist.

This, I think, is truly the great divorce, greater and sharper than Henry's and certainly than mine. It is the divorce of things and the signs of things from words and names, the triumph of nominalism, our culture's concession that it knows nothing of God, and that God, for all we know, knows (or at least cares) nothing of us. Since

God is no longer assuredly in things and intimately so, we are estranged not only from Him but from his creation, from things themselves; and even his "gifts and creatures of bread and wine" are
nothing more than what we call them, nothing more than names.

For all these reasons and for his unmaking of the only world they
knew, Henry's subjects came to hate their king, who, in their understanding of kingship, should have been their father and protector.
Someone—these things could not be said publicly or owned up
to—is supposed to have remarked that if Henry truly knew how his
people felt "it would make his heart quake." But this is how divorce
is: It breaks children's hearts, and brokenhearted themselves, the
children have an inclination to visit the same affliction on their children, as Cranmer might have put it, "unto the generations."

*     *     *

Around this time, amid the rubble and smoke of Cranmer and
Henry's Reformation, another ancestor appears, this time from the
line of my maternal grandmother, Martha Baker Griggs. His name
was John Baker; he came from Sissinghurst, Kent, and he served as a
member of Parliament from a number of constituencies, including
the City of London, during the 1520s. In 1535 he found himself a
member of the Privy Council, the king's inner circle of ministers
and advisers, numbering twenty persons and including both Thomas
Cromwell, Henry's Lord Privy Seal and chief secular henchman,
and Thomas Cranmer.

It is in relation to Cranmer that John Baker—about whose middling place in Tudor history my grandmother Griggs and her sisters
used to make a great fuss—enters the story I've been recounting.
Like Cranmer, he seems to have had good adaptive capacities, the
ability to sense which way prevailing opinion was drifting, adopt it,
and survive—in his case, right up to his death from natural causes at
the beginning of the reign of Elizabeth I. Unlike Cranmer, he was
by instinct a religious traditionalist, but this does not seem to have
troubled or impeded him overmuch.

As I said, John Baker joined the Privy Council at the height of
Cromwell and Cranmer's pro-Reformation influence in the mid-
1530s. By the close of the decade, however, Henry, prompted by the
accelerating international pressures the pope had arrayed against

him, had begun to wonder if he had gone too far. In the middle of 1540, Cromwell had been removed and Cranmer, although still secure in the king's affections, was in the ideological minority on the council. The traditionalists now saw an opportunity to topple Cranmer and roll back the Reformation, and they took it. Various anti-evangelical measures were put through Parliament and a campaign was launched to root out and remove pro-Protestants from influential roles, with particular attention to Archbishop Cranmer's household and home diocese in Kent.

John Baker, being from that county, was given the assignment of locating and interrogating evangelicals in the district, and where necessary, bringing them up on charges of heresy. In fact, only a few were charged and fewer still executed, because the real purpose of John Baker's investigations was to put pressure on Cranmer. Cranmer did send Margarete back to Germany, for fear his marriage would be discovered, and various accusations were lodged against him—that his sister was a bigamist and that buggery was tolerated among his cooks and other household staff—but nothing was proved. Love also once again intervened: Henry married Catherine Parr, who was to be his last queen and whose religious inclinations were evangelical, if moderately so. She proved to be the balm of Henry's final years, a peacemaker and mediator who brought together all his three children at court for the first time. Moreover, she provided a countervailing Protestant force to the Privy Council's traditionalist majority, thereby assuring the survival of Cranmer's reformed church and of Cranmer himself.

John Baker survived, too. He continued his heresy-hunting, and in 1546, assisted by a torturer in the Tower of London, interrogated some evangelicals who provided evidence that there were heretics among Queen Catherine's inner circle at court. Catherine successfully threw herself on the mercy of her spouse and survived, as did Cranmer and John—now Sir John—Baker. That same year, as King Henry's death now appeared imminent, the balance of power at court swung back toward the evangelicals. The traditionalist Howard family of East Anglia (whose shrines in the vicinity of Somerton had been vandalized fifteen years before) overplayed its hand in trying to control what would become the regency of Prince Edward when he succeeded his father. The elder Howard, the duke of Norfolk, and his son, the earl of Surrey, were sent to the Tower. John Baker participated in the arrests. Surrey was executed, and his father then threw himself on the mercy of the king, now on his deathbed, but to no avail. He was kept in the Tower for the next six years.

When Henry at last died, on January 28, 1547, at two o'clock in the morning, John Baker was in attendance. His signature was on Henry's will, a will that—whether the king understood it or not—was designed to assure a Protestant succession by disowning Mary, Henry's Catholic daughter by Catherine of Aragon.

In the final moments of Henry's life, Thomas Cranmer was sent for. It might have been an awkward final meeting: The king could have asked for the last rites of the old faith and Cranmer, now a thoroughgoing Protestant, would have been loath to perform them. In the event, however, the king had lost his capacity to speak by the time Cranmer arrived. Instead, Cranmer merely asked Henry to give him some sign that he trusted in God; that he had simple faith. Henry is said to have squeezed his old friend Cranmer's hand as hard as he could manage, and then he passed away.

In this way, by the king's speechlessness, did the new faith triumph over the old. Or so it seemed. But in fact, though it disowned Mary, Henry's will provided for a thoroughly Roman Catholic passage into eternity: invocations to Mary and the saints, a requiem mass, and a huge bequest to allow two priests to pray full-time for his soul. By this mixture of intention and accident, Henry died with a foot in each faith, in the world he had destroyed and the new one he had made. For his part, Cranmer is said to have mourned the king deeply, and to have grown a long white beard—in the style favored by Lutheran clerics on the Continent—as a symbol of his loss.

With Henry dead and the boy king overseen by an evangelical regency council, the work of the Reformation could pick up where it had left off ten years before. There was another round of iconoclasm following the explicit and wholesale ban on all images. In addition, the overtly Protestant Thirty-Nine Articles of Faith were promulgated, Cranmer's Book of Common Prayer finalized, and some sixty editions of the vernacular Bible published. Clerical celibacy was officially abolished and Margarete could at last come out of hiding. Sir John Baker remained on the Privy Council, presumably turning his energies to prosecuting papists rather than evangelicals. What is surprising is that he remained on it and even gained greater power, when the boy king died in 1553 and his half-sister Mary became queen by popular acclamation.

Sir John Baker flourished under Mary's restored Catholic regime, hunting down evangelical heretics and finessing the exchequer's accounts—the kingdom's finances were in total disarray—in order to keep the queen solvent. His old acquaintance Cranmer did not fare so well. He was arrested shortly after Mary took power and was subjected to a long series of examinations, disputations, and trials both for treason and for heresy. But the newly reinfranchised Catholic powers did not necessarily want Cranmer dead. Although Mary, who had been declared illegitimate through Cranmer's work on her father's behalf, bore him understandable animus, the new government knew that a recantation of his heresies by the arch-Protestant himself would be the greater coup in aiding the old faith's restoration. In time, after two years of imprisonment and house arrest in Oxford (where the sharpest Catholic theological minds in Europe took turns having at him in debate), Cranmer admitted his errors on topics ranging from the pope to transubstantiation in a series of published recantations. He threw himself on the mercy of both the queen and the pope and went to confession and received the Eucharist at mass. But by this time, almost three years after Mary had ascended the throne, it was too late. His fellow defendants Bishops Nicholas Ridley and Hugh Lattimer had already been burned for heresy, and the queen could not be persuaded to relent against the man who had made her mother a whore and herself a bastard. Thomas Cranmer was burned on March 21, 1556, recanting his recantations as the flames consumed him; but words, at last, had failed him.

*        *        *

Around this time, between the death of Henry and the restoration of Catholicism under Mary, evidence of the other half of my ancestry, my father's family, the Clarks, begins to emerge. They, too, came from Suffolk, from a village called Westthorpe about twenty miles northeast of Somerton, and there was also a contingent of them from the vicinity of Hadleigh, about twenty miles southeast. I've found three Clarks from this time who seem likely to have been of my father's family, and their stories are germane to the larger history I've been recounting.

There was a Thomas Clark, an evangelical who was burned for heresy at Bury St. Edmunds in 1546 in a crackdown that was apparently part of the traditionalist attack on the Protestant circle around Queen Catherine Parr. In 1553, early in Mary's reign, there was a man named John Clark of Hadleigh who, when his local priest, Rowland Taylor, resisted the reimposition of the Roman mass, brought in a traditionalist priest from another parish and erected an altar outside the church for him to use. When the altar was torn down during the night by some of John Clark's evangelical neighbors, he and a group of fellow traditionalists locked Taylor out of his own church while the imported priest said the Roman mass inside. After twenty years of Reformation and conflict, the divisions among the faithful of England were too deeply drawn to vanish in a simple restoration of the old faith. Protestantism had attracted sincere and fervent adherents, especially in East Anglia: In the Stour Valley, close to the Griggses, evangelicals were still refusing to receive the Catholic Eucharist in 1556, three years into Mary's reign. Then, only two and a half years later, in 1559 when Elizabeth took the throne, that mass was again supplanted by the Protestant rite.

As compared to these first two, I know a little more about a third possible ancestor, also called John Clark. He was a fellow of Magdalen College, Oxford, and thus—unlike the Lutheran-leaning Cambridge men, such as Cranmer—was what his entry in *The Dictionary of National Biography* calls "a steady adherent of the old form of religion." He had traveled on the Continent and spoke Italian and French as well as Latin, and became the secretary of Thomas Howard, duke of Norfolk, and then tutor to Thomas's son Henry Howard, earl of Surrey. He was the author of at least three books that we know of: *A Treatise on Nobility* (designed, perhaps, to secure the favor of the Howard family prior to his employment by them), and also the rather bafflingly titled *A Declaration Briefly Conteyning As Well the True Understandynge of the Articles Ensuynge as also a Recitall of the Capital Errours Against the Same—Predestination, Free Will, Faythe, Justification, Good Woorkes, Christian Libertye*.

The third, *De Mortuorum Resurectione* (On the Resurrection of the Dead) was written in 1547; it seems to have been prompted by the arrest and execution of his pupil Henry Howard, and is dedicated to him. The book, approximately thirty pages long, is printed in four parallel columns, one each in Latin, English, Italian, and French. An orthodox restatement of Catholic doctrine on death and the Last Judgment, with particular emphasis on the heavenly reward that will be attained by those who keep the old faith and do good works on earth, it is a tract designed to comfort people like the bereaved and dispossessed Howards.

For all his linguistic gifts, John Clark was not a gifted prose stylist like Thomas Cranmer, but he was earnest in his belief and hopeful in his loss. Of the dead he wrote:

In Christ's celestiall kyngdome they shall shyne as the sonne. There they shall se God the eternall fountaine and forme of the soverayne beautie of the soverayne pleasoure of the soverayne goodness, continually communicatynge hymselfe to all creatures, to whom thynges past do not passe, ne thynges to come do succede, almightye, incomprehensible, whome engelles desyre to behold. There shal be none lame, ne blynde, none deformed or imperfecte, the lyfe shall know none ende, ne love quale, joye diminishe, ne youth ware old, dolor shall not be felte, groning not hearde, ne sorowfull thynge seen.

I also know a little of John Clark's fate. In the spring of 1552, he came to the attention of the authorities and specifically to that of Sir John Baker, who had been involved in rounding up the other members of the Howard contingent. He was accused of "lewd prophecies and slanders" and sent to the Tower. He hanged himself with his belt in his cell on May 10.

It was said that books on necromancy had been found in his rooms when he was arrested. This was one of the stock charges brought by heretic-hunters, but perhaps, erudite and now isolated as he was, he did in fact have such books. As the enchanted world of the old faith was suppressed, the magical found outlets in other places, and, as the rise of Protestantism went on, particularly in the occult and the searching out of witchcraft.

In any case, John Clark left this life guilty of despair and of suicide in the eyes of his own faith. And for that, a place in heaven that he envisioned in his book may well have been denied him. Like his probable cousin Thomas Clark, burned for his evangelism five years earlier, I think of John as a victim of King Henry's great divorce. And perhaps he was also a more direct victim of John Baker, whose descendant, my mother, would marry Clark's descendant, my father, and bear me, exactly four hundred years, one month, and a day after John Clark's death.

That the great divorce went on for some time and goes on still is evident enough. Once the divorce between Protestants and Catholics was complete—if a divorce is ever a completed act rather than an unsalvable wound, an unraveling without end—there were divorces between Protestant groups and within those new denominations yet more divisions, down to this day; down to the time of the divorce between those descendants of John Baker and John Clark, my parents; down, indeed, to my own.

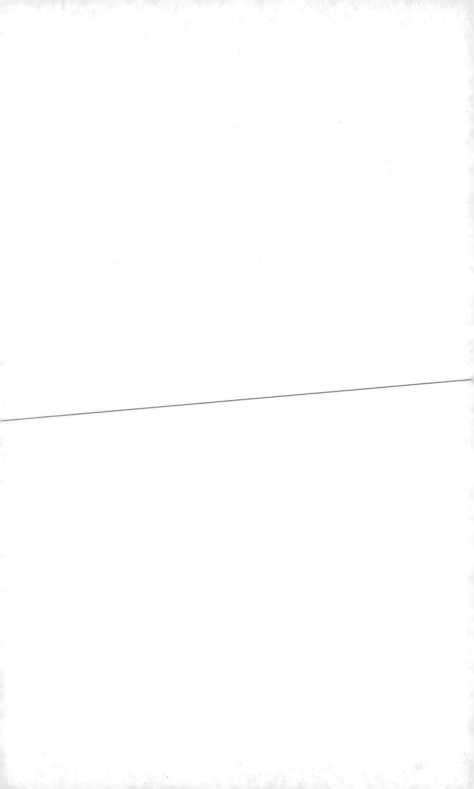

# PART II

# THE WILDERNESS

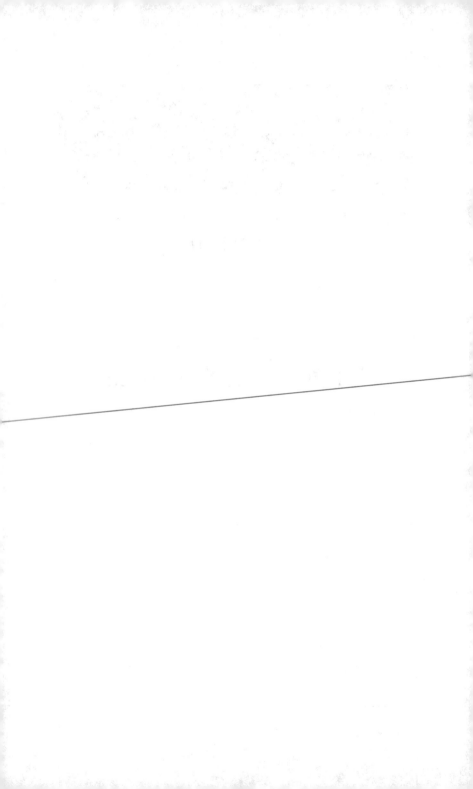

# ONE

fter we had gone to Somerton, I took my children to Stepney in the east end of London. It is by no means beautiful or pastoral, but it was the last place in the old world my Clark ancestors knew before they set off for New England, for the New World, for what they imagined was the wilderness.

In fact, for perhaps the better part of its current inhabitants it is Stepney that is now the new world, for they immigrated here from India and Pakistan in the last few decades. They probably do not see Stepney as a wilderness, though they easily might. Their saris provide nearly the only color among the grim housing estates built on block after block jointly flattened by the Luftwaffe and postwar urban planners and architects; moreover, they have faced and still face the hostility of Stepney's aboriginal population.

Those aboriginals figure largely among the models for London's archetypal East End urbanite, the Cockney, but when the Clarks came here sometime in the 1500s, Stepney was still a village distinct from the capital. It was principally known as a home to sailors and sea captains who berthed their ships on the Thames, half a mile away; and it was also a center of Protestant religion. The vicar of its church, St. Dunstan's, had been burned as a Lutheran heretic in 1541, and his successors upheld the Puritan tradition well into the next century.

St. Dunstan's sits on a seven-acre green, studded with London plane trees whose shade was a relief after our two-mile forced march through the heat, fumes, and ugliness of Mile End Road. The church was cool and much older than I had been given to believe:

Established in 952, it is exactly a thousand years older than I am. The last English-born Clark in my line was baptized here four hundred years ago, on March 8, 1599. His name was Thomas Clark. His parents had been married in this same church a year before. His mother's name was Mary Morton and his father was John Clark; John was a Puritan and a mariner, a man of the sea.

The font where Thomas Clark was baptized—where Mary held him while the vicar touched his head with water and John watched—still stands on the north aisle of St. Dunstan's; and to judge by its bulky Romanesque columns and rounded arches, it is much older than most of the present building. I stood a long time at the font and thought of Andrew's baptism six months before, and my own baptism thirty or so years ago, and of how impossibly far away America seemed, and of how much farther it must have seemed when John sailed the ocean at a top speed not much faster than a good jog. As far as I knew, I was the first of Thomas Clark's descendants to return here and stand where the vicar spoke his name and blessed him with water and set the voyage of his life in motion.

Thomas and his parents were fiercely Puritan, and I, in the custom of converts, can be a little overzealous, which is to say puritanical, in my new faith. The walls of St. Dunstan's are covered with funereal monuments, nearly all dedicated to sailors, decorated with carved anchors, ropes, and ships, and rigorously Protestant in their biblical inscriptions, in their protestations of the virtues possessed by those to whom they are dedicated. But in the back, behind and to the left of the altar, is something that reminded me that this, once, had been a Catholic church: a small carving of the Annunciation, heavily worn not by vandalism but merely by time, perhaps by the touch of hands. As in many Annunciations, Mary is seated, listening to what the angel is telling her. She is not quite surprised, although she has looked up from her sewing or her reading to find the angel before her. It is as though she has been waiting for this, has been biding her time, and now it has come. Now she waits, listening to the angel, wondering how to respond, waiting for her answer to come, attending the arrival of her own assent. And then, expecting, she will wait for her child to be born. All this time, before and during and after the angel's coming, she has been waiting. She has been, as it were, looking out to sea.

# TWO

fter Queen Mary died in 1558, her half-sister, Elizabeth, succeeded to the throne and England was Protestant again, at least in name. Catholic priests and bishops were removed from office, Cranmer's prayer book was reimposed, and the roods and images were destroyed or put back into the attics and storerooms from which they had emerged in 1553. But the queen herself had both a crucifix and candles in her private chapel, and these stood not on a simple communion table but on an altar, the very existence of which implied that when holy communion was held there, something more than a simple memorial of the Last Supper was taking place.

Queen Elizabeth's religion was scarcely Roman but neither was it fully Protestant, at least not in the eyes of those who had waited out Mary's reign in exile in Holland, Germany, and Calvin's Geneva and who had every expectation of returning home to build a truly reformed church. But the queen wanted—and, as head of the church, got—a compromise. Or a muddle, from the standpoint of the Protestant hard-liners, the Puritans, in London and East Anglia. She wanted, for example, vestments; not the chasubles and copes whose rich embroidery had been famed throughout ecclesiastical Europe as "opus anglicorum," but, at a minimum, white surplices. That alone was too much for the Puritans, for whom all ceremony and adornment were distractions from rather than means to the contemplation of God. Anything other than the reading of the Bible or

its explication in sermon was beside the point, if not downright in-
jurious to faith.

Thomas Cranmer had said, "Holy scripture containeth all things
necessary to salvation," and his Puritan successors took him at his
word. By 1571, they had condemned Cranmer's own prayer book,
itself considered radically Protestant in the 1540s, as "a popish dung-
hill," an antibiblical repository of liturgical relics. A later Puritan
would put it most succinctly: "The Bible, I say, the Bible only is the
religion of Protestants."

Elizabeth's bishops did their best to gain acceptance among the
people for the queen's compromise between the old faith and the
new, now the official church of England, and for the most part they
succeeded. But for the Puritans the authority and even the existence
of the bishops was itself unscriptural and therefore illegitimate; and
as for the queen, no temporal ruler had any business coming between a Christian and his Bible in the first place.

That notion of the necessary liberty of the religious conscience
could extend itself into the economic and political realms, and thus,
although not hugely influential among the populace at large, Puritanism was especially attractive to the emerging class of Elizabethan
yoemen, gentry, and merchants—the people who today would be
called entrepreneurs and small-business owners—seeking to maxi-
mize their freedom and power in Parliament and in the marketplace;
people who held small or medium-sized lands or were involved in
the shipping business; people like the Griggses and the Clarks.

By the last quarter of the century, Puritans in Parliament formed
a significant minority, in which virtually all the representatives from
Suffolk were numbered. What little influence Catholicism or even
moderate Protestantism held in the county was gone with the dis-
grace and execution of the duke of Norfolk, the surviving son of
the suicidal John Clark's pupil Henry Howard. With the eclipse of
the Howards, control of local parishes fell into the hands of Puritan
gentry like the Polley family, who dominated local affairs around
Somerton (and whose memorials and funereal monuments fill the
churches the Griggses worshiped in). Liturgical practice in the
neighborhood and throughout the Stour Valley as often as not ignored the strictures of the prayer book in favor of Puritan reading
and preaching. When the old priest at Lawshall, about a mile from

Somerton, continued despite protests to remember the dead in his communion prayers, much of the congregation simply and quietly left, hiring their own minister and forming their own congregation.

In this manner, Puritanism gained power in East Anglia, never openly flouting the authority of the established church but steadily accreting influence and new adherents. Catholics also operated an "underground" church, but could accomplish little in Suffolk. Around 1590, a Jesuit despaired, "In other places, where a large number of people are Catholics and nearly all have leanings to Catholicism, it is easy to make converts. . . . By contrast, in the districts I was living in now Catholics were very few. They were mostly from the better classes; none, or hardly any, from the ordinary people, for they are unable to live in peace, surrounded as they are by most fierce Protestants."

By 1590, the Stour Valley contained the largest "conference," or association, of Puritan clergy in England. When I try to imagine what prompted my ancestors to become Puritans, I have to assume that even for those who had no personal conviction of the truth of Puritan doctrine, the pressure around Somerton to conform to it must have been enormous. Catholicism must have been unthinkable, and even the practice of officially sanctioned Anglicanism would have been a source of suspicion to one's neighbors.

The Puritans, then, were too large and influential a minority to simply be suppressed by the church or the crown, although the idea of creating a separate colony in Ulster where Puritanism might be at least isolated from the rest of the nation had been mooted as early as 1572. Moreover, most Puritans styled themselves reformers who had every intention of remaining part of the official Church of England. They simply wanted to bring the church into closer conformity with what they believed were biblical ideals. But for some, the Gospel seemed to demand a more radical kind of reform. To those who believed, as they did, in double predestination—that God had by his foreknowledge preordained some of humanity as the elect who would be saved and consigned the rest to damnation—it seemed to follow that the true church must consist only of those elect, and that membership in the church and certainly admission to its sacraments ought to be confined to those who could demonstrate that they were among the chosen. By contrast, every person in England was considered a member of the Church of England, and was a member of his or her local parish by virtue of being born in its vicinity. It was one thing to hijack the prayer book liturgy and quietly substitute Bible reading, psalm singing, and preaching in its place—as was common in East Anglia—but it was another to exclude subjects of the queen from attending what was in law her church because they could not prove their sanctity to the satisfaction of local zealots. As doctrine, this was at best dubious; as politics, it openly defied the state's authority over the church and was thus treasonous. Those who espoused it were called Separatists, and unlike more moderate Puritans, they were harried into exile, first in Holland and at last to Plymouth Colony. Thomas Clark and his family were among them.

The triumphalist view of the Reformation I was taught when I was a child saw the Plymouth "pilgrims" as heroes in the quest for freedom of conscience and religious and personal liberty. But viewed from the standpoint of their more moderate brethren, such as my Griggs ancestors, the right they sought was the right to exclude whomever they saw fit from practicing religion at all—at least in the parishes they dominated. John Robinson, a Separatist preacher, explained that "the scriptures do expressly debar men of lewd and ungodly conversation of all fellowship, union, and communion with God." The mere presence of the ungodly corrupted the church just as "a little leaven leaveneth the whole lump."

The Separatists did not hold this belief out of a scrupulous or superior opinion of themselves, but because they genuinely feared for their souls. The open, universal communion of the Church of England defied Scripture and so invited God's wrath. Even without suffering harassment from civil and ecclesiastical authority, the Separatist wing of the Puritan movement saw the advantage and even necessity of leaving England. As early as 1597, four Separatists— among them a John Clark who was likely the father of Thomas Clark—joined an expedition to Newfoundland with the idea of establishing a Puritan colony on an adjacent island called Ramea. But on their arrival the Puritans were cheated by cod fishermen trading in the area, set upon by local Indians, and attacked by a French warship. Having barely escaped the New World with their lives, they decided instead to settle in Holland. Ten years later a further attempt was made to establish a Puritan colony, this time on the coast of present-day Maine, but this, too, was aborted. Finally, in 1620, a ship called *Mayflower* successfully landed Separatist emigrants at Plymouth on Massachusetts Bay. Her third officer was John Clark.

He was remembered at Plymouth for lending his name to Clark's Island outside Plymouth harbor, where a scouting party from the *Mayflower* slept the night before they made their final landfall in November 1620. A storm had come up and Clark was apparently the man who found them a place to shelter:

> Though it was very darke and rained sore, yet in the end they gott under the lee of a smalle iland and remained there all that night in safetie. But they knew not this to be an iland till morning, but were divided in their minds; some would keepe [to] the boate for fear they might be amongst the Indians; others were so weake and cold, they could not endure, but got ashore, and with much adoe got fire (all things being so wett) and the rest were glad to come to them for after midnight the wind shifted to the north-west and it froze hard. But though this had been a day and night of much trouble and danger unto them, yet God gave them a morning of comfort and refreshing (as usually he doth to his children), for the next day was a faire sunshininge day and they found themselves to be on an iland secure from the Indians, wher they might drie their stufe, fixe their peeces, and rest themselves, and gave God thankes for his mercies in their manifold deliverances.

John Clark did not remain at Plymouth, but recrossed the Atlantic with the *Mayflower* on her return voyage and died of a fever in Virginia two years later. His son Thomas, baptized at St. Dunstan's, Stepney, twenty-one years before, came over with the second wave of colonists from Holland in 1623 and stayed for good. By then Plymouth was an established community, and there was talk that the newest emigrants were not made of the same stuff as the "first comers"; that after only two years in existence Plymouth Colony was already losing some of its original mettle. Governor William Bradford complained of having to remind some would-be Christmas revelers to get back to work. They should not have needed to be reminded that neither Christmas nor Easter nor any of the holy days of the old church calendar was celebrated in Plymouth. Much of the supposed grim repressiveness of Puritan society is overstated—the Puritans enjoyed drinking, dancing, and lovemaking about as much as the respectable burghers of any age have, and evince a remarkably tender affection for their spouses and children—but Plymouth did not tolerate either sloth or popery in any form.

Thomas Clark seems to have been an unremarkable member of that community. He was perhaps a little less pious than some and a little more ambitious than most. He was granted an acre of land by the Eel River when he arrived, and then not much is heard from him for about seven years, during which time he was presumably farming and adding to his landholdings. Then, in 1631, he married Susanna Ring, who had been born in Holland to a prominent Separatist family from Suffolk. A year later, Thomas was listed as one of the "freemen" of the colony, meaning that he had demonstrated signs of being among the elect to the satisfaction of the church, had been admitted as a member, and was therefore entitled to vote and to exercise the rights of a full citizen, a status attained by less than a quarter of the adult population. It also gained him certain economic advantages: For example, when Cape Cod, just south of Plymouth, was opened to settlement, Thomas Clark was among those allowed to purchase a substantial piece of it at an insider's price.

With rights, of course, came responsibilities. Thomas served as a constable, a deputy, a surveyor of highways, a soldier in the first Indian war in 1637, and a juror. The law seemed to exercise a special attraction for him, and one account of the colony makes mention of his "legal pretensions," including his ability to draw up indictments and suits, using both English and Latin terminology. It would be only a slight exaggeration to say that Thomas Clark would just as soon sue you as smile at you. Over the years, he sued his neighbors for theft, for nonpayment of debts, for borrowing his boat, for moving boundary markers on his property, and for blocking the road to his house. He sued both men and women, the living and the dead (or at least their estates), the low ("Peter, Indian," to whom Thomas lost by failing to appear and was ordered to pay sixteen shillings and sixpence) and the high (Deacon Samuel Fuller, surgeon, worthy of the church, and overseer of Thomas's wife's family estate).

I cannot say whether this litigiousness made Thomas Clark a popular figure around Plymouth, his attendance at court being nearly as constant as his attendance at church. In 1638, he himself was sued four times (for slander, among other things) and brought up before the court on a charge of "barratry," the false provocation of legal discord. But most of Thomas's legal scraps involved property and trading, the absolute freedom of which Puritan society was still undecided. In 1639, for example, he was fined for "extortion, in buying a paire of boots and spurs for ten shillings and selling them againe for fifteen shillings." Ever watchful for opportunity, Thomas obtained a license to sell "strong waters," a substance with which he was to have tragic acquaintance, having served as a coroner's juror in the death of Robert Willis, who

> being up the greatest past of the night att the house of James Cole of Plymouth, with other fishermen and some of the towne of Plymouth, and having drunk beere and stronge waters, and almost at the break of day, going on boarde the boate to which he belonged to goe out on fishing, and being in the stern of the said boate, and assaying to thrust the said boate away from another boate that was by her, or endeavouring to hang his rudder, he fell over board into the water, and soe was drowned ended his life.

Thomas was himself charged and acquitted of drinking after hours at James Cole's tavern a few months later. He was left chagrined by the law on other occasions. In 1639, he sued the self-styled preacher Samuel Gorton, only to have the case made moot when Gorton was exiled to Rhode Island for his heretical religious fanaticism.

It is rather a shame that Clark and Gorton never got a chance to confront each other in court, for they manifest two aspects of Puritanism carried to their extremes. Gorton's heresy was called antinomianism, which literally means "antilegalism," a belief that subjective, individual religious revelation—the conviction, say, that one has been ravished and taken over by the Holy Spirit—is superior to the wisdom or rule of any human institution like the church. Puritanism, after all—true to its nominalist roots—admitted that neither objective knowledge of God nor of one's own election to salvation was obtainable. On the other hand, it held that humans are saved only by grace through the operation of the Holy Spirit. Did it not follow that the spirit might leave some trace of its presence in the souls of the elect; that it might even speak to and through them? And if that was the case, who had the right to disagree with such a soul?

Having to a great extent denied the possibility of objectivity in spiritual matters, Puritanism was hard pressed to respond to unorthodox assertions of subjective truth. Gorton, for example, denied the existence of the Trinity. He had no personal revelation of it; moreover, it wasn't mentioned in the Bible, the only source of revealed truth the Puritans subscribed to. And in that, people like Gorton exposed Puritanism's great internal contradiction: Puritan theology asserted that the Bible and only the Bible contained the truth, but simultaneously denied that human beings had any sure ability to apprehend that truth. The logical—or rather, illogical—outcome of Luther's individual soul perusing *sola scriptura* in order to ascertain what Christ meant to him was the private but irrefutable looniness of people like Gorton.

The problem at the crux of Gorton's antilegalism was the same as that of Thomas Clark's legalism. For the law, at least as understood in Plymouth Colony, was descended from the Bible: The convenants between God and his people were paralleled by those among the elect in civil society, and the laws and legal judgments of that society were founded on Scripture. In that respect, the law had the same aura of sole and ultimate truth in the secular realm as the Bible did in the sacred. When Thomas Clark turned to the courts, it was as if he were turning to the Scriptures. He and his fellow Puritans believed in the law as they believed in God. Both the Bible and the law were books, records of covenants and contracts obeyed and abjured and of the rewards and punishments that followed from them. The Puritan mind conceived of God as the Word in a most literal sense— took the Word at its word, as spoken, written law; and so, we might say, took law as something akin to God. When Thomas Clark had recourse to the courts—meditating on statute and precedent, casting his charges and affidavits in Latin and English—he might almost have been at prayer, seeking God's truth even though the law of his own mind declared it to be beyond his understanding.

# THREE

Wandering among Thomas Clark's lawsuits and the ungraspable certainties of Samuel Gorton (or his Boston counterpart, Anne Hutchinson), it is easy to regard the Puritan worldview as inherently flawed, as an intellectual and spiritual dead end wholly lacking in either appeal or reason. But it is not that easy. For one thing, Puritanism chose to grapple openly and unflinchingly with questions no branch of Christianity has ever dealt with successfully; for another, its misgivings about the possibilities of human knowledge opened the hearts of its adherents to a range of emotional experience that, while tending toward the bleak, could also encompass the sublime.

In 1611, Thomas Griggs's Suffolk neighbor John Winthrop had a dream that he recorded in his diary:

> In my sleepe I dreamed that I was with Christ upon earthe, and that beinge very insistant with him in many teares, for the assurance of the pardon of my sinnes etc. I was so ravished with his love towards me, farre exceeding the affection of the kindest husbande, that being awaked it had made so deep an impression in my hearte, as I was forced to unmeasurable weepings for a great while, and had a more lively feeling of the love of Christ than ever before.

So Winthrop believed and yet, as a good Puritan, must have been afraid to believe, for an excess of faith—of assurance about God's love and one's own salvation—spoiled faith. In the paradoxical calculus of the Puritan economy of salvation, it was better to be pessimistic than optimistic. The recipe for gaining God's love was to presume his indifference, while loving—and, necessarily, fearing—Him all the while. Moving believers between poles of despair and exaltation, all the while suspending them in a state of perpetual uncertainty, it was not a faith for the faint of heart.

In fact, within ten years of Winthrop's dream, the church authorities in England determined that on balance it would be better if those in their charge remained untroubled by the knowledge of such a tortuous and difficult doctrine. Thus preachers under the rank of dean or bishop were prohibited to "presume to preach in any popular auditory the deep point of predestination, election, reprobation, or of the universality, efficacy, resistibility, or irresistibility of God's grace." In effect, this edict forbade the preaching of the core of Puritan dogma, and men like Winthrop must have despaired of continuing to practice their religion openly in England. Although not Separatists, they began to consider emigration, even as other events began to move them toward that decision.

The East Anglian economy, whose century-long boom had enriched the Griggses while inclining them toward Puritan individualism, began to sour in the 1620s. The cloth trade collapsed, bad harvest followed bad harvest, and taxes had to be raised to care for the poor and for the victims of fresh outbreaks of the plague. Meanwhile, King Charles and his bishops, while not in any overt sense suppressing Puritanism, made clear their intention of moving the Church of England in a more "Arminian" or high-church direction, with greater emphasis on sacraments, ceremony, and authority, all elements of crypto-Catholicism as far as Puritans were concerned.

The Puritan temperament was reluctant to ascribe any good fortune to God's will, for fear that such an explanation would prove to be a manifestation of spiritual pride (and thus perhaps prompt God to retaliate in anger). But in times like the 1620s, it was quick to attribute bad fortune of every kind to divine displeasure. The medieval mind had assumed that since God was good, the good that occurred in the world was an expression of his presence, while evil had no real existence, but was merely a privation of the good, a nec-

essary concomitant of free will, in which God permitted his creatures the godlike freedom to say no to Him.

Puritanism turned this disposition upside down. Bad fortune was
almost always taken to be a direct expression of divine anger, while
good fortune tended to be construed as indifference—God choosing
to leave you alone—rather than favor. Moreover, the Puritans replaced the medieval enchanted, created world—God's corporeal
self-expression, which seemed to partake of the Creator's own time-
lessness—with a fallen, even hostile environment where the clock
was always ticking, and always, needless to say, running down. It was
as though the Puritans had substituted pessimism for optimism and
time for space, exchanging an organic universe for one segmented,
even fragmented by events and destinies. In keeping with their devotion to the word and the law, they were obsessed with history,
with uncovering the hidden narrative in which each individual was
an actor, and which ended in either damnation or salvation.

That same narrative itch applied itself to larger phenomena, and
so, when hard times came to East Anglia, a Puritan pastor remarked,
"As sure as God is God, God is going from England." And John
Winthrop wrote, "I am veryle persuaded God will bring some heavy
affliction upon this land, and that speedyle." The following year, in
1630, he was on his way to New England, leading a migration that
would bring twenty thousand people across the Atlantic. Thomas
Griggs, aged thirty-six, and as his father had ordained "broughte up
up to perfectly reade and understand the English tounge and also
readily and cunningly write and caste an account," was among them.

*       *       *

The first Griggs to arrive in Massachusetts was Thomas's cousin (or,
perhaps, uncle), who came over in 1635 on a ship called the
*Hopewell*. The seven-week crossing was so stormy that the crew
girded the ship with cable "that they might keep her sides together."
For most emigrants, the crossing was doubtless the most terrifying
experience of their lives; and having been through a fair approximation of hell at sea, they were prepared to see New England the way
John Winthrop, now its governor, did, as a godly "city on a hill" in
a fallen world. Scarcely had they come ashore and settled in the out-

lying section of Boston called Roxbury, than a torrent of sermons—
New Englanders could expect to listen to fifteen thousand hours'
worth over a lifetime—reminded them of the holy work of history
to which they had been called as participants:

> The Lord looks for more from thee than from other people;
> more zeale for God, more love to his truth, more justice and
> equity in thy wayes. Thou shouldst be a special people, an
> onely people, none like thee in all the earth.

Although they were not Separatists (and with the Atlantic between them and England, they were in any case free to run their
churches as they saw fit without fear of interference), the Massachusetts Bay colonists took their purifying mission perhaps even more
seriously than did their brethren at Plymouth. Going Governor
Bradford one better, they eliminated not only all holidays such as
Christmas, but also traditional names of the months, since these
were pagan, or popish, or both. Only full members of the church
had citizens' rights, but in Massachusetts candidates to become "visible saints" were subject to a scrutiny that was extreme even by
Puritan standards. In Roxbury in 1636, the year Thomas Griggs
himself arrived there, an obviously pious woman named Susannah
Bell found herself flummoxed at the rather opaque question, "What
promise the Lord had made home in power upon me?" Unable to
respond with a specific example of a biblical covenant that her conversion had impressed on her, she was turned away. She spent a further year in anxious study and prayer and was at last accepted.

That anxiety, only seven years into the Massachusetts Bay's existence, was palpable in Roxbury and throughout the colony. At
Salem (whose church Thomas Clark's erstwhile legal defendant
Samuel Fuller helped set up), the minister was by 1635 refusing to
take communion with anyone but his own wife, for fear of sharing
the sacrament with those who might not be among the elect. And
fear of not being among the elect, of being inexorably condemned
to damnation could drive people to despair, and even beyond.
Winthrop recorded the case of a Roxbury woman who had given
birth to a stillborn infant, an event that Puritans regularly interpreted
as a sign of divine anger: "She fell withal into great horror and trem-

bling, so as it shook the room, and crying out of her torment, saying Now she must go to everlasting torments." Some persons, finding the anxiety unbearable, attempted to simply preempt the entire
question of their destiny. Winthrop recorded the case of a young
mother who

> having been in much trouble of mind about her spiritual es-
> tate, at length grew into utter desperation, and could not en-
> dure to hear of any comfort, so one day she took her little
> infant and threw it into a well, and then came into the house
> and said, Now she was sure she should be damned, for she
> had drowned her child.

But in New England certainty was as dangerous as uncertainty.
Thomas Griggs had been settled on his twelve acres for scarcely a
year when another inhabitant of Roxbury, Anne Hutchinson,
loosed New England's great doctrinal controversy. Like Plymouth's
Samuel Gorton, Hutchinson maintained that she was saved and had
received the direct inspiration of the Holy Spirit. But she went further, opining that, in contrast to her own experience, the bulk of the
New England churches were pursuing a covenant of works rather
than faith in their emphasis on obedience to civic and pastoral authority and close scrutiny of their parishioners' beliefs.

On the face of it, this does not seem like a crisis that would shake
a community to its core, but it did. For one thing, Hutchinson was
extremely intelligent and learned, and could equal and sometimes
best the Colony's finest theological minds in argument and scriptural
citation. Moreover, she had eminent defenders, in particular John
Cotton, perhaps the most distinguished preacher in New England.
That she managed all this and did so as a woman made her presence
in the colony explosive. The people of Roxbury wanted her out of
their community and pressed the authorities to bring her to trial for
heresy.

Cotton was eventually persuaded to give up his defense of
Hutchinson. He was brought around to the view that God's relation
to New England and its institutions and clergy was itself a "covenant
of grace," not a human vehicle for obtaining God's favor by works,
but a divinely ordained event in the history of revelation and re-

demption. In that respect, Hutchinson's indifference to communal and clerical authority and its control over the faithful was a threat and a challenge to New England's fundamental understanding of itself. But it was probably her offense against the doctrine of *sola scriptura* that sealed Hutchinson's fate, for when pressed she admitted that she believed that the Holy Spirit directly spoke to and inspired the elect without benefit of preaching or the Bible. That was enough to justify sending her into exile in Rhode Island. The primacy of the spoken and written word—Puritan "logocentrism"—could not be challenged in New England, even if that logocentrism inevitably tended toward a personal religion like Hutchinson's, making the believer, barred from any knowledge save "what Jesus through the Bible means to me," accountable only to herself.

Antinomianism therefore did not disappear, and the faithful had to be eternally watchful against it. In the 1640s the pastor of Roxbury Church, John Eliot, recorded the case of a neighbor of the Griggses named Mary Dummer, whose persistence in her heresy Eliot clearly regarded as a fate worse than death:

She was a godly woman but by the seduction of some of her acquaints she was led away into the new opinions in Mrs. Hutchinson's time, and her husband removing to Newbury, she there openly declared herselfe and did also (together with others) seduce her husband and perswaded him to returne to Boston; where she being young with child and ill, Mr. Clark (being of the same opinions) unskillfully gave her a vomit [purgative], which did in such manner torture and torment her with the riseing of the mother [miscarriage] and other violences of nature that she dyed in a most uncomfortable manner. But we believe God tooke her away in mercy, from worse evil which she was falling into and we doubt not but she is gone to heaven.

I do not know if the "Mr. Clark" who caused Mary Dummer's death is an ancestor, any more than John Eliot knew if his surmise about her salvation was correct. Eliot was perhaps a more compassionate minister than most in New England (he virtually alone among the clergy concerned himself with the salvation of the Indians and translated the Gospel into their language), but many felt the spiritual anxiety of their parishioners, their fear that their faith was faulty or false. One minister worried aloud, "If Christ gives such peace, how then comes it to pass that many a gracious soul meet with so much trouble in spirit, that the soul hath lost his peace and sense of the favour of God[?]"

It is hard for me, and, I suppose, for most people today, to imagine how the Puritans would keep faith with a God and a religion that demanded so much and gave so little; still more, why they would want to. In our time, belief—like seemingly everything in our culture of consumer individualism—is a choice, and not one that comes very easily to most people. But for the Puritans disbelief was simply not an option, not because religion was mandated but because the reality of God's existence—and his pleasure or displeasure—was self-evident, the first principle of reality. God existed and had power over your life whether you liked it or not. Amid all the boundless uncertainty of the world, that one thing was absolutely certain.

The Puritans, then, did not have a problem in believing in God as we do, but a problem in believing in themselves, in the adequacy of their own paltry human faith. Faith was not simply the prerequisite to salvation, but was salvation itself, the greatest gift, the absence of which was sheer nonexistence, the place called hell.

John Eliot thought Thomas Griggs had the gift. Thomas had lost his wife, Mary, scarcely a year after they had come from Suffolk, and then lost their daughter in 1645, when she was twelve. The following year, Thomas himself died, aged forty-seven, leaving three older children and twelve acres in Roxbury. Compared with Thomas Clark, Thomas Griggs was modest in both means and civic standing. The principal bequest in his will is of "a white backt cow." His virtues clearly lay elsewhere. John Eliot recorded in his book:

Month 3 day 23 Dyed Brother Griggs who lay in a long affliction of sicknesse and shined like gold in it, greatly glorifying God and magnifying his grace in Christ.

# FOUR

I n the years following Thomas Griggs's death, the guardians of
New England's spiritual welfare were beset by a growing sense
of entropy, of "declension." Writing not long after Griggs's
death, John Eliot wrote of the fever that had taken Thomas and so
many others,

> God's rods are teaching. Our epidemical sicknesse of colds
> doth rightly by a divine hand tell our churches what our epi-
> demical spiritual disease is. Lord help us to see it, and to have
> such colds in the height of heat of summer shows us that in
> the height of the means of grace, peace, liberty of ordinances
> et cetera yet may we then fall into malignant and mortal
> colds, apostacys and coolings. This visitation of God was ex-
> ceeding strange. It was sudden and general, as if the Lord had
> immediately sent forth an angel, not with a sword to kill, but
> with a rod to chastize, and he smot all, good and bad, old and
> young, as if there were a generall infection of the aer.

Thomas Scotto, whose daughter Mehitabel would marry Thomas
Clark's son Andrew, was appointed by Governor Winthrop "to see
that the Graves be digged five foot deep." His brother Joshua Scotto
would write a tract called "Old Men's Tears" lamenting that "New
England is not to be found in New England, nor Boston in Boston."
The Reverend Samuel Mather, the elder brother of Increase Mather
and the uncle of Cotton Mather, wrote in 1650, "It is too plain to

be denied that there is a dying spirit in New England to the ways of God." Scarcely twenty years after the great exodus out of England and the new covenant between God and his elect in Massachusetts, it seemed almost for nought.

The divinely ordained history that the founders of New England had believed they were destined to enact now seemed a delusion. In Plymouth, William Bradford, the recorder of that history in his colony, gave up writing it. He thought he might devote himself to the Word in a more literal way, by learning Hebrew: "Though I am growne aged, yet I have had a longinge desire to see, with my owne eyes, something of that most ancient language and holy tongue, in which the Laws and Oracles of God were write; and in which God and the angels spake to the holy patriarks of old time; and what names were given to things from the creation."

Bradford felt that most of the people of Plymouth Colony had broken faith with the covenant they had come to America to carry out. He might have expected as much from the second generation, but even "old comers" like Thomas Clark seemed more devoted to commerce than religion. In 1654 Clark was again brought up on charges "for taking of six pounds for the bare loane of twenty pounds for one yeare, which wee conceive is great extortion, contrary to the law of God and man." Not that Thomas was in any way looking back. In partnership with his sons Andrew, James, William, Nathaniel, and John, he had expanded his activities northward to Boston and southward to Cape Cod, where he bought up fishing rights and land. Andrew managed Thomas's affairs in Boston, while James, John, and William oversaw Plymouth and the Cape. Nathaniel was installed as an apprentice and clerk in a law office.

Just as there was nothing irreligious in his frequent recourse to the courts, so Thomas Clark would have denied that he was turning his back on God in his devotion to business. No less a divine than the great Richard Mather had made clear that prosperity was a gift from God, a sign of his favor; and by the same token poverty, unless wholly the result of forces beyond human control, was a sign of disfavor and even a sin. In the future, some preachers would assert that New England, "the new Israel" was meant to be "a plantation of religion, not of trade," but by then this was not a view with much support among the laity.

In the 1650s, with "declension" so evident, heresy seemed much more of a threat than the accumulation of wealth. On Cape Cod, whose leading minister, Barnabas Lathop, had recently married Thomas Clark's daughter Susanna, there had been talk of "a pernicious plot of the Devill to undermine all Religion and introduce Atheisme and profaneness" in the form of Quakerism. In Plymouth, Quakers were thrown in jail and publicly whipped; in ever-zealous Boston, they were executed.

The Griggs children of Roxbury, meanwhile, remained devout in the mode of their father. John Eliot received John and then Joseph into the church as full members in 1652. When John married Mary Patten of Cambridge in 1658, she too was received into the Roxbury church. But they had been married less than a year, and Mary had just been delivered of their first son, John, when she was called back to Cambridge to testify in a lawsuit between her old neighbors living on Garden Street.

Rebecca Gibson was three years older than Mary, and lived across the street from the widow Winifred Holman, to whose son Abraham she had formed an attachment about the same time John Griggs and Mary were getting engaged. It seems that Rebecca's parents broke off the courtship, and instead betrothed her to Charles Stearns, a widower. It was then that the troubles began.

"The last winter before this I was afflicted with Mrs. Holman's hens," Rebecca's father, John Gibson, reported. "I could not keepe them out of my barne and from destroying my corne." The Gibsons' own hens began to "runne about the house as if they were mad." Winifred Holman also had a rooster, "all milk white save only a little grey on the winges," and both Gibson and his son tried to drive it away by throwing stones at it, but neither could hit it. Gibson's son said, "Here is the devilishtest bird that I ever saw in my life, and I asked him why he did say so and he said I never threw halfe so often at a bird in my life but I did not hit it, but this I cannot hit it." Then they saw the rooster fly away to Widow Holman's house. But in the evening Rebecca came outside "and saw this bird under her house. She thoght it were a catte but she going towards it perceived it was a white bird and it did fly along the house and so away to Mrs. Holmans." The bird was also seen flying in the night "when it was too late for birdes to be abroad."

It did not end there. "My wife has been much troubled with her wheel when she set herself to spin for the necessity of her family. Sometimes she could make no worke on it and she thought it might be out of kilter and we both used what means we could with it but it was never the better." Then, without explanation, the spinning wheel worked again, and then it would not. "One time amongst the rest she set herself to worke and was much troubled that she could make no work on it. She began to feare there might be sumthing that myght be the cause of it. She set her wheel away and went out and found [the widow Holman's daughter] Mary Holman at the oake turning round."

Another time, Mrs. Gibson went out to the well where she saw Mary Holman holding a bowl. Catching her eye, Mary raised the bowl over her head and let the water slowly spill out. When Mrs. Gibson returned home she found Rebecca "crying so immoderately that the teares fell so fast from her eyes that my wife was fayne to stand and wipe them from her face with her apron and her mother asked her wherfor she cryed and she sayd she could not tell but she sayd she could not [stop herself]."

Later, after they had brought a suit against the widow and Mary Holman for bewitching Rebecca and the widow had countersued for slander, the Gibsons thought it might have been the stockings. The widow had got hold of a pair of Rebecca's stockings, and when Rebecca got them back and put them on, she began to have dreams and fits. "She cryed out and sayd a snake stunge her under her arms and when she was out of her dystemper she sayde she saw a thynge lyke a great snake come into the house with a thynge lyke a turtle upon its backe and it came upon the bed to her. And another time when one of our elders were at prayer she barked lyke a dogge and though we held her mouth close with our hands yet she would speake saying that Mrs. Holman and Mary Holman were witches and bewitched her and her child."

Mary Griggs gave a deposition at the trial stating "we have known this Winnefret Holman, widow, this many years, but never knew anything in her life concerning witchery. But she hath always been a diligent hearer of any attender to the word of God." That testimony was added to the other testimony, and it is not easy to tease out the sequence, the history, of events; of whether first came the hens or the tears or the stockings and the snake with the turtle riding on its back. But in the end something like this seems to have happened:

> After [Rebecca] had 2 exterordary fits which she had never had the like before Mary Holman asked her why she did not get sum helpe for them and she answered she could not tell what to doe. She had used means of physicians and could have no helpe and the sayd Mary sayd that her mother sayd if she would put herself into her handes she would undertake to cure her with the blessings of God.
>
> Our daughter telling us of it and we not suspecting them, we wished her to go to see what she would say to her and she sayd her daughter was a prating wench and did love to prate but yet she did prescribe some herbs to her that she should use. After this my daughters child grewe ill and Mary Holman coming in often asked her whather child ayled and she sayd moreover that her mother and she took notice that the child declined ever since the 3rd of Jenuery and expect it will come to the grave but if you will put it into my handes I will undertake to cure it.
>
> After this Mary Holman borowed a sclit [cutting] of hair and when she brought it home the child was asleepe in the cradle and a boye rocking it and the mother of the childe was gone for water and the boye sayd that Mary Holman came to the child as it was asleepe and took it by the nose and made the blood come and set it a crying that the mother heard it and before she came in Mary was gone over the gate. When she came in and saw the child in such a case, she shooed the boy for making the child cry and he sayd it was Mary Holman that did it and went away as fast as she could.

After that, Rebecca's child began to waste away and Rebecca had more fits: "She was afrighted with Satan and thought that she saw him stand by the bed's side so that she cryed out with a loud voice all night to the lord for helpe saying Lord helpe me, lord helpe me that she was heard a greate way off." On other occasions, Rebecca had to be restrained, held down in bed while she cried that she was fighting against the devil, against "Mrs. Holman's black chest and Mrs. Holman's oak, but what she meant by them we cannot tell. Concerning the child it does decline and fall away daily according to Mary's words and yet we cannot perceive that it is sicke at all but will suck and eat."

By the time the matter came to trial in Charlestown, the child was dead; and we might expect, given our own view of Puritan credulity and superstition, their penchant for imagining the worst of any situation, that the Holmans were condemned by the court. But it was a jury trial, and the jury chose, as it were, to dismiss all the suits by splitting the difference. It found for the Gibsons in the defamation case against them and fined Winifred Holman fifteen shillings and tenpence court costs. Then it found for the Holmans in the suit against Rebecca, but leveled a fine against her of only eight shillings and fourpence, noting that "the defendant was by Gods hand deprived of her natural reason when she expressed these words charged on her"; that she was, in fact, insane with grief. John Gibson, who wrote the history we have been reading on his daughter's behalf, was made by the court to swear that "he is heartily sorry for his evil thereby commited against God, and wrong done to the said Mary Holman and her friends, and doth crave the forgiveness of the said Mary Holman of this trespass."

Such skepticism in the face of charges of sorcery or heresy was not uncommon. For all its fears of "declension," the New England authorities were loath to embrace accusations of active evil or ungodliness. Perhaps, by the logic of their own theology and their own sense of history, they should have been more vigilant. But in the same year as the Holman trial, for example, two witnesses in Plymouth swore they heard a man named John Newland say that "hee is as holy as God is holy, and as perfect as God is perfect, as George Barlow affirmed." But this George Barlow was known to another witness: "Thomas Clark affirmed in open court that George Barlow is such an one that hee is a shame and a reproach to all his masters; and that hee, the said Barlow, stands convicted and recorded of a lye at Newbury."

Like Mary Griggs, Thomas Clark denied that the evil was real, that evil had manifested itself as a thing a man could see and touch. Thus far, the New England Puritans had resisted the notion of evil

possessing a life of its own. Ill fortune was not accidental, but prov-
idential or the result of human failing. Evil had no agency or substance of its own. Yet as declension rolled onward and human sin
mounted, how angry could God become before He deserted his
people and left them to their own devices and those of a fallen world
freed from his control? And if he did—if the promised land reverted
to wilderness—where would they be? Whose spirit would they be
among? Whose hand would be upon them?

# FIVE

From 1660 onward the journal of John Eliot, the Griggses' pastor in Roxbury, records a crescendo of providence: "dreadful thunder and lightening in the night" that knocked down a house and left its occupants unharmed but overcome "by a great stink of Brimstone"; a comet that lingered in the sky for three months; another lightning strike that turned a dog to ash but left the boy standing next to it untouched; a whirlwind in Dedham and Dorchester that sucked water out of the river and spun it in skeins through the air; hailstones as big as eggs, as big as fists; corn and wheat blasted and burned in the fields. There was more in 1666, a year fit for the Antichrist:

> It pleased God this summer to arm the Caterpillers against us which did much damage in our orchards and to exercise the Bay with a severe drought. The churches in the Bay sought the Lord by fasting and prayer, our church at Roxbury began the 19th of the fourth month. The Lord gave rain the next day. At which time happened a sad accident at Marshfield, for in that town a certain woman sitting in her house and hearing dreadful thunder crackes, spake to her son and said Boy, shut the door, for I remembr this time four years ago we had like to have been killed by thunder and lightning. The boy answered, Mother, it is all one with God whether the door be shutt or open. The woman said again, Boy, shut the door. At her command the Boy shut the door, but immediately there

came down a Ball of Fire from heaven, down the chimney and slew the old woman and the Boy and an old man, a neighbor that was present, and a dog that was in the house, but a little child that was in the armes of the old man escaped; and a woman with child being present was sore amazed.

It pleased God that our wheat was Mildewed and blasted this year also.

That was not the end of it: "It pleased the Lord this Summer to visit the country with the small pox, which greatly encreased in the winter and proved very afflictive and mortal unto many." Nor was there much relief in 1667. On New Year's Day, then March 25—what once had been Lady Day in the old religion—Samuel Ruggles (whose family was soon to intermarry with the Griggses as well as the Holmans of Cambridge) was standing by the Roxbury meeting-house with his oxen and cart. A lightning bolt struck the oxen dead in their harness and tossed Ruggles through the air, burning the shoe from his foot. The contents of the cart itself were intact, and among them a chest apparently untouched, containing pewter and linen. But upon opening it, "the pewter had small holes melted in it and the linnen some of it singed and burnt."

In Roxbury the providences came from without, from the sky, but at Plymouth they issued from within, out of men's minds and mouths. People like John Newland might be accused by other people of claiming to be as great as God, or of lesser but scarcely less serious things:

> James Clark complaineth against Sarah Barlow and Marcye Bartlett, in an action of slaunder and defamation, to the damage of two hundred pounds, for reporting that they saw the said James Clark kiss his mayde and use other uncivil carriages that he acted towards her in the field upon the Lord's day.

Sarah Barlow was, of course, kin to George Barlow, whose veracity had been impeached by James Clark's father, Thomas, in the Newland matter. In the event, James was outraged, and thinking big (as was the Clarks' wont when money was involved) sued the women for two hundred pounds each, a small fortune. The court found for him, but fined the defendants "ten shillings apeece," the same penalty it leveled against James five months later for drinking at the notorious Cole's tavern "on the Lords day, in the time of publick worship of God."

The offenses and slanders and slights accrete in the 1670s: William Walker is made to pay double to Thomas Clark for stealing a bolt of cloth from him, and ten shillings more "for telling a lye about it." Walter Winser is fined five pounds for selling liquor to the Indians, while Philip, the Indians' "chief sachem," pledges his subjection to "the King Majestic of England, this government, and the lawes thereof," and as proof of it "will bring in or cause to broughte in yearly one wolfs head unto thye Treasurer." A month later, the court authorized that Indian lands be opened to white settlement "whereunto our collonie have a right." There was also the case on which James Clark sat as juror in which John Buck and Mary Atkinson were found guilty of committing adultery and "uncleaness" and so sentenced "to be publickly whipt att the post or pay each of them a fine of ten pounds in currant silver money of New England; moreover, John Buck was to pay "the sum of three pounds a yeare, for the tearme of eight years, unto the said Mary Atkinson in good and currant merchantable corn, at prise currant, to be for and toward the bringing up of the child begotten in the said acte of uncleaness."

This was doubtless the source of much talk in Plymouth, but it was no marvel. But what to make, in a long season of wonders and providences—epidemics and earthquakes and comets cleaving the sky—of the very fish of the sea, so to speak, committing mass suicide, taking their own lives? John Eliot could only imagine, for it happened once on the thirtieth day of the fourth month and then again, like the arc the comet inscribed in the night, on the first three days of the fifth month: "The fish in the fresh Pool at Watertown in great abundance came to the shore, faint, drooping, pining and dying, many scores of cartloads were observed on the south side of the pond, and within four or five dayes they were rotten and much consumed."

It was not long after that "the warr with the Indians brake forth, the history wheroff I cannot, I may not relate. . . ." There were things surpassing wonders, past providences; and these, Eliot seems to have thought, were unspeakable.

*          *          *

It was left to Increase Mather, son of Richard, father of Cotton, to write the history of King Philip's War, in per capita terms the most devastating conflict in American history. Nearly ten percent of the adult males in the colony were killed, and six of its fourteen towns were abandoned or burned to the ground. The source of the war is the familiar prototype of all of America's subsequent conflicts with its native population: a misunderstood or broken treaty, white settlement on native lands, and the arrest of Indians for real or imagined retaliation against whites, in this case the murder of a Christianized Indian who had been informing against Philip.

The Indians attacked the town of Swansea between Plymouth and Rhode Island in June 1675. In August, the authorities at Plymouth ordered 112 Indian men, women, and children sold into slavery in the West Indies, among them Philip's nine-year-old son. Clark's Island was their internment camp. Philip's people made alliances with neighboring tribes and, advancing through guerrilla-style raids and incursions, the war spread westward into the Connecticut River Valley. By the spring of 1676, as Mather writes, it had come home to Plymouth.

March 12: This Sabbath eleven Indians assaulted Mr. William Clarks house in Plimoth, killed his Wife, who was the Daughter of a godly Father and Mother that came to New England on account of Religion and she herself also a pious and prudent woman; they also killed her sucking Childe, and knocked another Childe (who was about eight years old) in the head, supposing they had killed him, but afterwards he came to himself again. And whereas there was another family besides his own, entertained in Mr. Clarks house, the Indians destroyed them all, root and branch, the Father and the Mother and all the Children. So that eleven persons were murdered that day, and under one roof; after which they set the house on fire. The leader of these Indian was one Totoson, a fellow who was well acquainted with that house, and had received many kindnesses there, it being the manner of those brutish men, to deal worst with those who have done most for them.

William Clark had been in town, perhaps at church, perhaps about his father's business. We do not know what kind of relationship he had with Totoson, or what the Indians intended by attacking his house. They might have logically assumed he was the proprietor of Clark's Island, although it was in fact owned by the town. At any rate, they left him his son Thomas, his grandfather's namesake, if only by mistake and with a section of his brain exposed. His grandfather prevailed on the best surgeon in Boston to patch the child's skull with a plate of silver, and he was known thereafter as Silver-headed Tom.

The war ended that summer—"God turned his Hand against our Heathen enemies and subdued them wonderfully"—and Totoson was tried and given "the centance of death, which was, that his head should be severed from his body, which was immediately accordingly executed." The head of Philip himself was brought to Plymouth "in great triumph . . . soe that in the day of our praises our eyes saw the salvation of God."

The mood of triumph was not indulged for long. The church at Plymouth declared days of repentance and prayer:

> Whereas the Holy and Righteous God hath in many wayes in yeares lately past changed the course of his favourable dispensations against us, we desire to be deeply humbled in his sight under his mighty hand and to reflect upon our owne hearts and ways with serious Consideration, whereby we see abundant cause to judge ourselves as being guilty of many evills for which the Lord may Justly be provoked to avenge the quarell of his Covenant upon us. . . . For these and other evills that might be mentioned, wee desire to lye in the dust before God and to abhore ourselves and unfeignedly to repent in his sight and humbly to acknowledge that God is Just and Righteous in all the evills wee have been visited with, yea that He hath punished us far less then our iniquities do deserve.

For the clergy at least, the war afforded an opportunity for spiritual renewal, a chance to stop declension in its tracks, particularly among "the rising generation," the children and grandchildren of old comers like Thomas Clark.

Providence cooperated: In the summer of 1668 a smallpox epidemic was visited on Boston. Increase Mather's son Cotton, then age fifteen, wrote his uncle John Cotton, the pastor of the church in Plymouth: "To have coffins crossing each other as they have been carried in the streets—To have, I know not how many corpses following each other close at their heels—To have 38 dye in one week—6, 7, 8 or 9 in a day. Yet thus it has lately been, and thus it is at this day."

Cotton's father used his pulpit to inspire more terror than pity: "Death waits for you," he told his congregation. "There is now a Mortal and Contagious Disease in many houses; the Sword of the Lord is Drawn, and young men fall down apace slain under it." After the epidemic came another comet, whose import was not lost on Increase Mather: "God will ere long pour down the Cataracts of His Wrath upon a sinful Nation, which hath of late been found guilty before the Lord of Signal Apostasy, Debauchery, and above all of nefandrous Contempt of the Pure and Powerful Dispensation of the Gospel."

Mather aimed his words at the young, not only because they were most in need of reform, but because their parents' history was already made, already recorded, while that of the rising generation was still but a thought in the mind of God. The young therefore might save history, might yet redeem New England from the wilderness. It was doubtless terrifying to have crossed the Atlantic crowded into a heaving, disintegrating ship like the *Hopewell* fifty years before. But was it less so to be burdened with the weight of both heaven and hell, the future and past? Increase preached the following to the children of his congregation:

> Go into secret corners and plead it with God [for] if you dye and be not first new Creatures, better you had never been born; you will be without excuse before the Lord, terrible witnesses shall rise up against you at the last day. . . . As for many of you, I have treated with you privately and personally, I have told you, and I do tell you, and make solemn Protestation before the Lord, that if you dye in a Christless, graceless estate, I will most certainly profess unto Jesus Christ at the Day of Judgement, Lord, These are the Children,

whom I spake often unto Thy Name, publickly and privately, and I told them, That if they did not make themselves a new heart, and make sure of an interest in Christ, they should become damned creatures for evermore; and yet they would not repent and believe the Gospel.

# SIX

I came godless to Cape Cod in 1969, age seventeen. I took LSD on the beach and in the stunted, sandy-floored forest, and the bark on the pine trees shimmered and moved like a lava flow, like the uncertain and amorphous particles from which it seemed to me the world must have been made. I had come to live with my stepmother, my dead father's second wife, because my own mother couldn't cope with me. The pursuit of faith and goodness I had taken up at age twelve no longer interested me, and my interest in justice and politics had waned in the face of the more urgent business of finding myself as a sixteen-year-old. I was not bad, but I was not good, and God existed only insofar as I could conjure Him up, name Him; and I could scarcely say who I myself was.

I was part of the "rising generation" of the time, and found the preachments of my parents as terrifying as my contemporaries of three centuries before must have found Increase Mather's, with one crucial difference: I did not find them terrifying because I took them at face value and accepted them, but because I believed I could see through or around them—view them, I might say today, ironically. And what I saw was a social, political, and cultural order whose final end was at best a life of stultifying conformity and spiritual torpor and, at worst, a nuclear holocaust.

Convinced of this, I went looking for anchorage in a world adrift, hoping to find myself, as the argot of the day had it, by getting lost as much as I could in the woods between Harwich and Brewster, trawling for a self on the sandy, pine-needled forest floor.

I would have approved—or, rather, "related to"—the very language I just described this search with, a rhetoric of simile and approximation, for I knew at best only what things were "like" entirely in relation to me with scarcely a clue as to what they in fact were. I was prepared to admit this, and took a certain pride in it, knowing only that the world was essentially mine to discover. Among the things I didn't know was that these woods had been, at one time, Thomas Clark's.

Even now, I am aware that genealogy is too often the province of cranks and snobs and is of about as much interest to strangers as an account of one's last outpatient surgery. The scope of adolescent curiosity is, moreover, notoriously circumscribed; and in the 1960s we had the watchword of "relevance" to defend us from unappetizing concerns and points of view. That narrowness—if it is narrowness—is usually chalked up to the teenaged personality's narcissism, selfishness, and egotism, character flaws that will be outgrown. On the other hand, it seems to me that no one is as open and genuinely vulnerable to beauty as an adolescent. In terms of sheer devotion and hunger, art (particularly in the form of music) mattered as desperately to me then as it ever has in my life. Considering that vulnerability, adolescents take an enormous risk in being as open to the world as they are, since the social and psychic stakes they are grappling with are so terribly high: ostracism versus acceptance, dependence versus liberty, and—so it seems when you are in the midst of it—being versus nonbeing. It is a rigorously bipolar, yes-or-no universe, insistent on certainty—Am I in or out? Okay or fucked up?—and yet certainty is the very last thing it affords. In that, and in its curious mix of cocksureness and credulity, it is more than a little like Puritanism.

That correspondence between my life and Thomas Clark's is something I would have strenuously denied. The one thing I knew was that I was against repression, and who was more repressive, more utterly uptight than the Puritans? Nor would I have approved of Thomas's acquisitiveness as manifested in the swath of Cape Cod, from present-day Brewster to present-day Harwich, nearly from the north shore to the south, that he took title to. Had I known, I might have thought that taking LSD in Thomas's woods was a fine piece of guerrilla theater, a liberated rejoinder to his restricted, capitalistic worldview. But then, what did I know of Thomas's world? I had never seen a comet or a whirlwind or an execution or the shore of Massachusetts Bay before any white man had stepped upon it or a shilling piece stamped with King Charles's head. Perhaps Thomas and I had in common a sense that neither of us could say for sure whether we were bound for heaven or hell, or which of those two these woods might be.

It was after King Philip's War that Thomas moved to the Cape. He and his son Andrew had both taken wives in Boston; Thomas his second, after the mother of his children died sometime in the 1650s. He married Alice Nichols in 1665, but she lived only six years after that. Thomas sued her family for her estate and gave the house they had shared to Andrew and his wife, Mehitabel Scotto. But by 1678 Andrew and his family, together with his father, were back in Plymouth. Andrew served in two coroner's inquests with his brother William—both for drownings preceded by drinking at Cole's. William himself had remarried a year and a half after his wife and children's deaths at the hand of King Philip's warriors. Nor does that experience seem to have turned him utterly against Indians. In 1682, he took on an Indian named George as a servant and laborer, bailing him out and standing surety against various fines he had run up in scrapes with the law.

Thomas, meanwhile, was bringing suit against a partner in his Cape Cod bass fishing venture, and sometime in the 1680s moved to Harwich with Andrew, leaving his affairs in Plymouth under the control of his son Nathaniel. Nathaniel was very much his father's son. He was the arch-lawyer of the family, and in 1684 or '85, he married one of the richest widows in Plymouth, Dorothy Lettice Gray, whose husband had recently left an estate in excess of twelve hundred pounds.

Nathaniel was well into his forties by the time of this, his first marriage. In that he departs from the uxoriousness of the rest of his family, but perhaps he was too much occupied with his legal and political connections, which were considerable. He was secretary to the Colony Court, and certainly played a major role in drafting the *Book of Laws* of 1685, the great formal codification of Plymouth's statutes and ordinances. In that same year King Charles died and his successor, James II, decided to impose direct rule on Massachusetts. A governor was to be appointed, and Nathaniel Clark was named a member of his council. In the midst of these triumphs, however, Dorothy, Nathaniel's wife of scarcely a year, moved out of their house and filed the following document with Plymouth Court:

> I am sorely afflicted that I have this sad occasion to petition to God and you, for in that Mr. Nathaniel Clark hath not performed the duty of a husband to me, for he is misformed, and is always unable to perform the act of generation. And therefore your petitioner humbly prayeth that I may be divorced from him, for our lives are very uncomfortable in the sight of God.

Nathaniel responded by drafting a cease-and-desist petition of astonishing complexity (certainly much more complicated than my own divorce decree three hundred years later). Besides specifying what portion of their house Dorothy might occupy, it divied up their property and obligations in minute degree, down to one hogshead of rum and three barrels of cider to be reserved "for his own drinking." Nathaniel evidently believed it would be a long, hard winter. He was right.

The court affirmed his petition and also directed that Nathaniel's "body be viewed by some persons skillful and judicious, and therefore doe request that Mr. John Cutler, Mr. Thomas Oakes, and Mr. William Avery, physicians, shewing himself unto them, that they would give their judgment of him." The doctors found no abnormality, and the court denied Dorothy's petition for divorce. Now it was left to the church to heal the breach. Dorothy agreed to confess her misstatements and "failings," and the church elders "declared themselves to be well satisfied." Then it was Nathaniel's turn:

> The elders then speaking a few serious words to Nathaniel Clark as a child of the church, he [Clark] brake forth into a wicked passion and spake vile words, intimating that the church would cleare the guilty and condemn the innocent, abusing also Paul's words to the mariners, that it were better

and nearer to salvation to be out of such a church than in it, etc., which carriage and words of his were highly offensive, and so declared by the Pastour to be, but at the present it was meete not further to proceed upon.

During the period that followed, Nathaniel and Dorothy seemed to have reached some sort of peaceful accommodation. Nathaniel's brother John's son was admitted to full church membership; less happily, Nathaniel's stepdaughter by Dorothy, Susanna, was admonished for "fornication" with John Cole (of the tavern-keeping Coles) prior to their marriage.

Meanwhile, Nathaniel's ship at last came in, in the form of the arrival of Governor Edmund Andros, whom he was to serve as councillor. In addition to enjoying periwigged, London-style high living at Andros's mansion in Boston, Nathaniel, flush with power and influence, determined to get his own back at Plymouth. Specifically, in 1687, he asked the governor to deed Clark's Island over to him, although it was town property and no Clark had previously laid claim to it. Andros complied, but this and other high-handed conduct on his part alienated much of the colony's population. Ultimately, all the councillors save Nathaniel boycotted their sessions with Andros, leaving Nathaniel perhaps more powerful but also more isolated.

Not long afterward, James II, found to be a crypto-Catholic, was deposed in the "Glorious Revolution" of 1688 and replaced by the solidly Protestant William and Mary. The immediate response of New Englanders was to overthrow Edmund Andros, put him in chains, and ship him back to England on the next available boat. They sent Nathaniel Clark with him.

The new occupants of the English throne, heavily lobbied by Increase Mather, established a colonial regime more acceptable to New England. Nathaniel Clark returned home unharmed but stripped of power. He also had to face condemnation and trial in Plymouth as "a publicke enemy to and disturber of the peace of this colony." His brothers William and John posted his bail, and it was once again left to the church to make the peace.

Plymouth church, it might be said, had a bellyful of the Clarks that summer of 1689. First, James Clark's daughter (also named Susanna) was publicly admonished for fornication, and then William was condemned for his role in his brother's expropriation of Clark's Island. And Dorothy stood accused of striking the pastor's son as well as "joyning with and encouraging her husband to get Clarks Island from the town and at last setting her hand to the sale of it."

The pastor's son, Josiah Cotton, had been climbing a tree on Dorothy and Nathaniel's property, and, in Dorothy's account, "she tooke the lad gently downe from the tree and he came downe upon his feet." But witnesses averred that Dorothy had in fact "pulled the lad out of the tree with her hand and then threw him over the fence." Dorothy explained that the boy's subsequently bloodied face was the result of his mother, Mrs. Cotton, "putting a key into Josiah's mouth." The church elders did not find these explanations terribly convincing, and ordered Dorothy to prepare an act of repentance.

Then it was time to deal with Nathaniel. Pastor Cotton sent two elders to bring him to the meetinghouse, but they returned saying, "'He would not come, he had nothing to say to us, nor would have any thing to doe with us.' Upon which the Pastor declaring to the church sundry of his scandalous wicked words and practises, and that now he had practically disowned his relation to the church," Cotton ordered the elders to go fetch him again. Nathaniel refused them again, saying, "he should not come, for he could not speake, because he was under bounds" since the matter had been, and still was, in his mind, under the jurisdiction of the court. Nathaniel thought he could trump the church with the law, but in this case the covenant between civil and sacred legalism went unrecognized:

> July 7: Nathaniel Clark made it manifest his Rejection of the church, in that he came not to the publick worship, nor did attend on the church, wherefore after many brethren had particularly exprest themselves as Judging him worthy to be rejected for his not hearing the church, there was then a vote called for and universally consented to, that he should be disowned. The elders did then declare that whereas Nathaniel Clark had like Esau despised his birthright, by many words and carriages contemned the church, they therefor disowned him and cutt him off from his relation to the church as an un-

profitable branch; and the elders prayed after, and the Pastor added a word of counsell and admonition to all church children.

Dorothy Clark was received back into the church a year later, in May 1690. Nathaniel Clark died in January 1717, excommunicate, doubtless angry and sure of his rights under the law.

# SEVEN

W hat Thomas Clark made of his son's troubles we do not know. He lived another eight years after Nathaniel's trial and expulsion from Plymouth church, dying in 1697 at the age of ninety-eight years. Nathaniel had epitomized Thomas's legalist side, just as Andrew embodied the opportunistic businessman, building and operating mills on Stony Brook and Bound Brook, which ran through their woods; trying to corner the Cape bass fishery; and reestablishing the Clarks as merchant mariners and sea captains.

I am descended from Andrew—Nathaniel Clark died childless— but as an adolescent I might well have shown some of Nathaniel's character traits. I had his sense of injustice, his feeling, as he told the church elders, that the authorities would as likely as not "cleare the guilty and condemne the innocent"; and I had some of the petulance he displayed when things went against him. I also had some of his delusions, his capacity to overvalue his own rights and capabilities. And at times, like him and like Dorothy, I had a tendency to lie if I felt the ends I sought justified it.

That year I spent in and around Thomas Clark's woods, I imagined myself an artist, although in what medium I had not decided. I had painted a little and not very well, and I was drawn more to crafts, albeit crafts that claimed a strong aesthetic component, that married beauty to a sense of community and social justice in the spirit of William Morris. There was nothing original about that impulse. It was fundamental to the 1960s urge to connect the search for personal authenticity—for finding oneself—to the building of an "alternative" community. Maybe those were contradictory goals, but they did not seem so at the time. Similarly, I liked the idea of one's work also being a kind of spiritual discipline, a search for "enlightenment" (which I saw as pretty much identical with the search for self).

There was an influential book at the time, M. C. Richards's *Centering,* which approached making ceramics on the potter's wheel in this very spirit. I don't recall much about it now except that it melded the Zen Buddhist spirit that the English art potter Bernard Leach had brought to Western ceramists with what was becoming known as humanistic psychology. As I understood it, making pottery was an honest and beautiful craft that sustained the community and through which you could "see God." I wanted to be a potter.

As it happened, my stepmother had a friend who operated an arts-and-crafts summer camp, and through her I secured a job assisting the ceramics teacher, a pretty college student from New Jersey. Through the summer she taught me what she could in exchange for cleaning up and doing chores around the studio. I was not a gifted potter—I was in too much of a hurry to acquire the qualities that I understood to go with being a potter, as opposed to learning how to make good pots—although I made one or two pieces that bordered on the competent. I was a little stymied by the teacher, on whom I had a crush, but who took me no more seriously as a potential lover than she did as a Zen potter.

I had other interests: Dilettantism was no crime in 1969. We viewed everything as a potential outlet for self-expression, and in the search for identity, the more self-expression the better. Someone had told me that the French government had an apprenticeship program for would-be stained-glass artisans. In exchange for a commitment to work for a set number of years doing restoration and repair in the great Gothic cathedrals, the program would provide training, room and board, and a stipend. I never found out if such a program really existed, but that same summer I thought I would try working with glass.

In retrospect, my interest in stained glass, like my interest in ceramics, had something to do with what I saw as its spiritual dimension. Although I was no longer a practicing or believing Christian, its aesthetic dimension still had resonance for me. As perhaps they are for most adolescents, the hungers I felt for beauty, for love, for sex, and for God were interdependent, interconnected, and almost indistinguishable from one another. In any case, I got a book about stained-glass crafting from the library and set about figuring out what would be involved in manufacturing a little piece of Chartres on Cape Cod.

I discovered through the yellow pages that there was a dealer in stained-glass supplies not far away, just outside Plymouth, an expedition that could be managed in half a day or so. But during the week, the only time the glass store was open, I was supposed to be working at the camp, and I knew that my stepmother, who in any case was openly skeptical about my various artistic enthusiasms, would not countenance my skipping work and going away on my own to Plymouth. But stained glass—although I knew nothing about it— had taken on the imperative force of a love, of a longing that could not be denied. Without much conscious calculation, I told the owner of the camp that my stepmother wanted me to take a day off to run some errands for her; and I told my stepmother that the owner of the camp wanted me to pick up some supplies for a putative stained-glass workshop at the camp. That these two were close friends who talked virtually every day did not occur to me.

I came home from my trip with two exquisite pieces of glass, both imported from Europe; one a brilliant blood red, the other a deep amber-straw, each about a foot square. They were like jewels, I wanted to show them off. Instead, the moment I walked in the door, I was confronted with my lie, which I had already, in my excitement, forgotten. But the adults in question were furious. The owner of the camp announced that she would take me back only as a favor to my stepmother, and my stepmother herself made it clear that in her estimation I was beneath contempt. She had of her own generosity taken me in when few if any members of my family wanted much to do with me, and I had repaid her with deceit, betrayal, and the humiliation of being played for a sucker in tandem with one of her best friends.

I was put under house arrest, leaving only to go to work. And there was more. Phone calls were made to my grandparents and my mother. In the collective judgment of the adults responsible for me, with this incident—and perhaps others that I wrongly believed they were unaware of—I had crossed the line from the merely "difficult" to the "disturbed." I needed help, and it was made clear to me I was going to get it.

My stepmother was a Catholic—the only one ever to marry into either side of the family as far as I know—and she sent me to her parish priest. He had had some training in counseling, she explained, and had volunteered to see what he could do for me. Despite my earlier flirtation with Catholicism, I had never spoken to a priest at any length in my life. And although I now consciously rejected Christianity as irrelevant to anything that mattered to me, I found the idea of speaking about myself to a priest immensely intimidating, a cross between the confessional (about which, like most Protestants, I had rather strange ideas) and a police detective's rubber hose. I also thought that by dint of his sacred office and sheer jesuitical smarts he would see right through me, and the prospect terrified me. Not knowing what else to do, I dipped into a Teilhard de Chardin paperback, figuring it might make a good icebreaker, or better still, a screen behind which I could secure myself for at least a little while.

When at last this conference took place, I broke down. Virtually the instant the door to the priest's office closed, I poured forth what now seems to me a massive confession, a tsunami of sin and confusion and woe. It was not just this lie that I had been caught out in that distressed me, but my entire life. Because the truth was, my whole life was full of lies; or, more exactly, I felt I no longer could say what was really true and what were the stories I had concocted to improve on reality, to make myself a little more of what I wanted to be.

In the press of events, I probably exaggerated the extent of my confusion about what was real and what was not. But I felt utterly lost, and at that time of my life, feeling *was* reality. The priest saw how unhappy and mixed up I was, and allowed that my situation was beyond his own counseling skills. During the entire conversation, he never proposed any religious solution to my problems, although I expected he would, and indeed perhaps hoped that he might—whether I wanted to dismiss the suggestion or to fall upon it wholeheartedly, I cannot say. Instead, he sent me to Dr. Freed.

*          *          *

Dr. Freed wasn't a medical doctor, but a psychologist with a Ph.D. However, as far as I was concerned he was just as intimidating as the priest, and their function and authority were nearly indistinguishable. Since I had made a hash of finding myself, it now seemed to me, they would uncover my self by a kind of medical intervention, a forceps delivery of my miserable, shamefaced authentic self into the glare of the world.

I have always been overawed by credentialed professionals, and this feeling seems to run in the family. Although the Clarks seem to have an almost primal attraction to the law, they haven't to my knowledge produced any distinguished jurists, doctors, or—with one exception—clerics. The same, on the whole, is true of the Griggses. On both sides, then, we are much impressed by such people, although until I stumbled across him on my own, I never heard anyone mention Dr. William Griggs.

William was a nephew of Thomas Griggs in Roxbury, and seems to have been born in the old country. Exactly how or where he received his medical training is unclear, but he was on record as a physician in the town of Chelsea in the 1650s and in Gloucester in the 1670s. By 1690 he had finally settled in the town today known as Danvers, but which was at that time called Salem Village.

His wife was born Rachel Hubbard, and although all their own children were grown by the time they settled in Salem, they took in Rebecca's grandniece Elizabeth, rather, I suppose, as my stepmother took me in. And like me in 1969, Elizabeth was seventeen in the winter of 1691–92.

She earned her keep by cooking and cleaning for the septuagenarian doctor and his wife. Happily for Elizabeth, there were younger people living in easy reach: Mercy Lewis, another servant girl who lived at Thomas Putnam's together with Putnam's daughter, Ann; Mary Walcott; and Betty Parris and her cousin Abigail Williams, who lived with Betty's father, Samuel, the pastor of Salem church. They did the things that adolescent girls do together, waiting out their arrival in three or so years at what the Puritans considered marriageable age; and with that mingling of jest and credulity common to teenagers, they cast fortunes to see "what trade their sweet harts should be of."

Was Elizabeth a "trial"—as adolescents are so often said to be—to Dr. and Mrs. Griggs? Probably not, at least not until the Reverend Parris's girls, Betty and Abigail, got sick. Parris had been appointed pastor at Salem two years earlier, and in his very first sermon took on the themes of election, covenant, and declension:

> Learn we to adore, and in our very souls to magnify, the free grace of God in Our Lord Jesus Christ for the gracious distinction he is pleased to make between us in New England and millions of others. . . .

Parris believed in the privileges and responsibilities that went with the New England covenant, and he was stringent in reminding his parishioners about them. He was not an easy or popular man, nor did he feel it was his business to be. He worried, like all his colleagues, about the rising generation, the troubled youth of New England. And then hell broke loose under his own roof.

Betty and Abigail became alternately listless and manic, and then the convulsive fits began, the unstoppable itchings and scratchings, the shrieking and babbling in tongues, the hiding under tables and chairs, the trances and lunatic poses. He fetched Dr. Griggs—who knows how many times?—and at last the doctor opined that the girls must be "under an evil hand." Parris employed every weapon at his disposal: days of fasting, of repentance; marathons of prayer in which he got neighboring ministers to join him. But none of these means was effectual. The problem was not within his house, but without, out in the world, or beyond the world altogether.

Once the matter was given over to the law, the Griggses' niece Elizabeth Hubbard, now herself afflicted, was the first of the girls to testify:

> The deposition of Elizabeth Hubbard, aged about 17 years, who testifieth and saith that on the 28 February, 1692, I saw the apparition of Sarah Good, who did most grievously afflict me by pinching and pricking me, and so she continued hurting me till the first day of March. . . . Also several times

since, she hath afflicted me and urged me to write in her book. Also I saw the apparition of Sarah Good go and hurt and afflict the bodies of Elizabeth Parris, Abigail Williams, and Ann Putnam. . . . Also in the night after Sarah Good's examination [by the legal authorities] Sarah Good came to me barefoot and barelegged, and did most grievously torment me by pricking and pinching me. And I verily believe that Sarah Good hath bewitched me.

Beneath these words Elizabeth made her mark in the shape of a hook, signing herself not in Sarah Good's book but in the book of law, the book of the New England covenant. She and the other girls did the same against Rebecca Nurse and Bridget Bishop and John Willard until there were over a hundred persons accused in and around Salem. That is not to say that Satan—for who else could it have been?—did not fight back. Elizabeth testified

that the last second day [May 2, 1692], at night, there appeared a little blackbearded man to me in blackish apparel. I asked him his name, and he told me his name was Borrous. Then he took a book out of his pocket and opened it and bid me set my hand to it. I told him I would not. The lines in the book was red as blood. Then he pinched me twice and went away.

The next morning he appeared to me again and told me he was above a wizard, for he was a conjurer, and so went away. But since that he hath appeared to me every day and night very often and urged me very much to set my hand to his book and to run away, telling me if I would do so I should be well, and that I should need fear nobody, and withal tormented me several ways every time he came, except that time he told me he was a conjurer. This night he asked me very much to set my hand to his book, or else, he said, he would kill me, withal torturing me very much by biting and pinching, squeezing my body and running pins into it. . . .

Eliz. Hubbard declared the abovewritten evidence to be truth upon her oath, that she had taken. This she owned before the Jury of Inquest, August 3, 1692.

That is my brave cousin Elizabeth, who would not sign Satan's book, but kept the covenant, the true book, always before her; or, if not that, did as she was told. I remember how it is when everything and nothing feels quite real, how truth might be nothing more than the gaps between bloodred lines in a book, and how much comfort there is, at last, in filling those lines with what the pastor or the doctor says is best.

For Elizabeth's trouble and that of the other girls, two dozen persons died at Salem, mostly by hanging. With one, Giles Corey, also accused by Elizabeth, a new method was tried:

> Giles Cory was prest to death. . . . [He] pleaded not guilty to his Indictment, but would not put himself upon Tryal by the Jury (they having cleared none upon tryal) and knowing there would be the same witnesses against him, rather chose to undergo what Death they would put him to. In pressing, his Tongue being prest out of his Mouth, the Sheriff with his Cane forced it in again, when he was dying. He was the first in New England, that was ever prest to death.

That is how it is when they bury you alive with stones: Your tongue will come out, and who knows what it will say?

Within a few years, it all seemed a terrible mistake, although at the time, the best and most pious minds in New England—Increase and Cotton Mather, Governor William Phipps, Deputy Governor William Stoughton—had applied themselves to the bewitching of Salem's rising generation, which Increase had himself characterized as "lamentably degenerate" in comparison with their parents. But by 1697, many of Samuel Parris's parishioners would not receive communion from him, from hands that now seemed stained with "Innocent Blood," and he was dismissed from his pulpit. That same year, old Dr. Griggs passed away. His will left nine books on "physick"; it was from these, or from something deeper and more experiential, that he had been able to make his diagnosis of "an Evil Hand."

*        *        *

Dr. Freed owned the works of Sigmund Freud and his followers. He never showed them to me, but I concluded it from other evidence.

He was trained as a psychologist but fancied himself a psychoanalyst. Our sessions—he insisted on at least two per week—were called "the analysis," or more informally, "the work," which consisted, as far as I could see a pattern in it, in my saying whatever came into my head while he sat opposite me puffing his pipe. Sometimes he took a note on a small pad he kept on the end table that held his tobacco pouch and pipe cleaners, and sometimes he seemed to look away, out the big picture window that stood between us, with an amused expression on his face. That expression bedeviled me and mocked me, implying that everything I said was a lie or an evasion; that it was not the truth, it was not what he or the "work" required.

I knew Dr. Freed wanted something—this analytic "truth"— from me and I tried desperately to give it to him, although it seemed wholly beyond me to grasp what exactly that truth might be. It was something that I was hiding or withholding, and the job of the analysis was to uncover it, to confess it; and by thus naming it, rather as in a fairy tale, I would make it disappear. It—this unknown truth— had something to do with sex or my mother or wishes I had concerning her or others (even against Dr. Freed himself) that I must feel were unspeakable, even to myself. So in fact, this truth was mine to speak. Despite my protestations that I had not the slightest idea what it was, I was willfully refusing to speak it; I was the agent of my own despair. The disease that afflicted me was myself.

But the only truth I could speak with certainty was that I was unhappy, that the world was self-evidently beautiful, and didn't I deserve to partake, if only a little, of that beauty? I honestly did not think I was concealing anything at all, unless it was the depth of my sense that I was condemned. I would have given anything to know and be able to say what the truth of me was, but as things stood I was irretrievably, almost by predestination, among the neurotic, the sick, the psychically damned.

Still, I went on talking to Dr. Freed, hoping that I might stumble across the thing we were searching for; that Dr. Freed would suddenly turn away from the window toward me, his quizzical, skeptical smile evaporating, and he would look at me deeply and say, "Yes, that is it." But this never happened, and so we met over the course of a year in a state of steady stalemate, looking out the window; and sometimes—I am sure this is true—we would remark to each other how beautiful the view was. Dr. Freed was proud of his window and of his view, in a rather self-satisfied way, as though he possessed the secret of the view's beauty just as he presumably possessed the secret of the truth about me.

That window is what I remember best about our sessions. It gave onto a huge marshy bay facing east and beyond it was the Atlantic and beyond that the old world of Thomas Griggs and Thomas Clark and all its dissatisfactions. That is not to say that I thought about them, or about any of my ancestors at the time, but I did start to think about my father, whose absence from the time I was two and whose death when I was five was the great lack, the great privation of my life. He had loved Cape Cod—it was here that he came when he was stricken with polio; here that he came to die—and he loved to sail. I had been told that on the eve of World War II, when he was about the same age as I was while I "worked" with Dr. Freed, he took part in nighttime civilian anti–German submarine patrols in his little sloop. This was the kind of thing—a good and exciting thing— that I wished I could do myself, and so when I looked out on the water I imagined him and felt a sort of communion with him, though I couldn't recall him as much more than a shadow to one side of my infancy. I even began to imagine that to recover him, to know him, would be to recover myself, to know the truth of me at last. But my imagination was scarcely that large, and it seemed to me that my imagination and its desires were what had gotten me in all this trouble to begin with.

So I used to look out at the bay and the ocean on the ride home from my sessions with Dr. Freed. And more and more, it seems to me that that was what Dr. Freed and I mainly did during those sessions at which we were going to uncover the truth about me: We looked out to sea and waited, as though the answer might come like a ship appearing on the horizon. I was expectant, I suppose, because hope was all that stood between me and the sense that I had been annihilated; between living and drowning. And in that, I feared the sea as much as I hoped that it or something sailing upon it might deliver me.

# EIGHT

I was a watcher, waiting apprehensively on the sea's edge, but for my Clark ancestors the sea was the field in which they labored. Andrew Clark's son Scotto was a miller at his father's Stony Brook mill, but the next generation, born at the turn of the century, returned to the water. Scotto's son, also named Scotto, was a master mariner working out of Harwich, and nine of his eleven sons were sailors or whalemen; of the nine, five died at sea. The death of the second eldest, Tully, was reported in the *Massachusetts Gazette* of October 3, 1765:

> A son of Capt. Clark was killed by a sperm whale near George's Bank a few days since. The whale struck the boat at the bows with his head with great force, throwing the young man, who stood there ready with his lance, into the mouth of the whale, which turned and made off with him; he was heard to scream by his father, who commanded the boat, as the fish's jaws closed upon him.

This kind of incident did not deter the likes of Scotto Clark. It is said that when his last child was born and proved to be a daughter, "he wept, because he thereby yet lacked one boy to make up the crew of two whale boats." He wept, we might say, because he had no more sons to give to the sea.

Give, the Clarks did: Those who did not die of natural causes were without exception killed at sea, a half-dozen or so in each generation. It was as if they were predestined to this fate when they were baptized. For while the girls were routinely given names like Mercy, Patience, Temperance, and Thankful—names of comfort and consolation—the boys were christened with the names of men who came to bitter or terrifying ends: Samuel, Lot, and especially Isaac, the son whom God asked Abraham to sacrifice.

Captain Isaac Clark was my grandfather's grandfather and was even in my generation still regarded as the family patriarch. During the Revolutionary War, he worked as a privateer, expropriating the cargoes of foreign ships or, alternatively, running the embargo lines himself, sneaking American goods into friendly European ports. His ship was called *Financier,* a name that would no doubt have pleased his great-grandfather Thomas. He was taken prisoner three times by the British, but survived the war to make a lucrative career in hauling cargo from far and exotic ports. On one voyage he sailed as far as Siberia in pursuit of furs, and returned with a load of Siberian timber from which he built the family's house, which still stands in Brewster on Cape Cod. He died in 1819 together with his son, also named Isaac, on the coast of Africa, having written his daughter Temperance that "the voyage is not profitable, that it will bring no golden eggs, and that the family must look to God in his grace to provide the things that are needful."

I do not know to what extent this remark, which proved to be his last words to his family, is a commmonplace or an expression of convinced faith. The eighteenth century marks the emergence of distinct secular and sacred realms in American society, the end of the Puritan vision of a divinely covenanted "city on a hill" in which the law of the state and that of God were one thing. It is as though, around 1700, having confronted evil outright at Salem and been stymied by it, the theocracy of William Bradford, John Winthrop, and the Mathers simply collapsed. By this time, not only did their notion of the New England covenant seem unable to guide the application of the law and the affairs of state, but it could scarcely direct the spiritual lives of the people credibly. Solomon Stoddard of Northfield, the father of the "Great Awakening" of the 1730s and 1740s, confided in 1699 that the faithful were in a perpetual state of confusion about the status of their redemption:

[Wondering] whether they are sincere saints, they labor in it for many years; and one minister gives signs, and they try themselves by them, and another gives signs and they try themselves by those; and sometimes they think they see signs of sainthood and sometimes the signs of hypocrites; and they don't know what to make of themselves.

By the early 1700s, New England Christianity was devolving into two camps: on the one hand, the proto-evangelical hellfire preachers represented by Stoddard and most famously by his heir Jonathan Edwards, who emphasized an affective spirituality based on a personal subjective experience of sinfulness and redemption; on the other, the Harvard-centered "Brattle Street Liberals," who proposed an accommodation between Christian faith and the celebration of human reason that was then gaining ground in Europe. The latter, notably in the person of John Leverett, the future president of Harvard, emphasized a cooler, more intellectual religion that is the ancestor of Unitarianism, Episcopalianism, and "mainstream" Protestantism. Man was a rational creature created by a rational God, they said: It followed that such a God was moderate and reasonable. Christians should not fear so much for their salvation; they should— contradictory as this sounded—put their faith in reason.

The Brattle Street Liberals had an affinity with the "republic of letters" envisioned by the intellectuals and deists of the Enlightenment, with men like Jefferson who would found the American republic. But while reason is sweet—while it fosters moderation, dispassionate thinking, toleration, and an optimistic view of human potential—it makes for rather tepid religion. The appeal of preachers like Jonathan Edwards (who was no intellectual slacker) and his successors was, by contrast, to the heart rather than the mind. By the sheer power of rhetoric and charisma, such evangelists successively revealed the Christian's authentic inner self in all its abject, shameful misery—and then its only possible means of redemption, the mercy of Jesus Christ. But unlike the earlier New England assessments of "signs" of election and the like by elders and ministers, the knowledge of this redemption was almost entirely experiential and subjective: If you felt you were saved, you were, for most purposes, saved in fact. The personal, affective logic of the Great Awakening, sustained not by the authority and structure of the Puritan congregation but by revival meetings and itinerant preachers, led inexorably to something very much akin to the antinomianism that so terrified the first generation of New Englanders. Each individual was left to define, for better or worse, the inner truth of his soul.

Edwards himself balked in the end at the kind of "personalist," individualist religion the Great Awakening had spawned. Like most ministers, he worried that the unregenerate would falsely claim to be saved; but it was equally likely that the truly elect might falsely fear they were damned. The dilemma of predestination—of knowing one's redemptive fate—had not been removed, but was merely rendered wholly rather than partially subjective. The elders and ministers of the previous generation could offer some assurance, some informed judgment about one's spiritual health, but now, when salvation was afforded solely by a "personal savior," no one could authoritatively judge anything about anyone.

My own family illustrates the point. Thomas Griggs, the great-grandson of the emigrant Thomas Griggs, "owned the covenant" at Roxbury Church in 1744 together with his wife, Margaret, shortly after their marriage; and given Thomas's age—twenty-eight—this must have been, at least in part, a recognition of some kind of positive conversion experience. On the other hand, Captain Isaac Clark's uncle Barnabas Clark of Boston is mentioned in 1749 in the records of the New North Church as being one who "labored under such doubts and fears with respect to the Lord's Supper, that they were afraid immediately to approach unto it." Barnabas's scrupulosity is indicative of how spiritual self-doubt could flourish among Christians emancipated from pastoral authority. But the fact that scarcely a quarter of churchgoers bothered to receive communion at all tells us something more about the now private rather than corporate nature of religious observance. The Eucharist had been reduced to a symbol under Protestant theology and reserved for the elect few under the Puritans; now more and more New Englanders were, unlike Barnabas, simply indifferent to it as an institution, as they were increasingly indifferent to all traditional church institutions and authority. (Thomas Griggs's cousin Joseph, for example, was publicly censured by his pastor, the Reverend Abiel Stiles, in

1757, and appears not to have been bothered a whit by it.) Conversion, not communion, was the critical Christian experience, and took place only in the confines of the individual human heart.

What began in the churches was completed on the battlefield and in the statehouse: The creation of the world's first truly secular, liberal democracy, "liberal" here being understood in its traditional emphasis on individual liberty and free enterprise. Even though its founding was to set in motion yet a further erosion of their influence, the clergy blessed the new republic as the culmination of the task of the covenant begun in New England a century and a half earlier. The Rev. William Emerson, pastor in Concord, Massachusetts, great grandfather of Ralph Waldo Emerson, rallied his congregation and their militia in a series of sermons that promised "the Lord will cover your head in the Day of Battle and carry you from Victory to Victory," for the fight ahead was no mere political conflict but the final working out of proof to the world "that there is a God in New England."

Exactly what effect the Revolution had on my ancestors I cannot say, though there is evidence of more mobility and risk-taking in the recorded events of their lives. The Griggses moved into Connecticut, and Elisha Clark, one of the few sons of Scotto Clark to survive his father's obsession with whaling, moved to central Massachusetts to farm, tired, perhaps of the sea. His son Scotto married Rebecca Emerson, the Reverend William Emerson's niece. But in this new age of freedom and opportunity, even love was not without peril. In a watershed moment in the Griggses' family history, Mary Griggs, the daughter of George Griggs successively of New Roxbury, Woodstock, and Pomfret, Connecticut, eloped with a certain Captain William Wyman, expressly defying and shaming her stunned parents.

There were other novelties. Chester, the son of Captain Stephen Griggs of Woodstock, born the year before his father went to war in 1776, is mentioned in village records as having died "unmarried and insane." This is the first instance of the word "insane" I came across in my research, and I wonder whether it is itself a product of the new, secular republic; whether one hundred years earlier Chester might have been referred to as "possessed" or "under an Evil hand"; whether the communal universe in which tangible evil moved among the citizenry had been displaced by the private realm of one individual's mental health.

Of course, the word "insane" is joined to "unmarried" and that, too, may be germane. I suppose he never married because he was insane and no one would have him; but then, at the time I was seeing Dr. Freed, I might well have believed that he went insane because he was unmarried, because no one would love him. I felt deeply unloved and unlovable myself. I was a senior in high school that year, and had a date with a freedom-loving girl who, I was assured afterward, had been itching to "ball" me. My friends were perplexed as to why this hadn't been obvious to me and why I hadn't taken advantage of the opportunity; so, too, was Dr. Freed. None could fathom that *I* could not fathom the possibility that anyone could be interested in me in that way. When graduation drew close, Dr. Freed urged me to remain on Cape Cod to continue to work with him on these and other "issues"; he suggested I could do a "prebusiness" major at the local junior college. I suppose I should have paid attention to this counsel, as he had my best interests in mind. He wanted me to complete my "analysis"; he wanted me to build the foundation for a good career; he wanted to get me laid.

Instead, I went to California, to art school. I had no more gift for art than I did for love, but I needed beauty, the intimation of the profound, just as desperately. Happily, the school, on the border of Berkeley and Oakland, had an open admissions policy, in keeping with the spirit of the times. Just as important, I needed to get out of New England, which felt like a weight of stones crushing the breath from my body, the quintessence of what I would have then called plastic, fascist, life-denying Amerika.

The word "Puritan" occupies a lot of territory in the American imagination, usually in connection with a killjoy, repressive attitude toward sex. So too, more recently, does psychology and psychoanalysis; and also, more often than not, in connection to sex, albeit in a more tolerant if earnestly pathologizing pedantic mode. Neither characterization is fair or accurate, nor is the commonplace that psychoanalysis and its relations are the cure for Puritan repression. This is scarcely scientific, but the evidence I have adduced here suggests that my family enjoyed at least as much sex under the reign of Cotton Mather as it has under that of Freud.

For my purposes the similarities between modern "depth" psychology and Puritanism are more striking than the differences. In both, what dwells "intime," deeply, in the human soul is not the divine but the atavistic and unspeakable: depravities, secrets, and wounds. In my work with Dr. Freed, the world was divided as surely between the neurotic and emotionally healthy as Thomas Clark's world was split between the unregenerate and the elect. These distinctions between states of the soul or the psyche—which may or may not be the same thing, but overlap a great deal—are not in themselves invalid, although they admit only two possibilities out of the many in a complex universe. But both depend on a substrate of hidden knowledge—the mind of God or of the subconscious—that is difficult or impossible to apprehend with any accuracy, and in that respect it is no easier to know one's authentic self and the state of its health than it is to know whether one is saved.

Moreover, while both Puritanism and psychology insist on this necessarily nonobjective reality, neither is very comfortable with its ramifications for the believer or client: spiritual self-knowledge unapproved by the clergy or elders is the result of pride or antinomianism; self-knowledge unapproved by the therapist or analyst is "resistance" or delusion.

It is easy to press this comparison too far; and to say there is nothing useful or true in either Puritanism or psychology is to employ the same dualism I might well condemn in them. Let us merely say that, by virtue of their presuppositions about the dark underpinnings of the world, the mind, and what the latter can know about the former, it is too easy to find oneself in the position of the woman who threw her child in the well in order to put an end to the agony of her uncertainty. Sadly, and doubtless unintentionally, the Puritan economy of salvation can push one to and over the brink of hell; and the healing of psychology could drive a person to depression, our secular name for despair.

Perhaps what connects these respective regimes is not only Western philosophy but Western religion, or at least the residue of it. To quote the Bible in order to refute Puritanism (or Protestantism in general) is not the homeopathic remedy it may seem, but an invitation to spend eternity caught in an infinite and regressive loop of counterinterpretations. But I am going to do it anyway, in this one instance. There is an account in the Gospel of John in which Jesus encounters and subsequently restores the sight of a man blind from birth. Seeing this man—or rather, in a sense, not really seeing him at all—everyone around Jesus asks, "Who sinned, this man or his parents, that he was born blind?" The only explanation anyone can imagine is that this misfortune is the result of either predestination or willful misbehavior; or, in psychological rather than Puritan words, of a childhood trauma (the memory of which may be repressed) or of self-inflicted wounds—of "acting out" or "neurotic ideation."

Jesus' stunning, baffling reply is "Neither this man nor his parents sinned. He is blind in order that the works of God should be made manifest in him." Jesus is saying, I think, that this man, in his very blindness, is a sign, a sacrament of grace. In this transformation, Jesus has turned what others in their dualism could only see as judgment or punishment, as pathology or abnormality, into glory, into health. And then, bringing that grace to fruition, he restores the man's sight. The aftermath of this incident goes on for several more chapters, and is among the things that inexorably lead to Jesus' crucifixion. As much as the healing itself, Jesus' refutation of the prevailing legalistic orthodoxy affronts everyone.

I could at this point say that the Puritans, who knew the Bible much better than I ever will—who, we might say, worshipped the Bible—must have missed the point of this story. But I do not think the Puritans were inept at exegesis, or reached the understandings of Scripture that they did as a result of either folly or cussedness. I am always struck by the Puritans' bravery, both physical and intellectual; by their willingness to face the terrors of the sea in coming to New England and the no less daunting terrors of the implications of their understanding of God, which they followed unflinchingly to their logical conclusions.

Not just all faith, but all knowledge starts with a few unprovable axioms that must be accepted in order for belief or thought to proceed. In the case of Puritanism, these included the impossibility of knowing anything about God except through Scripture (and that only imperfectly) and a view of creation that saw man as so depraved that there was no reason his creator should redeem him save on a whim. That alienation of man from God found its darkest expression in the notion of double predestination, whose ultimate implication is that God knowingly creates some people for salvation and some for damnation; that God created hell and populates it with creatures he intends from the beginning of time to be damned. This grotesque, I might say satanic, God is a creator no one could or should believe in.

This is perhaps an extreme if, to my mind, perfectly consistent following through of the ramifications of Puritanism. Nor can the doctrine behind it be dismissed simply because it leads to such a dismal and unacceptable conclusion. The problem of harmonizing divine omniscience with human freedom will not go away, but this solution to it is a dead end. It led the Puritans not to a city on the hill but into a wilderness from which they could make no exodus.

To the extent that America retains traces of Puritanism—and I cannot but believe societies carry the cultural material of their ancestors just as individuals do the genetic material of theirs—it seems to me that this may have less to do with sex or pleasure than with a profound preoccupation with individual merit or fault. Believing each of our own fates to be individually earned or deserved, we live in dread of both community and the self, lest that self be proven unregenerate, lest its self-inflicted yet somehow predestined shame be disclosed to the world. In our manic adulation of "achievement" and "success," in our dread of failure, loss, and death, and in our fear of pollution by the sick, the sinful, and the unfortunate, we live in the terror, the wilderness, of our forefathers. We are the Puritans' children, their bewildered rising generation.

In reading and writing about these ancestors there were times I felt literally, physically oppressed by them and their world, by a nauseating, heavy lassitude from which I felt I could not rise. Before I began, I might have chalked this up to a somatic reaction to the burdensomeness of Puritan repression and its dark vision of human worth and redemption, to the suffocating heap of words, books, and laws in which its reality is encoded. A New Englander of my grandparents' generation, John Dewey, likened his similar feelings to a wound:

> The sense of divisions and separations that were, I suppose, borne in upon me as a consequence of New England culture, divisions by way of self from the world, of soul from body, of

nature from God, brought a painful oppression—or rather, they were an inward laceration.

I think Dewey was right, but I must wonder if what I feel is also a kind of cowardice, an incapacity to stomach the trials the Puritans subjected themselves to in offering up themselves and their children to the mercy of an arbitrary God as surely as my ancestors offered their sons to the sea. If the Puritans were right, they did no less than peer into the mouth of hell without blinking. That is not something my faith requires me to do, and I have to wonder if my faith is a defense, an avoidance of what I would rather not face. But the handmaiden of faith is not doubt, the relentless testing and analysis of faith, but hope, or so I have to believe. The Puritans were brave to confront doubt as they did—to assume nothing about God or his intentions toward them—and they faced doubt straight on. Just as the sea consumed Scotto Clark's sons, it swallowed them whole.

# PART III

# THE NEW AGE

# ONE

n 1816, an ancestor of mine, Susan Chaffey, stitched a piece of needlework of the sort customarily undertaken by girls of her age—seven years—and now I have it on the wall next to my son's bedroom door. It came from my grandfather Griggs's house by way of my grandmother, who was a descendant of Susan Chaffey, herself a descendant of Sir John Baker, the Tudor chancellor and inquisitor of heretics.

The needlework bears the title "A Curious Piece of Antiquity On the Crucifixion of Our Saviour and the Two Thieves" across the top, surrounded by a border of what seem to be pink and green flowers; or perhaps they are butterflies. It is indeed a "curious piece," for it is no ordinary, straightforward sampler—a showpiece designed to show what skills a young needleworker and potential wife and mistress of the house had mastered—but a triple acrostic. The words of Christ and the two thieves, laid out to form their respective crosses, provide the vertical elements: From right to left, "If thou art the Christ, save thyself and us;" "O God, my God, why hast Thou forsaken me;" and "Lord remember me when thou comest into thy kingdom," these last being the words of the "Good Thief," who was the subject of my Bible essay when I was twelve.

The horizontals with which these words intersect and interlace are formed of the following doggerel:

> Behold O God **in ri**vers of my tears
> I come to thee, bow down thy blessed ears

To hear my plaint and let thine eyes that keep
Continual watch behold a sinner weep.
Let not, **O God, My God,** my sins tho' great
And numberless bet**w**een thy mercy's seat
And my poor soul **h**ave place, since we are taught
Thou **Lord remembe**rest thyne **if thou art** sought
I co**m**e not Lord, wit**h** any ot**h**er merit
But **wh**at I by my saviour **Ch**rist inherit.
Be th**en** his wound**s** my balm, his st**ri**pes my bliss
His **th**orns my dea**th** be ble**st** in his
And th**ou** my bles**t** redeemer **sa**viour, God,
Quit my ac**co**unts, with**h**old thy **ve**ngeful rod.
O beg for **me** my h**o**pes on **t**hee are set;
And **Chr**ist forgive me, since t**h**ou'st paid my debt.
The liv**in**g font, the li**f**e, the wa**y I** know
And but **to** thee, **O** whither **s**hall I go?
All ot**h**er helps are vain, g**r**ant**e** thine to me
For in th**y** cross my **s**aving hea**l**th I see.
O hear**k**en then th**a**t I with **f**aith implore
Lest **s**in and death sink for me evermore.
Lastly O **G**od, my way**e**s direct **a**nd guide,
In **d**eath defe**n**d me that I **n**ever slide.
And at do**om**'s day let **m**e be rais**d** again
To liv**e** with the**e** sweet Je**sus** say amen.

It is not much as poetry or even as prayer, but as a piece of needlework it is an astonishingly complex task for a seven-year-old to undertake, and, to our eyes, a rather pointless one. It is more trouble to read than it is worth; for a scarcely literate child, it must have been a hellish ordeal to write, never mind to stitch, serif by serif and stroke by stroke. I can picture Susan by the fire, perhaps with her mother looking on, guiding her, badgering her, while she works, her little fingertips sore and ruddy. But that is all: The cultural and religious imperatives that impelled her to create this thing are beyond my imagination. I cannot fathom *why* she ought to be doing this.

That is not to say that Susan's "curious piece" does nothing for me, or doesn't speak to me; but what it says is a little outside my reach. The pieties seem conventional, and perhaps they are nothing more than customary banalities of early-nineteenth-century "affective" Christianity. But perhaps I am simply deaf to the conviction and the truth that underly them, my imagination being as stunted as my faith. At the least, I suspect that Susan at age seven knew more about Christ and the two thieves than I did at age twelve, and more than I do now.

The closest I can come to comprehending Susan's needlework is to see it as art; to view its apparent pointlessness (if that is the right word to use in connection with an object fashioned with a needle) as the surface of something designed to illuminate the profound; to lay, in its acrostic horizontals and verticals, an interpretive, imaginative grid over the Christian mystery; to impose symmetry on the ever-shifting ground of human faith. But this explanation is simply too much to ascribe to the work of a seven-year-old, even if my own modern and mature assessment of it is so obviously too little.

I am more at home with another written exercise that is part of my family history, composed just two years earlier by a man of about twenty-five named Aaron Bigelow. Aaron Bigelow's piece—a leaflet of fifteen pages he had privately printed in Boston in 1814, during the War of 1812—aspires to no art. Rather, its creator has a grievance, which is to say that he has a "self" as we today understand the term, and his creation is that self and its self-expression. In this, Aaron Bigelow is thoroughly modern and we—or at least I—can relate to him.

His grievance concerns Susan Griggs, a granddaughter of Thomas Griggs, whom we met in the previous chapter "owning the covenant" at Roxbury Church in 1744. Thomas's son Samuel married Beulah Hammond—a deeply pious woman, as we shall see—and they settled in Brookline, and had nine children. Susan, or "Sukey," as she was known in the family, was the fourth-born and the first daughter.

According to his book, Aaron Bigelow met Susan in July 1808, when she was eighteen years old. "Pleased with the girl," he asked permission to call on her; both she and her parents consented. By Thanksgiving, Aaron was sufficiently pleased to propose marriage. Susan responded that she felt she was still too young to make such a commitment, but conceded that in "a year or two she should have no objection" to marrying. Aaron, sensing some reluctance, pressed her: "I said to her, If you do not like me well enough to marry me, say so, and we will part friends, however unpleasant it might be to me to be deprived of the pleasure of visiting her."

Aaron found Susan's father congenial enough, but was a little wary of her mother, whose overbearing, overdevout influence seemed to be the chief source of Susan's reluctance. But through the winter he remained confident that their engagement would sooner or later come to pass, that something would bring matters to a head, as indeed something did:

> From this, time past altogether with us like time upon the wings of the wind, until the 15th of April 1809, at which time Susan came to Mr. Whiting's of Boston, where I boarded, and where she spent a few days with her cousin; I then waited on her to her fathers in Brookline at the same time. However, we went up as far as Wiswalls tavern in New-ton at her request, as well as for my own gratification; where we called and took a cup of coffee. While there, we conversed on the former subject of marrying, she observed that all matches were foreordained by God; she arose, went to the desk, took up a bible, opened and read as follows, 15th chapter of Paul the Apostle to the Romans, 5, 6, and 7, verses; "Now the God of patience and consolation, grant to be like minded one towards another, according to Christ Jesus; that ye may with one mind, and one mouth, glorify God, even the Father of our Lord Jesus Christ; wherefore, receive ye one another, as Christ also received us to the glory of God."
>
> She shew me the passage which she accidentally opened to, and replied, She was now convinced she was made for me. We then returned on the way to her fathers, talking upon the subject until we arrived at Davis' hill in Brookline; we stopped, I said to Susan, I do not wish to have any more difficulty or suspense in this business, as you have placed your trust in God who is the maker of all matches, you will now be able to decide the question on principles of religion; and as your mother places the result of all cases in the hands of

her maker, it may give her satisfaction to hear your determination in our case, predicated upon that principle.

Susan replied, What I just saw at Mr. Wiswalls is a strong evidence that I shall marry you, as if I had heard a voice from the clouds, or seen an angel from God sent by the almighty to join our hands in marriage.

That seemed to settle the matter as far as Aaron was concerned. By summer, his and Susan's relationship had grown deeper:

I continued to visit her until the 10th of July following when at her fathers house in the afternoon, there was an appearance of a sudden shower, I went out and assisted the old gentleman in getting in some hay, after which feeling somewhat fatigued, went upstairs and lay down upon the bed; soon after Susan came up and asked what was the matter. I told her nothing. She replied, My aunt Cory and a cousin are below stairs, they will not however stay long and I will return again. When they were gone Susan returned, fastened the chamber door, and came to the bed and asked me if I wished her to lay down with me. I replied yes, at which she threw herself on the bed, putting her arms around my neck and appeared anxious on account of my indisposition. She said she was happy to think it was in her power to contribute to my happiness, and called me her husband, and said I had never condescended to call her my wife. She was truly loving and agreeable, and gave me all the satisfaction that unmarried lovers ought to expect.

Susan and Aaron continued to enjoy such intimacies, apparently without the knowledge of her parents, although Aaron seemed to believe their silence constituted assent. He was mistaken. One evening the following May, Aaron and Susan

returned to her fathers late in the evening; the family were in bed. We set up about an hour, when I took her by the hand and gently led to the bed, where we affectionately enjoyed each others embraces until morning, when Susan appeared to be very sick at the stomach. I got up and brought her some cold water, at which time her mother entered the chamber. Susan! exclaimed she, I am surprised to see you here, why did you not go into your own chamber? You have no business here. Susan replied, We have not injured each other. If you have done no hurt, said the old lady, You had no business to be here with Bigelow. I am astonished at your conduct.

Aaron made an exit downstairs, pursued by Mrs. Griggs, who harried and berated him, saying that, modest as their means were, she should sooner part with twenty dollars than have her husband learn what she had discovered. Aaron retorted that he considered Susan "no otherwise than my wife" and was prepared to marry her then and there.

It is unclear what if any response Mrs. Griggs made to this assurance, but whether because some understanding had been reached or out of sheer recklessness, a week later Aaron again spent the night with Susan at her father's house, where she gave him "all the satisfaction I could enjoy from my intended wife."

Two weeks later Aaron went to visit "my sweet Susan and found her very ill":

> I asked her what was the matter. She said she had been ill ever since I had been there before. I asked again what ailed her. She replied she believed I had brought her into trouble, and asked me if I thought we had done right to do as we had done before marriage.

Aaron kissed her, and swore that he was prepared to marry her "at any moment." This calmed Susan, but over the following days Aaron became convinced that "her mother at this time had become so inveterate as to conduct herself very inimical towards me, and from her conduct I thought it was her determination to prevent my marrying Susan."

On the fourth of July, 1810, Aaron spent the night again with Susan "little thinking it was to be the last time." But, once Susan's mother had apparently assured herself that Susan was not in fact pregnant, "the old lady's hypocritical plans which had long been smothered, was now about to burst forth with double fury on the head of one who was more anxious for the happiness of her daughter than it was possible for her to be herself." Although, according to Aaron, Mrs. Griggs had previously exhorted him to attend church more regularly and quoted him the Bible verse that "it is easier for a camel to pass through the eye of a needle than for a rich man to enter the kingdom of heaven," she had been investigating his financial situation. And although Aaron does not describe it, it seems that Mrs. Griggs discovered that he had recently undergone some kind of setback in his business:

> About the 20th July, I went to visit my intended wife, but to my astonishment and grief, was received with coldness. I asked Susan if she had heard of my late misfortune. She replied, Yes, that I must take my leave of her, as her mother was determined I should never marry her. I asked her what she would do in that case under certain delicate circumstances. Susan replied, I must do as well as I can. My mother says if I marry you I shall have more troubles instead of less. . . . At which time Mrs. Griggs came into the room saying, Well, Mr. Bigelow, your property is all gone. I have been praying that something may happen to you to break up your courtship with Susan. There is now a door open, and I am heartily glad of an opportunity to put a stop to your marriage.

Aaron replied, "If this is the fruit of your religion, I have been deceived of your character. If you can rejoice at my misfortune, which has a natural tendency to destroy not only my peace but that of your daughter, you must be a very unnatural mother."

> Then Susan entered and said with tears in her eyes, I am sincerely sorry for your loss, my affections for you are the same, but what shall I do? My mother utterly forbids my marrying you, and we must part, and I hope that God will be our companion, and that we may finally be happy.

Aaron Bigelow's little book circulated in sufficient numbers to end up in not a few libraries, if only as a "curious piece of antiquity." It would be nice to say that its intended purpose was to somehow win Susan back, and that it succeeded in accomplishing this. But Aaron married another woman in 1820, and of Susan there is no trace in the records of Massachusetts: no sign of her marrying, bearing children, or dying; no sign of her having ever thereafter existed at all.

In any case, the explicit purposes of Aaron's book were twofold. First, to warn off any other suitors:

> I now feel it is a duty to myself and my God to caution any gentleman against paying any attention to the said Susan under the pretence of marrying her in my absence, on the peril of being posted as a paltroon, or to meet me like a man with such weapons as he may choose, should I live to return from the United States service, in which I am now engaged.

Yet this is stated almost as an afterthought, and reading the book makes it clear that Aaron's second purpose is what most preoccupies him: "to make a statement of . . . the reprehensible conduct of Mrs. Griggs, the mother of Susan, who professes to be a follower of Jesus." This is not a theme that Aaron, who makes no claims of piety for himself, is prepared to let rest for long, and he takes particular pleasure in quoting Scripture against Mrs. Griggs: "For if 'by their fruits ye shall know them,' will not the world judge her a nominal and not a real professor of christianity?" The exposure of her hypocrisy is no less than a crusade for Aaron:

> The reader must now judge after the facts here stated for the truth to which I am accountable to my God; whether the veil which Mrs. Griggs attempts to throw over her true character by her professions of Christianity is sufficient to screen her even from the scrutinizing eye of the world, much less from Him who searches the hearts.

In Aaron Bigelow's book we are much closer to our world than to the New England of even one hundred years earlier, where disputes of this kind would have been dealt with in the meetinghouse by the church elders on behalf of the community. Now the dispute is viewed as a wholly private matter—of legitimate concern only to the individuals directly involved, and presumably to be settled according to their lights—which is nevertheless to be aired in public through what we today call the media. To my mind, the content is as modern as the form of its dispersal: the legalistic assertion of injury and grievance and the claim to individual rights—in this case, to Susan's hand in marriage—on the one hand; on the other, a new notion of what constitutes virtue, in which the crucial measure of a Christian soul is not inward conversion but outward conduct.

We are a long way from the Puritans. Consider, for example, the case of Joseph Moody in the 1730s, only eighty years before Aaron first courted Susan Griggs. Joseph Moody was the uncle of Rebecca Emerson, whom Scotto Clark would marry (they would name their firstborn child Mary Moody). Joseph was the son of an eminent minister; aided by an exceedingly melancholic temperament, he took Puritan notions of the abjectness of the human soul to heart as few ever would. In his diary—written in Latin and then ciphered into a private code—he excoriated himself for his inability to feel a true conversion, for his lustful thoughts about women, and his frequent episodes of "self-defiling." A typical entry runs: "Sat. 2 Wind fresh S. . . . Extreme insensibility took complete possession of me. . . . Nevertheless divine Jesus wilt thou not, through thy spirit, come to the aid of my worst of souls?"

Joseph was, like Aaron, unlucky in love. Already betrothed by his parents to a woman named Lucy, he fell hopelessly in love with a cousin, herself engaged to another. Stifling his feelings, he married Lucy and eventually came to love her, only to see her die in childbirth. Now the father of a brood of children and himself pastor to a church, he stunned his congregation by appearing before them with his face covered by a veil which he thereafter refused to remove, speaking either through the veil or with his back turned. He explained this was the only appropriate mien for one who was, at bottom, "nothing but a *shadow*."

A legendary figure in New England, Joseph Moody was perhaps the ultimate expression of Puritan self-abnegation, of the wish to erase, even annihilate the self. Aaron Bigelow, for all the regret his story may provoke, was impelled in exactly the opposite direction; and the only self annihilated in his orbit was doubtless that of Susan Griggs, who found herself the object of talk if not of pity, and thus unmarriageable, unalterably stained in a new age that was losing its ability to believe in redemption but not, needless to say, in sin.

# TWO

U seful as the Bible proved to be in exposing the likes of Mrs. Griggs, it seems to have been less able to provide the answers sought by young people like Aaron Bigelow in the early nineteenth century. Perhaps, in truth, the questions had changed; rather than concerning the soul and its fate, they took up the heart and its wishes and feelings, its self-expression in love and conduct. To interpret its mysteries required not preachers and theologians but poets and novelists. It was Stendahl who said, ten years after Aaron and Susan's courtship, that "in love everything is a *sign*," as though speaking of the explication of Scripture or the sacramental universe of the Middle Ages.

Nor were faith's prospects much aided by reason, although the great theological project of the eighteenth century in general and of the Brattle Street Liberals in particular was the provision of exactly such an undergirding. The result in New England was the triumph by 1820 of what was to be known as Unitarianism, the tolerant and reasonable faith propagated by Harvard's best minds against the pessimism of Calvinism and the irrationality of affective religion. Yet in Cambridge itself in 1820, an eighteen-year-old girl named Lydia Maria Francis could write (even as her brother was finishing his degree at Harvard Divinity School), "I wish I could find some religion in which my heart and understanding could unite."

Thirty years later, as the adult Lydia Maria Child, Lydia Francis would achieve fame as a writer and abolitionist. In 1820, however, she had a neighbor and protégée even more precocious than she. The neighbor girl wrote this letter that same year:

My Dear Father,

Yesterday I wrote you a short epistle in Latin, now I sit down to address you in my native language. I am half way through the fifth book of Virgil. In my last lesson I got the whole of the fourth book and Uncle Elisha said I got it extremely well. Who would believe that it was February? The winter has passed very quickly to me. Shall you be here the first of April alias April fool day? I remember when I was only 6 years old that morning you told me to look out of the window and see that little bird perched on a tree. I looked and was very much surprised to see none. . . .

I have spent five days in Boston and returned the day before yesterday. My aunt carried me to Dr. Clarkes. He has lately failed in trade and boards out. After much research we at length arrived at Mrs. Mansfields. A ragged, dirty little boy came to the door. Does Dr. Clarke board here? The boy scratched his head. Do'nt know ma'am. In he went and presently returned with a Wo'nt you walk in. Well we went in and were ushered into the greasy kitchen from that were introduced to a narrow wet passage into a back door to a neat parlor. The Doctor is a healthy man about 3 and 40. Mrs. Clarke is a pretty, interesting woman apparently on the verge of thirty. She has five children, 4 sons and one daughter.

I saw a head of her daughters painting which looked very natural. Five or six pencils and brushes lay upon a window sill—and a portrait was upon a wooden frame. I saw also a beautiful landscape. This young lady's name is Sarah. She has a singular taste for painting—

[My brother] William Henry is sitting on the rug singing "Phosannur in de sidest." The little rogue alias student of roguery does this in imitation of us. These words are in the Chorus Anthem Hosanna in the highest.

Miss Kimball informs me that Miss Mary Elliot went through Virgil in thirty days and I have studied with renewed vigor ever since [because she] shall surpass me if possible. I

shall finish this letter with the Lords prayer in Latin. Farewell
I am your affectionate daughter

Sarah M. Fuller

Noster pater qui estis in coelo sis sacrum tuum nomen, tua
voluntas esto factus in terra ut in coelo, da nos eum diem nos-
trum quotidianum cererum et da veniam nobis nostra peccata
ut da veniam eis qui peccant nobis duco nos non tempta-
tionem et trade a peccato tuum imperium, potestas et gloria
semper. Amen

PS Correct it for me papa will you? I had almost forgot,
Thank you for your pen.

Sarah M. Fuller—who in a previous letter told her father, "I do
not like Sarah, call me Margaret alone, pray do!"—was ten years old.
Her father, Timothy, who, together with history, would defer to her
wish to be called simply Margaret, was a Harvard-educated Unitarian and Cambridge's U.S. representative for four terms. From Margaret's infancy, he had personally supervised her education. She was
reading history and biography by the time she was six and had mastered French and Greek grammar before she was ten; the girl who
she worried might overtake her in Virgil was five years older than
she. The ragged if genteel family of Clarkes Margaret reported visiting were descendants of Thomas and Andrew Clark. The young
artist was Sarah Jane Clarke, two years older than Margaret and a girl
whom Margaret decided she did not much like; of Sarah's brother
James Freeman Clarke we shall hear more.

Margaret's precocity was outstanding, but, in 1820s Cambridge,
also a matter of degree. Latin and Greek were the foundation of all
true education, and boys normally entered Harvard at age fifteen.
Neither Margaret nor any other woman could attend Harvard; that
her erudition should equal and generally exceed any Harvard grad-
uate of her generation was therefore remarkable in itself. But the
form of her mind was as unique as its content, embodying her father's Unitarian ideals to an almost extreme extent. Unitarian theology was a response to both the pessimism of Calvinism and the high
emotion of evangelical, affective religion. To counter them it put its
faith in an optimistic view of human potential and in rationality. In-

deed, it found God nowhere so evident as in reason, as in the mind. Unitarianism's most eminent preacher, William Ellery Channing, saw the mind of God mirrored in the mind of man: "The creation is a birth and shining forth of the Divine Mind, a work through which his spirit breathes. In proportion as we receive this spirit, we possess within ourselves the explanation of what we see." Mary Moody Emerson, Scotto and Rebecca Clark's cousin Ralph Waldo Emerson's aunt, opined that Channing had gone "clean out of his reckoning," but that was a minority view, at least in Cambridge. Putting aside the perfection of the soul for what might be called the perfection of the mind, Harvard Unitarianism saw scholarship and education—particularly literary education—as a kind of Eucharist, a communing with and partaking of the divine. Timothy Fuller, despite his son William's chanting of the "Sanctus" on the parlor rug, had no use for most varieties of liturgical or spiritual practice, but the acquisition of knowledge and the improvement of her mind were the rigorous monasticism to which he consecrated his daughter from birth.

Immersed so early in the classical world of Latin and Greek, Margaret was by adolescence more Stoic than Christian. She later explained that for her the Bible could not compete with pagan stories; it simply wasn't literature. By the time she was a teenager, Margaret, or at least her mind, was perfect in her father's estimation. "She has no faults," he is recorded as saying, and he bought her Maria Edgeworth's popular child-rearing manual so she could help inculcate the same excellence in her young brothers and sister.

At the end of her father's program of training, Margaret had a unique ability to engage men as intellectual equals, and she was a passionate, funny, and opinionated raconteur. Perhaps for that same reason, she did not have much luck in attracting men as romantic partners; and she was afflicted with a kind of mother-hunger, a desire for a consuming union with a woman more beautiful and big-hearted than she. Although she was consistently generous and kind, she felt, and often seemed to the outside world, at a perpetual remove from others, lost or trapped in the capaciousness of her own mind. Lydia Maria Child would later say, "Margaret's egotism is the consequence of her father's early injudicious culture—never *allowed* to forget *herself*."

# THREE

D r. Samuel Clarke had indeed "lately failed in trade," as Margaret had written her father, and not for the first or last time. A man of many parts and many occupations—doctor, pharmacist, sheep farmer, inventor, schoolteacher—he was fortunate in having a detached and insouciant demeanor. After the setback that had landed the family at the boardinghouse Margaret visited, he invested the last of his fortune in a chemical factory in Newton that subsequently burned to the ground. At the scene, he remarked to his son, James Freeman Clarke, "We may call this, I suppose, the abomination of desolation." He died shortly thereafter.

Widowed and financially ruined, Mrs. Clarke took in boarders and farmed out James to his grandparents, the Reverend and Mrs. James Freeman. James's grandmother was descended from John Eliot, the Griggses' pastor in Roxbury; his grandfather was an eminent Unitarian divine who proceeded to give James a home education not unlike that being received by Margaret Fuller. "Before I was ten years old," James later wrote, "I had read a good deal of Ovid, some odes of Horace, a little of Virgil, the Gospel of Matthew, and had gone as far as cubic equations in algebra. I had also read through the 'History of the United States,' Hume's 'England,' Robertson's 'Scotland,' Ferguson's and Gibbon's 'Rome.'"

If the substance of James's education was similar to Margaret's, the style was not. A genial and patient instructor, James's grandfather made study "almost as entertaining as play." The intellectual ethos of James's childhood was scholarly and by no means without rigor, but also easygoing, even eccentric. James's great-uncle Dr. Jonathan Homer was the famously absentminded pastor of Newton church and was known to walk the streets in his gingham dressing gown. According to James,

> If he met you on the road he would begin to say aloud what he was meditating. For example, he might begin, without preface, thus: "Why Beza should have given that rendering of Corinthians I cannot say. Possibly he may have found it in Erasmus, though I have not been able to trace it in either of the early editions. Sir Isaac Coffin has promised to send me the first Geneva; but Tyndall would be better." Having made these cursory remarks he would pass on.

Perhaps of necessity, therefore, James's family was also exceedingly tolerant, not merely of eccentricity and nonconformity but in more substantive ways. They were abolitionists at a time when this was by no means a widespread position in "liberal" Boston. James's mother helped establish a home for black pensioners and on her deathbed said to her daughter, "Sarah, I wish carriages to be sent to take the old colored women to my funeral. I think it will be a great amusement to them. They do not have many amusements."

James, exactly the same age as Margaret Fuller, grew up a happy and a precocious child if also a somewhat dreamy and isolated one. The Freeman house was on a hill, and James sometimes imagined it was an island: "We could see the distant line of ocean on one side, and the pale blue horizon of far-off hills on the other, [and] I supposed, in my simplicity, that this circle of blue was the all-surrounding ocean, and that all the solid land was contained in what met my eyes." The house was full of books, and it was said that many of these had come from the family's ancestral home on Cape Cod where they had washed up in a shipwreck. So it was that James might picture himself at sea or a castaway, reading a volume of Shakespeare that had washed up at his feet like a message in a bottle.

James was sent to Boston Latin School at age ten, and thence to Harvard in 1825, when he was fifteen. He was part of the distinguished class of '29, among whose members were Oliver Wendell

Holmes, William Henry Channing, and James's cousin William Greenleaf Eliot, who would found Washington University (as well as be grandfather to the poet T. S. Eliot). James had another cousin in the class, the future congressman George Davis, and it was on this account that he was reacquainted with Margaret Fuller. By James's senior year, when they were both nineteen, Margaret was already known as the sharpest and most unconventional young mind in Cambridge, and that alone might have drawn them together. But the fact was, Margaret was in love with George Davis, and James had fallen in love with Margaret's friend Elizabeth Randall while on the rebound from the loss of an earlier girlfriend, Louisa Hickman. It was natural that they should compare notes and share whatever intelligence each had of the other's love interest. Moreover, since James's maternal grandmother was born Sarah Fuller, it appears they were related. In April 1830, James sent Margaret a copy of one of Sheridan's plays together with a letter asking her to investigate this connection, and the next day received the following reply from the normally late-rising Fuller:

Half-past six, morning—I have encountered that most common-place of glories, sunrise, (to say naught of being praised and wondered at by every member of the family in succession) that I might have leisure to answer your note even as you requested. I thank you a thousand times for "The Rivals." Alas!! I must leave my heart in the book, and spend the livelong morning in reading to a sick lady from some amusing story-book. I tell you of this act of (in my professedly unamiable self) most unwonted charity for three several reasons. Firstly, and foremostly, because I think that you, being a socialist by vocation, a sentimentalist by nature, and a Channingite from force of circumstances and fashion, will peculiarly admire this little self-sacrifice exploit. Secondly, because 'tis neither comfortable to the spirit of the nineteenth century, nor the march of mind, that those churlish reserves should be kept up between the right and left hands, which belonged to ages of barbarism and prejudice, and could only have been inculcated for their use. Thirdly, and lastly, the true lady-like reason—because I would fain have my correspondent enter into and sympathize with my feelings of the moment.

As to the relationship; 'tis, I find, on inquiry, by no means to be compared with that between my self and ⸺ ⸺, of course, the intimacy cannot be so great. But no matter; it will enable me to answer your notes, and you will interest my imagination much more than if I knew you better. But I am exceeding legitimate note-writing limits. With the hope that this epistle may be legible to your undiscerning eyes, I conclude.

Your cousin only thirty-seven degrees removed,

M.

The missing name was, of course, George Davis, but the dashes are the only expression of reticence in the letter, an otherwise typically brassy performance by Margaret's endearingly haughty and cajoling intellect, the drum majorette of "the march of mind." As for heart, it was not easily separable from "reason" (as opposed to the sense-bound "understanding") in the Anglo-German Romantic worldview that was becoming the rage among young Cambridge. James's heart was sufficiently touched by Margaret's flirty invitation to "enter into and sympathize with my feelings of the moment." He immediately proposed that they rendezvous the next day at a wedding in which Elizabeth Randall was to be a bridesmaid, for while to see "the fair Elschen" among the bridal party would be "a feast for the eyes," "mind and heart desire the nourishment" that only chatting with Margaret could afford.

In the usual manner of bright young minds, James and Margaret tossed around catchphrases and concepts from books they had not read. In his very next note James, for example, alluded to "the accelerated activity of the human intellect." But they had a better excuse than most for adopting this pretense: The essential authors in question—Goethe, Schiller, Schelling, Novalis, and the rest—were often not available in translation or were available only through English popularizers such as Coleridge and Carlyle. Margaret and James wanted to read these things desperately and they would, together.

The attraction of Romanticism is easy to understand, accommodating as it did both their loftiest intellectual aspirations and their scarcely postadolescent erotic fretting and mooning. Poetry by itself was heady stuff—Margaret claimed "my whole being is Byronized"— and too much could carry off one's "oversoul" entirely. In one of the autopsies of his breakup with the divine but difficult Louisa Hickman he wrote to Margaret, James allowed that "Louisa was a girl of strong feelings, which she indulged and fed by constantly reading poetry when young." But Romanticism went deeper than literature; it was more than an artistic movement or even a philosophy. For those trapped in what Ralph Waldo Emerson was just then calling "the corpse-cold Unitarianism of Brattle Street and Harvard College," it had the force of a new faith, or at least a counterreligion whose American variant would be called Transcendentalism.

But as in Romanticism, there is perhaps a tendency among the young for the self to have no boundaries, and accordingly for the intellectual, the psychological, the spiritual, and the erotic to be all mixed up together, to merge into one striving, one question. Any religion worthy of the name ought to offer a response to such a quest, ought to be able to contain and comprehend the amorphous unity of all the things that the self felt so deeply and intensely. But Unitarianism, in its devotion to rationality, in its compulsion to keep the hounds of subjectivity and pessimism at bay, had lost its capacity to speak about such matters. Even so eloquent a Unitarian as Emerson— seven years Margaret and James's senior and the junior pastor at Boston's Second Church, the onetime church of the Mathers—turned to poetry, even if it was only to suggest that the self's yearnings were ultimately self-consuming; that they led in the end back to the self:

> Then take this fact unto thy soul—
> God dwells in thee—
> It is no metaphor nor parable
> It is unknown to thousands and to thee
> Yet there is God.

Poetry could accommodate that mystery—itself no more than Channing's theology taken to its logical conclusion—in a way that religion no longer could. But for all its capacity to evoke inchoate feeling, poetry was dumb when it came to the practical force of spirituality: What did faith actually accomplish in this world or the next, morally or redemptively? God was a vague presence, a comfort to those in need and inclined to lean on Him, but not of much utility to a young person like Margaret:

> Loving or feeble natures need a positive religion, a visible refuge, a protection, as much in the passionate season of youth as in those stages nearer to the grave. But mine is not such. My pride is superior to any feelings I have yet experienced: my affection is strong admiration, not the necessity of giving or receiving assistance or sympathy. When disappointed, I do not ask or wish consolation—I wish to know and feel my pain, to investigate its nature and its source; I will not have my thoughts diverted, or my feelings soothed; t'is therefore that my young life is so singularly barren of illusions. I know, I feel the time must come when this proud and impatient heart shall be stilled, and turn from the ardors of Search and Action, to lean on something above. But—shall I say it?—the thought of that calmer era is to me a thought of deepest sadness; so remote from my present being is that future being, which still the mind may conceive. I believe in a God, a Beauty and Perfection to which I am to strive all my life for assimilation. From these two articles of belief, I draw the rules by which I strive to regulate my life. But, though I reverence all religions as necessary to the happiness of man, I am yet ignorant of the religion of Revelation. Tangible promises! well defined hopes! are things of which I do not *now* feel the need.

Margaret wrote this in a letter to George Davis at the beginning of the end of their romance. George was as intellectually daring and conversationally brilliant as Margaret, and notably irreligious. With perhaps a measure of desperation, she was trying to assure him that in this, too, they were soul mates; that she was at worst holding on to a latent deism as an old-age insurance policy. This, however, was not to save the relationship, and she and James Clarke continued to commiserate over the respective loves who refused to love them back. George Davis had not yet tipped his hand, but Elizabeth Randall had at last made her feelings—or the lack thereof—known to James. He was devastated and begged Margaret in letter after letter to *explain* it to him—this one and Louisa, the one before, and all his failings in love. Wearily, Margaret tried:

> I will endeavor to satisfy you—Elizabeth's conduct was not "systematick" that is to say, she did *not* reason with herself and lay down a *plan* for her conduct with regard to you. Her conduct was in each instance the spontaneous expression of impulses which were however invariable in their action. After seeing you a process of this kind would always ensue—"I am sorry I am not happier in James's society; how he has left me dissatisfied and pained. I admire some things in him [but] I do not nor never shall love him; but why should I pain him?" After this half compunctious fit there was an invariable revulsion of argument of this sort—"James does not really love *me;* if he *did,* if he loved me understandingly, he would read the language of my actions at once! He could not be interested and engaged when I am wearied and sad; his pain would be too great; no! 'tis a phantom that he loves! Why should I by grateful patience continue the illusion? Let him see me petulant and weary as I feel, and this film must be brushed from his eyes." —These pros and cons would pass after every interview when her mind was not engrossed by some powerful interest.

Astute and sagacious as this analysis was, James, perhaps understandably, could not take it to heart, any more than Margaret herself could when her own rejection came. Unlike Margaret, James found that faith came easily—perhaps thanks both to his disposition and his upbringing—but not self-confidence. Writing to her of a character in William Godwin's novel *Mandeville,* he reflected, "Brought up from his infancy in the solitude of his uncle's house and without any companions his own age, to whom he could freely talk, and on whom he could first try and exercise his active powers, he never was a boy—neither was I, for I was similarly brought up till I was ten years old. The effect of this must always be the same—to substitute self communion for action—and is always in my opinion bad."

Heartbroken and diffident, James imagined himself unique, but he had in fact put his finger on the principal psychological malady of his generation, as Emerson understood it: "The young men were born with knives in their brain, a tendency to introversion, self-dissection, anatomizing of motives." Margaret had previously attempted to shore up James's ego in a letter regarding her estimation of his "character and situation," of the person, the embodiment of Romantic ideals that she believed he was capable of becoming:

> I have greatly wished to see among us such a person of genius as the nineteenth century can afford—i.e., one who has tasted in the morning of existence the extremes of good and ill, both imaginative and real. I had imagined a person endowed by nature with that acute sense of Beauty (i.e., Harmony or Truth) and that vast capacity of desire, which give soul to love and ambition. I had wished this person might grow up to manhood alone (but not alone in crowds); I would have placed him [in] a situation so retired, so obscure, that he would quietly, but without bitter sense of isolation, stand apart from all surrounding him. . . . I wished he might adore, not fever for, the bright phantoms of his mind's creation, and believe them to be but the shadows of external things to be met hereafter. After this steady intellectual growth had brought his powers to manhood . . . I wished this being might be launched into the world of realities, his heart glowing with the ardor of an immortal towards perfection, his eyes searching everywhere to behold it; I wished he might collect into one burning point those withering, palsying convictions, which, in the ordinary routine of things, so gradually pervade the soul; that he might suffer, in a brief space, agonies of disappointment commensurate with his unpreparedness and confidence. And I thought, thus thrown back on the representing pictorial resources I supposed him originally to possess, with such material, and the need he must feel of using it, such a man would suddenly dilate into a form of Pride, Power, and Glory—a centre round which asking, aimless hearts might rally—a man fitted to act as interpreter to the one tale of many-languaged eyes!

James's response is lost, but we may guess that he felt, as he had said before to Margaret, "you overrated me." In his eyes, it was Margaret who, despite her sex, might venture to attain this role. And in any case, the Elizabeth affair was already coming to a head, and even as its pain dissipated, James lashed himself with the memory of Louisa Hickman and what he believed was her ill-considered marriage:

> George [Davis] brought me last night a letter from Louisa. It was good, quite so, but everything I see of her makes me melancholy. It is not the thing—it is not what her character promised. She has committed herself, irrevocably, to the unhappiness of a mistaken course. She is an example of one whose love of freedom and spirit of independence was the cause of her heart and mind entering into the worst slavery. She hung the manacles around herself, and believed herself therefore free. Alas, she soon found there was no backward step on the path she had entered, and now all her joys are those of remembrance; at the age of thirteen she would have scorned the thought. She knows nothing of me; she only recollects me with pleasure because I was her companion at a time when her spirit was triumphant, when she influenced and governed every body within her reach just as she chose, and nobody knew, or pretended to understand *her,* for she did not *choose* that they should—and now she fears to speak of that time, and bounds her recollections by last summer and [the confines of her] garden.

James concluded, "But to return to myself (to which subject I ever return with renewed interest), I think too, Margaret dear, that I must give up Love." And so he did, joined shortly by Margaret herself (who would write, two years after the breakup, "George is to me a walking *memento mori*—haunting my daydreams"). Together they determined to learn German and read the masters in the original. They would change the world. They would see God.

# FOUR

God, after his fashion, proved elusive, and as intransigent as love. James had faith glowing in him like a little flame that might gutter but that was never wholly extinguished. But Margaret's tougher mind wanted more than intuition or sentiment, nor was she inclined to deify nature as Emerson and his principal acolyte, Thoreau, would do. "The 'beauties of nature' never could console me," she wrote James during his convalescence from Elizabeth Randall. "I do hope that at this moment you are either calmly asleep or reading some good book or listening to some kind and interesting friend; not looking into the beautiful vague of the sky for an answer."

In this, Margaret was at one with Mary Moody Emerson who, wary of the Channingite excesses her nephew Ralph Waldo would take to even higher planes, preferred "to cast [nature] off and rely on that only which is imperishable." Of course, Aunt Mary's notion of the absolute was for her, because of the truth of revelation, more real, more concrete than nature; Margaret's was perfectly abstract, pure mind, a slippery thing indeed for intellects slighter than hers. Margaret and James's guide to Kant, Goethe, Schiller, and the rest was Thomas Carlyle, who was of a similar bent: "The Universe is but one vast symbol of God; nay if thou wilt have it, what is man himself but a Symbol of God; is not all that he does symbolical; a revelation to sense of the mystic God-given force that is in him?"

This was a reality long on symbols and mightily short on referents for them, so much so that it is easy to imagine that God Him-

self might be no more than the symbol-in-chief of a creation entirely devoid of substance, one of pure ideas and signs. But that did
not, at least initially, worry Margaret and James and their ilk, for
Carlyle and the Germans were nothing less than "a new heaven and
a new earth, a new religion and a new life," as James recalled. He
watched Margaret master German in not much more than three
months; he, as usual, was slower.

During this time, at which James was also making his way
through Harvard Divinity School, he and Margaret exchanged
billets-doux and set up breathless rendezvous as though in the throes
of a fiery passion, save that lovemaking was not the goal they had in
mind: "Dear James, Where are you, and what doing? and *why* don't
you come here? . . . I wish to talk with you now about the *Germans*."
For his part, James took walks around the ponds north of Cambridge and fancied himself Goethe's Wilhelm Meister at Lake
Geneva or the Bay of Naples. When he and Margaret talked about
these things he found that "our converse was more intimate (*inniger*)
than ever before. I felt as if our minds were embracing, and found no
discord in their centre."

It was Goethe who had said "feeling is all," and the erotic charge
in their correspondence seems unmistakable. Were James and Margaret in love, or, at a minimum, was the rebounding James infatuated
with Margaret? Even before this time, James's Grandpa Freeman,
seeing them together, thought so. James's mother recalled:

Father Freeman sat looking at them and when they were off,
he said, "Poor James!" "What's the matter, Father Freeman?"
said I. "Poor James!" said he, "he'll go and marry that woman
and be miserable all the days of his life. Don't you see what a
cross mouth she's got? She won't make him happy!"

But perhaps it was not so much Margaret's heart James was after as
her soul. The closing of one letter changes moods abruptly to reveal
concern, and an incipient mission for the pastor-in-training James:

Margaret! Late hour will be my ruin; it is nearly one A.M.
Good night. Tender dreams flit round thy couch, my dearest
and noblest friend. May thy heart find shapes to meet and re-

turn thy caresses, and mayst thou find in the society of thy night excursions the perfect sympathy which daylight brooks not. Be still my friend. Bear with my vanity, and many weaknesses, and childlike follies. Help me not to betray my beautiful soul. . . . Here is a quotation for you. Bon soir.

"Nobody is so lonely in the world as an atheist. He mourns with an orphaned heart, which has lost its great father, by the immense corpse of Nature, which no spirit of the universe moves and holds together, and which grows in the grave and mourns, until it crumbles from the corpse. The whole world reposes before him as the great Egyptian Sphynx of stone half buried in the sand, and the universe is the cold iron mask of shapeless eternity."

Margaret responded indirectly, by way of a commentary on a sermon James had sent her. She recast the matter he had raised in terms of the German Romantic agenda, first as a philosophical problem but ultimately as a question about the true, authentic self:

Do you really believe there is anything "all comprehending" but religion?—Are not these distinctions imaginary? Must not the philosophy of every mind or set of minds be a system suited to guide them and give a home where they can bring materials among which to accept, reject, and shape at pleasure? Novalis calls those who harbour these ideas "unbelievers"—but hard names make no difference— He says with disdain "to such, philosophy is only a system that will spare them the trouble of reflecting"—Now this is just my case—I *do* want a system which shall suffice to my character and in whose applications I shall have faith—I do not wish to *reflect* always, if reflecting must be always about one's identity, whether *"ich"* am the true ich etc.—I wish to arrive at that point where I can trust myself and leave off saying "it seems to me" and boldly feel it *is* so *to me,* my character has got its natural regulator, my heart beats, my lips speak truth.

The truth was, Margaret neither wanted nor felt she needed a redeemer or even a guide, a philosophical compass. Rather, she envisioned her own self refined to its purest essence, running off its own transcendent energy. Anything less than that seemed a great privation. And while James strongly felt that "a full religious feeling alone can help her," he also sensed that a great part of her yearning and frustration was caused by the limits imposed on her by her sex. In his journal he ruminated on her astonishing gifts, but sadly admitted: "Yet what is the effect of these powers. She is not happy—it all ends in nothing—it produces no commensurate effect—she has no sphere of action. Why was she a woman?" James could not but conclude that, constrained by the world, Margaret ought to turn to the spirit, if not to God then to another soul: "She has nothing to do—no place in the world and fears she never shall have. At least as she cannot do any thing, she might have some one to reverence."

It seems to have been beyond Margaret's capacity to imagine an ultimate being that was not, in the Romantic spirit, coterminous with her own mind; a divinity to which she might submit and by which she might be comforted. God, after all, was not love but mind. Margaret had not been much blessed with earthly love either, but it—or rather the loss of it—produced her first and perhaps only experience of the numinous. It came on Thanksgiving Day, 1831. Since her breakup with George Davis that summer, she had been physically sick with the loss and was bled and given medicine by a doctor for her anxiety, headaches, and lassitude. She was somewhat better by autumn, revived by her burgeoning friendship with James and the first phase of their joint study of the Germans. On Thanksgiving she agreed to attend the Unitarian services with her father, not out of any interest but, as ever, to please him. Once inside, her mind wandered:

> I almost always suffered much in church from a feeling of disunion with the hearers and dissent from the preacher; but today, more than ever before, the services jarred upon me from their grateful and joyful tone. I was wearied out with mental conflicts, and in a mood of most childish, child-like sadness. I felt within myself great power, and generosity, and tenderness; but it seemed to me as if they were all unrecognized, and as if it was impossible that they should be used in life. . . . I looked around the church, and envied all the little children;

for I supposed they had parents who protected them, so that they could never know this strange anguish, this dread uncertainty.

Afterward, Margaret excused herself from her family and went walking in the fields for what must have been two or three hours. Then, among the dead and clotted leaves and the jelling cold, it came:

> I did not think; all was dark, and cold, and still. Suddenly the sun shone out with that transparent sweetness, like the last smile of a dying lover, which it will use when it has been unkind all a cold autumn. And, even then, passed into my thought a beam from its true sun, from its native sphere, which has never since departed from me. I remember how, a little child, I had stopped myself one day on the stairs, and asked, how came I here? How is it that I seem to be this Margaret Fuller? What does it mean? What shall I do about it? I remembered all the times and ways in which the same thought had returned. I saw how long it must be before the soul can learn to act under these limitations of time and space and human nature; but I saw, also, that it *must* do it—that it must make all this false true—and sow new and immortal plants in the garden of God, before it could return. I saw there was no self; that selfishness was all folly, and the result of circumstance; that it was only because I thought self real that I suffered; that I had only to live in the idea of the ALL, and all was mine. This truth came to me, and I received it unhesitatingly; so that I was for that hour taken up into God.

So came Margaret's epiphany at age twenty-one, born of the loss of George Davis. James, meanwhile, continued to flay himself with the memory of his lovers. He dreamed of Louisa Hickman and then wrote poems about the dreams, and continued to visit Elizabeth Randall, whose every action was a sign of his own transcendent awfulness:

> I went into town and called on Elizabeth. The whole harmony of my day destroyed by this call, for I purposed to be

quite agreeable and was more stupid than ever, if that is possible. It is my cruel fate to be ever disagreeable when I most
wish to please. Elizabeth was quite worn out before I departed. She put her fair forehead into her sweet fingers and
uttered a sigh—or shall I call it a yawn?—which destroyed as
I before stated my equanimity for that night, and indeed for
half the next day.

Louisa was as much in James's thoughts as Elizabeth, if not more,
but was far, far away in the West with her husband. Then in the winter of 1832, a year after Margaret's Thanksgiving experience, word
reached Cambridge that Louisa had died at the age of twenty-one.
Her body was returned east and entombed in her husband's family's
mausoleum in Newton. Some months later, when the body was still
not much decayed, James obtained the key. He went late, deep in the
night, with a lantern. Inside, he removed the screws one at a time—
they were already seized fast in the wood—from the outer box and
then from the inner coffin. He spent a long time in the tomb, perhaps all night, alone with Louisa, watching her, just the two of
them.

That spring of 1833, James graduated from Harvard Divinity
School. He decided to go west, where in the evangelical wilderness
not a word of Unitarianism, never mind Transcendentalism, had
been heard. There was a minister's post available in Louisville, the
city where Louisa had died the previous year.

# FIVE

Eighteen thirty-two, the year when James Clarke was twenty-two and opened Louisa Hickman's coffin, was the year he met his cousin Ralph Waldo Emerson. Emerson had opened the coffin of his wife, Ellen, dead a year, earlier that spring. This was not something bereaved husbands or lovers routinely did, and so it may have been in imitation of his newfound friend that James paid his midnight visit to Louisa. That experience seems to have precipitated his uncharacteristically bold decision to go west, and it may have had a similar effect on Emerson: That summer he resigned his ministry at the Second Church, ostensibly over his doubt that Jesus had in any formal sense instituted the Eucharist as a sacrament. He felt into a fit of melancholia that persisted through the autumn, and then, on an impulse, he boarded a ship for Europe, bound for Italy, and Rome in particular. He would not be the last in his circle to make the voyage.

In parallel with himself and Emerson, the women in James's life were also striking out in new directions. Margaret's long career crisis seemed at last to resolve itself. Since the autumn, James had pressed her to think of herself first and foremost as a writer—"You are destined to be an author. I shall yet see you wholly against your will and drawn by circumstances, become the founder of an American literature!"—but Margaret remained diffident. However, it was not wholly unheard of for a woman to pursue such a career; one of Margaret's heroes was the Romantic critic and novelist Madame de Staël, and her childhood friend Lydia Maria Child was beginning to attract notice in print. But Margaret would scarcely settle for being merely a "female author": If she could not aspire to the level of a Carlyle or even a Goethe, it was not worth the bother. Accordingly, and with James's continued prompting, in 1833 she set herself a rigorous program of reading and, increasingly, writing with that goal in mind. And as aspiring writers male and otherwise were wont to do, she would support herself by teaching school or tutoring on the side.

James's sister, Sarah, had been in a quandary similar to Margaret's. An obviously gifted artist since childhood, she, too, wondered if her painting might constitute something more than a genteel avocation. She went to see Washington Allston, a painter renowned in Boston, who, upon examining her portfolio, recommended with "no hesitation" that she set herself up as a professional landscape artist. Sarah's sense of mission was also bolstered by her deepening acquaintance with similarly talented and ambitious women, Margaret among them. She and Margaret had previously regarded each other warily, but now, with James departed for Louisville, they found themselves drawn together. After a few meetings, Margaret wrote, "*Dear* Sarah. I not only *like* her but *love* her now. . . . I am no longer too much for her and she, I think, is quite frank with me." Sarah's circle of friends also included the Peabody sisters from Salem (who were cousins to the Griggses there): Elizabeth, Mary, and Sophia. Elizabeth and Mary were boarders with Sarah's mother, but it was Sophia, herself a painter and the high-strung, sensitive, and slightly impetuous last-born darling of her family, who became Sarah's most intimate friend.

As Sarah blossomed in Boston, James was increasingly miserable in Louisville, his sole consolation being his correspondence with Margaret. He was appalled by the filth, the lack of any intellectual stimulation or moral consciousness, the coarse language and coarser thought of the inhabitants, and, not least, the pervasive and corrosive ethos of legal slavery:

> Last night I was much shocked by the cold-blooded and unfeeling way in which a Natchez man described his exploits in flogging negroes. He told, with a truly fiendish glee, how he flogged a man nearly to death a day or two before on suspi-

cion of stealing. But my head is full of stories about hangings
and murders.

Nor was his mission as a Unitarian minister preaching reason and
optimism going well in the fundamentalist, hellfire atmosphere of
Kentucky:

> One day a Louisville lady, Mrs. W., asked me to come and see
> her, and told me she had no faith in Christianity as a Divine
> revelation, but felt unhappy and wished to attain this faith if
> it were possible. Her objections seemed to be so formidable
> that she thought they could not be answered. Inquiring as to
> their nature, I found that they all rested on the doctrine of
> the infallible inspiration of the whole Bible. She supposed
> that if she doubted or disbelieved any part, even of the Old
> Testament, she must give up the whole. And as there were
> many things, especially in the Old Testament, that she was
> unable to accept as literal verity, she imagined that she must
> not believe in Jesus Christ.

James itched to be in Boston, even if unbelief there was not
merely present but strident, right under his mother's roof. Elizabeth
Peabody wrote her sister Mary about another Clarke boarder, Horace Mann, whom Mary herself would eventually wed: "The truth
is he does not believe in revelation at all; he does not believe that Jesus Christ rose from the dead, nor any of those things." That was not
to say, Elizabeth added, that Mann did not consider Jesus a very fine
fellow indeed—"He thinks him the most extraordinary person that
ever existed and his instructions as the finest and most worthy of
consideration"—and their friendship continued in its unabated
warmth, as did that of Elizabeth and Sarah. Elizabeth, whom Henry
James would portray as the archetypal New England bluestocking
and do-gooder Miss Birdseye in *The Bostonians,* was more interested
in garlanding the world with progress and enlightenment than in orthodoxy:

> Sarah Clarke has written me some divine letters . . . which
> have done me a world of good, for she speaks as if I had been

to her a creative and enlarging and softening influence, from
first to last, and Mr. Mann spreads sunshine round my heart
by his brotherly tenderness, his stimulating approbation, and
by expressing that I interest his mind and beguile his sorrows.

If Elizabeth Peabody had a male equivalent, it was surely Bronson Alcott, the by turns charismatic and difficult schoolmaster and
all-purpose Transcendental mystic. In 1834, two years after the birth
of his daughter Louisa May, he founded the Temple School, with
Elizabeth as his assistant and Sarah Clarke and Sophia Peabody as art
teachers. Eschewing both rote learning and corporal punishment, it
was a precursor of what would be called a "free school" a century
and a half later, not only in its teaching methods but in its tendency
to founder on ideological and interpersonal differences. Two years
into its existence, Elizabeth and Alcott had a falling out over—
among other things—the life-extension "science" of health crank
Sylvester Graham, and Margaret Fuller replaced her as head teacher;
within a year, Temple School was closed, the victim of public out-
cry over Alcott's published statements on his "intuitive" method of
teaching children religion, which Harvard's Andrews Norton (also
known as "the Unitarian pope") described as "one third absurd, one
third blasphemous, and one third obscene."

This sort of excitement in Boston did nothing to ease James's
sense of isolation, with his correspondence with Margaret his only
tie to "the march of mind." Even that relationship was strained by a
misunderstanding during a short visit home in the summer of 1834,
when he ran afoul of Margaret's habitual itch for feeling slighted and
she charged him with the gravest crime she could imagine—behaving toward her like George Davis. A barrage of letters at last soothed
her, and at one point he had even persuaded her to add the Bible to
her reading list and she in turn reported back that she was indeed beginning to be persuaded of the necessity of belief. James exultantly
reported to his college classmate William Henry Channing that
Margaret "has become regenerate." Whether that was really the case
in any formal Unitarian (never mind Christian) interpretation of the
term is doubtful, but James needed something to bolster him. Finally, after a further year in the wilderness of Kentucky, he conceived the idea of launching a Transcendentalist magazine edited

from and for the West. It was to be called the *Western Messenger,* and in the summer of 1835 he returned to Boston to round up contributors.

James came home to find his sister, Sarah, a closer part of the circle gathering around his friend Emerson. Sarah was already well acquainted with Emerson's new fiancée, Lydia Jackson, whom she had previously described as eminently suitable for her intended groom in a letter to James: "She is a soaring Transcendentalist. She is full of sensibility, yet as independent in her mind as—who shall I say?— Margaret F."

Oddly, the one person in the Transcendentalist movement whom Emerson had not by this time met was Margaret. Emerson was already playing the role of "Sage of Concord" to some extent, and tended to wait for people to present themselves to him for inspection and approval; for her part, Margaret, scarcely shy, may have sensed that her mind might finally meet its match in Emerson. Sarah Clarke had repeatedly recommended her to Lydia—now rechristened the more euphonious "Lydian" by Emerson—who was quickly being understood as the most efficient means of influencing her new husband. James, too, urged his two closest friends to meet each other, but then he and Margaret had a second falling out.

Partly at James's behest, Margaret had earlier in 1835 tried her hand at fiction, and produced a short story called "Lost and Won," which was published in the August 8 issue of *The New England Galaxy,* just at the time when James was back from Louisville. The characters consisted of Emily, a young woman of a nonconformist and literary bent; Davenant, her conniving, treacherous lover; and Edward, Emily's well-meaning but diffident and bookish cousin. The plot turns on Davenant's cruelly abandoning Emily for another woman, subsequently realizing Emily's superior qualities, and returning to beg her to reinstate him in her feelings—a proposal she righteously and triumphantly rejects in favor of a better and kinder rival, leaving Davenant to fester in crabbed and eternal bachelordom.

James—whom Margaret had in all sincerity asked to comment on the story's literary merit—needed no assistance in reading the dramatis personae as respectively Margaret, George Davis, and himself. Foolishly, before returning West, he seems to have put it around

Boston, Cambridge, and Concord that this was the key to the story, driving the not untouchy Margaret to heights of fury. James had unthinkingly betrayed her twice over: first, in publicly venting and revivifying her humiliating history with George Davis; second, and much more gravely, by not treating her writing as art, but as a mere disguised anecdote and settling of scores.

Clarke and Fuller were not the only ones touched by the exposure of a roman à clef that year. *The New England Magazine* published a short story called "The Minister's Black Veil," clearly based on the case of Emerson's darkly eccentric forebear, Joseph Moody. The author was from Salem; he would soon cross Emerson's path through his acquaintance with the Peabody sisters and, in particular, Sarah Clarke's bosom friend, Sophia. His name was Nathaniel Hawthorne, and Emerson took an immediate and understandable dislike to him.

# SIX

A little shamefaced, James had Sarah write Margaret on September 29: "It is not as you suppose through his means that the meaning of the tale was made public as the only person he told of it besides George was Ellen Sturgis. . . . James begs me to say that he was exaggerating when he proposed to tell all the world about it and that among us all, we have not told more than three people." But the apology was overtaken by events: The following day Margaret's father suddenly and unexpectedly collapsed and died. Six weeks later, James's beloved Grandfather Freeman also died. Death, as ever, seemed to overshadow love and all its petty outgrowths. The matter of Margaret's short story was forgotten, and she and James—both scarcely twenty-five years old—turned pensive, huddling together for comfort in their friendship. The news of his grandfather's death had reached James on the Ohio River:

> But to what purpose this talk about rivers and mud banks, in which, after, all I take not a copper farthing's interest. I wish to talk to you. . . . What matters it from what part of infinite space the voice comes to you, so it be a loving kindly voice, whose tones are of old well-known and well-prized. Have we not thought the same thoughts, felt the same feelings, taken in the same impressions, worked them up into the same or a very similar knowledge?

Inevitably, too, the precocious isolate, island-bound boy whom James felt himself fundamentally to be and whom he fully revealed only to Margaret, came out strongly:

> I fear I am rather too apt to talk in this pseudo-pathetic, Byronizing strain. However it never seems to me ridiculous to talk so, nor does it strike people in that light, for it commonly produces the desired effect, namely, of inducing them to take me to their heart, pat me on the head, and say, "Dear child, it shall have its piece of sugar by and by." And then I feel quite satisfied again, wipe my eyes, go to play or to work as circumstances demand, and am willing to wait a little longer for my piece of sugar.

Margaret was not so inclined to imagine herself inadequate or immature as a matter of routine, but now she was effectively responsible for her mother and four siblings. She suddenly felt very old, her self not defined by the future she had pictured herself fashioning, but by the past, by memory and by history. She wrote James back, mentioning that yet another worthy of the older generation, a family friend and neighbor, had since passed away:

> Judge Dana too who was with me the morning you bade me farewell now lies in the church yard by the side of my Father. Verily the honored elders of the land are passing away in a crowd and leaving us their parts to play. Can we do it?—Can you, my friend, fill the place of your independent, candid and beneficent grandfather? Can I make good to my fellow creatures the loss of my pious, upright and industrious Father? Once I was more presumptuous but now I have attained more accurate ideas of the obstacles to be overcome in life.

James replied to say that this, too, had been on his mind:

> What you say about our not being able to fill the situation of our forebears and fathers struck a chord of thought in my mind which had just been vibrating. How much goes to form

such a character as your father's, or as my grandfather's. How much disappointment. How many hours of heartsickness to subdue unjust and selfish pride, and to teach dependence on God and man. How much patient effort and labor to form the habits of useful and practical wisdom . . . And all this we, in our ignorance, scorned and passed by unheeded. We thought, because we were young, and our thoughts new to *us,* and our will strong, we thought shame of their calm and steady activity, and hoped by the application of some great ideas, to move society to its very centre.

Despite this momentary hesitation, the latest of New England's rising generations could not help but feel the imperative to remake their parents' world, or at least their religion, which was much the same thing. To the Transcendentalist preacher Orestes Brownson, Unitarianism was "negative, cold, lifeless, and all advanced minds among Unitarians are dissatisfied with it and are craving something higher, better, more living, and lifegiving." But the discontent went beyond mere intradenominational dissension to the entire culture: "Society as it is is a lie, a sham, a charnel house, a valley of dry bones."

Neither James nor Margaret would put the matter so strongly. James wanted to get the *Western Messenger* solidly established, and Margaret had decided to dedicate herself to writing a book about Goethe. But then Margaret at last met Emerson. Sarah's and James's entreaties and recommendations had had their effect. Margaret went to Emerson's house in Concord for a day, and stayed three weeks, and thereafter nothing was the same.

\*          \*          \*

Emerson, too, had been recently touched by death. His beloved younger brother Charles died in May 1836, aged twenty-eight, on the eve of his wedding. The habitually sunny Emerson was devastated, as Sarah Clarke reported to Mary Peabody: "I looked away, I could not help it, for it seemed like intruding on his sacred sorrow to demand so much as a look of recognition—but I could not help seeing that the seraphic smile was quenched—Ah Mary—when such a bright planet shoots from the horizon, how dark it leaves us!—and how uncertain and shadowy become the things of time and sense."

When Margaret arrived in July, Emerson's grief was more subdued and Margaret's company eased it still more, in a manner Emerson later found a little intrusive and disconcerting:

> I still remember the first half-hour of Margaret's conversation. She was then twenty-six years old. She had a face and a frame that would indicate fullness and tenacity of life. She was rather under middle height; her complexion was fair, with strong fair hair. She was then, as always, carefully and becomingly dressed, and of lady-like self-possession. For the rest, her appearance had nothing prepossessing. Her extreme plainness—a trick of incessantly opening and shutting her eyelids—the nasal tone of her voice—all repelled; and I said to myself, we shall never get far. . . . I believe I fancied her too much interested in personal history; and her talk was a comedy in which dramatic justice was done to everybody's foibles. I remember she made me laugh more than I liked; for I was at that time an eager scholar of ethics, and had tasted the sweets of solitude and stoicism, and I found something profane in the hours of amusing gossip into which she drew me. . . .

Emerson had just finished "Nature," the essay that would prove to be his masterwork and Transcendentalism's chief manifesto. Although it arguably contained few ideas with which James or Margaret or anyone with an acquaintance with Carlyle and the rest would be unfamiliar, "Nature," in Emerson's characteristically emphatic and urgent poetic style, turned them into a religious and cultural imperative, the fusillade in an apparent revolution. Andrews Norton and Emerson's and James's other old teachers at Harvard were scandalized. One of the newer members of the faculty, Francis Bowen, reviewed it—not entirely unfairly—as follows:

> General truths are to be obtained without the previous examination of particulars, and by the aid of a higher power than the understanding. The hand-lamp of logic is to be bro-

ken, for the truths that are *felt* are more satisfactory and certain than those that are *proved*. The sphere of intuition is enlarged, and made to comprehend not only mathematical axioms, but the most abstruse and elevated propositions respecting the being and destiny of man.

What appalled and frightened Harvard delighted Margaret and James. Emerson's philosophy was inseparable from Emerson's self, and in him they saw what they saw in their own friendship. James would write Margaret, "Whatever we owe to those who give us confidence in ourselves, who make us believe we are something distinct and can do something special, who arouse our individual consciousness by an intelligent sympathy with tendencies and feelings we ourselves only half understand—all this I owe to you." James concluded, "You gave me to myself."

As for Emerson, James later wrote:

How nobly he has stepped forward into the arena, and how confounded are those who thought his brain turned and that he was a mere dreamer, to see that he is the most practical man about. . . . Every thought bears fruit with him, and has relation to life. . . . He asserts the necessity of self-reliance in an age when imitation and sympathy predominate; he defends the individual man, when we all get melted together in masses; he advocates and heralds the "triumphant reign of the first person singular" in a time when the first person plural is all in all. Everything with him revolves round this point. "Think for yourself your own thoughts" is his intellectual rule. "Act out yourself" his ethical maxim. "Believe in the God within you" his religious faith. This *"I by myself I"* is the red thread of all his cordage.

Nor was Emerson finished. A year and a half after the publication of "Nature," he was permitted to give a lecture to the graduating class of the Harvard Divinity School, a venue where Norton and the rest of the faculty apparently believed he could not cause too much harm. They were wrong.

In his Divinity School address, Emerson did not simply propound a philosophy uncongenial to Harvard Unitarianism, but seemed to attack Unitarian doctrine at its foundations. Norton and even Channing had clung—against all the evidence of their rationalism—to the precept that Jesus was at least partly divine and that his performance of miracles evinced that divinity. Against that, Emerson maintained that Jesus simply "belonged to the true race of prophets [and] saw with open eyes the mystery of the soul. Drawn by its severe harmony, ravished with its beauty, he lived in it, and had his being there." But, said Emerson, Jesus was divine only insofar as God manifests his divinity in every man. Sarah Clarke was in the audience and afterward called Emerson's address "a strain of high music rising from sweet melody to awful grandeur . . . not so much sublime as divine." Andrews Norton, too, found an analogy to music, sputteringly referring to it as "this incoherent rhapsody."

The breach had now been publicly made, the rising generation had declared its independence and was not a little overconfident of its rightness and likelihood of success. Margaret wrote James with amusement, "You know how they have been baying at Mr. Emerson, 'tis pity you could not see how calmly he smiles down on the sleuth-hounds of public opinion." In a letter to her brother, Sarah cooked up a witty scenario in which Dr. Palfrey, the dean of the Divinity School, "recommends that school to be closed for a few years, and to be reopened only when the pestilent effect of Mr. Emerson's address shall have been dissipated by the abstinence from theological studies, or when those who have been poisoned by the infection shall have all died off." In the meanwhile, according to Sarah, the Transcendentalist and Unitarian radical George Ripley "says they are going to appoint you Bishop of the West, and make you overlook the whole land, and detect the first sprouts of liberal Christianity anywhere they may shoot up."

Despite both the outrage of Norton and Palfrey and the crowing of the Transcendentalists, Emerson had said no more at the Divinity School than many people in and out of Harvard had been saying for years—no more than what Horace Mann had confided to Elizabeth Peabody at Mrs. Clarke's boardinghouse—but he had said it straight out to the face of the Unitarian pope in the Unitarian Vatican. Yet it was not much more than Channing had on many occasions implied, and far from being a departure from the Unitarian theology, merely took the assumptions of that theology to what many would regard as their logical conclusion. For if the divine was evident in all things in general, as both Unitarians and Transcendentalists seemed to maintain, it followed that the divine could not reside in any one place or person in particular, for example, in the sole person of Jesus. God was, so to speak, everywhere and nowhere.

This notion of pantheism does not seem far removed from Aquinas's conception of "deus est in omnibus rebus, et intime," but there was a fundamental difference. To say that God manifested himself *in* things was not to say that God *is* those things, which remain material signs of a spiritual being. But, as Orestes Brownson had observed two years before, the history of Protestantism was the history of the defeat of the spiritual by materialism—or rather, the surrender of human reason to the apparent limits of its knowledge of the divine—and Unitarianism "is the last word of Protestantism," whose reason-bound, materialist theology must necessarily in the end render God Himself matter rather than spirit. To recover the spiritual, Brownson believed, quite presciently, people would now either have to turn to the religions of Asia, or revert to Roman Catholicism, as Brownson himself would do some years later.

Brownson's conversion was doubtless delayed by his Transcendentalist suspicion of authority, which he saw as the repressive handmaid of rationalism and materialism with its insistence on submission to "facts" and "reason." In his and Emerson's program, the legacy of Protestantism would be countered by the individual meeting the divine on his or her own terms, constrained only by what felt right to the private heart and the free conscience. But by some accounts that very individualism was itself part of the Protestant legacy, every bit as much a part of Luther's problematic gift to Christianity as rationalism and materialism. In England, in the same year Emerson addressed the divinity school, the Oxford theologian John Henry Newman (who would, like Brownson, convert to Rome) gave his "Lectures on Justification":

> Luther found Christians in bondage to their works and observances; he released them by his doctrine of faith; and he left them in bondage to their feelings. . . . For outward signs

of grace, he substituted inward; for reverence towards the Church, contemplation of self.

Together, Brownson and Newman suggested that the "last word" in the Protestant revolution was neither Unitarianism nor Emerson's joyous personal idealism, but something much darker: a materialist divinity and a solipsistic humanity; God reduced to mere dust, man to lonely incoherence—something eerily close to the modern depictions of "the death of God" and of human existence as alienated and absurd that would be current a century later.

\*        \*        \*

Having met and been conquered by the vital force that was Margaret Fuller, Emerson felt compelled to open his Transcendental Club, originally consisting of himself, Unitarian minister George Ripley, Alcott, Brownson, and others, to women. Meetings were now held at Mrs. Clarke's rooming house, and were attended not only by Margaret but also by Sarah Clarke and Elizabeth Peabody. There and elsewhere, Margaret's conversational style was less chat than an intellectual and psychological onslaught. James habitually referred to her interlocutors as her "quarry," whom Margaret would subdue and conquer through charm, brainpower, and a sometimes unnerving capacity to penetrate deep into the psyches of others. Sarah recounted how

> Encountering her glance, something like an electric shock was felt. Her eyes pierced through your disguises. Your outworks fell before her first assault, and you were at her mercy. And then began the delight of true intercourse. Though she spoke rudely searching words, and told you startling truths, though she broke down your little shams and defenses, you felt exhilarated by the compliment of being found out, and even that she had cared to find you out.

That was not to say that Sarah, any more than her brother, found no flaws in Margaret. Her self-confident manner, joined to the obdurate sharpness of her intellect, could too often render her more intense, more hard and sheer, than others could easily bear. Sarah, like James, who was still absent in the West, aimed to soften her a little, chiefly through exposure to art, to which Margaret was indeed amenable. And art for her tended to lead somehow back to religion, or to the vision she had met on Thanksgiving Day, 1831: "A Christ, by Raphael, that I saw the other night, made me more long to be like Jesus, than ever did a sermon," she wrote of one painting. Another Raphael moved her to consider the somber weight of the Christian redemption: "I am not one of the lovers of sorrow, but one of these forms makes me feel the might of the Cross and forbids to reject the blood, the cup of gall and vinegar, nay even the irritating ignominious crown of thorns." These reactions and impulses, however, remained sporadic—verges of spiritual experience over which Margaret could not quite permit herself to fall—but her aestheticism remained constant. It was the closest she came to the numinous, the sole object to which she could comfortably bring faith.

Emerson, too, followed art, if less instinctively than Margaret, and grew in his appreciation of both Sarah and her work, one of whose paintings now hung at Concord. Sarah was a good Transcendentalist, but also a New Englander with little nonsense about her: she was, he noted in his journal, "a true and high minded person, but has her full proportion of our native frost." Nor was Emerson averse to offering advice: He thought Sarah an altogether more gifted artist than her mentor Washington Allston—who was only "an inarticulate sound" rather than "a Titanic genius"—and badgered her to sever her connection with him in order to "satisfy the wants of your own soul." Sarah wrote James of her dilemma, which was at the crux of Emerson's ideal of self-reliance:

> Mr. Emerson asked me a question such as I might have expected from him: he asked me, "How can Mr. Allston help you? But *how* can he help you?" Clearly he disbelieves in any help but self-help. For my part, I have arrived at that time of life, as mother's phrase is, when I do not disdain to receive help from an Allston. To be sure, it is far grander to get out of your difficulties alone and have all the glory of it; but meantime one might starve in the forest, before one could find the way out.

In this as in other matters, James was inclined to defer to Emerson, whom he had been vociferously defending in the *Western Messenger* against his Unitarian opponents. Although still isolated in Kentucky, James had lately been joined in the West by his Harvard classmate William Henry Channing, who had taken a pastorate in Ohio, and the two grew close, perhaps as close as he and Margaret were, given the distance between them. For her part, Margaret assumed that she and James remained intimates so mutually trusting that she felt no compunction in sending James's old letters to her young friend Caroline Sturgis together with a jaundiced outline of his tragic but compelling romantic history (including moments passed over above):

J. had three loves: 1st Louisa. A girl with creamy skin, bright, not loving, blue eyes and long curling locks of gold. She had some talent and a good deal of natural melody of character. She was one of those who act a part all the time in real life, not for the sake of being seen by others but to gratify natural dramatic propensities. James was the hero of one of her little melodramas. There was no real love in it, but it was pretty, and did pen a picture on the wall of life's vestibule. This was a love of fancy!

Next came Eleanor. This was one of what Mr. Emerson calls "urns of expression." She had one of the untouched bosoms like those in your book. She had . . . [the] secret eye, the mantling cheek, the timid consciousness of possible womanhood. Her long chestnut hair fell around her like a veil, so that young men were naturally tempted to try to make her come out. No one can predict what will be the fate of these water-sprites when they get their souls by wedlock. They may become heroines, sirens, or angels, or as likely domestic cats or spaniels. Eleanor became the latter. This too was not love, but only fancy, now tinged with passion. Both these maidens loved J. as much as he loved them. He got as good as he gave. Then came Elizabeth, a premature woman, a morbid, sickly but fascinating child. Half passion, half devotion, by turns sinner and saint. She was worthy to be loved. J. loved her at first little more than the previous but, as she did not return it, it became a deep passion and gave the needed crisis to his character.

Needed or otherwise, Margaret's own character faced a similar crisis a few months after writing these words in February 1839. In addition to being fond of Caroline Sturgis, Margaret had formed a strong attachment to Anna Barker, a magnetic young beauty from a wealthy New Orleans family. At the same time she found that her feelings for another friend, the handsome aspiring Transcendentalist Sam Ward, had turned into an erotic attraction she had not felt for any man since George Davis. Just as she was preparing to declare herself to Ward, whom she privately called Rafaello, she learned that he was already in love with Anna Barker and that the two were on the verge of announcing their engagement. Ward not only rejected Margaret but threw over art in favor of commerce. In order to support Anna in her accustomed style, he gave up literature and painting for a job in business. Once again both devastated and humiliated by love, she was further hurt by learning from a friend on the street that James Clarke had just gotten engaged without a word to her.

A few awkward, stiff letters passed between Margaret and James about this apparent miscommunication, and Margaret politely and bravely bestowed her blessing to the union, just as she would eventually to that of Sam Ward and Anna Barker. Why James had never said anything to Margaret about Anna Huidekoper, the daughter of a Pennsylvania Unitarian minister and *Western Messenger* contributor, is difficult to gauge. It does not seem to have been the kind of relationship that prompted the Goethian outpourings that Louisa and Elizabeth had inspired. Instead, James found Anna austerely pretty, steady, and kind, and she had presented herself at a moment when it seemed that marriage ought not to be deferred any longer. Perhaps James felt a little sheepish at having taken not a soulmate but simply a wife.

There were few women less like Margaret than Anna; and it had never been clear—least of all to Margaret and James themselves—what was the exact nature of the elusive but unmistakably erotic charge that underlay James and Margaret's friendship, but now it was submerged forever as James became a husband and, in October 1840, a father. Margaret busied herself with her "Conversations"—

a sort of lecture series and Transcendental Club exclusively for women—and the editing, at Emerson's behest, of the new Transcendentalist magazine, *The Dial*. When James at last moved home to Boston in late 1840, his and Margaret's relations were cordial, courteous, and not without warmth in the manner of old friends between whom much has passed, but for whom some matters are best left unrecalled. Things were not the same, of course, as they had been ten years ago when James had first addressed her as "cousin mine"; or even at the end of 1838, when Margaret had written James, both of them all of twenty-eight, "In few natures does such love for the good and beautiful survive the ruin of all youthful hopes, the wreck of all illusions." Sarah, scarcely two years older, had a similar sense of the world being all before them and yet simultaneously passing them by:

> But shall we ever learn the art of life? I am now thirty-one, and that is much, as the Turks say; but I feel like a beginner in everything. It is well and I am grateful that life so renews itself day by day; but it fills me with surprise. It is true the misty enchantment of morning has dispersed, but life seems fair before me still. A golden sunshine is in the world, and, though its wholeness is broken by some shadows that are all too black, sometimes I lose sight of them, and then they are as if they were not. One cannot at this age enjoy the world with the unoccupied heart of childhood.

Or could one? Hardly six months later Sarah conceived a new painting, a great and numinous dawnscape:

> I shall try to represent that mystic hour when the whole earth is full of reflected light, but the sun is yet unrisen; when everything seems like preparation and expectation, and the landscape has a beauty that disappears the instant the sun is above the horizon.

We do not know if she ever undertook to paint it, although doubtless Mr. Emerson pressed her to do exactly that.

# SEVEN

Emerson had, in any case, taken every other matter relating to the advance of the Transcendentalist cause in hand. He had founded *The Dial*—a magazine for the "hundreds of girls and boys who are dissatisfied with the existing state of things in the planet," as Sarah wryly put it—and installed as editor Margaret, who had filled the first issue with poems and pieces by herself, Emerson, James, and Sarah, among others. Margaret's "conversations" with what Sarah now styled an "infidel association" of women were at least as rigorous and tough-minded as anything Emerson himself might ordain. Sarah reported the case of one participant at a conversation who defended the right of women to determine their opinions solely on the basis of feeling since the intellectual sphere was not native, either by nature or by male exclusion, to women. "I am made so," says she, "and I cannot help it." "Yes," says Margaret, gazing full upon her, "but who are *you*? Were you an accomplished human being, were you all that a human being is capable of becoming, you might perhaps have a right to say, 'I *like* it therefore it is good'; but, if you are not all that, your judgment must be partial and unjust if it is guided by your feelings alone." In Margaret's mind Transcendentalist self-reliance should brook no exceptions for the "weaker sex."

Nor was Emerson himself softening his public utterances. In the wake of his January 1840 Boston lecture series "On Religion," Sarah created another of her characteristic whimsies:

Mr. Palfrey was seen to go into the lecture room with the others, but no one discerned him coming out; after such research and inquiry the next morning the door keeper confessed that he found a small pile of ashes on one of the seats about as large as a pea's head; and that no Mr. P. was thenceforth met with. "This is a fact," as Miss Edgeworth says.

Lumping the dean of the Harvard Divinity School with the preachy, fuddy-duddy Maria Edgeworth gives a fair sense of the estimation the Transcendentalists now held of their opponents in New England's old guard. Not just the ideas but also the talent were firmly located in the Concord camp. By 1838 the twenty-one-year-old Henry Thoreau was a fixture at Emerson's house, doted on by Lydian, adored by the Emerson children, and universally regarded as positively aflame with potential. In the same year, Sarah met two more additions to the circle in the company of her best friend Sophia Peabody:

> That evening I saw Hawthorne for the first time. He came with Jones Very, both new treasures of Elizabeth [Peabody's] discovery. . . . Hawthorne, shrouded in a cloak, Byronic and very handsome, looked gloomy or perhaps only shy. Mr. Very had written poems which were remarkably spiritual and savored of Swedenborg.

Hawthorne had not yet moved to Concord, and even when he did, would always be a reluctant member of the Transcendentalist community. He and Emerson disliked each other more or less on sight, he found Thoreau ugly (not an entirely unfair estimation), and he thought Margaret Fuller haughty and overbearing, if also fascinating, to judge by the frequent appearance of characters based upon her in his work. The whole Emersonian project struck him as naïve and pretentious, blinded by idealism to the world and humanity as they really were, an exercise in folly and even madness.

The case of Hawthorne's companion on the night Sarah met him, Jones Very, could be said to bear this out. Very had been a classmate of Thoreau's at Harvard and had stayed on after graduation as a tutor in Greek and a divinity school student. He was indeed capable of "remarkably spiritual" poetry, as in "The New Birth":

> 'Tis a new life—thoughts move not as they did
> With slow uncertain steps across my mind,
> In thronging haste fast pressing on they bid
> The portals open to the viewless wind;
> That comes not, save when in the dust is laid
> The crown of pride that gilds each mortal brow,
> And from before man's vision melting fade
> The heavens and earth—Their walls are falling now—
> Fast crowding on each thought claims utterance strong,
> Storm-lifted waves swift rushing to the shore
> On from the sea they send their shouts along,
> Back through the cave-worn rocks their thunders roar,
> And I a child of God by Christ made free
> Start from death's slumbers to eternity.

Such poetry—printed by James, an early admirer, in The *Western Messenger,* and quickly taken up by Emerson and Margaret—recounted an experience of spiritual transformation both powerful and personal, a sort of inundation by the spirit that sat uncomfortably with Harvard Unitarianism, as did Very's intimations that he felt his verse was somehow being dictated to him by the divine. His identification with Christ—pressed in an essay on Shakespeare and in mystic utterances made around Cambridge—became so extreme that his teachers and classmates feared for his reason. James, admittedly at some distance from events at Harvard, allowed that Very might tend to "perhaps an extravagant pushing of some views to their last results," but this was common among "earnest religionists." Emerson, too, regarded Very as "eminently sane." When at last the crisis came, Elizabeth Peabody reported her version of events to Concord:

September 24th 1838

My dear Mr Emerson—
     The very day poor Very was carried to the Insane Hospital (for you have doubtless heard of his misfortune) he came to

see me, to deliver his Revelation and told me he had sent you his Essay on Shakespeare. I have been in hopes to hear ever since he went to [McLean Asylum in] Charlestown that he was sick of a brain fever which would prove his insanity but a temporary delirium but I have not and so I suppose it is water on the brain. It was probably produced by intense application. He was superintending the Greek class out of which he has got a great deal of studying and he has the idea of a great moral responsibility which arose I suppose from his success in awakening the sentiment of duty in others. Besides he has been a year or more in his divinity studies, and writing besides. I have feared insanity before. *These impulses* from above I think are never sound minded. I wonder whether something might not be written by a believer in the doctrine of Spirituality which would show the difference between trusting the Soul and giving up one's mind to these *individual illuminations.*

. . . He was so gentle and harmless in his hallucination that one almost forgot how wretched he was—that such a beautiful light had gone down in darkness. He spoke of going to you and telling you his discovery and when he went to the hospital his greatest grief seemed to be that he was so persecuted he could not give you his revelation. He was promised that you should be informed that he was there. . . . He used Christ's words all the time and in the whimsical manner an insane person might. But the thought that has pressed itself on my mind *most* is how some people have taken it all as nothing but *transcendentalism* which shows in Very entirely, they do not apprehend *the ground of a real belief* in *Inspiration.* What a frightful shallowness of thought in the community that sees no difference between the evidence of the most manifest insanity and the Ideas of Reason!

Elizabeth was right that those doubtful about Transcendentalism would make use of Very's commitment. Richard Henry Dana, Jr., a childhood schoolmate of Margaret's who was about to become famous as the author of *Two Years Before the Mast,* opined that Very "is very intimate with Emerson and the other Spiritualists or Supernaturalists, or whatever they are called, or may be pleased to call themselves, and his insanity has taken that shape accordingly. I am told some of them are absurd enough to say that he is not insane but that the world does not understand him. Would that their insanity were no worse than his, but madness is in their *hearts*."

Bronson Alcott, never one to speak with moderation, admitted that Very was, in fact, insane—"Insane with God, diswitted in the contemplation of the holiness of Divinity"—but this was exactly the sort of talk people like Dana cited to prove their point about the Emerson circle. In any case, Jones Very was released from McLean's Asylum in time to attend Emerson's Boston lecture "The Doctrine of the Soul" in December and to buttonhole Elizabeth Peabody on the notion of the unreality of physical evil and thence of pain, such as that which Jesus might have experienced on the cross. James Clarke was also present at the lecture, and promised he would look into obtaining Very a pastorate in the West. No such position ever materialized; Very remained in New England and completed a number of further stays at McLean's. James did, however, eventually edit the complete edition of Very's poems and essays.

The intense if unorthodox spirituality evinced by Very cropped up elsewhere, most surprisingly in Margaret, where it coincided, perhaps scarcely by accident, with her devastation at the romance between Sam Ward and Anna Barker, who were to be married in October 1840. Margaret's most intimate correspondents during this time were Caroline Sturgis and, increasingly, James's close friend and Harvard classmate William Henry Channing. In a letter to Caroline, Margaret revealed a sense of a personal relation to the incarnate Jesus that was far removed from the abstractness of her earlier pronouncements on religion:

> Cary, I was much moved by what you say of Jesus—He will yet be your best-beloved friend; with all the blurs, that a factitious, canting world places between us and him, with all the love for liberty of the speculative mind, we cannot at last dispense, we cannot get away from the divine character, the profound sympathies, the exalted ethics of that Man of Sorrows.
>
> I partook of communion last Sunday for the third time, and had beautiful thoughts about the bread and the wine which some day I may tell you.

Not much later, Margaret said to James of the arch-Romantic hero Shelley that "the unhappy influences of early education prevented his ever attaining clear views of God, life, and the soul," as though she might have been describing herself. "At thirty"—and Margaret had just turned thirty herself—"he was still a seeker, an experimentalist. . . . Had Shelley lived twenty years longer, I have no doubt he would have become a fervent Christian, and thus have attained that mental harmony which was necessary to him."

Margaret did not intend to wait twenty years. As the Barker-Ward wedding day approached in the fall of 1840, she craved an epiphany through which she would be at last stunned into real conversion, but more and more she realized that she needed a guide, a sort of priest, to bring her to the moment. At one time, James might have been the person, but time and his new wife had altered their relation. In particular, as Margaret wrote William Henry Channing, he was now a father of a son, christened Herman:

> This news made me more grave even than such usually does. I suppose because I have known the growth of James's character so intimately. I called to mind a letter he had written me of what we had expected of our fathers. The ideal Father, the profoundly wise, provident, divinely tender and benign, he is indeed the God of the human heart. . . . When I recollect how deep the anguish, how deeper still the want, with which I walked alone in hours of childish passion, and called for a Father often saying the word a hundred times till it was stifled by sobs, how great seems the duty that name imposes. . . . Could the child keep learning his earthly as he does his heavenly father from all best experience of life till at last it were the climax: "I am the Father. [If] you have seen me, ye have seen the father."

The only person Margaret knew who could conceivably fill such a role for her—who, to her mind, had almost an obligation to help her—was Emerson.

The problems and complexities of love and friendship had in part launched Margaret's search for religious truth, and were to shadow her all along its course. For her relationship with Emerson—

on her part, intellectually competitive and emotionally filial; on his, impressed but wary—was hardly straightforward. But in what was now almost a religious rapture, Margaret was blind to the tensions between her and Emerson. Around the time of the wedding between the man she had once called "Raffaello" and the woman she now dubbed "his Madonna," she told Caroline of a Marian ecstasy of her own, a maternal counterpart of the idea of fatherhood the birth of Herman Clarke had prompted in her:

> The life that flows in upon me from so many quarters is too beautiful to be checked. I would not check a single pulsation. It all ought to be—if caused by any apparition of the Divine in me I could bless myself like the holy Mother. But like her I long to be virgin. I would fly from the land of my birth. I would hide myself in night and poverty. Does a star point out the spot? The gifts I must receive, yet for my child, not me. I have no words, I wait till he is of age, then hear *him*. . . . Yet the cross, the symbol you have chosen seems indeed the one. Daily, hourly it is laid upon me. Tremulously I feel that a wound is yet to be given.

This was no more extreme and rather more lucid than Jones Very in his sanest moments, but Emerson could not grant Margaret—could not see in her—the spiritual authenticity he saw in Very. In his journal at this time he had already written:

> Margaret is a being of "unsettled rank in the Universe." So proud and presumptuous yet so meek; so worldly and artificial with the keenest sense and taste for all the pleasures of luxurious society, yet living more than any other for long periods in a trance of religious sentiment; a person who according to her own account of herself, expects everything for herself from the Universe.

This egocentricity, he told her directly, this failure to undertake the "pure acquiescence," was inconsistent with "the only authentic mode" of religious life. Margaret was stunned: She could scarcely consider him a friend, still less a Father or spiritual director. She replied with sorrow and bitterness:

> If you have not seen this stair on which God has been so untiringly leading me to himself, you have indeed been wholly ignorant of me. Then indeed, when my soul, in its childish agony of prayer, stretched out its arms to you as a father, did you not see what was meant by this crying for the moon; this sullen rejection of playthings which had become unmeaning? Did you then say, "I know not what this means; perhaps this will trouble me; the time will come when I shall hide my eyes from this mood?" Then you are not the friend I seek.

In the end, within a month, she took this blow, too, as a sign of her spiritual progress, as a lesson in seeing the difference between the mind and the heart, and their sometimes agonized intersection in the soul. She wrote Caroline as though she were at prayer: "O these tedious, tedious attempts to learn the universe by thought alone. Love, Love, my Father, thou hast given me. I thank thee for its pains."

*  *  *

Not long before this episode—and probably not for the first time or the last—James said to Sarah of Margaret, "What a sphynx is that girl! Who shall solve her?" But he was thinking not of religion, but of politics, and of Margaret's "natural affinity for the mass": her sense, despite her intellectual hauteur, of democracy and populism, that "man is not made for society, but society is made for man." She, James thought, rather than Emerson, for all his idealism, had the potential to be an activist.

Politics, or at least social justice, was increasingly on James's mind. He had become close to Wendell Phillips, the prominent abolitionist and all-purpose firebrand. Moreover, Transcendentalism, like the liberal wing of Unitarianism, was becoming politicized. The antimaterialist Orestes Brownson had just published an influential article called "Democracy and Reform" whose calls for equity and justice had been cautiously reiterated by Emerson in his latest lecture series, "The Present Age." None of this meant that James or his associates were giving up their fundamental philosophical elitism—their belief in the superiority of the cultivated, educated mind—but they saw a need for society as a whole to be restructured in ways consistent with their idealism. In 1841, James would establish his own Unitarian congregation in Boston, the Church of the Disciples, and the idea of reform would be central to its existence. James planned, for example, to institute a weekly lecture series whose contents he sketched in his journal:

Reforms: Their relation to the Church, to the Age, by J. F. Clarke. 2. The Temperance Reform, Its history, idea, and present state. What is wanted now, What ought the church to do? By E. H. Chapin or John Pierpont. 3. The Peace Movement, by Theodore Parker or S. J. May. 4. The Anti-Slavery Movement, by Wendell Phillips. 5. Reforms in prisons, poorhouses, hospitals, insane asylums, etc., by Dr. S. G. Howe, or J. A. Andrew. 6. Social Reform, by W. H. Channing. 7. Educational Reform, by Horace Mann.

This program resembles the agendas of Unitarians (and liberal Christians in general) more than a century later, for which James and the Church of the Disciples are in many regards the original model. There is also something familiar about the belief many of his circle held that reform must be brought to bear just as strongly on traditionally private relations and institutions—the family, for example—as on civic ones, the sense, especially prominent among those like Margaret who had begun to perceive women as a discrete class, that "the personal is political."

To that end, George Ripley began to organize the community known as Brook Farm late in 1840. Sarah wrote James that "our colony of friends will probably settle at West Roxbury and try the experiment of life on a new plan and a true plan." But even its earliest stages were marked by a dissension—usually over ideological matters rather than practical ones—that would only increase over time. Sarah drolly reported that with only six families signed up, there was already tension between Unitarians of Ripley's own radical stripe and those of a more conservative bent: "The practical Christians have filed off, resisting the resistance to non-resistant principles in the Ripley party." But by the New Year of 1841, the community was ready to go forward. Sarah produced a lengthy account of its plan:

> There are perhaps a dozen families, all good men and true—farmers, teachers, mechanics, and preachers—who wish to unite with Mr. Ripley and commence a new way of life. . . . The plan is to have one large house with suites of apartments, two bedrooms and a sitting room, then to have some small cottages at about five hundred dollars each for other families; another building close at hand for cooking, etc.; a washing establishment moved by steam or a horse; a large apartment for eating, another for social purposes, wherein a soiree will be held two or three times a week, and all the inhabitants admitted and urged to come; a library to which all will have access. The government is to be popular, not patriarchal, for Mr. Ripley would never do for a patriarch. The farming is to be conducted on the most liberal and scientific principles of English husbandry, and the earth is to yield her increase in a style hitherto unknown in New England. Wealth is to flow in rapidly, but without corrupting the members of the community, for the luxuries are to be common to all and appropriated by none. . . . I have no doubt it will be realized if even on a very small scale. It is astonishing what a wide-spread desire there is for a new mode of life. Every day, almost, Mr. Ripley has a letter or a visit from some one who has for years nourished a desire for this thing and has been sure it would happen at last.

Nor did the urge for communal living end there: "I will tell you what Mr. Emerson's plan is: he is not going to join the Ripley set, but take to his own house several destitute friends—Mr. Alcott and family, Christopher Cranch and wife (he who believes in God), George Bradford (your admirer)—and adopt them all into his family, make his property a common fund for their support, and all unite in common labor to assist each other. . . . Does it not strike you that this is the beginning of a truly Christian life?"

Perhaps so, but only Thoreau would move in with the Emersons on any permanent basis. Brook Farm began with seven members, including Margaret's brother Lloyd and Nathaniel Hawthorne (whose friendship with the Peabody sisters had sharpened its focus into a special attraction toward Sarah's best friend, Sophia), but grew to nearly thirty by the spring of 1841. A number of these were part-timers, including the West Roxbury Unitarian minister Theodore Parker, the eccentric Catholic convert Charles King Newcomb, and Margaret herself, who took up temporary residence at the suggestion of her mother. Margaret's visits to Brook Farm were sporadic, and rendered trying by the unwanted romantic attentions of Charles Newcomb, whose chanting before the homemade shrines in his room was also beginning to unnerve the other communards. Nathaniel Hawthorne, not by nature a deeply social being, was taking the notes that would be the basis ten years later of his novelization of life at Brook Farm, *The Blithedale Romance.*

Theodore Parker was meanwhile attracting attention with his writing. The previous year, in the first issue of *The Dial,* Margaret had published an article by him adapted from his sermon "The Divine Presence," which, Sarah had told James, "is considered utter heresy and abomination by Dr. Norton and others." On May 19, 1841, Parker outdid himself with a sermon entitled "A Discourse on the Transient and Permanent in Christianity," which prompted one writer to the *Boston Courier* to proclaim he would rather have every Unitarian church in New England demolished than permit the likes of Parker to preach from a single pulpit.

Parker, like Emerson at the divinity school, did not say much more than had been said or thought before, but he said it as a minister of the Unitarian church from a Unitarian pulpit. He began, uncontroversially, by declaring that Christ surely did not expect his original followers to accept the Old Testament writings of their forefathers in any literal sense; it followed, he then suggested, that modern men and women should read the New Testament in a similar fashion, conscious of the limitations of its historical context.

That declaration doubtless made some of the congregation nervous. What followed was stronger still:

But still was [Jesus] not our brother; the son of man, as we are, the son of God, like ourselves? His excellence—was it not hu-

man excellence? His wisdom, love, piety—sweet and celestial
as they were—are they not what we also may attain? In him,
as in a mirror, we may see the image of God, and go on from
glory to glory, till we are changed into the same image.

God was man and man is God, Parker seemed to be saying, but
in either case the person Jesus was human rather than particularly
divine. Having disposed of that matter—having denied the fundamental proposition of what most people understood to be Christianity—he burned his final bridge: The church, Unitarian or
otherwise, had no right to impose any belief or doctrine on anyone;
Christian religion was what any man said it was to *him*:

Christianity allows perfect freedom. It does not demand all
men to *think* alike, but to think uprightly, and get as near as
possible to the truth; not all men to *live* alike, but to live holy,
and get as near as possible to a life perfectly divine. . . . But
there is no Christian sect which does not fetter a man. It
would make all men think alike, or smother their conviction
in silence.

Much of Boston reacted precisely by wanting to smother Parker,
but not everyone agreed: James, himself the city's most popular
preacher, according to Elizabeth Peabody, thought the "sermon
blazes with fire from the bush. It is the best defense of true Christianity I have ever seen." With most preaching venues now closed to
Parker, however, James took it upon himself to invite him to use the
pulpit at the Church of the Disciples. But even James's tolerant and
liberal congregation found this hard to accept, and he had to call a
parish meeting to ease their fears. That he was able to do so successfully says much about the man and the minister James had now become. Personally popular and unassuming, perfectly tolerant,
cultured, and intellectual yet endowed with an innate faith, he could
support a Parker or an Alcott and frequently hold views identical
with theirs without diminishing his own standing or credibility in
either Unitarian or Transcendentalist circles. He did not have the intellect of Emerson or of Margaret, but he had endless faith, not perhaps in any particular doctrine but in the notion that life and the

world were at bottom good, and life and the world appeared, by and large, to return the compliment.

It was not so easy for others. At the same time as Parker was being excoriated for his sermon, James's closest male friend, William Henry Channing, publicly resigned from the ministry, citing his disbelief in the authority of either the Bible or the Christian church as an institution. Elizabeth Peabody wrote a friend in Northampton: "You know about Wm. Channing, I suppose. He has a rough path to walk what with the revilings etc. with which his confession is met. His friends say some that he is mad and others that he is wicked." Channing was in turn Margaret's closest correspondent at this time, and was in no position to shore up her own faltering belief. The intensities of a year before, when she had felt within herself Christ and Mary's joys and agonies as bodily facts, had been replaced by shadows, by occasional glimmerings in the form of mere ideas.

Then, in January 1842, as though a knell tolled over the previous year, Emerson's beloved eldest son, Waldo, died at the age of five. Emerson wrote Sarah: "I have no skill, no illumination, no 'nearness' to the power which has bereaved me of the most beautiful children of the children of men. . . . It is nothing to me but the gloomiest sensible experience to which I have no key, and no consolation, nothing but oblivion and diversion." He also wrote Margaret and bared his devastation to her as though none of the tensions between them had ever occurred:

> My little boy must die also. All his wonderful beauty could not save him. He gave up his innocent breath last night and my world this morning is poor enough. He had scarlatina on Monday night. Shall I ever dare to love any thing again? Farewell and farewell, O my Boy!

Margaret too had loved Waldo. She recorded in her journal a conversation between him and his mother, which showed him possessed of a mind a little like Margaret's, vast and fearful of the vastness it sensed in the world:

> "Mamma, may I have this bell which I have been making to stand by the side of my bed?"

"Yes, it may stand there."

"But mamma, I am afraid it will alarm you. It may sound in the middle of the night, and it will be heard over the whole town, it will sound like some great glass thing which falls down and breaks all to pieces; it will be louder than a thousand hawks; it will be heard across the water, and in all the countries; it will be heard all over the world."

Later in 1842, Margaret spent several weeks at Concord, and she and Emerson resolved their differences, or at least established a middle ground upon which they could get along. "We agreed that my god was love, his truth," she wrote. As for religion, "What is done here at home in my heart is my religion. . . . I belong nowhere. I have pledged myself to nothing. God and the soul and nature are all my creed, subdivisions are unimportant. As to the church, I do not deny the church—who can that holds communion on themes of permanent interest as I do with several minds? . . . With William [Channing], with Sarah Clarke, I am in church."

Such a religion—really a restatement of the religion Margaret had devised for herself years before, perhaps even as a child—would have to suffice for her, although for one whose self-confessed God was love, it provided slight solace for a broken heart. At times, Margaret was inclined to resign herself to the bitterness of the estrangements and loss that had so often filled her cup: "I have no belief in beautiful lives; we are born to be mutilated." But then she could see it a little otherwise, as she wrote of Waldo Emerson's death to William Channing, himself bereft of faith:

I loved him more than any child I ever knew, as he was of nature more fair and noble. You would be suprised to know how dear he was to my imagination. I saw him but little, and it was well; for it is unwise to bind the heart where there is no claim. But it is all gone, and is another of the lessons brought by each year, that we are to expect suggestions only, and not fulfilments, from each form of beauty, and to regard them merely as Angels of the Beauty.

# EIGHT

That summer, on July 9, James officiated at the wedding of Nathaniel Hawthorne and Sophia Peabody, with Sarah standing as witness. Hawthorne had given up Brook Farm some time before, and the couple arranged to rent the Old Manse in Concord, the house of Emerson's grandfather William. By way of a wedding gift Emerson had Henry Thoreau, the universal Transcendental handyman, plant a vegetable garden on the property. That goodwill did not prevent Emerson from confiding to his journal a scant two months later that Hawthorne's "reputation as a writer is a very pleasing fact, because his writing is not good for anything, and this is a tribute to the man."

Hawthorne's opinion of Emerson was equally sardonic. In his own journal, Hawthorne describes lying down for a nap and employing a copy of *The Dial* "as a soporific," and of Emerson dropping by "with a sunbeam in his face":

He seemed fullest of Margaret Fuller, who, he says, has risen perceptibly into a higher state since their last meeting. He apotheosized her as the greatest woman, I believe, of ancient or modern times, and the one figure in the world worth considering.

Hawthorne did not like Margaret any more than he did Emerson, but he had to put up with her more, by virtue of his wife's intimacy with Sarah Clarke and Sarah's intimacy with Margaret. Those of the Concord circle were adept at this kind of benign hypocrisy, long practiced in New England. And that legacy, in all its breadth and weight, was at the heart of the tension between Hawthorne and Emerson. In Hawthorne's mind, Emerson simply wished to wave away the past and the reality of evil by dint of idealism and "self-reliance," to deny the continuing influence of the Puritan pessimism that Emerson's own character betrayed: the emotional chilliness beneath his outward cheeriness, the distance at which—despite the constant stream of boarders and acolytes passing through his life—he kept his heart from other people.

In earlier confessing his admiration for Sarah's "native frost," Emerson perhaps admitted that the Puritan strain in the New England soul was not entirely without value, or at least was not to be easily dismissed. Sarah herself told Margaret that "she had at one time a tendency towards Calvinism" and she and Margaret had "agreed that there is in the depths of the experience a misgiving lest there should be an inflexible justice unsoftened by Love which might exact to the utmost the penalty of sin, forcing us to suffer in proportion to our capacity for evil"—a fair definition of the New England God. And that understanding of evil was not so very far removed from what the Transcendentalist mind came up with unaided. When Margaret went walking with William Henry Channing's cousin Ellery by Walden Pond and encountered some snakes, Ellery said "they were the *criticism* of the Universe, handsome, easy in motion, cold and odious."

Emerson, too, had written, "I acknowledge (with surprise that I could ever forget it) the debt of myself and my brothers to that old religion . . . which taught privation, self-denial, and sorrow." But for Emerson that was as far as it went, or ought to go, whereas for Hawthorne—no believer in any doctrinal sense—even after the theology had been abandoned, the dark cast of the Puritan mind necessarily remained, if only as the history upon which the present grew. But its residue in Hawthorne, in the form of skepticism, was intolerable to Emerson:

> [It] esteems ignorance organic and irremovable, believes in the existence of pure malignity, believes in a poor decayed God who does what he can to keep down the nuisances, and

to keep the world going for our day. It believes the actual to be necessary; it argues habitually from the exception instead of the rule; and if it went to the legitimate extreme, the earth would smell with suicide.

Yet Emerson could not make the problem go away. With or without Hawthorne as a neighbor to remind him of it, it was as fundamental as existence itself. Emerson admitted as much to himself the summer after he had had Thoreau plant the newlyweds' garden: "It is very unhappy, but too late to be helped, the discovery we have made that we exist. That discovery is called the Fall of Man."

\*          \*          \*

The following summer of 1843 James Clarke performed the marriage of another Peabody sister, that of Mary to Horace Mann. James remained a Transcendentalist, but one acceptable to an increasing segment of more conventional Boston society, and he rather feared the complacency that might come with this position. Margaret had cautioned him, "You have chosen your path, you have sounded out your lot, your duties are before you. Now beware the mediocrity that threatens middle age, its limitation of thought and interest, its dullness of fancy, its too external life, and mental thinness." For his part, James admitted he had lost some of the fire of his youth, although others had not. To Margaret he wrote, "William [Henry Channing] and [Ralph] Waldo [Emerson] were obedient when young, and we were rebellious. They now are disposed to spurn restraints, which we are not indisposed to accept. Is it not so?" Perhaps, for Margaret at least, it was not entirely so.

She was just beginning to enter her social activist–reformer phase. In the spring she wrote an article for *The Dial* called "The Great Lawsuit," a protofeminist analysis of woman's present estate in a male-dominated society, which would form the basis of her book *Woman in the Nineteenth Century* in 1845. That summer she traveled to Niagara Falls with Caroline Sturgis and James and Sarah, continuing down the Great Lakes to the frontier town of Chicago where the younger Clarke brothers, William and Abraham, had a drugstore. James returned home, but sent Margaret fifty dollars, which allowed her and Sarah to continue traveling through the Illinois prairie and north into Wisconsin and Michigan, writing and, in Sarah's case, sketching. William Clarke accompanied them through the Rock River country, and Margaret wrote James:

> I have become a friend to your brother William too. I always thought I should and now I am. I do not know whether he is the most engaging companion, or most to be loved as a man; he is so open and free and sprightly, yet large and noble in all his feelings.

On the way home, Margaret stopped in New York, where she met Horace Greeley, the editor of the *New York Tribune,* and the Swedenborgian Henry James, Sr., father of the then-infant sons William and Henry.

The record of Margaret's journey was published the following year, 1844, as *Summer on the Lakes,* with engravings by Sarah added for the second edition. The book is scarcely a travel book by modern standards, but a discursive compendium of poetry (including a long piece by James), imaginary dialogues, and Romantic musings which do not seem to have much to do with the landscape over which Margaret and Sarah traveled. But the book was well received—save by Orestes Brownson, who described Margaret as "a heathen princess, though of what god or goddess we will not pretend to say"—especially by Horace Greeley's *Tribune,* who offered Margaret a job as a staff critic and reporter on the strength of it.

The *Tribune*'s self-described mission as an "Anti-Slavery, Anti-War, Anti-Tobacco, Anti-Seduction, Anti-Grogshop, Brothels, Gambling Houses" organ of the people did not seem to have much in common with Margaret's Goethian "march of mind." But in the course of *Summer on the Lakes* Margaret had also interviewed the women of immigrant families as well as the native people they were displacing, and wondered aloud about the effects of industry and economic exploitation on the frontier. That mixture of idealism and activism was exactly what interested Greeley, and he was anxious to have Margaret on his staff.

Margaret was flattered but unsure. At last free of economic constraints, now that her youngest brother had attained his majority and her sister was married (to Ellery Channing), Margaret had imagined that her first priority would be the trip to Europe she had for so long postponed. But Greeley had offered her a handsome salary and the chance to do literary and journalistic work that seemed the logical outgrowth of everything she had striven for, and to do it from a position of influence and power in the nation's greatest city.

There also was the matter of William Clarke, who had arrived in Boston that spring. Clarke had written to her earlier from Chicago and described her affect on him as "one who learned to hold a strange masterkey over my thoughts and character." Margaret then wrote a poem to him:

> May generous love glow in his inmost hear,
> Truth to its utterance lend the only art;
> While more a man, may he be more the child;
> More thoughtful be, but the more sweet and mild;
> May growing wisdom, mixed with sprightly cheer,
> Bless his own breast and those who hold him dear.

William prolonged his stay in Boston from April into May. Margaret was now deeply in love with him, referring to him as her "*herzens kind*"—her heart's own child, her companion in a "mutual visionary life." But by the end of the month, William had made his position clear and returned to Chicago, leaving her a poem that read, ". . . hope will linger long / But the time has come to sever what to join were wrong."

Later, Margaret wondered aloud to Caroline Sturgis:

> In the case of mein herzens kind, too, was it not a well grounded hope? Had not he all? The exquisite sense, the recreative genius, the capacity for religion planted in an unsullied youth. My love for him was, indeed, pure; how could there come a shadow? I know it will pass, but how could it come? How could aught of Death poison one sultry day these pure waters?

Margaret loved William as a man—a man younger, less "finished" but more vital than most she knew—but also as a kind of son, and for that reason the relationship, although intense, did not end as bitterly as those with George Davis and Sam Ward. When William was gone her pain was akin to "the deserted heart of an old person;" her love had been "a holy mother's joy in this birth of the soul," and now the boy was a man and had of life's necessity moved on and away.

Margaret was thirty-four years old, a spinster by anyone's reckoning, as was Sarah, thirty-six and feeling adrift after the recent death of her teacher Washington Allston. She told Margaret how it was to age:

> As life advances she sees two faces, one spotlessly fair like the Virgin in [Raphael's] the Madonna del Pesce, a beauty not so much eloquent with soul as serenely the untouched fairness of virgin womanhood. As soon as this has appeared to her, it is suddenly displaced by one of an ugliness exactly opposed to this. And, as the years pass, the beautiful face becomes more beautiful, and the ugly one more ugly.

Margaret and Sarah visited Sophia Peabody Hawthorne regularly at Concord that summer, and it was Margaret's greatest joy to hold Sophia and Nathaniel's newborn daughter Una in her lap, against her breast. She gave Sarah an engraving of Raphael's *Descent from the Cross* with a poem she had written to accompany it:

> Virgin Mother Mary mild:
> It was thine to see the child
> Gift of the Messiah dove,
> Pure blossom of ideal love,
> Break, upon the guilty cross
> The seeming promise of his life!
> Of faith, of hope, of love a loss
> Deepened all thy bosom's strife
> Brow down bent and heart strings torn
> Fainting, by frail arms upborne.

Sometimes Margaret and Caroline Sturgis shared a bed and Margaret awoke, her incessant headache stilled, thinking the two of them might be Mary and Elizabeth in the hills of Judea, awaiting the births of Jesus and John. And she wrote to herself, "Yes, it is only love, that heaven on earth, that can make any mortal cease for a moment to be lonely: that divines, and its knowledge is divine. Sages must be alone, children and lovers are not. But it is no easier to be always a lover than always a child: so the soul of a mortal must often be alone." And Mary—whose image pursued Margaret, who would not leave her mind—most loving, most loved, was in the end most alone of all.

Margaret's *ideas* about God and religion had not changed, but these signs—of the virgin and her son and their love and her desolation—preoccupied her, waking and sleeping; these and worse. She had decided to accept Greeley's offer and go to New York. The Monday before she was due to leave, she

slept from 8 till 7 next morning and had a good sleep, except for a terrible dream about Caroline. I thought she was lost on the sea-shore and that I vainly attempted to go and save her. My feet seemed rooted to one spot and my cloak of *red silk* kept falling off when I tried to go. At last the waves would wash up her dead body on the hard strand and then drew it back again.

Death came by drowning, as William's love came by "pure waters," like the flood of Jones Very's dementing faith. Margaret went to New York, half-driven, half-pursued, knowing that whatever she chose to believe, in whatever guise, God hunted her.

# NINE

Margaret spent two years in New York. In the spring of 1845, *Woman in the Nineteenth Century* was published to both widespread praise and condemnation of its program of Emersonian self-reliance and self-development for unleashing women's untapped potential. Both William Henry Channing and Lydia Maria Child were in New York, William as a minister to the city's slums and Lydia as editor of the *National Anti-Slavery Standard*. Each encouraged her engagement in social issues, and Margaret investigated and wrote about prisons, insane asylums, prostitution, mistreatment of immigrants, and child labor. By 1846, a journalist named Edgar Allan Poe was writing a profile of her, portraying her as the journalistic conscience of New York.

That was not to say Margaret had forgotten literature. As the *Tribune*'s chief reviewer, she wrote a generous review of a first novel called *Typee* by Herman Melville. Later that year, on August 4, Melville married in Boston, and his bride, Elizabeth Shaw, chose to receive her wedding day communion from James Clarke. Three days before, James had seen Margaret off from Boston harbor on the Cunard ship *Cambria*. Abandoning the wealth and fame she had accrued in New York, she was going to Europe at last. By now, Brook Farm had closed and Transcendentalism in Concord seemed less a vital force than a sideshow presided over by a beleaguered Emerson. That year Hawthorne wrote, "Never was a poor little country village with such a variety of queer, strangely dressed, oddly behaved mortals, most of whom took upon themselves to be important agents of the world's destiny, yet were simply bores of a very intense water." But in Europe, the land of Raphael and Goethe, Margaret was sure it would be otherwise: The mind and history were advancing together, and the revolution was under way.

*       *       *

Margaret's reputation, as well as letters of recommendation from Emerson, had preceded her arrival in Europe, and shortly after landing in England she had met Wordsworth, Carlyle, and others of note. But she was most taken by Giuseppe Mazzini, the exiled Italian republican leader, a revolutionary "whom holiness has purified, but nowhere dwarfed the man." Traveling on to France, she met George Sand and another exiled revolutionary, the Polish poet Adam Mickiewicz. Margaret formed an immediate and passionate attachment to Mickiewicz, who in turn saw Margaret as a feminist Romantic-revolutionary prophet, "a spirit who has known the old world, who has sinned in the old world and who seeks to make known that old world in the new. Her base is in the old world; her sphere of action is in the new world; her peace is in the world to come. She is called upon to feel, to speak, to move within these three worlds." He also advised her to reconsider her commitment to remaining a virgin, which she had recommended in *Woman in the Nineteenth Century* as a means by which women might preserve their autonomy. Thus exhorted to revolutionary action—"Your mission is to contribute to the deliverance of the Polish, French, and American woman"—she left at last for Italy, her perennial goal, her soul's home.

Margaret arrived first in Genoa, sailed on to Naples and by Easter week was in Rome, which was celebrating not only the spring holidays but the political reforms taking place under the new pope. Pius IX, who as sovereign of the Italian Papal States was Rome's and central Italy's secular ruler, seemed likely to introduce a more representative government and perhaps even to loosen the church's control in favor of a republic of the kind favored by Mazzini. Margaret, filing reports to the *Tribune,* doubted this—the pope "is not great enough," she opined after seeing him in a procession—but was herself distracted by other events during Easter week. Having attended vespers at St. Peter's, Margaret lost her companions in the crowd on the piazza and, appearing bewildered, was approached by a good-looking Italian who asked if he could be of assistance. The man was Giovanni Ossoli, age twenty-six, son of an aristocratic family with a long tradition of service to the papacy but who himself was of re-publican sympathies. Unable to find a carriage, Ossoli walked Margaret all the way back to her hotel in the Corso and kissed her hand in farewell.

She could not but be drawn to him, but in the atmosphere of the Roman spring she was also attracted to others. She met an Ameri-can painter in his early twenties named Thomas Hicks, and sent him a letter with the salutation "Dear Youth" and the message "I want to know and to love you and to have you love me." Hicks painted Mar-garet—a book in her lap and a statue of Eros peering over her shoul-der—but his attentions ceased there. Margaret meanwhile visited Florence and that autumn toured northern Italy, using Goethe's *Ital-ian Journey* as her guidebook. She spent the winter in Rome, read-ing, sightseeing, and growing closer to Giovanni Ossoli.

The new year, 1848, proved to be the year of revolution throughout Europe, with the governments in Sicily, Paris, Prague, and Vienna falling. The collapse of the latter, which ruled northern Italy, prompted rebellion in Milan and thence down the peninsula. In April, Margaret addressed her *Tribune* readers as follows:

> To you, people of America, it may perhaps be given to look on and learn in time for a preventative wisdom. You may learn the real meaning of the words FRATERNITY, EQUALITY; you may, despite the apes of the past who strive to tutor you, learn the needs of a true democracy. You may in time learn to reverence, learn to guard, the true aristocracy of a nation, the only real nobles—the LABORING CLASSES.

At least in her rhetoric, Margaret had taken up Mickiewicz's ad-vice, and she had also followed it in another particular: She and Gio-vanni Ossoli had become lovers, and she had been pregnant with his child since January. The Romantic individualist-idealist was gone together with the virgin, and so too, for the moment, were the Marian visions and intimations of the divine that had shadowed her. That summer she wrote Emerson and put to rest any residual questions about the conflict between them eight years before:

> Some years ago I thought you very unjust because you did not lend full faith to my spiritual experiences, but I see you were quite right. I thought I had tasted of the true elixir, and that the want of daily bread or the pangs of imprisonment would never make me a complaining beggar. . . . Those were glorious hours, and angels certainly visited me, but there must have been too much earth—too much taint of weakness and folly—so that baptism did not suffice. I know now those same things, but at present they are words, not living spells.

On the one hand, for Margaret the political—the reality of approaching guns—had subsumed the personal; but then, the personal, more real than even that reality, overshadowed everything. On September 7, 1848, in a remote village away from Rome, she gave birth to a son and named him Angelo.

Two months later, Pius IX abandoned Rome, and a provisional government called an election for the New Year. Margaret had returned to Rome that winter, and a letter from James reached her there, wondering what had become of her and when she was returning home. "If you do not soon return we shall all be Catholics," he wrote, alluding to the latest round of Transcendentalist defections to the Roman church, and in particular that of Orestes Brownson. Margaret wrote back, assuring him that "spirits that have once been sincerely united and tended together a sacred flame, never become entirely strangers to one another's life." She hoped he might come to Europe soon, as indeed he was then planning. His sister Sarah was already well along with plans to come to Italy, perhaps to stay there permanently, and Margaret urged her to set off despite the unstable political situation. Neither to James, nor indeed to anyone at home save Caroline Sturgis and Sarah (whom she had sworn to secrecy) had she mentioned Ossoli or the baby Angelo, although both the infant's frail health and the advisability of remaining in Rome constantly worried her.

On February 15, 1849, the Roman Republic was declared by

the city's interim secular government. France, Naples, Spain, and Austria responded by calling for the reimposition of papal rule, and the siege of Rome was under way in April. Margaret tended the wounded in the makeshift hospital established in the pope's abandoned Quirinal palace. She and Giovanni sent Angelo out of the city to be tended by a wet nurse—who, they discovered, neglected the baby in favor of her own child. When Margaret was reunited with him, he was malnourished and listless.

Throughout much of this time, although she filed optmistic reports on the progress of the republic for the *Tribune,* Margaret was dejected. In March, she wrote William Henry Channing:

> Father of light, conduct my feet
> Through life's dark, dangerous road;
> Let each advancing step still bring
> Me nearer to my God.

These clumsy lines from some hymn I learned in childhood are always recurring. Ah! How very sad it is, that all these precious first feelings that were meant to kindle steady fire on the altar of my life were wasted. I am not what I should be on this earth. I could not be.

Three months later, with the collapse of the republic and its supporters, including Margaret and Giovanni, expelled from Rome by the occupying armies, she told William the truth:

I am so much merged now in the young growth of my child. For I am a mother now, and the spirit of my little one embellishes more and more its frail temple, so frail it requires great care from me to keep it fixed on earth. His smiles are an exceeding rich reward, and often give my heart amid the cries of carnage and oppression an even bird-like joy. Yet for his possession also, whether given or lent, a great price is exacted.

The pain was not only maternal but social. By autumn, when Margaret, Giovanni, and Angelo settled in the relative calm of Florence, her relationship with Ossoli was common knowledge in Italy and word had spread to America. Elizabeth Barrett Browning, who had met Margaret in London and herself was now settled with her husband, Robert, in Tuscany, remarked, "The American authoress, Miss Fuller has taken us by surprise at Florence, retiring from the Roman field with a husband and a child above a year old. Nobody had even suspected a word of this underplot, and her American friends stood in mute astonishment before this apparition of them here." It was, and remains, unclear whether Margaret and Giovanni ever formally married—something then exceedingly difficult in Italy between a Protestant and a Catholic—and Margaret's detractors at home were quick to seize on this as evidence of her advocacy of "free love," among other feminist heresies. Nor were people always kind about Giovanni, who was regarded even by the Brownings—great friends of the Ossolis over the next nine months—as attractive but "with no pretension to cope with his wife on any ground appertaining to the intellect."

The Brownings had a child about the same age as Angelo, and the two played together while their mothers talked. But Margaret found Florence less alluring than her beloved Rome, particularly as the fall turned to winter and the days grew frigid and the long nights were lit by "cold, statue-like moonlight, such as we have in New England, such as I do not remember in all my life of Italy." November, she told Sarah, who had put off her travel plans on account of the siege, to come to Italy by next spring, or risk missing her altogether. It seemed inevitable that she and Angelo and Giovanni—now, along with his family, ruined financially in the wake of the siege—must return to America if they were to survive. She wrote of all this and more on a late November evening on the Piazza Santa Maria Novella in a letter that is without a salutation, but which may have been written to James:

> I crossed the river for my afternoon walk, to see Mr. and Mrs. Browning. They have a beautiful little baby, two or three months younger than mine, so we have this in common with so many other sympathies.
>
> Now Ossoli is gone out, and I am alone in my little room, beside a bright fire. I have your letter before me, and I am

thinking how much I wish for you instead. Though your letter is very dear, and does me good, you are one of the persons I have wished so much might know about me without being told. I have thought a great deal about you, and things you used to tell me, and remembered little traits and pictures of your children that would surprise you. How pleasant it would be to talk over all these now and here; for you are quite right, it is in Italy we should have met. I wish I did know how to write to you about myself, but it is exceedingly difficult. I have lived in a much more full and true way than was possible in our country, and each day has been so rich in joys and pains, actions and sufferings, to say nothing of themes of observation, I have never yet had time to know the sum total—to reflect. My strength has been taxed to the uttermost to live. I have been deeply humiliated finding myself inferior to many noble occasions, but precious lessons have been given, and made me somewhat better, I think, than when you knew me. . . . I thought I knew before what is the mother's heart, I had felt so much love that seemed so holy and soft, that longed to purify, to protect, to solace *infinitely*; but it was nothing to what I feel now, and that sense for pure nature, for the eager, spontaneous life of childhood was very partial to me before. My little one seems nothing remarkable. I have no special visions; but to be with him, to take care of and play with him, gives me such delight, and does me so much good, that it is only now I feel poverty a great evil. . . . Should I succeed in cutting my way through the thorns and stand in a clear place at last, I shall be tired out and aged perhaps, or my little one will be dead. This last seems very probable, for Heaven has thus far always reclaimed the children I most loved. You ask my plans: they are very unsettled. . . . I suppose I will have to return to the U.S. . . . I hardly know how I am to get there either; even in the most economical way, direct from Leghorn or Genoa, is two hundred dollars for us both. I am very sick and suffer extremely at sea. I suppose it would be worse in these poor accommodations than it was in the steamer, and Ossoli is untried. We cannot afford to take a servant, and what would become of the baby if we were both sick. I never think of the voyage without fearing the baby will die in it.

*     *     *

James had in fact come to Europe that previous summer, but not, as Margaret wished, to Italy. And in speaking of the deaths of the children she most loved, she was speaking to him. On February 15, the day the Roman Republic was declared, James's firstborn son, Herman, aged nine, died of scarlet fever, as had Waldo Emerson seven years before. Five days before falling ill, the boy had dug a path through the snow that remained visible for two weeks after his death, and William Henry Channing remembered him standing on the doorstep, holding a volume of Plato. Then the fever struck him, and on the third day he was dead.

James's grief was quieter, slower in its gestation than Emerson's. He went about his business, and left in July on the trip he had planned to Europe. He was named a delegate to the peace conference held in Paris that August under the auspices of Louis Napoleon, whose army had so recently driven the Ossolis from Rome. Louis appeared and Victor Hugo presided, and afterward James felt "the Peace Congress probably did just as much good as any man could reasonably expect." And then James left for the Alps where, if going to Italy was still ill-advised, he could yet, at long last, walk in the footsteps of Goethe, seventy years after the master himself had walked.

It was with Goethe that James and Margaret had begun together, when they were nineteen. It was Goethe, through Faust, who had given definition to the God they sought:

> Who has the right to name Him? . . . The all-embracer, the all-sustainer, does he not hold and sustain you, me, Himself? Does not the sky overarch us, is not the earth solid beneath us, do not the eternal stars climb the heavens all around? Fill your heart with it, so great is it, and when you are utterly filled with that bliss, then call it what you will—fortune, heart, love, God! I have no name for it. Feeling is everything, names but sound and smoke, clouding heaven's fire.

And the poem on the "Descent from the Cross" that Margaret had given Sarah was surely little more than her paraphrase of Gretchen's words before the shrine of the Mater Dolorosa:

> O Bend Thou,
> Mother of Sorrows; send Thou
> A look of pity on my pain.
>
> Thine heart's blood welling,
> With pangs past telling,
> Thou gazest where Thy Son hangs slain.
>
> Thou, heavenward gazing,
> Art deep sighs raising
> On high for His and for Thy pain. . . .

And it was the "Jungfrau," the Virgin Mother, who had stalked Margaret's heart, who as the Transcendental feminine provided Faust's final "verklärüng," his transfiguration, the heavenly "clearing" of his vision:

> All earth comprises
> Is symbol alone;
> What there never suffices
> As fact here is known;
> All past the humanly
> Wrought here in love;
> The Eternal-Womanly
> Draws us above.

James spent a day hiking around the base of the Alp called the Jungfrau, and then, the next day, he went into a little church and collapsed in grief: "The memory of dear Herman came over me so strongly that I thought my heart would break." The other people in the church who "noticed my convulsive sobs must have thought me some great sinner, awakened and convinced. . . ."

Before he turned back, at the crest of the Alps, he might well have imagined he could see all the way into Italy, where Margaret, too, was preoccupied with her child:

> During the siege of Rome I could not see my little boy. What I endured at that time in various ways not many would survive. In the burning sun I went every day to wait in the crowd for letters about him. Often they did not come. I saw blood that had streamed on the wall close to where Ossoli was. I have here a piece of bomb that burst close to him. I sought solace in tending the suffering men. But when I saw the beautiful fair young men bleeding to death, or mutilated for life, I felt all the woe of all the mothers who had nursed each to that full flower to see it thus cut down. I felt the consolation too, for those youths died worthily. I was the Mater Dolorosa, and I remembered that the midwife who helped Angelino into the world came from the sign of the Mater Dolorosa. I thought, even if he lives, if he comes into the world at this great troubled time, terrible with perplexed duties, it may be to die thus at twenty. . . . It seemed then I was willing he should die. But when I saw him lingering as he did all August and July between life and death, I could not let him go unless I would go with him. . . . I resolved to live day by day and hour by hour for his dear sake and feed on ashes when offered. So if he is only treasure lent, if he must go as sweet Waldo did, as *my* children do, I shall at least have these days and hours with him. Now he is in the highest health and so gay—We cannot but feel happy in him, though the want of money is so serious a thing. . . . I suppose we shall find ways. The governor of the world must have his alms days every now and then; we will eat the charity soup ourselves and buy pap for Nino. If I can but be well, there's the rub always.

But Goethe must have the last word: "The Gods, the unending ones gave everything to their darlings in full—all joys unending, all pains unending, in full." As for the other consolations she had sought, Margaret wrote a Quaker friend in New York, "You are a

Christian. You know I never pretended to be, except in dabs and sparkles here and there."

\*          \*          \*

The voyage Margaret so dreaded began on May 17, 1850. The Ossolis had spent their last night in Florence with the Brownings, and then boarded the *Elizabeth* under the command of Captain Seth Hasty, carrying a small complement of passengers and one hundred and fifty tons of Carrara marble. A week out of port, Captain Hasty fell ill and was relieved at the helm by his second officer, Henry Bangs. The Atlantic crossing passed without incident in fine weather, and on July 18, Bangs announced that he expected them to make landfall at New York harbor the next day. At two-thirty in the morning, the *Elizabeth* ran aground on a sandbar off Fire Island, and battered by swells fed by a tropical storm off the Carolinas, began to break up.

The *Elizabeth* was coming apart in her midships, but the forecastle remained intact. Bangs ordered the crew to help the passengers move there, but his order was refused, and he and the second mate assisted Margaret, Angelo, and the rest across the broken flooded decks. But by morning, the forecastle itself was beginning to break up, and although the *Elizabeth* was but four hundred yards from shore, the surf was too high and rough for lifeboats to reach her. Meanwhile, a crowd numbering in the hundreds had gathered on the beach, and the looting began: paintings, casks of olive oil, castile soap, and bolts of silk were hauled away and sold on the streets of Patchogue, the nearest town.

At noon, most of the crew had abandoned ship. The few remaining tried to persuade Margaret to lash herself to a plank and let the surf carry her to shore while Giovanni and a crew member swam Angelo to safety. Instead Margaret gave up her own life preserver to one of the sailors still remaining and stood fast, refusing to be separated from Angelo. In the end, as the forecastle was being torn apart by the rising gale, the ship's carpenter seized Angelo and swam for shore with Ossoli, where all three were later found drowned. Margaret was last seen standing in what remained of the forecastle. A great wave broke over her, and she was swept into the flood.

The news reached New England a few days later, and Emerson sent Henry Thoreau down to Fire Island to see what could be done, to retrieve "all the intelligence and, if possible, any fragments of manuscript or other property." But there was little that had not been lost, destroyed, or hauled away by the scavengers: only pieces of Margaret's writing desk, and a few papers of no consequence.

Later, Giovanni's coat was found on the beach together with a body which, since the others had all been recovered, was presumed to be Margaret's. Henry Thoreau went to identify it, but found it had been so abraded and beaten in the surf that neither its sex nor any other characteristic could be distinguished: "Simply some bones washed up on the beach," he recorded. "They would not detain a walker there more than so much seaweed." He paid to have the cadaver buried and the spot marked, and returned to Concord. In his journal he wrote, "I do not think much of the actual, it is something that we have long since done with."

In a letter to a friend, he expanded on the thought:

I have in my pocket a button which I ripped off the coat of the Marquis of Ossoli, on the seashore the other day. Held up, it intercepts the light—an actual button—and yet all the life it is connected with is less substantial to me, and interests me less, than my faintest dream. Our thoughts are the epochs in our lives; all else is but as a journal of the winds that blew while we were here.

By Thoreau's reckoning, all that mattered of Margaret was in her thoughts, in the march of mind she had so desired to manifest, and there would not be much point in pursuing her memory, in weighing the facts and accidents of her life. In that respect, perhaps it is Thoreau—to whom she was never close and whose peregrinatory, asynchronous prose style she told him she could not read "without pain"—was her one true heir: More than any Transcendentalist's world, Thoreau's was fully emptied of "God" or "meaning" beyond what the mind could bring to it. Nothing but thought stood between life and death, between existence and nothingness. Actuality, what men had imagined was real, was mute; it scarcely cast a shadow.

But Thoreau (perhaps) aside, the others were preoccupied with

Margaret. It is not clear, for example, what Emerson hoped to accomplish by sending Thoreau to Fire Island, except to respond to the sense that he or an emissary ought to be in the place where she had died, as though to watch over it, to gather and take possession of the relics. In the same way, Emerson quickly conceived the idea for a biography or memorial volume; and he, James, and William Henry Channing worked on this project for the next eighteen months. When it was published in 1852, their *Memoirs of Margaret Fuller Ossoli* became the best-selling book in the United States until it was displaced by *Uncle Tom's Cabin* later that year.

By the standards of the time, the *Memoirs* is a quite frank account of Margaret's life, quoting at length from letters and journals that give a fairly explicit picture of Margaret's crises of the spirit and the heart. But what was beyond mention was the question whether Margaret and Giovanni had been truly married and whether Angelo was legitimate. When Sarah Clarke at last made her own journey to Italy a year after Margaret's death, she and her traveling companion, Julia Ward Howe (to whom James in 1861 would casually suggest that she try writing some new words to the tune "John Brown's Body") tried to investigate the matter, but found no evidence to settle it. For all their radicalism, there were some proprieties and conventions that the Transcendentalists were unable to dismiss. At one point James had described Margaret's drowning in the wreck of the *Elizabeth* as her "euthanasia." He had feared before she ever left for home that neither her work nor her life could flourish in America; worse, that her antifeminist critics would try by means of the Ossoli affair to destroy her reputation, and would succeed. The motto he, Emerson, and Channing chose for the *Memoirs* suggested as much: "Et quae tanta fuit Romam tibi causa videndi? Libertas!"—"And what was the great reason for your seeing Rome? Freedom!"

Whether because of it or by coincidence, Transcendentalism as a movement ended around the time of Margaret's death. The work of abolishing slavery seemed a much more pressing matter, and absorbed the energies of those who might otherwise have taken up the life lived at Concord and Brook Farm. With minor adjustments, Emerson's philosophy of the self could be, and soon was, made to seem but the latest in exhortations to the traditional American virtues of hard work, individualism, and good cheer. Even Transcendentalist pronouncements on religion did not look so disturbing once the chief preoccupation of the churches and clergy became morality rather than the mechanics of redemption. Compared with the business of enforcing godly conduct in this world—compared with abolition, temperance, and the protection of women and children—arguments about the exact nature of Jesus's humanity or the operations of miracles were rather beside the point. In spite of Thoreau, actuality rather than idealism—the practical sorting out of the nation's civic, economic, and social arrangements that would culminate in war within ten years—had triumphed. In 1855, James bought the abandoned Brook Farm, five years later, he turned it over to the Massachusetts 2nd Regiment as a camp and training ground.

As Emerson rather dolefully put it in his journal not long after Margaret's death, "After us, mysticism should go out of style for a very long time."

# TEN

The great reason for my seeing California was indeed freedom; just as crucial was the pursuit of what I understood to be the transcendent. But to arrive, as I did, in 1970—when Haight Street in San Francisco was largely the province of tour buses and dealers in heroin and methamphetamine and Telegraph Avenue in Berkeley had been rebuilt as a riotproof pedestrian and bus mall—was like turning up in Concord five years too late. Later in the year, I went up to Mendocino and visited a commune set on twenty or thirty acres, a Brook Farm in the redwoods. The buildings were handsome and well constructed, but mostly empty. Of the two dozen or so original communards, only three or four remained, the rest having tired of conflicts and power struggles over the division of labor, the governance of the community, and the manners in which its members would be or not be permitted to eat, meditate, and have sex.

I was not discouraged by this. I had escaped New England, the control of my family, and the probings of Dr. Freed. I was enrolled in art school, and the faculty's absorption in "process" and "conceptual" art left my lack of either visual acuity or skill in draftsmanship and the like blessedly unexposed. Talking about art was, at this historical moment, as good as making art, and talking was something I could do. The things I said do not now seem to me to be either interesting or clear, but, as in art, coherence and clarity were less important than authenticity, in particular personal authenticity. Every individual was the creator, audience, and sole critic of his or her own self, and the self was one's magnum opus, in my case my only opus. I was, to adopt a description normally considered unflattering, full of my self. That is not to say that I was primarily "selfish" (though I doubtless was), for a fully realized, "actualized" self was the greatest good one could offer to others. True morality and every other virtue followed from it; the personal was political, and politics was experiential, subjective. You could not, said the prime psychological truism of the time, love others until you loved yourself. Every person was his or her own redeemer; once redeemed, those selves could collectively save the world.

It seemed a time of great consequence. I was in hot and earnest pursuit of love, art, justice, and the divine, and they were all not only connected, but were, in me, in the bildungsroman that was my young life, a single seamless thing. I knew nothing of either Goethe or the literary genre of yearning and identity he created in which to be young, to be an artist, to be in love, and to be a spiritual seeker were the same task, one's life's work. Everything I felt seemed magnified in the larger world and mirrored back to me, for at that moment what concerned the young seemed to concern and consume the world entire. The primacy of self-fulfillment and self-emancipation—the right to construct oneself freely, without political, economic, social, or even psychological hindrance—was evident in the movements against war—not just against the war in Vietnam, but against any war—and racial discrimination, in feminism, and in the "sexual revolution." More than nations or societies or institutions, selves had rights that could not and must not be brooked or abridged.

That was not to say that I had no use for institutions and the values they conferred, but I wanted their benefits without their restrictions. Thus my girlfriend and I moved in together, living as man and wife without marriage, an act that seems to have shocked our friends and families in 1970 nearly as much as it did Margaret Fuller's one hundred and twenty years before. Similarly, I attended school, but with the understanding that it was a resource, a collection of tools, from among whose parts I might pick and choose to construct an education that was, according to my own lights, coherent and useful to me.

I took the same approach to religion, which, like everything else, was difficult to separate from the other aspects of my life, from art and politics and love. But my religion was mostly colored by psychology, by the notion of "personal growth." I wanted, not unreasonably, psychotherapy without Dr. Freed—without psychotherapists—and I wanted religion without priests. I wanted, as Margaret had wanted, and as Walt Whitman would write five years after her death, a religion in which "every man shall be own priest . . . through the divinity of themselves." That religion would be more or less identical with therapy, for surely what gave solace to the soul gave solace to the mind. What were evil and despair but a "negative head trip"; what were redemption and enlightenment but "self-actualization"?

To that end, I read deeply in Eastern religion, or at least in Western popularizers of Eastern religion, like Alan Watts. In retrospect, Watts is a figure I find sympathetic. An Englishman with a literary education, he was an ex-Anglo-Catholic Episcopal priest who moved to San Francisco during the late-fifties Beat era and became a popular speaker and prolific author. I think the first book of his that I encountered was called *The Book: On the Taboo Against Knowing Who You Are,* the very title of which left my scalp tingling. It was an amalgam of Zen Buddhism, the sociology of Paul Goodman (another seminal figure in my reading), and what was becoming known as humanistic psychology. Watts claimed to be and no doubt believed himself to be a serious scholar and practitioner of Zen Buddhism, but I am not sure Watts's Buddhism would be very recognizable to anyone in the East; stripped of monastic and intellectual rigor and adapted to Watts's home just north of San Francisco, it might as well have been called Marin Buddhism.

That was of no consequence to me. The point about Watt's theology—which he called a joyous cosmology—was that it equated personal authenticity and freedom with the quest for the transcendent, with enlightenment itself. Being truly yourself, whoever that was, in the here and now, exercising perfect authenticity with perfect freedom, would unite you with the Godhead, whatever that was. There was some work involved, some variety of meditation, but I could never quite get myself to remain still enough to perform it. I was serious, but I was also eager.

This was a pretty solipsistic theology, but it did have an outward-looking component: nature worship. Along with Watts, Herman

Hesse (whose work seemed more or less a novelization of Watts), and their ilk, another important component in my reading was the coffee-table-sized Sierra Club books with their luminous landscape and nature photographs by Eliot Porter and Ansel Adams. I wrote my high school senior thesis based almost entirely on one of these, featuring photographs of the Big Sur coast with quotations from the California poet Robinson Jeffers. Jeffers was doubtless a crank and a misanthrope, but to me his self-styled quasi-monasticism—he lived in an isolated stone tower overlooking the Pacific—was an ideal in which the union of the self and nature was identical to the self's union with God. I did not ask myself why the parts of creation that I deemed beautiful were good and those deemed otherwise—including, for Jeffers, most other human beings—were not; nor did I think much about the possible contradiction between pursuing radical individualism on the one hand and universal truth on the other. In this I was consistent with the Emersonian, Thoreauvian Transcendentalist ancestry of the sixties, which despite its present-day critics, is nothing if not American.

I had only a passing acquaintance with Emerson and Thoreau, and little knowledge of their own fascination with Eastern philosophy and nature, or of their benign dilettantism, of which I and the sixties also partook. The fact was, I was too impatient to read them, but I did grasp the spirit if not the letter of one aspect of their thought. I wanted my self-education itself to be transcendent; I wanted a little of this and a little of that—Zen, LSD, backpacking, throwing pots, taking thirty-five-millimeter pictures, and growing zucchini—to add up to everything. My favorite book of all was *The Whole Earth Catalog,* which to me did indeed seem to contain everything worth knowing about, which turned browsing among my various curiosities and desires into the closest thing I could imagine to meditation.

Although I was much drawn to solitude—providing it didn't mean being alone too often—I was also open to persons and group activities that promoted "growth" without impinging on my autonomy. Thus, I sat and drank peyote tea at the weekly "Monday Night Class" of San Francisco's all-purpose guru and acid chaplain, Stephen Gaskin, and attended Esalen's evening encounter groups at San Francisco's First Unitarian Church. I saved up money to enroll in a weekend-long Esalen smorgasbord of encounter, Gestalt therapy, and psychodrama, billed as "A Time to Grow," forty-eight hours of soul-baring, truth-telling, and centering. But, racking my brain to recall what transpired there, I can only remember that among the participants was a twentyish woman in an advanced state of pregnancy. I could not take my eyes off her. Pregnancy, infants, and children in general were not much in evidence in the parts of San Francisco and Berkeley I frequented, but the rarity of her condition was not as striking as the presence, the weight and gravity, it lent her amid the existential posturing that surrounded her. She, the Madonna, the mother biding her time, awaiting her delivery, was, in a room full of people proclaiming their authenticity, the one thing that was real.

That I recall this, and not much more, is not meant to be evidence that I dismiss that time and what happened during it as so much nonsense. It is a popular position to take these days, but reflects, I think, not a wish to expose past self-indulgence and hypocrisy, but a deeply cynical age's unease at the memory of one far less so. The years from, say, 1961 to 1974 were idealistic, not necessarily in the reality of their goodness and virtue, but in their belief that goodness and virtue were possible, and that fairly ordinary people could aspire to them and bring them into being. I can only speak for myself, but I was in deadly earnest in my enthusiasms and crusades, my reading, filmgoing, and absorption in music, and in my use of psychedelic drugs. Rightly or wrongly, I saw all these things as aspects of a crucial quest to find myself, and thus find the good and true. If anything, I wish I had taken the whole business, and myself, less seriously. I may have been a fool, but I was a sincere one. What may truly offend the era's present-day critics is not its falsity or pretensions, but the sheery corny, unironic wholesomeness of its credulity. It is akin to what made Hawthorne uncomfortable about Emerson, and what would have made him positively cringe about Whitman.

I do not know whether in all this I was truly fashioning a self (and a lens through which to comprehend myself and the world) or merely a scrapbook of enthusiasms. As time went on, the view did not grow sharper, but more diffuse, but I didn't mind this. It was like the beauty I saw in nature: You couldn't pinpoint exactly which aspects of a view made it beautiful; you only knew that somehow the whole was beautiful, and the vagueness, the seeming ineffableness of it, made it more so; that vagueness suggested that God was somehow manifest in it. My own sense of self was most complete when I could insert myself into these tableaux, which didn't need to be of Sierra Club purity to be affecting, to become not just views but epiphanies.

There would be a time at the end of my adolescence, when I was about twenty, when driving on the Pacific Coast Highway on a mid-summer day with "Stairway to Heaven" playing on the radio would seem like heaven—not in actuality, perhaps, but in possibility, the possibility of effectuating all my desires. And that feeling seemed as true a sensation of the good and the real as I could recall in a long time. I had come, after much searching and every best intention, to mistake craving for wonder. I was now, at last, an adult. My Goethe years were done.

Perhaps this says something about why the neo-Transcendentalist program of the sixties was no more explicitly successful than its original a century and a half ago, at least not for me. Beyond failing to end poverty, war, and injustice, it seems somehow to have diminished the very credulousness—the capacity for belief and faith—that created and, for a while, sustained it. In my own case, the grab bag of notions I assembled—what would then have more kindly been described as an eclectic, alternative spirituality—simply lost its ability to console or even interest me very much. My fabrication of it entailed burning such other bridges as I had, Christian or otherwise, and so I was left with my "self," such as it was. And perhaps this reflects something of the position of our age generally. For I had wanted the substance, the essence of the institutions with which I had grown up—church, family, and so on—without the nuisance of their form, their restrictions and rules and expectations.

But the very modes of authority and tradition that I found objectionable were what give these institutions their structure and shape, and without them they tend to collapse. My memory of those days is rather like that: shapeless, atomized, a world of discrete, isolate selves who, for all their good will and better intentions have individuated themselves to the extent that only the self is real, and nothing outside it can be believed in or even taken at face value.

This is a species of doubt of a different magnitude than the doubt Margaret or the other Transcendentalists (save those like Emerson and James Clarke endowed with an instinctive and unshakable Christian faith) experienced. They were always mightily convinced of some kind of divinity, and rarely lacked for signs and intimations of it. But my disbelief was starker than that, a sort of impotence. I wanted to believe, but I could neither detect nor imagine anything to believe in, and I could not decide whether this condition was evidence of a failing on my part or a failing on God's—a failure to exist. And this was how many people, some of them my ancestors and their acquaintances, felt after the wreck of the *Elizabeth*.

# ELEVEN

**W**as ever anything so tragical, so dreary, so unspeakably agonizing," thought Sophia Peabody Hawthorne, "as the image of Margaret on that wreck alone, sitting with her hands upon her knees and tempestuous waves breaking over her? But I cannot dwell upon it." The Hawthornes had moved to the Berkshires in western Massachusetts in May 1850 at the suggestion of Caroline Sturgis, who had the idea of turning the vicinity of Lenox into a Concord West; and already Sam and Anna Barker Ward and Ellery and Ellen Fuller Channing had taken up residence there. Caroline pressed Emerson to abandon Concord, or at least to make the Berkshires home while he worked on the *Memoirs,* but he remained at home and collaborated with William Channing and James Clarke.

James's friend and college classmate Oliver Wendell Holmes was meanwhile also summering in the Berkshires, and among his neighbors locally were Evert Duyckinck, editor of the *Literary World,* and one of his regular contributors, Herman Melville. It seemed only fitting that Melville and Hawthorne meet, as they did the first week of August and nearly every day thereafter.

To Melville, Hawthorne's writing was a revelation, not only in its craft but in its underlying sensibility, and Melville found Hawthorne the man just as compelling. Melville and Hawthorne—men who struck other people as dark, moody, and inscrutable—found each other easy to know, with the same preoccupations and same slightly detached view of a troubled and troubling world. Shortly after they met, Melville contributed an anonymous review of Hawthorne's *Mosses from an Old Manse* to the *Literary World,* remarking on its "mystical blackness" and "Puritanic gloom":

> Certain it is, however, that this great power of blackness in him derives its force from its appeals to that Calvinistic sense of Innate Depravity and Original Sin, from whose visitations, in some shape or other, no deeply thinking mind is always and wholly free. For, in certain moods, no man can weigh this world, without throwing in something, somehow like Original Sin, to strike the uneven balance.

No one has ever understood Hawthorne better; nor has anyone been a better foil for him than Melville, with his manic engagement with the world and his droll appreciation of its dark absurdities. The two men forged a friendship of deepest intensity that summer and fall, talking, walking, drinking, and writing; in Hawthorne's case, *The House of the Seven Gables;* in Melville's, *The Whale,* better known as *Moby Dick.* When Melville was not visiting Hawthorne's house, he was pressing Hawthorne to visit his:

> Do not think you are coming to any prim nonsensical house— that is nonsensical in the ordinary way. You won't be much bored with punctilios. You may do what you please—say or say *not* what you please. And if you feel any inclination for that sort of thing you spend the period of your visit in *bed,* if you like, every hour of your visit.
>
> Hark—There is some excellent Montado Sherry awaiting you and some most potent Port. We will have mulled wine with wisdom, and buttered toast with storytelling and crack jokes and bottles from morning till night.
>
> Come—no nonsense. If you don't, I will send Constables after you.

But the chief business of their relationship was theological, and in particular the problem of theodicy—of squaring a reputedly good God with a clockwork creation chockablock with evil: "The reason the mass of men fear God, and at bottom dislike Him, is because

they rather distrust His heart and fancy Him all brain like a watch."
To comprehend this was Melville and Hawthorne's great task and
calling—"I feel the Godhead is broken up like the bread at the Supper, and we are the pieces. Hence this infinite fraternity of feeling"—but it was an impossible one, a doomed attempt to say the
unsayable.

> We incline to think that God cannot explain His own secrets,
> and that He would like a little information upon certain
> points Himself. We mortals astonish Him as much as He us.
> But it is this *Being* of the matter; there lies the knot with
> which we choke ourselves. As soon as you say *Me*, a *God*, a
> *Nature*, so soon you jump off from your stool and hang from
> the beam. Yes, that word is the hangman. Take God out of
> the dictionary, and you would have Him in the street.

That it was a doomed attempt made it no less attractive to
Melville and Hawthorne, who were nothing if not aficionados of
doom and fatalism: "Though I wrote the Gospels in this century,"
Melville told Hawthorne, "I should die in the gutter." Provided the
writing was going well, they could live with that. Melville had high
hopes for *Moby Dick, or The Whale,* published at the end of 1851 and
dedicated, of course, to Hawthorne. Hawthorne himself had published *The Scarlet Letter* in 1850, *The House of the Seven Gables* in 1851,
and, in July 1852, *The Blithedale Romance,* his roman à clef based on
Brook Farm and Margaret Fuller in the form of the sensuous, brainy,
and inscrutable Zenobia. *Moby Dick* did not sell well, but Hawthorne
was now a phenomenon, as Melville reported to him:

> This name of "Hawthorne" seems to be ubiquitous. I have
> been on something of a tour lately, and it has saluted me vo-
> cally and typographically in all sorts of places and all sorts of
> ways. I was at the solitary Crusoeish island of Naushon (one
> of the Elizabeth group) and there, in a stately piazza, I saw it
> gilded on the back of a very new book, and in the hands of a
> clergyman. I went out to visit a gentleman in Brookline, and
> as we were sitting at our wine, in came the lady of the house,
> holding a beaming volume in her hand, from the city—"My

dear," to her husband, "I have brought you Hawthorne's new book."

The husband and wife were Mr. and Mrs. Newell, and the gentleman drinking with Melville was their boarder, George Griggs, the younger cousin of Susan Griggs, onetime fiancée of the rejected pamphleteer Aaron Bigelow.

George Griggs (who was also related to Sophia Hawthorne) was a lawyer in Boston and a friend and protégé of Judge Lemuel Shaw, Melville's father-in-law. Herman's older sister Helen was a frequent guest of the Shaws and through them became acquainted with George Griggs, to whom she soon became engaged. In January 1854, Helen and George were married by James Clarke, who had similarly offered the communion service on Hawthorne's wedding day.

By family accounts, George Griggs could be gruff and parsimonious, but Herman appears to have been fond of him. He frequently boarded at the Griggses' house in Longwood, and George used his political and legal connections to find work or a government appointment for Herman, whose books after *Moby Dick* had been neither critically nor commercially successful. But it was difficult to convince anyone to take on the increasingly melancholic, inebriate, and eccentric Melville, and in 1856—with his wife, the Griggses, and the rest of his family at a loss to do anything for or with him—Judge Shaw agreed to underwrite a recuperative voyage to Europe and the Middle East for him.

Hawthorne had had better luck than Melville with the political spoils system, having secured himself a consulship in England after the election of his college friend Franklin Pierce to the presidency in 1852. Upon landing in Liverpool, Herman went straight to Hawthorne. It was an awkward reunion: Hawthorne, like Herman's other friends and family, had tried and failed to get him an appointment, and, as Hawthorne wrote in his journal, Herman now seemed diminished, less diverted than put upon by his usual preoccupations:

Melville has not been well of late; he has been affected with neuralgic complaints in his head and limbs, and no doubt has suffered from too constant literary occupation, pursued without much success latterly; and his writings, for a long while past, have indicated a morbid state of mind. . . .

He stayed with us from Tuesday till Thursday; and on the intervening day, we took a pretty long walk [on the seashore] together, and sat down in a hollow among the sand hills (sheltering ourselves from the high, cool wind) and smoked a cigar. Melville, as he always does, began to reason of Providence and futurity, and of everything that lies beyond human ken, and informed me that he had "pretty much made up his mind to be annihilated"; but still he does not seem to rest in that anticipation; and, I think, will never rest until he gets hold of a definite belief. It is strange how he persists—and has persisted ever since I knew him, and probably long before—in wandering to-and-fro over these deserts, as dismal and monotonous as the sand hills amid which we were sitting. He can neither believe, nor be comfortable in his unbelief; and he is too honest and courageous not to try to do one or the other.

From England, Melville took a ship to Constantinople and thence to Egypt and, at last, to Judea and Palestine. He came to Jerusalem as Margaret had come to Rome, seeking liberation, but found there instead the wellspring of his annihilation, the incarnation of his despair. He recorded them in his journal:

The color of the whole city is grey and looks at you like a cold grey eye in a cold old man—its strange aspect in the pale olive light of the morning.

Judea is one accumulation of stones—Stony mountains and stony plains; stony torrents and stony roads; stony walls and stony fields, stony houses and stony tombs; stony eyes and stony hearts. Before you and behind you are stones. Stones to right and stones to left. In many places laborious attempt has been made to clear the surface of these stones. You see heaps of stones here and there, and stone walls of immense thickness are thrown together, less for boundaries than to get them out of the way. But in vain; the removal of one stone only serves to reveal three stones still larger below it.

There is at all times a smell of burning rubbish in the air of Jerusalem.

Is the desolation of the land the result of the fatal embrace of the Deity? Hapless are the favorites of heaven.

*Wandering among the tombs*—till I began to think myself one of the possessed with devils.

The mind can not but be sadly and suggestively affected with indifference of Nature and Man to all that makes the spot sacred to the Christian. Weeds grow upon Mount Zion.

The Holy Sepulchre—ruined dome—confused and half-ruinous pile—labyrinths and terraces of mouldy grottos, tombs and shrines. Smells like a dead-house, dingy light. —At the entrance, in a sort of grotto in the wall a divan for Turkish policemen, where they sit crosslegged and smoking, scornfully observing the continuous troops of pilgrims entering and prostrating themselves before the anointing stone of Christ, which veined with streaks of mouldy red looks like a butcher's slab. —On the same level nearby is a kind of gallery, railed with marble, overlooking the entrance of the church; and here almost every day I would hang, looking down upon the spectacle of the scornful Turks on the divan, and the scorned pilgrims kissing the stone of the annointing—The door of the church is like that of a jail—a grated window in it—The main body of the church is overhung by the lofty and ruinous dome whose fallen plastering reveals the meager skeleton of beams and laths—a sort of plague-stricken splendor reigns in the painted and mildewed walls around. In the midst of all stands the Sepulchre. . . . From its porch issues a garish stream of light upon the faces of the pilgrims who crowd for admittance into a space which will hold but four or five at a time. . . . Wedged and half-dazzled, you stare for a moment on the ineloquence of the bedizened slab, and glad to come out, wipe your brow glad to escape as from the heat and jam of a show-box. All is glitter and nothing is gold. A sickening cheat. The countenances of the poorest and most ignorant pilgrims would seem tacitly to confess it as well as your own.

As though to follow the historical progress of Christian religion, Melville went next to Rome:

Tiber a ditch, yellow as saffron.

Silence and loneliness of long streets of blank garden walls.

No place where a lonely man will feel more lonely than in Rome.

This day saw nothing, enjoyed nothing, but suffered something.

*          *          *

Herman Melville returned home at the end of 1857, and his family persuaded him to take to the lecture circuit with an account of his travels, which he did with some small success during the next two years. But what hope for him was there, knowing what he did? The Christmas after he returned from the Holy Land, George's cousin Leverett Griggs, Presbyterian pastor of the First Church of Bristol, Connecticut, preached a sermon "On the Doctrine of Annihilation," which was subsequently printed and perhaps sent to Longmeadow; and perhaps it could have thence been passed on to Herman by his sister. But what good could it have done? Cousin Leverett said what Herman already knew:

My subject is one of solemn interest to such as have not made their peace with God. You have been created in the image of your Maker—capable of knowing and enjoying Him. Hitherto you have been laboring to defeat the great object of your existence, and the result is you are strangers to all substantial bliss.

Yes, that was it—but what of it, if one was paralyzed, too weary, as if weighted with all the stones of Judea, to believe; to strike through to it? In two years there would be a war, in five Hawthorne would be dead, in seven, the Shaws and the Griggses would think Herman was insane and counsel his wife to leave him; in eight, his eldest son, Malcolm, would die from a shot from his own pistol. Whether the death was deliberate or accidental, Malcolm's plan or God's, no one knew, not Herman, perhaps not even God.

*               *               *

Melville had scarcely left Rome when Hawthorne arrived in 1858, and stayed for the following year. Sophia was reunited with Sarah Clarke, who was living permanently in Italy along with a contingent of American women artists and onetime Transcendentalists. They were drawn both to Roman culture and, frequently, to the Roman church. Just as Hawthorne arrived, Anna Barker Ward underwent a noisy conversion, leading Emerson to decry "this running of the girls into Popery," which he despised every bit as much as Harvard Unitarianism. The American colony at Rome fascinated Hawthorne—it was like Brook Farm and Concord of the 1840s transplanted to the ruins of the Caesars, to the studios of Renaissance artists—and before he left he had begun a novel based on it, *The Marble Faun.* While in Rome, he also did some further investigation of Margaret Fuller's life and domestic arrangements during her final years in Italy. When *The Marble Faun* was finished, its plot line turned on the illicit and tragic relationship between Miriam, an exotic and brilliant American exile, and Donatello, an unscrupulous member of the Italian nobility fallen on hard times. It was, despite much effort during the years after the Hawthornes returned to America, his last novel.

New England was not kind to Hawthorne on his return from Europe. Abolitionist feeling, always strong in Boston, ran high as the war began, and Hawthorne's association with the now disgraced compromiser Franklin Pierce rendered him persona non grata. He accomplished little with his writing, and in the heat of the war, his other work seemed to belong to a now remote age. His health declined, and although not yet sixty, he was frail, white-haired, and bent.

James Clarke presided at his funeral in Concord on May 23, 1864, with Alcott, Longfellow, Holmes, and Emerson as pallbearers. The next day, Emerson recorded his thoughts about Hawthorne:

> I thought there was a tragic element in the event, in the painful solitude of the man, which I suppose could not be endured, and he died of it. I have found in his death a surprise and disappointment. I thought him a greater man than any of his works betray, that there was still a great deal of work in him, and that he might one day show a purer power. . . . It was easy to talk with him—there were no barriers—only he said so little that I talked too much. He showed no egotism or self-assertion, rather a humility, and at one time, a fear that he had written himself out. One day, when I found him on the top of his hill, in the woods, he paced back the path to his house and said, "This path is the only remembrance of me that will remain." Now it appears that I waited too long.

Melville learned of Hawthorne's death only after the funeral. They had not seen each other since the day in England when they had sat among the sand hills, smoking and talking about God. Herman—now entering his own long decline into poverty, obscurity, and despair—reread *Mosses from an Old Manse,* the book that had brought them together fourteen years before, annotating and writing in the margins. He underlined the phrase, "He will pass to the dark realm of Nothingness, but will not find me there" and wrote next to it, "This trenches upon the uncertain and the terrible."

# TWELVE

Hawthorne and Melville, together and separately, had tried to say the unsayable, and had in their own estimation failed. But even as Hawthorne was buried and Melville consigned to the oblivion of the unread, it seemed to more and more people that it was only artists, poets, and their ilk who had any possibility of addressing the sacred. Horace Bushnell, who was with Leverett Griggs at Yale—a redoubt of Calvinist divinity set up in opposition to Harvard—and became one of his generation's preeminent theologians, concluded that apprehending religious truth involved "not reason, or logic, or a scientific power, so much as a right sensibility," an "aesthetic talent" that could grapple with the "signs and images" through which God communicates Himself. Neither systems of doctrine nor systems of morality could constitute true religion, although the construction of these was precisely how most Christian churches sought to maintain a foothold in the later nineteenth century.

But no matter how the basis of belief was presented, it was hedged in by one or another objection. On the one hand, science and reason could not offer convincing proofs of religion; but on the other, to demand belief without them seemed to fly in the face of the spirit of the age—of progress, and especially moral progress, through the search for and discovery of knowledge. Appeals to authority—even the authority of God Himself—and tradition met a similar kind of resistance, for they impinged not just on reason and progress, but on individual intellectual and spiritual liberty.

It was thus that by 1865, the Transcendentalists had triumphed not only in the cause of abolition, but in religion: Concord had defeated Harvard Divinity. In that year Charles Eliot Norton, the son and heir of the Unitarian pope, Andrews Norton, would write:

> The relation between God and the soul is original for every man. His religion must be his own. No two men think of God alike. No man or men can tell me what I must think of Him. If I am pure of heart, I see him, and know him— Creeds are but fictions that have nothing to do with the truth.

The latest of New England's rising generations took unbelief as a matter of course. Young William James and his brother, Henry, had been carefully tutored in religion as students in Newport, Rhode Island, by George Griggs's nephew, the Reverend William C. Leverett. To judge from a letter written by William James a few years later, the tutorial does not seem to have done much to inculcate the Christian faith: William wrote that "if we have to give up all hope of seeing into the purposes of God, or to give up theoretically the idea of final causes, and of God anyhow as vain and leading to nothing for us," then friendship, a clear conscience, and an active life of accomplishments would suffice just as well. Another contemporary of the Jameses, Henry Adams (related to both the Clarks and the Grigges, and conceivably to everyone else in New England) declared that a faith that countenanced a God who could stand by while Adams's young sister died subject to "a fiendish cruelty known to man only in perverted and insane temperaments could not be held for a moment." Such a religion "made pure atheism a comfort."

Most Americans, however, were unwilling to adopt either atheism or Emersonian individualism in lieu of organized religion. Belief was hard, but the churches could offer a moral if not a truly spiritual home, providing a guide to a way of life—centered on hard work, thrift, temperance, Bible study, and love of family—that would ensure happiness and peace in this life, even if it could not guarantee salvation in the next. As Charles Eliot Norton noted, "The question of the existence of God must be regarded as one that has no intrinsic relation with moral character." People sensed this, even if their pastors were unwilling to address it directly, and looked where they could for answers to more transcendent concerns. James Clarke, in fact, achieved his first national best-seller by responding to this need, expanding an article in the *Atlantic* entitled, "Buddhism—The Protestantism of the East" into a book called *Ten Great Religions.* Foreshadowing Alan Watts and other popularizers of Eastern religion by nearly a century, James suggested that Westerners could supplement the slight sustenance of contemporary Christianity by recourse to Eastern mysticism. Such eclectic, personalized "spirituality," neither assenting to a unified body of doctrine nor abandoning faith altogether, constituted the religion of an increasing number of people. Atheism, then as now, was not an option for the vast majority of them, for the problem was not the impossibility of God but the difficulty of belief. In 1870, the English Darwinian Thomas Henry Huxley invented a name for this crippled faith: agnosticism.

Disbelief—or the incapacity to believe—thus itself became a kind of religion, the final fruit of Luther's unknowable, individualized God. But this affliction scarcely touched one of its principal authors, Emerson. In 1873, at the age of seventy, he took his family to Europe: to London, for a last visit with his old friend Carlyle; to Paris, where Henry James served as guide and was "a sort of son" to Emerson; and to Rome, where Lilly Ward, the daughter of Sam and Anna Barker Ward, tried fervently but without success to convert Emerson's daughter Ellen to Catholicism. From Rome, they traveled to Egypt and sailed on the Nile in the company of Henry Adams and his wife, Marian. In Rome they had visited Sarah Clarke, who thought Emerson looked "wonderfully improved" by the journey. He was eternally himself. Charles Eliot Norton, who had sailed home with the Emersons, thought he was perhaps too much so: "His optimistic philosophy has hardened into a creed, closing the avenues of truth. He cannot accept nothing as fact that tells against his dogma. He refuses to believe in disorder and evil."

Emerson and Norton, the son of perhaps his greatest detractor, had walked on the deck together, and Emerson, refuting yet another of young Norton's skepticisms, said that even polar magnetism, the itch of the needle to find north, was an example of the divine spirit to be found in nature. He took out his pocket compass and showed it to Norton. "I like," he said, "to hold the visible god in my hand."

*          *          *

By the time Emerson died in the spring of 1882, Sarah Clarke had moved home permanently from Rome. The last thing she had done before leaving was to sketch all the places in Italy "reputed to have known the tread of Dante's wandering foot," as her young acquaintance Henry James put it. (She and James had met in Rome in 1873, and James portrayed her as the painter "Augusta Blanchard" in his *Roderick Hudson*.) The drawings and the article Sarah wrote about following in Dante's footsteps were printed in a two-part piece in the *Century* magazine. On her journey, Sarah had spent a long time at the Scrovegni Chapel in Padua studying Giotto's frescoes of the life of Christ and his mother. She was particularly drawn to the angel who appeared to the women in the garden at Christ's resurrection. The angel seemed to Sarah the figure "most beautiful of all":

> I spent some time here alone, trying to copy the beautiful angel, but the light was insufficient, and the picture too high on the wall for me. I even procured a permission to put up a scaffold, meaning to spend some days there in copying; but the weather changed, the chapel became too dark for my work, and as the rain continued, I gave up my plan.

The light, the light and its coming, "when everything seems like preparation and expectation." The light, and the want of it.

*          *          *

Sarah and James Clarke were old now, and almost everyone they had known when they were young was dead. Once James had said in a sermon:

> It is the young who are oftenest tired of life. As we live on, we seem to grow younger, not older; we find ourselves coming nearer to God and man; we grow more like little children in our hearts. . . . A man wonders that he ever could have been weary of life; he feels the infinite riches of the universe, and thanks God, in the depths of a happy heart, for the gift of existence.

James was happy, even as the young men like Charles Eliot Norton were unhappy. He sat on the beach near Cape Ann, listening to the surf, and felt "as if all the anxiety and worry of life were far away. Here it is always afternoon."

When he was seventy-two, James made a last trip to Europe, and on the way home he went to East Anglia to visit the churches and villages of his ancestors, the Clarks who settled in Plymouth, and the Eliots and Curtises of Roxbury. In Nazing, Essex, he climbed the church belfry: "In ascending I had to push my way through the remains of the nests made by many generations of rooks. As I looked down from the tower I saw Epping forest in the distance, and nearer, the common, where tradition tells us that Boadicea defeated the Roman army. In the little church are still shown the oaken seats on which John Eliot and William Curtis sat as boys."

The peace of these last years was interrupted in 1885, by an eruption of scandal and rancor disseminated in and by the media, now considerably more developed than when Aaron Bigelow excoriated Susan Griggs and her mother in the year James was born. Nathaniel Hawthorne's son Julian, whom Margaret Fuller and Sarah Clarke might have dandled on their knees in his infancy, published a biography of his father containing the following extract about Margaret from Nathaniel Hawthorne's journal:

> She was a person anxious to try all things, and fill up her experience in all directions; she had a strong and coarse nature, which she had done her utmost to refine with infinite pains, but of course it could only be superficially changed. The solution of the riddle lies in this direction, nor does the conscience revolt at the idea of thus solving it; for (at least this is my own experience) Margaret has not left in the hearts and minds of those who knew her any deep witness of her integrity and purity. She was a great humbug—of course with much talent and much moral reality, or else she could never have been so great a humbug. But she had stuck herself full of borrowed qualities, which she chose to provide herself with, but which had no root in her.
>
> There appears to have been a total collapse in poor Margaret, morally and intellectually; and tragic as her catastrophe

was, Providence was after all kind in putting her and her clownish husband and their child on board that fated ship. There was never such a tragedy as her whole story—the sadder and sterner, because so much of the ridiculous was mixed up with it, and because she could bear anything better than to be ridiculous. It was such an awful joke that she should have resolved—in all sincerity, no doubt—to make herself the greatest, wisest, best woman of the age; and to that end she set to work on her strong, heavy, unpliable, and in many respects defective and evil nature, and adorned it with a mosaic of admirable qualities such as she chose to possess, putting in here a splendid talent and there a moral excellence, and polishing each separate piece and the whole together till it seemed to shine afar and dazzle all who saw it. She took credit to herself for having been her own redeemer, if not her own creator.

Sarah and James launched a letter-writing campaign in the New York and Boston newspapers, defending Margaret's character and quoting from Sophia Hawthorne's letters in Sarah's possession showing that Margaret had been a welcome guest in the Hawthorne household. Julian Hawthorne replied that none of this altered his report of his father's opinions and added, for good measure, his own estimation of Giovanni Ossoli as "a handsome animal, having scarcely the intelligence of a human being." The media war of reputations ended, probably, with Hawthorne's diminished, and with the world's view of Margaret—now being reinvented as a feminist heroine—more elevated. Julian, of course, disagreed: "The majority of readers will, I think, not be inconsolable that poor Margaret Fuller has at last taken her place with the numberless other dismal frauds who fill the limbo of human pretension and failure."

No one denied that Nathaniel Hawthorne had written these things, or thought them. James suggested that "Hawthorne wrote in his notebooks all sorts of hints and suggestions, as they occurred to him, as the ground for future imaginative characters." Hawthorne's journal entry about Margaret, then, was in fact a sketch of a Zenobia or Miriam in development, not an objective assessment of Margaret herself. Convincing or otherwise, this explanation underlined Hawthorne's troubled fascination with Margaret's character, or at least certain aspects of it, and in particular, her aspirations to unite in herself art and the spirit. Hawthorne, a truer New Englander than any of the Transcendentalists, could only regard these as ambitions and pretensions. She was in his view a Goethian hero: not the poet–priest–creator of worlds, but Faust, damned by hubris, by having tried to expropriate what belonged to God alone. "Sin, care, and self-consciousness have set the human portion of the world askew," Hawthorne had written in *The Marble Faun,* and our efforts to set it right tend to be both in vain and vainglorious: "We go all wrong, by too strenuous a resolution to go all right."

In that, we might think that Hawthorne could have felt some sympathy with Margaret. They also shared, perhaps unbeknownst to each other, a fascination with Mary, the Mater Dolorosa. In *The Marble Faun,* the foil to the tragic, Fulleresque Miriam is Hilda, an American artist whose initially aesthetic but finally spiritual absorption into the ethos of Rome ends with her becoming the custodian of a shrine to the Blessed Virgin, making a confession to a Vatican priest, and apparently undergoing a conversion to Roman Catholicism. But in the end, she remains what she is, a self-described "daughter of the Puritans." However deep her attraction to the consolations of Rome, and of Mary in particular—to the Puritan mind the most repellent and heretical aspect of the Roman church—convinced belief in them is not a bridge Hilda is capable of crossing. *The Marble Faun*'s Miriam represents one side of Margaret, but Hilda represents another no less real. That it should be Mary—the emblem of Christianity at its least rationalistic and most affective, tender, and corporeal—who would so intrigue the arch-intellectual Margaret Fuller and the post-Puritan pessimist Nathaniel Hawthorne is a curious thing. And it is either surprising or fitting that Hawthorne's younger daughter, Rose, did indeed convert to Roman Catholicism, taking orders as a Dominican lay nun and establishing an informal association of other converts she called Daughters of the Puritans.

By the 1880s, amid the literary "realism" of Howells and James, Hawthorne and his preoccupations were antique; and in the postwar experience of Charles Eliot Norton and Julian Hawthorne, Margaret—like all the leading Transcendentalists—might well seem pretentious and even ridiculous, especially by virtue of her sex. The seventies and eighties were a succession of political and business scandals, of which the best that might be said was that a great deal of money was made. The previous generation's devotion to beauty and "the march of mind" seemed a glib and cheaply bought idealism, which the current age, cleaved by conviction and doubt, by the idea of progress and the debilitations of agnosticism, could not afford.

James Clarke knew otherwise. He had the notebook Margaret had first given him when they were young, when she was in love with George Davis and he with Louisa, and they had addressed each other as "Cousin Mine." Inside the cover she had written, "Extraordinary, generous seeking/Be revered in thee the faithful hope that still looks forward/And keeps the life-spark warm of future action/Beneath the cloak of patient sufferance."

And she had been right about beauty and art, about God being in them, about how they took faith and gave faith back. It was a little thing—no more than the work of a girl like Susan Chaffey putting thread to linen, yet stitching revelation—but like Margaret's Mater Dolorosa, it suffered and saved the world. In the months before James died in 1888, he wrote Sarah, full of hope: "If we have been made by an infinite wisdom, we have been made for something more than just to begin a career and then to be cut off. That would be too inconsequential. Here are you, as much interested in life and art as ever. I, at seventy-seven, full of plans of work that would take a dozen years to complete. We are, my dear sister, just at the beginning, not at the end."

Then, just before the end, James wrote Sarah about one of her paintings:

> Sitting before your picture of "The Jungfrau" one afternoon lately, the sun stole over it, and brought out a multitude of lovely details, introducing new values and lighting up the great silver peaks till they seemed to swim in a rosy radiance. The light quivered over the vast mountains; and when a cloud went over the sun, the mists collected round the summits and hid them for a moment, and then drifted away, and

the snowy fields emerged again, and once more were bathed in the tender light. It was really like being on the spot. I enjoyed it so much that I wished you to know of it.

It has been a severe winter. Except on Sundays, I have not been to Boston for a month.

# PART IV

# THE WORLD BEFORE THIS ONE

# ONE

y grandfather Clark was born in 1868, about the date that it became clear to Thomas Henry Huxley, Charles Eliot Norton, and Henry Adams that religious faith was untenable; that, in a phrase popular when I was young, "God is dead." There is no evidence that anyone ever detected so much as a pious bone in my grandfather's body. That is not to say he was not a good man, but people thought he was good in the manner of the Stoics and just in the manner of the Roman law, both of which fascinated him. Classical Rome was his great avocation, and when he became tense or overworked or bored my grandmother would say, "Off you go to Rome," and he would board a liner for Italy once more.

He came by his indifference to religion naturally: His father, Charles Clark, was born in 1836, part of Henry Adams's generation of nominally Unitarian agnostics; and Charles seems to have shared Adams's penchant for despair, for feeling on the whole a little disappointed in life. His mother, Martha Pierce, was a Homer on her mother's side, and thus my grandfather, subject to the New England custom of turning family names into first names, was named Homer Pierce Clark. I am named Robert Homer Clark.

The Clarks—save for exceptions like cousin James Clarke—and the Pierces were middling merchants, grocers, and real estate developers, but the Homers cut a wider swath though New England. Martha's uncle Sydney Homer, for example, not only enriched himself in the import trade but distinguished himself as a patron of the arts, education, and public welfare, making endowments to a dozen or so hospitals and orphanages as well as to Harvard, MIT, the Unitarian church, the Society of Natural History, and the Boston Athenaeum. He also took a deep interest in his niece, urging the teenaged Martha to be ever more self-reliant. In response to a newsy letter from her, he suggested she could "make it better":

> You could have told me of the books you read, or better still of the thoughts you think. Have you no inner life, separate from the outward daily pursuits, or even from the events of outward life? Do you never think, Who am I, What am I, Whither do I tend? You have health and ability, and will naturally desire to attract and secure the love and respect of some person of character.
>
> This cannot be permanently done without some corresponding traits on your part: so do not let the Spring of your life pass in vain pursuit of things as vain. Above all, learn to *think* and practice the habit of thinking for yourself, not only of such things as are adapted for your sex, but also such as even concern the world; history, business, politics, and the art of expressing yourself neatly, clearly, and with kindness. I want to see you an honor to yourself and to your family. I am sure you have the ability if only you will exercise it.

This code, both Stoic and Emersonian, without a trace of religious sentiment, was what the Homers expected of Martha, and she seems to have met their expectations while passing them on to her son Homer. As for the "person of character" whose love she was to attract and secure, Charles Clark was a good man but perhaps of less stern stuff than the Homers.

Charles had gone to St. Paul, Minnesota, in 1858 to seek his fortune on the frontier in the hardware business. He returned to Boston in 1865, married Martha in 1866, and worked for her father's china and crockery import firm. In 1868, my grandfather Homer was born, followed by his sister Mary in 1871. But in 1872, perhaps chafing a little in his father-in-law's employ, Charles moved his family back to St. Paul and returned to the hardware business. His work involved a fair amount of travel around the Midwest, as he wrote his then four-year-old son:

> My Dear Little Homer,
>
> I have just received a letter from Ma Ma and she says you have received the letter I wrote you from Winona, so I will send you another.
>
> I shall take the sleeping car for Indianapolis tonight. I will get the lower berth if I can and if I cannot get a lower berth will take an upper one same as you and Ma Ma slept in when we went from Cincinnati to New York on the Atlantic and Great Western RR when you put your head over in the morning and said "Good Morning Pa Pa." I don't believe it will be such a nice car as that was, 'tho. I shall go from Indianapolis to Cincinnati and shall see Mr. and Mrs. Hunnewell and the dog and the horse and the chickens. Do you remember the night you and I frightened them all down after they had gone to roost? I hope baby [Mary] is well and does she laugh now when you talk to her?
>
> Pa Pa

Homer grew up uneventfully, save for an attack of polio that left him with a slight limp and deafness in one ear. He attended the Unitarian church his father had helped establish in St. Paul, went to public schools, watched the state capitol burn down in 1881, and in the same year saw Sitting Bull led through town captive after giving himself up five years after the battle of the Little Big Horn. Just as exotic were the standing-room-only lectures the following year of the Anglo-Irish aesthete Oscar Wilde.

The late 1870s and early 1880s were prosperous times, in which even someone as inadept at business as Charles Clark could make money. But in 1883 recession set in, and Charles found himself with piles of unsold goods and no way to pay his creditors, among them various members of the Pierce and Homer families. His firm went into bankruptcy and Charles slid into despair. Recognizing his parlous mental state, in 1884 Martha packed him and the children up for a year-long stay in Germany and Italy, financed by her family. It was only after the fact that she learned in a letter from a family friend that her husband had tried to kill himself:

> Am glad to hear that yourself and Charlie are so well and contented. I agree with you that you were wise in making the move that you did, as nothing but a change of scene and surroundings would have brought Charlie out of his *dangerous* mental condition. Did you know he tried to buy a pistol one day from Adam Decker and that Mr. Decker sent Mr. Mayo and the latter walked Charlie around town all one afternoon a day or two before you left with him? It was true, but is known to only four or five persons and I did not speak to you about it as you had plenty to think about already.

Charles, Martha, and the children returned home in 1885. Charles remained in a fragile condition, and while Martha's relations agreed to continue to support them, they refused to underwrite Charles in any further business ventures unless the family returned to New England where the Pierces and Homers could keep an eye on him. When Charles tried to borrow money, he was thwarted by credit reports like this one: "Clark is an old business man with a failure charged up to him several years ago while in the hardware business. He is said to have *nothing* in his own name but his wife is in comfortable circumstances and owns property to the value of $30,000 to $40,000." Charles could do nothing much for himself or his family. True to the feminism of Martha's uncle Sydney, it was arranged for Mary to attend Smith College after her high school graduation. Her brother Homer went out to work to support the family, captive to his father's failure, his Roman virtue, his death wish.

# TWO

We like to think that self-annihilation is an urge that belongs more to our time than to the naïve and innocent past; that suicide in the age of Charlie Clark, if not always hushed up, was at least rare. But that was scarcely the case, at least among New Englanders. It was in the air, it ran in families.

For example, Susan Sturgis Bigelow, the sister of Margaret Fuller's companion Caroline Sturgis, took arsenic and killed herself in 1854 despite being young, beautiful, and to all appearances happily married. And all three children of Caroline's other sister Ellen, who married Dr. Robert Hooper, would commit suicide. Caroline had taken special interest in the firstborn of these, her niece Marian Hooper, and took pains to inculcate in her the feminist, intellectual, and philosophical agenda that she and Margaret had shared. Marian was a bright and assertive girl, but prone to sudden alterations in mood seemingly prompted by nothing more than a spell of bad weather. At the age of twenty-nine, even as she was in the final stages of courtship by a young man from a distinguished family, she could write:

> This winter when the very cold weather came the sun began to warm me but I snapped my fingers at it and I tried to ignore it. By and by it got so warm that I tried to move and couldn't and then last Tuesday at about sunset the sun blinded me so that in real terror I put my hands up to my face to keep it away and when I took them away there sat Henry Adams

holding them and the ice has all melted away and I am going to sit in the sun as long as it shines.

Marian Hooper and Henry Adams were married the following summer, in June 1872. When not beset by depression, Marian was an exemplar of wit, talent, and vivacity; her friend Henry James used her as a model for two of his heroines—Daisy Miller, and Isabel Archer of *The Portrait of a Lady*. Independently wealthy and well-connected, she and Adams traveled in Europe and settled first in Boston (where Henry lectured at Harvard in law, history, and the Middle Ages) and then in Washington, D.C., where she maintained the capital's most stellar social and intellectual salon.

Marian's great passion was photography, then still a cumbrous art involving coating glass plates with wet chemicals that were exposed for minutes at a time. Marian was gifted at composing portraits and her position in the nation's capital afforded her a steady supply of celebrated and interesting subjects such as Francis Parkman, Oliver Wendell Holmes, and George Bancroft as well as sundry ambassadors, statesmen, and senators. In late 1884, her work came to the attention of Richard Watson Gilder, editor of the *Century*, then America's preeminent magazine. Gilder wanted to use Marian's work on a regular basis, a proposition that Marian was deeply flattered by but that Henry felt she ought to reject both by reason of her social station and her sex. Henry prevailed and, perhaps independently of the matter, Marian entered another of her depressions.

On December 6, 1885, Marian began a letter to her sister Ellen: "If I had one single point of character or goodness I would stand on that and grow back to life. Henry is more patient and loving than words can express. God might envy him—he bears and hopes and despairs hour after hour." Marian did not finish the letter. She found potassium cyanide among her darkroom chemicals, swallowed it, and lay down before the fireplace in her room. Henry found her, dead, twisted, and redolent of almonds, but still warm, an hour afterward.

The death of his sister in 1870 had convinced Henry that God was malign if He existed at all, but Marian's death set him in a different direction. Its pointlessness—they had been so very good and happy together—left her death beyond interpretation, past either ascribing meaning to it or depriving meaning from other things. Henry did two things in connection with it. He took a long trans-Pacific journey to Japan in the company of the artist John La Farge, and he contacted the sculptor husband of Martha Clark's cousin Augusta Homer about a memorial to Marian.

Augusta was married to the Irish-born Augustus Saint-Gaudens, whose work in association with the architects Henry Hobson Richardson and Stanford White had already marked him the nation's foremost sculptor. His best-known work would be the Boston memorial to the Massachusetts 54th Regiment and its commander, Robert Gould Shaw, cousin to both Marian Adams and Elizabeth Shaw Melville. Before leaving for Japan, Adams was agreed that Stanford White would lay out the plan for the memorial in Rock Creek Cemetery in Washington and Saint-Gaudens would sculpt a female figure that would be its focus.

In Japan, Henry's guide was William Sturgis Bigelow, the surviving son of Susan Sturgis Bigelow, Caroline Sturgis's suicidal sister. Like so many New Englanders, Bigelow found neither meaning nor solace in Western religion; he spent seven years in Asia studying Buddhism. Adams's interests were largely aesthetic—he was past seeking conversion—but he was drawn to the serene figure of Kannon, a female emblem of mercy, and he photographed several examples, which were passed on to Saint-Gaudens. Adams at one point referred to the memorial as "my Buddha grave," and he wanted it to have both the essence of the Kan-non and that of the Blessed Virgin in Dante's *Paradiso,* which he was then rereading.

Saint-Gaudens finished in 1891, five years after Marian's death. His sculpture was a seated female figure in bronze, deeply shrouded in folds of cloth, her benign but impassive face half hidden. To the eye uninformed of Adams's trip to Japan she is nothing so much as the Mater Dolorosa, albeit drained of outward grief, at peace by virtue of being at a great distance from this world.

Adams was much pleased by Saint-Gaudens's work, but he felt that few others could grasp it, seeing nothing in the statue but a figure "of despair, of atheism, of denial." And it was the most religious who understood it the least: "The worst of all is the clerical preacher. He can see nothing but Despair. He shows what his own mind is full of." As to what Saint-Gaudens himself felt the sculpture "meant," there is silence, even in the correspondence between him and Adams preserved by his son, Homer.

Adams may have guessed best when he said, "Like all great artists, Saint-Gaudens held up a mirror and nothing more." Adams allowed that although he asked for a "Buddha grave" the work was "not in the least oriental." But Saint-Gaudens had indeed held up a mirror, and held it up to the soul of Henry Adams, although the image in it would not be entirely clear for almost ten years after the completion of the sculpture.

In 1900, Adams composed a poem called "Prayer to the Virgin of Chartres." Five years before, he had begun a massive study of the art and architecture of Mont-Saint-Michel and Chartres cathedral, which rapidly developed into a consideration of medieval culture as a whole and of the Blessed Virgin Mary as the "dynamo" behind it. He never felt himself a genuine believer, but through the beauty and the art of the Middle Ages he was inundated by the possibility of belief. In Chartres, he wrote,

> Anyone can feel it who will only consent to feel like a child. Sitting here any Sunday afternoon, while the voices of the children of the maîtrise are chanting in the choir—your mind held in the grasp of the strong lines and shadows of the architecture; your eyes flooded with the autumn tones of the glass; your ears drowned with the purity of the voices; one sense reacting upon another until sensation reaches the limit of its range—you or any other lost soul, could, if you cared to look and listen, feel a sense beyond the human ready to reveal a sense divine that would make the world once more intelligible, and would bring the Virgin to life again . . . more eloquent than the prayer-book, and more beautiful than the autumn sunlight; and anyone willing to try, could feel it like a child, reading new thought without end into the art he has studied a hundred times; but what is still more convincing, he could, at will, in an instant, shatter the whole art by calling into it a single motive of his own.

That last was the rub, for while human self-consciousness provides an inverse proof of the art's divine origin, it also undoes our capacity to apprehend it. It is a kind of original sin: We cannot see God because it is in our deepest nature continually to blind ourselves to Him, to choose self-regard over the divine vision.

Thus is Adams's "Prayer to the Virgin" a series of pleas: "Help me to see!" "Help me to know!" "Help me to feel!" But in all that, he knew he was past help, that it was not the Virgin or God who was dead, but his capacity to believe, and that this failing was his own. A New Englander to his core, Adams saw that he was not once damned, but twice: first by the fact of his disbelief, and second by being the apparently willing author of his disbelief, which he exacerbated by merely giving it thought.

Adams was one of the smartest men of his age, but he missed an essential point, one that Augustine was also blind to until well after his final conversion: that the search for belief presupposes belief. We do not look for that which we are convinced does not exist. Our belief as belief is already real; it is intellectual certitude—which a mystery like the divine denies us by definition—that we lack, and mistake for true faith. But we cannot or will not see it so.

Everything in "Prayer to the Virgin of Chartres" and in *Mont-Saint-Michel and Chartres* makes this clear. The fact of the prayer presupposes the reality of the being to whom it is addressed. Mary is real; it is Adams who will not let her be real to *him,* and he assumes, child of the Reformation that he is, that this certitude is the only way man—alone and in the imperfection of his mind—can apprehend God. With that burden afflicting him, Adams finished his life with the sense that it was not God or Mary that was unreal but Adams himself.

It was love that was in fact the author of his pain, or so it must have seemed. First, he lost his sister to an agonizing death, and then Marian. He loved them, and against all justice, goodness and reason—against everything that surely love ought to mean—he lost them. It is not hate or even indifference that is the opposite of love, but death; for his love, Henry was repaid with death, and that was enough to kill God for him.

Perhaps it was this to which Saint-Gaudens held up a mirror, and in it was reflected the image of the Mary, both Mater Dolorosa and Virgin of Chartres, the woman and the love that he thought were lost to him. At the end of his life, when he wrote his autobiography,

*The Education of Henry Adams,* he had found a kind of faith in resignation to those facts, and enacted the self-consciousness that estranged him from the divine by writing about himself entirely in the third person. And there again, while holding it in the palm of his hand, he missed the point. He was writing about Thomas Aquinas by way of expounding his theory of the dynamo of history, and quoted the very answer to the question he could not quite see that he had since 1870 been asking: "To me," said St. Thomas, "Christ and the Mother are one force—Love—simple, single, and sufficient for all human wants."

It was not, I would guess, that Adams could not hear or understand these words. But for anyone not already disposed to accept them they not only are cold comfort for a broken human heart but also ignore what seems to be the essence of love as we experience it. Love dissolves the boundaries between human selves, and we find ourselves desiring nothing more from one another than that the other simply *be.* Thus in love we lack nothing; we are, so it seems, as gods. And love, too, seems to dissolve time: Love inevitably feels eternal, we claim it and pledge it to those we love forever. In that, it again seems to partake of the divine, perfect being, perfectly eternal.

That is how it seems, but that is not, of course, how it is with us. Where love is concerned, loss is death, whether by literal, physical death or by rejection and the mutability of desire. What seemed the very essence of being exists no more; what was eternal becomes evanescent. If in love we partake of the divine—if love seems proof of God's realness—then love's loss is the death of God. Every love is a conversion, every loss a lapse from faith. Except for those like James Clarke, in whom belief is the hardiest of perennials, faith is nearly impossible to maintain in the face of loss. In that circumstance, Thomas Aquinas's formulation seems glib, cruel, and even demonstrably false, for if God is love and love is dead to us, so too must be God.

In that light, the belief in the necessity and possibility of belief—excepting for himself—that Adams clung to was a kind of faith. He was able to find in Saint-Gaudens's memorial to Marian an affirmation of what he could not quite bring himself to see, a sign of what God found in Mary: pure assent, acknowledgment, a yes to his eternal being, which she accepted as Love, to which she herself responded as Love. It is possible to see Mary, in her waiting and in her acquiescence to God's will, as merely passive and weak, but that is not how Adams or Saint-Gaudens saw her. She contained, instead, the quiescent serenity and power of the Buddha. She was strong where Adams was weak, saying yes where he could say at best only "Perhaps," gainsaying death with love.

It is a hard thing to do. Consider another cousin of Martha Clark, an artist like Saint-Gaudens, Winslow Homer. Homer became known first as a magazine illustrator and then as a painter of Civil War scenes. After the war he specialized in bucolic if unsentimental Americana: children playing in rural settings; country schoolrooms; pretty girls playing croquet or lying in the grass reading novels. His favorite model was a woman named Helena de Kay, a painter herself, whom he loved and proposed marriage to. But he lost her to Richard Watson Gilder, the editor of the *Century,* whose interest in Marian Adams's photographs preceded her suicide. When Helena married Gilder in 1874, Homer painted a portrait of her and gave it to the couple as a wedding present. Then he moved away from New York to a remote house on the coast of Maine.

The painting is somber, almost funereal. De Kay is seated on a couch, dressed in black, facing the left edge of the frame, against a wall, in a pose reminiscent of Whistler's mother. She holds a book loosely, without interest, and her eyes are downcast, her expression dejected. On the floor at her feet and just behind her is a crushed and broken rose blossom. She is dressed in mourner's clothes, but she is a widow not to any person but to love.

It was a pointed gift, and enough of a burr in Gilder's flesh to cause him to write poems inspired by it that seem to wonder aloud whether Helena must not still somehow love Winslow Homer, although she and Homer never spoke again after her wedding. On her death, Gilder had the painting sold.

Homer had meanwhile largely given up painting people, moving gradually from nautical scenes set on his Maine coast to pictures of the coast itself and finally of waves, violent, dark, and turbid, pummeling the shore. Through the 1880s and 1890s when his work took this turn, he grew ever more isolated and his communications with the outside world consisted mostly correspondence with his gallery, his canvas and frame makers, and his liquor supplier, the Pierce-

Homer family grocery concern, S. S. Pierce. When asked what his pictures—novel to the late nineteenth-century sensibility in their depopulated and barren starkness—meant, he was silent where he was not sarcastic.

The year after Saint-Gaudens finished the figure for the Adams memorial, Homer conceived and painted a work he described to his dealer as important. He shot a fox, arranged its limbs as though in a skulking, weaving trot, and set it belly-deep in the snow above the shore. He painted it each day until the sun thawed it from this pose, and then reset and let the cadaver refreeze into the desired position during the night. When he was done rendering the fox, he painted two crows overhead, so dark that they seem to merge together and form a black-bottomed storm cloud, which is descending upon the harried fox.

Homer called the painting *The Fox Hunt* and it is perhaps the bleakest thing you will ever see, although it is in fact nothing more than a fox, two crows, and field of snow. What is so disturbing is neither the pose nor the action that is occurring, but the sheer projection of inevitable finality it inscribes, the incipience of blood on the snow, the death that is gelling into reality around the fox, which is more than a fox, which is life itself with death bearing down upon it. Here is the soul and all its aspirations, and here is God, or the utter and undeniable lack of Him. This, the wilderness, is our end. This is where love takes us.

# THREE

My grandfather Homer Clark went into the woods to find himself when he was twenty-one years old, in 1889. He aimed to take up a homestead on the shore of Lake Superior in northern Wisconsin. It would, he felt, make something of him; it would be good for the body and the mind. "I think it would be the best thing a fellow could do for health," he wrote his mother, "as I hear they all grow strong and stout. I don't think there would be much time to idle away, as it would keep one pretty busy cutting wood for his fire, preparing meals, shooting for meat and catching fish. Then I should take a lot of good books, scientific books etc."

He lasted a little over a year and a half. The forest and the ice-clotted lakeshore were bitterly cold in the winter and the woods were abrim with blackflies and mosquitoes in the summer. Neighboring homesteaders stole his supplies, and he was harassed by lumberjacks from the timber companies, who wanted the trees that stood on the homesteaders' claims. After a while, they simply went ahead and began to log Homer's land, and by the spring of 1891 he found himself cheated out of his claim entirely. What he believed was his to freely homestead, had become, by legal and political sleight-of-hand, property of the Cranberry River Lumber Company.

It is hard to say whether he was embittered by this. Bitterness is not a Roman virtue, whereas stoicism is of its essence. But when he returned home to St. Paul, he returned as it were to discover his roots in the lives of Thomas Clarke and his sons: He determined to master the law. He took a job at a law-book publishing house in St.

Paul, and by night he studied for his law degree at the University of Minnesota. Among all the theses submitted by members of his graduating class, Homer's alone had a Latin title, *De Donatio Causa Mortis* (Concerning Gifts Made by Reason of Death). But so successful had he been in his day job at West Publishing Company that he never actually practiced law. Instead, he became West's production manager. Within ten years he was sufficiently flush to buy back the Clark family home on Cape Cod, the house built by Captain Isaac Clark from Siberian timber. Its title had by death and financial circumstance passed out of the family. By 1908 Homer was chief financial officer of the West Publishing Company and he owned his grandfather's house. What he did not have, at the age of forty, was any experience of love; or at least, he had no wife to show for it.

This was a situation that had begun to attract some comment, and Homer set out to remedy it by paying court to a twenty-two-year-old Minneapolis debutante and Adams descendant named Elizabeth Dunsmoor. She was pretty in a petite and doe-eyed manner, outwardly cheerful and pert, but also sensitive to the point being at times almost agoraphobic, having lived in the shadow of a more vivacious sister. She became seasick at the sight of water, whereas Homer loved the sea. She was also as deeply religious as he was not. He was to find she would not be easily won.

He pressed his suit over the next two years, writing her at every opportunity as he traveled on behalf of West Publishing and made visits to his new ancestral home on the Cape:

August 7, 1909—written on board the packet Harvard enroute to Boston, via Long Island Sound and the Atlantic Ocean.

My Dear Elizabeth:

Oh how much I have been thinking of my dear Elizabeth these past couple of days and longing for a glimpse of her, and again and again mentally thanking her for those two letters that came the first of the week, making it a very happy time for me . . .

This is a glorious morning at sea and as we are three and a half hours late I have been enjoying the view of the back of Cape Cod from the ocean. The combination of sand cliffs, fog, water and a little green in the distance make a wonderful marine picture. I have been wishing you were here to see it.

You can't realize how much pleasure I get in going over in retrospect that memorable Saturday and Sunday with you—the many joyful little incidents. You were so wonderful and also so very pretty. Perhaps, best of all from my standpoint, you seemed so very happy.

Longing to see the girl who means everything to me, I remain

With greatest love,
Ever yours,
Homer P. Clark

Homer kept up this campaign assiduously. It was not that Elizabeth was, in the manner of the shy and neurotic, afraid of love. She was afraid of death, and with some reason. She was to lose five siblings to tuberculosis, and she lived in terror of infection and illness, of strangers, of the better part of creation. When she yielded at last to Homer's romantic onslaught she saw him perhaps as more father and protector than lover, but that was of no concern to him. Everything he felt was beyond measure, beyond time or imagining:

Never before have I had any conception of the wonderful happiness that true love can bring, how everything present or future revolves around the one central object of affection.

Somehow you have already wrought a great change in me and I am praying that you will consent to bringing about a still greater development.

Would that I had the power to express my intense love for you—it might help in gaining your assent to marry me, which is the one great object I am devoutly wishing for.

Back of it all there is that firm conviction that through pleasure and sorrow we could be very happy together, else much as I might desire it, I care too truly for you to urge you to give up so much for me.

This was the conventional rhetoric of love, but also of conversion—of change "devoutly" hoped for, of "firm conviction" and "assent"—if only Elizabeth would redeem Homer. This, and the promise that he would allow her to bring up their children as Christians, was sufficient for her. They were married in 1910.

There were no children for seven years. Elizabeth's mother sickened and died shortly after the wedding, and then her last surviving brother was stricken with tuberculosis. Finally, in 1917, Elizabeth and Homer had a son, Robert. Elizabeth lived in fear that now not only she but her son might die. After another pregnancy in 1921, she herself fell ill and she wrote Homer a letter to be opened on her death:

> My Darling:
>
> I haven't the slightest idea this letter will ever be needed but here is one more "I love you." You have made me so happy, dearest, and so proud to be your wife. I think you are almost perfect and it is happiness to be near you, to see and watch you and know of the worthwhile and unselfish things you do. I love you so much and am glad to be certain you will miss me if I don't come through. If you want to remarry that is entirely all right. I didn't used to be willing but now I am perfectly but only be sure that it is someone who will be just to my babies and not jealous of them.
>
> You know the one thing I still would like in the world is for you to if possible believe in one of the orthodox churches. If you can't dear, will you anyway have my babies taught these beliefs?
>
> I know the new baby will be a happiness to you and Bobbie we surely know all about. Love them both a great deal for me. Goodbye my dear one. I love you so much.
>
> > Devotedly,
> > Bessie

Bessie, as Homer now called her, did not die, and the letter remained unread until after her death and Homer's death, over seventy years later. The new baby mentioned in it was my father. He was named Thomas Clark, in honor of Thomas Clarke of Stepney and Plymouth.

\*          \*          \*

Homer and Elizabeth had three more children, all daughters. Of the five siblings only two inherited Elizabeth's strong faith. Nor, despite Elizabeth's fervent hope, did Homer ever convert; in fact, he resigned his membership in the Unitarian congregation in St. Paul when it hired a pacifist minister. He occupied himself with business and civic affairs and made his trips to Rome, where, as ever, he prowled the ruins. In 1934, he wrote my father:

> This morning I spent an hour in Hadrian's tomb and how you would have enjoyed the guns there but especially what they used before they had guns. There were crossbows, pikes—all sorts of swords. A machine with a steel bow 12 or 14 feet long which had to be pulled back with a windlass and shot an iron arrow 7 or 8 feet long. The string of the bow was bigger than the mainsheet of the Zephyrus [the family sailboat on Cape Cod]. There was a machine for throwing stones about as big as my head.
>
> On top some of the Popes had built a palace in which they could live in times of trouble and they had a covered bridge from the Vatican so they could go there without anyone knowing about it. Ask Mother to read you about it from Baedeker. There was and still is a moat all around it but no water in it. There were many battles about it. The walls of the oldest part are about forty feet thick. Am sending a picture of it and the bridge Hadrian built eighteen hundred years ago.
>
> This letter will go over on the Rex which is the fastest boat of all but they say that next summer they expect the Conte de Savoia to beat the Rex's record. They don't run them at full speed, it takes too much coal. Please do your best to get good marks.
>
> With much love<br>Daddy

At age twelve, my father shared his father's love of ships and the sea and also had a boy's interest in weaponry, which my grandfather used as a vehicle to share his own passion for Rome and Roman history. It's revealing, too, that what most sightseers refer to as the Castel Sant'Angelo—the medieval papal fortress that entirely covers the ancient site—my grandfather saw exclusively as Hadrian's tomb, as though its postclassical history were rather beside the point.

In 1938, my grandfather at last took my father, now sixteen, to Rome, traveling on the *Rex* in one direction and the *Queen Mary* in the other. His brother Robert, a senior at Yale, drove the Ford they rented to tour the countryside and my grandfather, of course, was the guide. Nearly seventy years old, he had yet to tire of the place where, as his fellow New Englander (and distant cousin) Charles Eliot Norton put it, "the American, exile in his own land from the past record of his race, finds the most delightful part of the record"; and he surely would have concurred with another relation, Margaret Fuller, that "those have not lived who have not seen Rome." But I am not sure, to judge by a letter he wrote home to his mother, that my father saw it that way:

Dear Mother,
Well we got to Rome just a little while ago. We have seen all sorts of junk. It was rotten riding in the car all day long with not much to do or say. This hotel is alright but it is like all the other buildings in Italy. Made with some poor looking stone, this building is made to look a little better than most of the old homes. We went into Pompeii and Herculanum, and we all liked Herculanum better. They had much more besides just the buildings in Herculanum. They had a lot more of Pompeii uncovered than of Herculanum. In Pompeii they had a lot of junk that said 350 BC or other times, but we did not know if it was real or not. We meet people all over the place that were on the Rex. Most everyone is going to the same places at the same time. Some of the places that we eat at you can't get much to eat, and I don't like spaghette.

My father also wrote that "we have not seen him yet," without saying exactly who "him" might be. My grandmother doubtless would have mightily disapproved of her sons being brought into any close proximity to the pope, so the personage in question was surely Mussolini, whose staff and allies frequented the neighborhood in which the Clark entourage was staying. A letter my grandfather wrote home to his young daughters at the same date mentions that "there are many officers here with striking uniforms and from different nations. There are three German Army officers here at this hotel. They have large arm bands of red with black swastikas on them. Mussolini has forbidden the use of auto horns in Rome so it is much quieter than it used to be."

Robert drove his father and his brother northward to the Channel. They were delayed on the roads by "no end of German army motorcycles and cars." The following year, the war began. Robert took an officer's commission in the navy even before the United States entered the conflict, and served in Europe and then in the Pacific. After Pearl Harbor, my father took a break from the middling Midwestern college he was attending to patrol the coasts of Cape Cod with the Coast Guard Auxiliary, sailing in the dark, looking for German submarines.

Then, in February 1943, Robert was reported missing in action on board the U.S.S. *DeHaven* in the Pacific. He had been the blessed elder son—smart, poised, handsome, and personable—and as my grandmother awaited word from the War Department, her worst and most long-lived fears flocked around her, her prayers helpless to deflect them. When word came that Robert's dead body had been recovered from the hulk of his ship, my grandmother saw that of the two babies she had written about during her illness in 1922, she had but one left.

Thomas's reaction to the loss of his brother was to put himself as directly and quickly in harm's way as possible: He joined the Marine Corps as an enlisted man. Whatever else he may have understood from his father about the Roman world and pagan virtue, he knew it was noble to die fighting *pro patria,* and that to bear death nobly was the essence of stoicism. But he knew something else more viscerally, something whose atavistic, exacting logic was perhaps buried deep within Hadrian's tomb: that for brothers in arms, the death of one brother cannot be redeemed by vengeance or heroism or victory, or by anything life contains, but only by joining death to death.

To remain among the living is a shameful exile, a coward's fate. War is the Eucharist of the unredeemed, pagan world in which death is always the final victor, and this is its inexorable theology.

By 1945 my father was a corporal and stationed in the Pacific, standing by for the invasion of mainland Japan. Given the nature of Marine Corps combat and the probable rate of casualties in the invasion, he as likely as not would have been killed. In the event, he was saved, so to speak, by the atomic bombs, which forced the surrender of Japan and preempted the invasion.

My father came home from the war and was discharged in October 1945. Like everyone in America in the wake of V-J Day, and particularly as is the wont of homecoming soldiers, he celebrated and drank a great deal. But his was a melancholy conviviality. His college girlfriend, a perky Iowan now working as an editorial assistant at *Look* magazine in New York, wanted to be reunited with him as soon as possible, perhaps to formalize an engagement, but he put her off, remaining in St. Paul. He spent his evenings sitting at the bar at a joint called Talley's Tap, losing himself in a sullen haze; and when he bothered to write her back, it was without much enthusiasm. When, after six months, her own letters came less frequently, he wrote her back to tell her that this proved his point—that she really didn't care for him all that much, as he had suspected all along. Sitting at the bar at Talley's with a faint smile on his face, twenty-four years old, brotherless and chasing oblivion, he learned to tell a good war story, or so his friends would later say. Then, one night in March, he turned around and saw my mother, and that, as far my grandmother Elizabeth was concerned, was the end of him.

# FOUR

My mother, Elizabeth Griggs, shared a name with my grandmother Clark, and something of her character; not, perhaps, a dread of death and infection borne of much bad luck, but a wary fragility, a sensitivity to slights underlain by a sense of love's tenuousness. She was a kind and willing girl, overshadowed by prettier, more confident sisters and a little in awe of her father, her brother, and men in general. She had grown up attending the family Episcopal church much as she attended school or dance class, and what little faith she had she lost in comparative religion and psychology courses at Vassar. The closest she came to an epiphany was an encounter with Eleanor Roosevelt in 1943 in the ladies' room of the Poughkeepsie railroad station. Emerging simultaneously from adjacent stalls, my mother exclaimed in surprise, "Mrs. Roosevelt!" and Mrs. Roosevelt, like the very angel of the lord, like the mother my mother had never felt she possessed, replied, "Yes, my dear?"

After graduation in 1945, my mother eventually joined the Unitarian congregation in St. Paul that my grandfather Clark had so recently resigned from. This move provoked some controversy in her family, less for doctrinal than for social reasons, and was a puzzling mark of feistiness in a heretofore notably unfeisty girl. The same was true of her embrace of liberal and even quasi-socialist politics, the result as far as anyone could tell of her transfiguration in the Poughkeepsie ladies room.

She and my father had known each other casually before they

saw each other at Talley's Tap. They had friends in common, and both came from well-thought-of families in St. Paul, the Griggses having emigrated to Minnesota from Connecticut at about the same time as Charles Clark and having established themselves in business, albeit more successfully than Charles had done. But by now Homer Clark had become one of St. Paul's civic elders and worthies. And although my mother and father were only two years apart in age, his father was thirty years older than hers. My grandfather Griggs could have been my grandfather Clark's son.

My mother thought my father was very handsome and she liked the way he let her chatter fill his silences so nicely. For his part, my father was in the depths of rebound from his breakup with his college sweetheart, yet conscious that all around him his freshly demobilized friends and contemporaries were marrying and starting families. He was also drawn to my mother's family, who, unlike his own, were socially active, comparatively informal and fun-loving, and who drank with exuberance. My mother and father were engaged within six months of meeting in Talley's and married four months after that, in a lustrous ceremony at the Griggses' Episcopal church for which my mother temporarily set aside the religious compunctions she had acquired at Vassar. In the wedding photographs, my seventy-eight-year-old grandfather Clark, straightening my father's tie, looks as dignified as a Roman senator; his wife looks alarmed, even frightened, a little lost among these swells and imbibers and their prattling daughters.

My parents had their first child, a daughter who rather oddly received the name of my father's college sweetheart, Barbara, exactly nine months after the wedding, and then another daughter two years later, named Martha for my father's grandmother Martha Pierce Clark and my mother's mother, Martha Baker Griggs. I was born two years after that, in 1952.

I do not remember anything of my father then, for he and my mother separated and divorced just as I was turning two. Wanting a change and a fresh start, my father did the natural thing and moved back to Boston and Cape Cod, to the sea that he loved. When he arrived, New England was in the throes of a polio epidemic, and within weeks he was infected; in two years he was utterly paralyzed, and in two more he was dead.

Before he died, I saw him twice more that I can remember. As part of my parents' divorce settlement, I was sent east for a few weeks each summer when I was four and five years old. I stayed with my father and his new wife, a childhood friend, the stepmother who would take me in as a teenager, just as she then took him in, doubtless knowing he was dying. He was by this time more or less completely immobile, and I remember him less as a person than as a looming presence shipwrecked in a hospital bed, his soft voice against the clicks and sighs of the respirator, his breaths rumbling out of the depths of him, a hulk that, in the manner of whales, by an urgent logic incomprehensible to us, has run itself aground and beached itself in order to die.

After he was gone, there was little contact between the Clarks and the Griggses; despite my last name, I was raised almost entirely in my mother's family. Not that the Clarks ignored me and my sisters, but the occasions on which we saw them—set visits corresponding with major holidays—were awkward and uncomfortable affairs, dictated by duty rather than affection. My grandmother Elizabeth had, after all, lost both her boy babies, just as she had always feared: one to the Japanese and one to my mother. For she could not help but see how the history of my mother and my father's love had unfolded. If she had not married him, she would not have failed him as a wife; and if she had not failed him as a wife, he would not have gone to Boston; and if he had not gone to Boston, he would not have become infected, and his lungs would not have been destroyed as my grandmother's five brothers' lungs were destroyed.

Like her great-uncle Winslow Homer, she knew how and where love takes us; and although she never lost her faith, her capacity for prayer, and belief in an afterlife, I doubt she believed any more than her husband ever had, scanning the evidence of his Roman ruins, that love is truly stronger than death. Perhaps she sometimes thought that the pagan world Christ was supposed to have vanquished leaches into ours, insinuates itself among our saved and redeemed creation, and when it does pines not after life but after death.

# FIVE

$\mathbf{W}$ hen I was a boy, my grandfather Griggs had a house in a forest of jack pine and spruce on Lake Superior in northern Wisconsin, and although I spent at most two months a year there, it seems to me the setting of my whole childhood. On three sides of the house the earth was stony and russet and flocked with pine needles; on the fourth there was a lawn leading down to the lake. The earliest photograph I possess of myself is set there: I am perhaps four months old, belly down on the grass, and my sister is entertaining me with a toy turtle. My parents are dressed as if for tennis; they are young and attractive and gazing at their children. How could we not have been—all of us—anything other than happy?

The house itself was sheathed in white clapboards with double-hung mullioned windows and dark green shutters. There was a front door surmounted by a pediment, a flagpole and a bull's-eye window. That no one ever used this front door speaks to my family's Puritan, New England origins; that the front door was at the side of the house speaks to some particularity I cannot quite put my finger on, a penchant for the oblique and the indirect, no matter how obviously straightforwardness might commend itself.

The house's true entrance was through the kitchen porch, itself reached by a one-by-twelve flung across the pine duff like a draw-bridge. In wet weather it kept our feet out of the puddles and gumbo; in dry, it served as a level track for the wheels of the barbecue and the croquet set as well as a place to clean fish, whose viscera the raccoons carried off into the woods.

It was by no stretch of the imagination a wilderness. Before us and before the house, the place had been logged at least once and perhaps more, and was studded with the random clearings and tangled forest understory that suggested that the land had not known much peace of late. Still, we were blessed in such wildlife as presented itself: Birds sang their hours on the edge of the woods; garter snakes patrolled the foundation of the house; and deer stood outside the dining room windows regarding my grandmother as she skimmed her toast with marmalade and warmed her feet before the tangerine coils of the electric fire.

It was not, in retrospect, very much, but to me then it was an enchanted world and there was nothing before it in my life that I could or would have wanted to remember. In the scent and the heat rising in the sunlight from the pine needles, in the ratcheting of the crickets and the rustling of the wind, in its minute and myriad particularities, it seemed to almost pulse with beauty and excitement, with an inexhaustible goodness. My wonder in the face of it was bottomless.

Nor was this sense confined to the natural world. In fact, my grandparents' landscape was primarily interior. The walls of the house—a compressed-sawdust compound called beaverboard—were painted in light pastel colors and the rooms were furnished with simple, slightly worn furniture. Since they'd first arrived in 1930, the house had not so much undergone decoration as it had accreted its details organically, their immutable and sedate permanence disturbed only by eruptions of my grandfather's indomitable bad taste. Despite being raised in a locally distinguished family and receiving a prep school and Ivy League education, my grandfather reveled in artificial flowers, Reader's Digest Condensed Books, novelty neckwear, and "Sing Along with Mitch" records. When company was expected my grandmother and aunts swept the public rooms like a bomb squad, excising polyethylene hyacinths, ashtrays emblazoned with amiable drunks, priapic duck hunters, pissing urchins and miniature toilets with fur-covered seats and pearl-encrusted trim.

My grandfather's bad taste was, I think, more than a lapse or a quirk. Despite defeat after defeat at the hands of his wife and daughters, he pursued his taste as though impelled by a driving vision, a creative, even spiritual quest. He was scarcely an artist: He sold in-

surance, which perhaps encourages the cultivation of dread and rumination on last things. And so perhaps he sought to make an often
senseless world cohere, to vanquish chaos and tragedy through
whimsy.

During my childhood he began to impose a few such talismans
and objets outside the house, as though trying to establish a point of
contact or a portal into the natural world—into the wilderness—in
terms that would be understandable to both it and him. He had a
small yellow-and-black sign painted with the legend "Hoochy
Goochy Gulchy" and nailed it on a tree next to the deep creek that
ran along the border of the woods. And between the kitchen porch
and the little cabin where the male grandchildren slept when they
were old enough, he set up a little painted-plywood mother skunk
and four kittens mounted on croquet wickets. After the summer was
over and all of us had gone back home to the city for the winter, I
would imagine the house empty, echoing and cold, and the skunk
and her kittens buried under the snow. Then, when we arrived at
the start of summer, they were the first thing I sought out; if any had
been knocked down in the nine months since I'd seen them last, I set
them upright. I was a child, the skunk kittens were as children, and
so too, I think, was my grandfather in his fashion. But each year
there seemed to be one less kitten, seemingly vanished together with
the previous winter's snow, and by the time I was old enough to
sleep alone in the cabin and too old to care about them any longer,
there were none at all.

When I was four or five years old, when my father lay dying on
the shore of the Atlantic, my grandfather Griggs had what was
known as a picture window installed in the southwest corner of the
house. I don't remember the carpenters coming, but they must have
been some days at work—tearing out the old double-hung windows
and their frames and fitting a six-foot-long header in their place—
and when they were done, our relation to the world outside the
house was irrevocably changed. What was once outside was now in
some sense inside; by day, the green light poured into the living
room, and at night the incandescence from our lamps streamed am-
ber like oil across the lawn and into the trees.

In the first few years after the window went in, whenever guests
came to visit my grandfather would guide them to it, beaming like a

new father at the hospital nursery. It was as though he had acquired a
Vermeer. In fact, he had merely ordered up the frame and the glass,
but there was no separating them from what they contained. Two
miles of water lay between us and the lake's opposite shore, a pal-
isade of ruddy stone cliffs easing into hills of aspen and birch. These
things had always been there, and I suppose we had always seen
them. They had been many things, not one thing, but now they
were bound together. Now we had what people called a view. It sat
in our living room like the handsome portrait of a favorite son, of
friend or kin of whom we were terribly proud.

It seemed as often as not my grandfather could be found at the
window, looking through it or standing just in front of it on the patio he had had built. He was a man of habits, dressed in brown ox-
fords, pleated trousers of gray wool or gabardine, and a yellow
V-neck sweater. If it was midday, he held a gin and tonic in a tall
frosted glass; if it was evening, he had scotch and water or an old-
fashioned with a maraschino cherry in it that looked like the sun going down in a forest fire.

The view turned him into a connoisseur of sunsets and he fed
bolts of Kodachrome through his camera to record them. He must
have made hundreds of exposures, all much the same: a border of
spruce, a horizon of water, and the dusk's strata layered over them,
saffron, crimson, and streaky as bacon. Later, as an adolescent, I
wondered what he saw in what seemed to me so little, the sun's imperceptible decline, the acres of ruched and dimpled water, as tire-
lessly regarded as by a sailor's wife. My grandfather had been to sea
once, when he was nineteen, on his way to France to drive an ambulance on the Western Front. His ship traveled in a convoy; when
it reached France, he wrote his mother a letter and told her how the
Gironde opened itself into the Atlantic above Bordeaux to receive
them. He spent a year around Verdun, ferrying the wounded and the
dying, swabbing out the blood from his ambulance, debating the
merits of Protestantism versus Catholicism with the local priest. He
met a beautiful girl with wavy bobbed hair and serene eyes in Eper-
nay. He returned to the Midwest for good in 1918, and he kept her
picture in the back of a desk drawer for the rest of his life. I think
this, like many things in his life, was a keeping of faith, just like
maintaining his voluminous correspondence and researching the

Griggs family genealogy, honoring the past, doing memory's labor. I never heard him utter a devout or pious sentiment, but he clearly believed the world was more good than evil, and he was mightily content in it. That he had once met a pretty girl in France and that he now had a picture window were signs of grace enough for him.

*     *     *

We were children then—my sister, my cousins, and I—and while our elders confined themselves mostly to the house, the patio, and the lawn, we pressed the edges of our place in the world a few feet at a time: to the ditch on the other side of the road; to the stony, driftwood-tangled cove beyond the breakwater; into the woods to the far verge of the property. The earth was terra incognita but benign; barring ill weather, a little more of it could become home each day. We cached pennies and dolls and whistles in the bases of trees, and the forest gave us gifts in return: shelter in the rain, stones and berries, and—once and best of all—the white, perfectly preserved skull of a squirrel. It was enchanted, in the root sense of the word, "cantare": The world sang to us, it rocked us in its great soft arms.

One day when I was about nine years old, on a morning like any other, I heard screaming in the forest. The sunlight fell in shafts between the jack pines, and the air was still and resinous and warm. My cousin Cathy ran out of the woods, shrieking, raking wasps from her hair. She fell among the pine needles and lay on her stomach, writhing. Welts bloomed like tiny strawberries on her arms and legs. The screen door to the kitchen porch yawned and slammed again and again. She was encircled by adults and her cries became sobs and keening. She had stumbled into a wasps' nest in the woods; the stings were few and scarcely toxic, and she would be fine. She would not cry again with such ferocity for another eight or nine years, when a boy she loved forsook her.

I think it was not her body but her heart that pained her; her heart was broken that day. She had believed, until then, that the natural world was good—that it was a friend, itself a child as innocent and well-intentioned as she, and perhaps even a guardian, a protector. Now she had discovered it was cruel, arbitrary, and venomous. It repaid faith with caprice, with wounds. And the betrayal reverberated through everything she believed and thought she knew. For if the world was not good, why had not someone told her? Why, more important, had no one protected her? We were children; our lives were grounded in our faith in the wisdom and beneficence of adults, and beyond them, in the goodness of God. We had been misled, and perhaps lied to. In memory, the anger and the sting of betrayal were tangible as stone, as sour in our mouths as iron, as sharp as copper. They inscribed themselves on our lives as private martyrologies and *kindermärchen*. As in a Grimm's fairy tale, we suspected we had been abandoned, left in the forest. No one would save us, and we were children lost among other children, in the woods among the stones, the berries, the wasps, and the tiny white skull, creatures forsaken by our creator.

Thereafter, we approached the forest with wariness, or, as we grew older, with cocky heedlessness that hid an anxious, fearful belligerence. Needless to say, we sought revenge. Insects of all descriptions could be found trapped in the kitchen porch, flailing against the screens, their motions increasing in pitch and frenzy as the afternoon heat rose. We beat them with rolled newspapers and fly swatters, hosed them with water and insecticides drawn from brown bottles, asphyxiated them in clouds of gas. They buzzed in fury and agony and wheeled their bodies in pointless circles, like draw horses tethered to a mill.

I think we understood that we were cruel, but our cruelty was irresistible, like candy, like the desires in our bodies that we could not name and that we were scarcely learning to tease and sate. I myself spent more and more time by the picture window, not looking out of it, but sprawled beneath it on the sofa, reading books about expeditions, sea voyages, and sailors' knots. Sometimes a wasp or a blackfly would find its way into the house. I suppose they were drawn to the light of the window, or to the illusion that it was a passage to the outside. Or perhaps it was not an illusion, for no one could deny that the outside was clearly before them in the window, no matter how obdurate and impenetrable the window itself proved to be. They buzzed against it like drillers on a rock face of diamond, perhaps in frustration, perhaps in incomprehension, perhaps in sheer terror. I heard them, and I would get up and find a canister of insecticide and pump it onto their bodies until there was not a trace of their voices, until the poison mounted up like sea foam on the windowsill.

\*　　　\*　　　\*

I can still see myself, a child clad in shorts and a T-shirt and high-topped sneakers, performing this liturgy of annihilation, and I know I could see myself doing it then. It was that very self-awareness, that watching myself do it, that gave the act its savor, the newfound thrill of performing on the stage of one's self-consciousness. And it was that that took my actions out of the childhood realm of mischief, disobedience, or thoughtlessness, past that of sin—of simply failing to be good—and into the realm of evil, of not merely causing misfortune but creating it, fashioning a self that was evil's author, setting that creature in motion as God did Adam, and watching it go about its work.

That was a discovery I made long ago, when I was a scarcely a decade old, in the world before this one. But it seems to me that every human life reenacts the story of Eden, usually in childhood—an age in which there is no evil or falsehood or death, where seeming and being are one beautiful and numinous thing, where we are both wholly free and completely in accord with the creation we inhabit. One's own self and its expression seem identical with the world's will, with God's word, his self-utterance. Then, as Emerson put it, "It is very unhappy, but too late to be helped, the discovery we have made that we exist. That discovery is called the Fall of Man." And in the Fall, what we steal is not simply the fruit of the tree of knowledge, but specifically that of self-knowledge and the kind of self-expression that follows from it. In my lifetime self-expression has been regarded as one of the highest goods, and so it often can be. But in the Fall, we cease to differentiate between our use of this faculty and God's. The product of God's self-awareness is self-expression as pure being, as that which is wholly good. It's because of this that the expression "God is love" is more than a syrupy truism. For in a rigorously philosophical definition, love is that which lacks nothing—which wants nothing for itself but simply wills the existence of its object—and is therefore perfect being, which is to say God. God's self-expression is the Love from which we and his creation are engendered.

Our self-discovery leads elsewhere, not to joyful self-contemplation but, at least in part, to the end of our innocence. The loss of innocence seems to me less the gaining of forbidden knowledge than the discovery of desire—the sense that far from being blessed by both unimaginable grace and freedom, we are inadequate and also enslaved by what we lack; and the amelioration of that lack becomes our life's work. This is the knowledge that initiates our discontent, our disenchantment, our sense that we have been stripped of grace, that we are no longer loved. And that is, perhaps, why desire so often feels like love, or like the longing for it.

I know it was at my grandfather's house, after the wasps, that I discovered desire. For a long time before that, and some time after, life and the world felt emptied out, hollow, comfortable for the most part, full, in fact, of temporary satisfactions, but devoid of wonder. It seems to me now to have been a continuation and escalation of that sense of betrayal, of unwanted and unbidden knowledge, that first came upon me that summer when I was nine. Thereafter, my life did not lack joy or excitement, but they came not through the mere acceptance of the gift that that earlier enchanted world had seemed to me, but through the fulfillment of desire; of discovering an urge and acting on it, of making what I wanted to happen happen.

I think desire was in my body before it was in my mind. I first recollect it from around age ten: lying half-awake in bed in the cabin, conscious of a tension in my body, a sort of vibrant, manic itch, a delicious ache that on the one hand demanded to be eased—but how?—and on the other to be perpetually sustained. For the first time in my life, I didn't want to get straight up and play or go into the house or out into the woods. I wanted to stay here with this feeling for as long as it would go on.

In retrospect, I know that I was merely pressing my proto-adolescent morning erection against the mattress, but it took me some time to connect what I was feeling with my genitals or even with my body in a specific way, still less with the bodies of others. And I think at least a year went by before I understood that the sensation could be induced, coaxed, manipulated, and brought to a kind of epiphany, albeit not one that truly sated the underlying desire. That was what I came to understand about it, and in a general way about all desire: that it is not an itch that can ever really be scratched, because its savor, its substance—everything that we crave in—depends on absence, unfulfillment, lack. What we truly covet is the hunger on the verge of being sated, the flash of the synapse between wanting and having. To possess it is to spoil it, and so we must start all over again.

Thus was desire a little akin to the wonder I had previously felt. Perhaps it is what grownups have, or at least cultivate, instead of enchantment. It has the joyful vibrancy of wonder, but not its placid givenness. Indeed, desire is not given but must be pursued, urged, and driven, its objects forever time-bound and scarce, and perhaps our pursuit of it implies something is in turn pursuing us, for which we believe desire is the remedy. We are unlikely to ask whether it is a fair substitute for what we have lost, but that itself is in the nature of the desire: to seem to be what we want. And to sense the lack, the unbeing, at the heart of desire is perhaps the adult equivalent of what I discovered in the woods when I was nine, my first loss of faith.

It was in the wake of these things that I underwent my first conversion, to Episcopalianism and being "good," at the age of twelve. Now, it seems nothing so much as an attempt to recover the inborn faith I had lost in the woods by my grandfather's house; an attempt, it also seems to me now, that was predicated not on love but on desire and so was as misguided as it was well-intended. When I saw myself, I saw what I was not and wanted to be. My conversion was less about a turning to God—the root meaning of the word "conversion" —than about the construction of a new self in which I was both creator and creature. This is not the intended task of religion, and it is not surprising that I drifted away from it and toward psychology and the neo-Transcendentalist program of the sixties and early seventies, which promised to bring about exactly the change I desired.

If my life of the next twenty years had a theme, it was self-discovery. Of course, I had discovered myself long before, but I had not much liked what I'd seen. My notion of my self was an autonomous person, not an object—a being whose essence was a given, created thing—but a subject. My person might be, as psychology taught, determined by the interactions of culture, politics, and power, but it was also somehow infinitely malleable if I wanted to undertake changing it. I did not see the contradiction in that, or wonder exactly what agent—which *me*—stood still performing all these operations while my personhood underwent its constant renovation and improvement.

I still visited my grandfather's house during these years, less perhaps for its current attractions than as a museum of the boy I used to be. But in my dreams it was still a refuge, still the world before this one, unfallen. Sometimes I held its image in my mind in the form of a snow cave, the den of a hibernating creature, a heart—somehow warm and without fear or care—beating in the middle of the still and frozen world.

In fact, I never saw snow at my grandfather's house until I was older, eighteen years old. During the winter, squirrels had invaded the attic, and my grandfather and his handyman got the idea to drive them out by burning sulfur candles. One night in March, one of the candles fell, or was knocked over, and the house caught fire. When it was wholly in flames, someone across the lake, two miles away, saw the conflagration and called the fire department. But it was too late. The next day the earth where the house had stood hissed and buzzed with the snow, melted from the center of the fire outward, ringing it at a distance. I came a few days later. I would have liked to find the mother skunk and her kittens at some distance from the house, fallen, perhaps half buried in the duff, but safe, but they had disappeared years before. There was nothing left but two chimneys, some broken pieces of pottery where the kitchen had stood, and a few black shards of glass in the southwest corner. Someone told me the picture window would have exploded like a bomb.

I always wondered if the fire broke my grandfather's heart, if it effected some transformation or epiphany in his life. But I never knew his secrets, least of all that of his vast and placid contentment. I do know, as it later emerged, that despite his career in the insurance business, he had never bothered to put an insurance policy on the house in the woods.

He built a new house in its place, but it was not the same. I had my own house by then, and a career and a wife and a child. These things occupied me, and gradually took the place of the conscious self-fashioning I had been so busy with during my adolescence and twenties. Or rather, they became my person, they were who I was, until the shape and buttressing they had given my life began to fall away in my thirties. In the space of two years, I lost my job, my marriage, and my financial assets. The month I turned thirty-nine a close friend was diagnosed with a brain tumor, which would have to be removed by a long and complicated but not terribly perilous operation. Her surgery was in Pittsburgh, and at the moment it was taking place, I was driving down a highway in Wyoming, on my way to a magazine writing assignment.

I did not want to do the assignment and I did not want to be in Wyoming. The road ran through treeless high country, still winterbound, and the snow snaked on and off the shoulders in ribbons across the highway. From the west, black-bellied clouds were pressing down against the horizon, moving toward me, bearing, perhaps, an imminent blizzard. I thought of that, of all the things that had recently befallen my life, and of my friend on the operating table in Pittsburgh, and I said, aloud, not having given Him a thought in years, "Please, God—no more."

There was more. The weather held, but my friend never awoke from her surgery. The tumor was larger and the operation more difficult than predicted. She lingered for a week, and then she died. I cannot say that, like Henry Adams with the death of his sister in 1870, I lost my faith at that moment. I had already lost my faith in any conscious form years before, and was, for lack of any other belief, a sort of fatalist. Fatalism—accepting that, lacking anything else, randomness and chance constitute a system—may be the dominant religion among educated, worldly-wise members of my generation. Provided your luck holds and you are not so old as to need to give much thought to death (which in this view merely returns the body to the soil, a kind of composting that is both appealing in its circularity and ecologically public-spirited), as creeds go you could do worse. If it's not strictly held—and it is not the sort of belief anyone bothers to hold systematically—moments of particular success can be construed, in the more traditional American manner, as having been deserved or earned. All in all, it is a swell religion for the fortunate and the smug.

When things turn really bad, however, no one wants to be a fatalist. The mind does not easily tolerate effects without causes, events without explanations. That is why jilted fatalists become cynics; there is, it turns out, a system, but it's rigged. Despair is a braver and more honest option, but no one can cling to it and survive: It enacts love and creation in reverse, ending in self-annihilation.

After that day on the highway in Wyoming, I flirted with both cynicism and despair. I took up cigarettes again and drank too much. I sat at bars as my father had done at Talley's Tap, and I fulminated. But at some level I understood that my calling out to God and his apparent lack of response could be proof of something other than his nonexistence: his callousness. A part of me was inclined to say, *This is what you get for your trouble when you ask God for a favor.* That proposition, with its anger and sense of betrayal, presumes something rather than nothing. It presupposes that its object is real. It is the position of Job, and also that of Jesus on the cross when he asks why his father has forsaken him.

In my bitterness and sense of grievance I had, therefore, opened up a kind of dialogue after years of silence. It was sporadic to be sure, and had nothing to do with belief per se, never mind with doctrine or religion. My inclination was to adopt a kind of modified fatalism, made sweeter and more bearable by a specific engagement with the natural world. I spent a lot of time hiking during this period, as well as reading in the genre known as nature writing. It came to seem to me that nature in its purity, its beauty, and even its apparent randomness and amorality gave the lie to the notion of a creation abandoned by its creator. Nature, I believed, must say something, must be a sign, an indication of something rather than nothing.

It was then that I went back to my grandfather's house. I was forty years old, and my grandfather had died the previous summer. His death—the death of the man who had been the closest I had come to having a father, and in relationship to whom I came closest to being a son—had been another among the losses that seemed in those days to define my life. My mother and her siblings had decided to sell the house, which was, of course, not the house of my childhood but the one he had built after the fire. Still, the woods and outbuildings remained, and perhaps there would be something on the property I would like to take as a keepsake.

When I arrived, the only thing I recognized from my childhood was the cabin where I had slept when I was old enough and where now no one had slept for years. I went in, pushing past the dense mob of spruce and pine that had then been mere shrubs and saplings, but that now, tall as me and taller, blocked the way and surrounded the cabin. Inside, the floor tipped like a ship in a gale and wallpaper dangled from the walls. Yet the smell was the same as it always had been: green Palmolive soap, damp sheets and chenille bedspreads, paper, dust, and scorched lampshades. The light was sparse, the windows blocked by the spruce trees outside.

Tacked to the wall was a map of the lake that must have been placed there before I was born, and the point of land where I was standing was visible upon it, though no larger than a mote. If there was a picture window in heaven overlooking this place, perhaps this was the view. Before it had first been hung, the map had been altered in a few respects: Someone had brushed the lake blue with watercolor and painted a beautiful Indian princess in the corner, her eyes and hair dark and shiny as coal. She had been my emblem of desire when desire first came to haunt my bones, after the wasps, before the fire, when I began to lie beneath the picture window; when I still believed, as perhaps my grandfather always did, that naïveté was the mark of innocence—of ourselves in what used to be called "the state of nature" —rather than of mere ignorance. But then it seemed to me also true that since we were in that way a part of nature—coequal with nature rather than its offspring—then nature could not itself be our true parent, our creator, our God. Nature was but a sign of something greater, not the thing itself. And so, in that moment, I found myself bereft of the closest thing to a god I had in those days been able to imagine.

On an impulse, I decided to take the map, along with some of my grandfather's papers and scrapbooks, home to where I live now, near a park that encircles a lake. The map seemed to be all that was left of the view I remembered here, a speck no larger than the black of the Indian princess's eye. I pulled out the thumbtacks, flyblown with rust, rolled up the map, opened the door, and pushed my way back out through the trees. They stood all around, thronging the cabin, like children waiting to be let in.

# SIX

When I left the cabin for the last time, with the map under my arm and the now disenchanted forest all around me, what I at last desired, I think, was an end of desire; a return to the simple acceptance of the world which is wonder, our initiation—before we can consciously do good or confuse it with desire—into love. But the only remnants I could find were some papers and a map. But I could not see that the map truly *was* a map—a map capable of taking me as close to that place as I dared to go—even as, leaving the cabin, I could not see the forest for the trees. Instead, I had the map put in a handsome frame and hung it over my bed, and I walked around the little lake in a park near my house, trying to recover the unnamable thing I was sure I had lost, and which wanting only pushed further out of reach.

That sense of having reached another dead end might have dejected me, but an upward turn in my fortunes pushed aside the questions it raised. In the first few years of my forties I prospered as perhaps I had never prospered before. I had at last put the malaise of my first marriage's disintegration behind me and begun to regain the trust of that divorce's victim, my ten-year-old daughter; I had published two books to good reviews; and, most crucially, I was sharing my life with a woman whose beauty, goodness, and love for me I could only marvel at.

I had been sitting, as was my habit, at a bar, as my father had been sitting at a bar almost half a century before, and I looked over my shoulder and there she was. Beyond that, Caroline's and my courtship was rather different from that of my parents. While I was drawn to her with all the urgency that passion usually affords, I also held back in some fundamental way. Certainly I was, by virtue of my previous experiences with marriage and child-rearing, a little reluctant to rush into anything, but, reassured by the self-evident rightness of our relationship, I moved toward them, albeit without much enthusiasm. It was not that I would not "commit," but that I would not assent; I could not put myself fully into a relationship with another person.

That connection between people, I now believe, entails a kind of faith, and I had no more capacity to "believe" in another person than I did to believe in a God. I do not mean that I was cold or timid or more than normally self-centered, and by this time my despair and cynicism were in remission. Even my fatalism was no longer overt, although I had never succeeded like my stoic grandfather Clark into rendering it into something noble. But I was surely lost in myself, or rather among my selves, not so much in that I was selfish—although I was, and remain exceedingly selfish—but in that I was unable to see anyone or anything except through the lens of self-awareness, as though in the mirror of my own consciousness of me. I could not apprehend other people as "you," but—watching myself watching them—as refractions of one or another "I."

This sounds like what the Modernists of my grandfather Griggs's generation—such as his childhood friend Scott Fitzgerald—called egotism, or what people in my own generation detected in a "culture of narcissism." Both those terms imply a disorder of character, what Henry Adams's contemporaries called moral insanity, brought on by a larger sense of dislocation and alienation, of estrangement from the world. Like these, doubtless its precursors, the affliction I am trying to describe seems at bottom less one of the conscience or the heart—our sense of rights, wrongs, and responsibilities—than of the imagination and the faculties of perception and knowing. You could almost say that after we have, through three centuries of reason and science, understood and mastered the universe, it does not seem quite real to us; and the part of that enterprise that studied human behavior, belief, and epistemology has conferred the same sense of unreality on our experience of ourselves. The most recent and perhaps ultimate manifestation of this, calling itself deconstruction, proposes that all perceptions are necessarily mere social constructions, usually self-serving and pernicious in origin. Logically speaking, however, the argument seems to swallow its own tail, simultaneously positing and dismantling the truth of what it asserts, deconstruction itself then being only another culturally determined illusion.

Three-quarters of a millennium ago, nominalism suggested that we could not truly know God or the world, and, working with what was left over, Luther reformed religion on the basis that at least we could know ourselves, and with that as the one sure place to stand, we could approach God (and, by extension, the other objects we wished to know) *sola fide*. Perhaps this pushed self-consciousness—God's gift and Eden's curse—beyond its carrying capacity. In any case, when the self was subjected to the same perceptual analysis, it, too, became unreal. Perceptions lost the ability to perceive. Neither the thing observed nor its observer, object or subject, was real.

The artists and intellectuals of my grandfather's and father's generation had to cope with the sense that the world was unreal, that human society and culture were deceptions, but they salvaged the individual being, "the existential hero," from the wreckage. That, I suppose, placed an even larger burden on what the self was supposed to bear—on what the self was supposed to mean to itself—while removing more and more of the external supports that once sustained it. More crucially, we might say it removed the *context* for the self. Things exist in relation to other things, are located by the locations of other things, and take on their qualities and character by contrast and comparison to other things. If nothing is real or fixed, if there is no unmoved mover—nothing to *push* against, be it God or mere created reality—and everything is subjective and in flux, it is awfully hard to have a real and authentic self.

That is a bit how the world seemed from my bar stool. I do not mean that I believed that nothing was real, but everything seemed elusive and slippery to the grasp, and this engendered certain habits of mind. This was in the early 1990s, which looks to me now to be a time notable for its posturing, a veritable golden age of poseurship. There was a great deal of moralizing, sanctimony, and humbug about "character" and "family values" among our civic leaders, and faux bohemianism—goatees, piercing and tattooing, pseudo-nihilist black clothing and black makeup, sitting in pretend Left Bank cafés pretending to write poetry or keep journals—among the young and cultural elite. I don't think this was entirely calculating or even meant to be taken seriously. That it really was a pose could be, in any case, readily admitted, since everything was ironic. And even the irony was itself a pose, or a least the main means available to interpret what was taking place.

Not too long ago, irony could be genuinely enlightening, it could open our eyes. Joined to the sensibility of a former time—that of a Dickens or a Flaubert or a Marx—it could be a scourge, an engine of moral outrage. If nothing else, it suggested an awareness of plurality and nuance; at worst it was a display of sophistication. But more recently, in its "postmodern" form, irony has become an empty parlor game. It is to ethics—to the problem of our human situation and how we ought to live within it—as the pun is to humor; clever, diverting, and instantly forgettable, it merely inverts rather than responds to the question. As a convinced view of the world— which I think is how it was being practiced by me and the people I knew—it is, to say the least, problematic.

Irony became the voice of universal agnosticism, of the incapacity to believe, to know, or to be certain of even one's own identity— it was the refusal to take the value or verity of anything at face value. And if this seems to you to be the way things are, then perhaps it is the only honest position to take, if it is in fact a position at all, since it must necessarily undermine and look askance even at itself. That corrosiveness is the problem with irony: In its postmodern form, it seems to lead inevitably to resignation, cynicism, or nihilism. The object of irony, after all, is to demonstrate what things are not, to falsify or undermine their claims to truth and reality. Its affinities are with what is *not,* with lack, privation, and nonbeing, and it thus plumbs the same depths as desire. Irony, as a worldview, empties the world and finally itself of meaning and being.

Agnosticism, to which irony gives expression, arose because the facts of science and of an undeniably amoral world seemed to render belief untenable. If belief depends on knowledge—in this case, on scientific proof of a God who manages his creation in accordance with our notions of justice—it will always be untenable, because belief, by definition, is not knowledge. It is something to which we assent rather than something we know. Belief has nothing to do with what God does and everything to do with what *we* do, with our willingness or refusal, our capacity or incapacity, to accept an unprovable proposition.

That is all very well and good, we might say, but cold comfort—it does nothing about the incapacity to believe. But we also know that, followed by means of irony to its conclusion, agnosticism is untenable on the grounds not of belief but of simple reason: Its logic makes it self-consuming. For agnosticism to be correct, we have to posit a reality based on nothing rather than something, on nonbeing rather than on being. Regardless of our notions about God or religion, we cannot do this. Revisiting the Middle Ages, we discover that both the nominalists and Aquinas, however seemingly opposed, were right: It is true that we cannot directly know reality, but it is also true that reality *is*.

Religion and philosophy suffer nowadays in comparison with science because they depend on unprovable assertions. But so, in fact, does science. The most fundamental and unfudgeable constituent of science, mathematics, requires postulates—untestable propositions to which assent must be given—to go about its business. Philosophy and theology require nothing more: We accept, despite our inability to prove it, that there is something rather than nothing. Anyone will rightly object that believing in reality does not entail belief in God. That is true enough, but it does entail belief in *being,* and from there it is a very short leap to God, if you want to make it. The fact of reality may not prove God, but it implies Him. Agnosticism self-destructs as both knowledge and belief; atheism is, of course, no more than another unprovable proposition that posits nothing rather than something, it might be true, or it might not.

That was the logic of my situation in the early 1990s, but what was crucial to it was more felt than thought. The assent to something rather than nothing says that there are indeed real entities outside ourselves—"it" and, most important, "you"—and these entities by context and relation make us real to ourselves. Being acknowledges being, making being, as it were, be; and that process of being in relation to itself, lacking nothing, is how we understand God to be love. That is why we say that love—not desire, lust, need, domination, or possession—"brings us out of" ourselves, perceives us and calls us out; gives its assent to us and asks only that we assent to it; that we acknowledge its "you" as it has acknowledged our "I."

Human love, of course, is never wholly like this divine love, but it almost always partakes of it, as anyone in love feels. Dante understood this and wrote the *Divine Comedy* as a demonstration of it: Loving Beatrice leads him to the love of God. Placing himself in relation to her "you" puts him on the path to relation with the ultimate "You," the Love who is Dante's creator. It is no wonder that we seek love so hungrily, that we feel ourselves nowhere so "real" as in its presence; that, to paraphrase Augustine on the soul's yearning for God, our hearts are restless until they find their home in it. Perhaps that is why those who are truly convinced of the impossibility of love are as rare as atheists; and why agnosticism toward love is untenable, is but a temporary refuge before we go out to seek love yet again.

So it was in this way that Caroline finally brought me out of myself, putting a "you" before me to which I had to give assent. That is the way in which love is a species of grace: It opens one to being. It is a quotidian miracle and, at least in my case, is worked slowly, quietly, incrementally. Acknowledging her acknowledgment of me did not transform me or cause me to be in some way "reborn." Rather, it put me in the world's path, compelled me, after assenting to her "you," to begin to acknowledge some of the world's givenness, its createdness and relation to love; to open my eyes a little and attend its signs.

On the whole, neither my forebears nor I was much for epiphanies, flashes of enlightenment, or visitations on the road to Damascus. When moments resembling such things occur, they are dreamlike; they slip away and we find ourselves perhaps stunned and blinking but exactly where we were before.

It is that way with my own adult conversion, and continues to be so. Insofar as it has a signal moment, a time after which my relation to faith and religion was visibly altered, it occurred over a period of several weeks in the summer of 1995. Caroline and I had been together for three years. She was pregnant and I was writing my first novel, trying to get it finished before our baby's delivery date. I would like to give the experience a certain dignity by saying that it transpired on my knees, or at least while I sat upright in a stiff and venerable chair.

But I was, in fact, slumped on a rather cushy chaise longue, my notebook computer on my lap, listening to music and writing, as I had been for six months. My previous book had been, ostensibly, a cultural history of the Columbia River, albeit an impressionistic one, but to me it had ended up feeling like an epic poem or a novel, an extended rumination on all the things in life and the world I could not make sense of. The book did not give me the answers I sought, but it framed certain questions. Its final pages, a description of an Indian site on a tributary of the Columbia, give a pretty accurate impression of what those were:

> There is a graveyard on the Klikitat River above the place where long ago a girl learned to weave baskets that could carry water without losing a drop. Among the headstones there are dolls, plates, cups, and garlands of foil. Each plot is set up like a place at the table for an honored guest. There are yellow and purple plastic flowers, and pinwheels stuck in the ground at the heads of the graves. The pinwheels spin in the wind and it seems as though they are ticking off the running down of this world like clocks for the dead.
>
> But perhaps they turn in some other course like the propellers of ships, for what can save the world but persistence, the unceasing ebb and flood of winds and the descent of water? What else can set the world right, when death ensures that no one endures in it for long, and that for the living, loss is as daily as bread?

I do not think this is fatalistic or stoic, but it is a tragic conception of the life we are given. It observes creation's entropy: Life ends rather than continues. It wonders what to make of disappointment and death. It seems like gloomy stuff, but I was not particularly gloomy at the time. I suppose that not only was I beginning to grasp the inevitability of loss in this world, I was no longer finding American culture's habitual distractions from this fact—shopping, careerism, achievement, shopping, therapy, situation comedies, and shopping—very diverting.

What I had stumbled across and was now a little mired in was the basic discovery that human self-consciousness makes: that of death and its particular inevitability and preordainedness. But self-consciousness is also a gift, the capacity to perceive ourselves and creation in relation to each other, to practice the "beknowing" I spoke of in reference to my medieval ancestors and to see the evidences through which God manifests Himself in the world. In this, we might say that something of God's mind, his self-utterance, is mirrored in our minds; and since that self-utterance is the ground of love—being regarding being and wishing it to be—it is also through this gift that we are able to learn to love. The highest and most precious aspect of this gift of self-consciousness is the capacity to love God and apprehend his love for us. This capacity is called grace and it is by its workings that conversions, even those as paltry as my own, befall us.

I had been sitting, as I said, for several weeks in the midst of writing a novel, and through the novel I was trying to puzzle out answers to some of the matters that had been weighing on me. The novel was the story of a Midwestern family, not much different from my own although not consciously based on it, set at a time when my grandfather Griggs was about my own age now. The family is settled and prosperous, and its members are self-assured in everything from their taste in clothes to their religion, which is less a matter of faith than of entitlement, unexamined, as is most everything in their lives.

I am not a "plot-driven" writer. Rather, I imagine characters as thoroughly as I am able and then let the world have at them and stand back to see what they do. In this case, the fictional family was besieged in a very short span by afflictions ranging from betrayal to adultery to near death. That was the plot, and how my characters were changed by it was my theme. I would now say that I was trying to explore the interaction of faith and love, and I would have to admit that I think it is probably the theme of all my books, and that as a writer, since I do not seriously expect ever to "solve" it, I am stuck with it. One reviewer, wiser to my work than I am, said the novel was about "how love leads to suffering, and, more interestingly, how suffering leads to love."

So I sat on my chaise longue and watched and waited to see the movements of my characters through these trials so I could record them, and if you had seen me from behind you might not have even known I was doing anything more than daydreaming. I might have been slumped in a beach chair, looking out to sea. I was trying to evoke my characters' Anglicanism, and the music I was listening to to get the mood right was some chant from the early sixteenth century, music written on the cusp of King Henry's Reformation, from the time of Sir John Baker and John Clark, the Protestant heretic-hunter and his prey. There were two pieces that I played over and over again, and they were in fact more in the Catholic than reformed tradition, although I did not know this. The first was called "Mater Christi Sanctissima." I did not pay any attention to the words at the time, either in the original or in translation, but they were as follows:

> Mater Christi sanctissima
> Virgo sacrata Maria
> Tuis orationibus benignum redde Filium
> Unica spes nostra Maria
> Nam precibus nitentes tuis rogare audemus Filium.
> (Most holy mother of Christ
> Hallowed Virgin Mary
> Gentle your son through your prayers
> Mary our only hope
> Sustained by your entreaties we dare to seek your son.)

The other piece was the "Magnificat," Mary's response to the Annunciation, to the revelation of her pregnancy and her assent to it:

Magnificat anima mea Dominum
Et exsultavit spiritus meus in Deo salutari meo
Quia respexit humilitatem ancilliae suae ecce enim ex hoc
Beatam me dicent omnes generationes
Quia fecit mihi magna qui potens est et sanctum nomen eius.
(My soul doth magnify the Lord
And my spirit hath rejoiced in God my savior
For He hath regarded the lowliness of his handmaid

Behold, from henceforth all generations shall call me blessed
For He that is mighty has done great things to me and
　　holy is His name.)

The point of recording these words here is not to show what I was hearing, but rather what I was not hearing. I know a little Latin, but hardly enough to translate and take in these things on the fly. I might say instead that perhaps, as Caroline's love—her "you"—had put me in a position to see other things beyond myself, so the music put me in the path—in a position of openness and susceptibility— to its subject. I cannot say. I just do not know.

But at some point during those weeks, there was an utterance in my head—neither a thought nor a voice—whose source was outside myself, and it said that, really, I was going to have to go ahead and believe, wasn't I? Although it was not in any sense a voice, never mind a vision, it seemed to have a tone of affectionate chiding about it, like a parent wearily but amusedly saying, *Come off it now— enough,* knowing in advance that I had no choice but to agree. And it was true: the sense of this utterance hung in the air before me all through those weeks, but even the very first time I knew what my answer was going to be. So that was my conversion and my assent: *All right, I give up, you're right, I'll surrender.*

That was clear from the start, and so, too, was the sense that this utterance, this verbal shadow that had fallen across me on the chaise, came from Mary. That this had happened to me was not, to my mind, a great piece of good fortune, but an embarrassment, an erup- tion of cringe-making, hot and sticky unalloyed conviction in my cool and sophisticated life that was as corny and unrepentantly middle-brow as my grandfather's plastic hyacinths and the *Sound of Music* Broadway cast album. If I thanked God, it was for not having sent me anything worse: a vision or a Lourdes that would threaten to overwhelm my stripped-pine, pseudo-Shaker lifestyle with stoups of tepid holy water, tinkling rosaries, flaming hearts, and weeping plas- ter figurines. I did not tell anyone about it, and even to Caroline I only allowed that perhaps, with a baby on the way, we ought to in- vestigate a church. A christening, a baptism, might be sort of, well, sweet.

I have now come to believe that Mary has a special affinity for overregulated, hyperintellectualized New England hard cases like Margaret Fuller and Henry Adams, precisely those people to whom Mary ought to be anathema. God likes nothing so much, I think, than to discomfit a Puritan, and that was what I had always at bottom been. Not for nothing did nineties poseurs like me so often dress in black.

More seriously, I have come to learn that Mary is, in addition to her other qualities, the human exemplar of assent: of waiting for God's grace to come and, against all our proclivities, of saying yes to it—acknowleging God's "you," returning his love with what love we, in our poverty of spirit, can muster. In scenes of the Annunciation, Mary is usually pictured seated with a book or needlework in her lap, having been interrupted by the announcing angel. The image suggests that the expectation and coming of this ultimate "you" are what we are made for, and that all our other labors are but ways to pass the time while we await it.

Mary is also seen as the figure that embodies the church, the vehicle through which Christians come to Christ, just as she was the means through which Christ came into the world. Mary, like the church, is both mother and daughter. That aspect of Mary proved to be as significant to me as any, for I quickly discovered that, when word of my conversion leaked out, people were less alarmed that I was a believer than that I apparently planned to follow that belief into a church, and the Roman Catholic church in particular.

The suspicion of organized religion is surely part of my generation's wariness of authority in general and of the repressive, antiindividualist reputation of churches in particular, a notion that goes back to the Transcendentalists. More than one person suggested to me, not always subtly, that I was going to give up my "right to think for myself," that I was surrendering my personal autonomy in exchange for a handful of comforting verities. I would, they feared, become blinkered and even bigoted, rigid and censorious, closed to any idea or experience that didn't conform or relate to church dogma.

I think they were right to worry, and I was worried myself. Belief has a tendency to congeal into certitude, into convictions sustained by prejudice rather than the hard and uncertain work of encountering what is fundamentally mystery. Worse is the habit

religion often inculcates of predicating the righteousness of its adherents upon the unrighteousness of everyone else, a sort of
Manicheanism. Even the gentlest proselytizing has always made me
extremely uncomfortable, so these were pitfalls of which I was
highly conscious.

But at the same time, it seemed to me inherent in what I was undergoing that I would end up in a church. As much as I shared and
often exceeded my friends' distrust of institutional authority, it did
not seem to me that the consumerist, salad-bar spirituality—a little
Buddhism, a little Native American legend or angelology, a little
Jung by way of Joseph Campbell— practiced by so many of my contemporaries had much to recommend it. Rather, it bore the same
evanescent quality as any other lifestyle accessory they might possess.
People spoke of "my spirituality" as they spoke of "my sexuality," as
if these were personal preferences and tastes unconnected to anyone
or anything else other than the self. That very use of the term "spirituality" came to make me nervous: "spirituality" of this sort is to
religion what the word "sexuality" is to love—the work of faith carried out without a "you," without a context, which I already had
come to feel was what had made it so hard to believe in the first
place. And faith, I think, is work; it is, as Mary shows us, the labor
of our lives. It needs a frame in which to occur, rules both to follow
and to test, an edifice both to shelter us and to push against, a community, a corporate "you" in relation to which we *beknow* ourselves.
The word "religion" means "rebind," to tie us again to that from
which we had our origin but were severed. Religion's raison d'être
is not to foster yet another private choice (even, I believe, if it is "a
decision for Christ"), but rather a connection to a "You" that necessarily exists in community. All the corruption, imperfection, and
disappointment contained in the history of the church does not
change the fact of that need, any more than miscarriages of justice
or misuse of the public weal mean that we do not require law or
government.

We are, it seems, stuck with religion not by choice, but rather as
we are stuck with family: Fairness and rights, personal opinion, and
the desires of the majority are relevant, but are finally outweighed by
deeper, sometimes almost atavistic ties. Thus do we put up with and
even at times love, say, Grandpa, who tends to be autocratic and not

to listen; the schemings, competitions, inconstant love and support, and festering grievances of parents, aunts, uncles, brothers, and sisters; the children who never grow up and leave home as well as those who run away, breaking our hearts and—prodigal as we all are in families—yet return.

So it was with wariness and yet an incipient sense of the need for religion to be in some way organized that I first approached the Catholic church. Shortly after Andrew's birth, I went to St. James Cathedral, Seattle's principal Catholic congregation, and asked what would be involved in having Andrew, er, baptized there. Was I a Catholic? Well, no, I admitted, and neither was Caroline, although I finally blurted out that I was "curious" about becoming one. We just thought we'd let Andrew go first. I was gently informed that this was not the way it was generally done. Once a baby was baptized into the Catholic faith, the church thought it was a good idea for the child to have some adults—at least one parent and a godparent—to guide him or her in the faith.

Oh, yes, I allowed, that made a certain amount of sense. It was suggested that perhaps I would like to attend the cathedral's Rite of Christian Initiation for Adults (RCIA) classes and test my own interest in the Catholic faith; then the matter of Andrew's baptism could be returned to. Thus thwarted, I found myself attending the first of many Wednesday sessions in the Cathedral Hall. The initial sessions were called "inquiries" and were conducted almost entirely in question-and-answer format. The RCIA process is a Vatican Two–ordained program that replaces the somewhat cursory "instruction" adult converts received in private meetings with a priest prior to their baptism or, if they were already baptized in another denomination, first communion. It is meant to be more systematic, and goes to some lengths to ensure that conversion is neither hasty nor poorly thought out. In my case, for example, the process lasted almost a year and a half, and at times, contrary to fears of friends who were convinced I was being aggressively recruited into a cult, I felt the church was really trying to discourage me from joining at all.

The people who attended the inquiry sessions ranged from theologically sophisticated intellectuals to immigrants who scarcely spoke English, and the questions ran the gamut from the arcane to the obvious. Just as noticeable were the long silences between questions, as people struggled awkwardly to formulate their queries, to shape, at least in my case, amorphous urges, intimations, and inklings into words. Over the weeks there were dozens and dozens of questions put and answered, but there is one I remember particularly well. An Asian woman whose grasp of English was slight, to say the least, timidly raised her hand elbow-high and stammered out, "Why do you people worship statues?"

No one laughed or acted amused. This is, I think, the question about Catholicism that everyone really wants to know the answer to, rather as we once wanted to know how exactly the astronauts went to the bathroom in space. I do not remember who answered—it was either Marianne, a refreshingly down-to-earth, even brassy, lay teacher, or the radiantly serene nun who ran the RCIA program, Sister Frances—or exactly what she said. In any case, someone explained that Catholics did not worship images, but honored (or reverenced, if you like) them as signs of the holy, as evidences of God and his saints. Images also function as aids to contemplation and to teaching, but above all as signs, as visible aspects of unseen things. Nor is a sign the same thing as a symbol: A graphic representation of flames is a symbol of fire, but smoke is a sign of it—something that is *of* the fire, but is not the fire itself.

This view of the way God's presence is visible in the world—the manner in which "Deus est in omnibus rebus, et intime"—is one of the fundamentals of Catholic teaching and is called sacramentality; and it (together with the way Catholicism alone among Western churches gives Mary her due) is among the faith's main attractions for me. So it was that an apparently naïve and foolish question posed by an uneducated woman who could barely speak my language got to the nub of everything I was trying to give voice to. I later came up with an analogy. In the sacramental view, we see God as we see light under a doorway. We do not directly see the source of light, the flame, but the sign of the light, not a symbol or words describing the light but its emanation, and that is as a fact to us.

The church's seven official sacraments are formally ordained rites that enact such signs. But properly seen, the world is abrim with sacraments, with signs, not only as phenomena and things but as persons. And I cannot but think that the woman who posed that question was, for me at least, a sign herself.

\*       \*       \*

About a year into the process of being received into the Catholic church, I went to Rome with my family. I had been to Rome once in my twenties and found it dirty, noisy, and hot—much as its critics have been saying for twenty-five hundred years or so—but now I began to see what my grandfather Clark saw. My touchstones there were less classical than his, but the distinction between these realms, between pagan and Christian, is not one that the city itself maintains. It is all here, from the Etruscans to the cellular phone, as jumbled and incoherent and tawdry as anyone's life fully recalled, the basement storeroom of Western civilization, a Gypsy encampment in a graveyard, the great and venerable scandal and folly that is Rome. Any Catholic who walks away from this place—our temples built on the ruins of other peoples' temples, and now themselves beginning to crumble—feeling triumphant and smug isn't paying attention.

Perhaps for clarity, and because I thought Andrew and Tessa might enjoy a break in the country, we went to Ostia. Ostia was the ancient port of Rome, where the Tiber met the sea. But in the sly way that natural and human history interact in Rome, over the course of a millennium or so, the river and the seashore moved, leaving Ostia marooned, a port without water. Today it is a remarkable well-preserved city of ruins, the lines of its avenues and alleys distinct, bordered with block after block of foundations and remnants of walls, columns, and stairs that go nowhere. There is enough here to imagine not just the fact of a city but something of its character and life: the houses, taverns, warehouses, inns, offices, chandlers and sailmakers, wine and oil merchants, customs houses; the sailors and transients and hustlers and slaves who poured through the streets.

Tessa found the amphitheater and struck poses on the stone stage apron. Andrew crawled among the ranks of seats and fallen barrels of columns, chasing lizards. On the way out we sat under a pine tree on one of the stone sarcophagi that are everywhere, scattered over the ground like washed-up freight, marble boxes incised with their customary wavy lines and cameos of dead gods. On a wall, perhaps ten feet away, I saw a marker in Latin, translated into Italian on a plaque beneath it. As far as I could make out—I had to use a dictionary and some books back in Rome to get the full story—it said that in this spot St. Augustine and his mother, Monica, had stayed while waiting for a ship to take them home to North Africa; and that before they could leave Monica fell ill and died in this place.

Augustine records this in some detail in his *Confessions*. It happened a few years after his conversion, after he had heard the child's voice that said, "Pick it up," and after he had been baptized by Ambrose in Milan. His mother had been with him all that time, and now that he had found his new life, it seemed to both of them it was time to go home; for Augustine to serve as a priest and later a bishop, and for Monica to enjoy the fruits of her old age, to enjoy the peace that came of her son no longer being a trial to her.

They were to be in Ostia for about two weeks, waiting for the ship, and they stayed in a house or an inn together with Adeodatus, Augustine's son by his concubine of pre-Christian days, whose name means "Given by God." Augustine and his mother passed those days in large part waiting and talking, "incumbentes ad quandam finestram unde hortus intra domum quae nos habebat prospectabatur, illic Ostia Tiberina," "leaning against the window, looking out into the garden of the house where we were staying, there in Ostia on the Tiber." In their talking they came to a kind of transfiguration, a vision launched upon but ultimately beyond words, in which everything in Ostia and in the world, in the past they had been recounting and in the present moment was entirely sacramental, was entirely his sign, his word "ut audiamus verbum eius non per linguam carnis neque vocem angeli nec per sonitum nubis nec per aenigma simultudinis sed ipsum quem in his amamus"—"so that we heard his word, not human tongues nor the voices of angels nor the sound of thunder nor any enigma of resemblance, but purely He Himself whom we love through these signs."

There seemed to be nothing more to say after that moment; indeed, Augustine's mother told him she now had everything she had wanted from life, his conversion and her peace. Then she fell ill, and at the sea's edge, where she had been waiting all that time, "ergo die nono aegritudinis suae quinquagensimo et sexto anno aetatis suae tricensimo et tertio aetatis meae anima illa religiosa et pia corpore soluta est"—"then in the ninth day of her sickness and the fifty-sixth year of her life and the thirty-third year of mine, that devout and holy soul was loosed from its body."

It seemed to me a sign in itself that my path had unexpectedly crossed Augustine's in this way. It is easier to want to make happenstance mean what we want it to mean than merely to let it be nothing more than a tap on the shoulder, a sign that at most says, "Here, pay attention." In any case, it made me think of my mother, whom I did not much think about at that time. My mother was in the fifth year of Alzheimer's disease when I was in Rome, and the thought of her was dreadful to me—not just the loss of her and the burden she would become, but the awful, trudging, incremental path her decline would take, as she was slowly flayed of her memory and her mind.

By the time you read this, she will doubtless be effectively dead to me, or rather I will be dead to her, for she will no longer know me. And she will ask as our old cousin Emerson did about Thoreau long after Thoreau was dead and Emerson himself had entered dementia: "What was the name of my best friend?" She will not know, and there will be no point, it will seem to us, in telling her.

After Ostia, after I came into the church, my mother and I reached an accommodation, one that had evaded us since I was a teenager and she could do nothing with me but put me into the hands of the woman who had nursed her ex-husband, my father, through his death. We talk every week—about the past, because my mother cannot remember what has just happened, but she still retains much of her life from thirty or forty years ago. I think in doing this we are doing something more valuable than passing the time with each other; I think we are tending and honoring the things we have loved, we are offering them our devotions as we do the saints and Mary the Mother of God.

Since I have been writing this book I have been asking her about the religious life of our family such as it is. She told me a few weeks ago, "Well, it wasn't about belief. It was about *going* to church. So I caused quite a stir when I went over to the Unitarians—because I wasn't in that family pew anymore," and I joined her in saying, "Second from the front on the left-hand side."

She stopped, and then she said, "Of course, a few years ago I started going back to the Episcopal church, to St. John's. It was mostly because of the prayer book, the beauty of it. The comfort of it."

I know this last part not to be true, and that is the way Alzheimer's is. What might have been or should have been insinuates itself into the histories that really took place. In fact, my mother has not been in a position to get out of the house to any church in several years, and the Episcopal church discontinued use of Thomas Cranmer's prayer book back in the 1970s. So she would be rather disappointed if she were to go to St. John's. It is better that she have "the comfort of it," as she does now, in the ruins of her mind, the Ostia in which she now passes her days.

After I became a Catholic, and as my mother's disease progressed, I often found myself wanting to take her the Eucharist; to send a priest, Catholic or Anglican, to her little apartment and give her communion. She has never asked for this and my presumption would not extend to actually arranging such a thing, although I still think of it often. But I have also learned that the church recognizes something called "the communion of desire": Those who hunger for the Eucharist but cannot receive it due to sickness or imprisonment or such circumstances receive it by a kind of proxy through those able to attend mass. Every mass enacts Christ's sacrifice for anyone who wants it, for "the beauty of it, the comfort of it." So I believe that my mother does receive communion after a fashion, and that she hears the liturgy said in an exquisite English that no one speaks anymore. That is the sign that we see between us, through the window, hanging over the garden, while the water is closing over the hulk of her memory, while we wait for her ship to come.

# SEVEN

I at last became a Catholic in 1997, at Easter. Along with fifty other converts, I took my first communion and was confirmed at St. James Cathedral during the Easter Vigil mass, late on the Saturday night before Easter Sunday. This is how, we were told, it was done in the earliest days of the church. We stood in the dark, listening to readings from Genesis through to the resurrection, and gradually, almost imperceptibly more and more candles were lit. Then we stood before Father Michael Ryan, the pastor of the cathedral, and Archbishop Thomas Murphy. Archbishop Murphy was dying of cancer; he would be buried in this very place only two and a half months later.

Normally, the archbishop would perform our confirmations, speaking words of committal to us and marking our foreheads with oil. But we had been told this would be done instead by Father Ryan: The archbishop was so weak, and the risk to him of infection in touching us so grave, that he would merely preside. But instead, the archbishop stood, beaming, and set his hand on each of our fifty heads. I was tired as I waited my turn. I had been in this church, late at night, for two hours already. I was not bored or unhappy or irritated, but neither was I going to have an epiphany or transfiguration here. I was only moved, turned a little from where I had been, quietly converted here and in a hundred inconsequential instances, rebound to what I had always been.

I reached the front of the line and Father Ryan told the archbishop my name, and then he raised his hand to my head and said the words. He was pallid and weathered in the way of the near-dead, but he smiled and I felt the pressure of his hand on my head. It was a hand reaching out of and through death to bring me into this new life. Love, aching and weary, was stronger than death after all.

\*　　\*　　\*

Andrew was baptized by Father Ryan in the full daylight of a Sunday morning a week later. Caroline and I stood on one side of the font, and his aunt, uncle, and maternal grandmother stood on the other. I held him, although at eighteen months, he was too big to be held on his back as baptized infants are. He looked busily around and when the water was poured on his head, he cried out with irritation, in a tone of affronted protest that made the congregation laugh. Then we moved down the aisle to the altar, where Andrew was to be anointed with oil, just as I had been in my confirmation. I was tense as I waited for Father Ryan to come around to us. Andrew's first outburst was more amusing than embarrassing, but, as his struggling in my arms seemed to indicate, he was now about to go into full toddler meltdown.

But when Father Ryan reached us, Andrew merely looked at him quizzically. Then Father Ryan signed Andrew's head with oil and said, "We now anoint with the holy chrism of salvation as Jesus Christ was anointed so you may live always as a member of His body," while Andrew continued placidly to regard him. We returned to our seats, where Andrew busied himself with the little pencils and pledge cards and such that are in the pew.

I would like to say that his sudden silence was more than a burst of composure, that it was an uncanny but real sign of his assent to the rite he was participating in. But that is too tidy and facile. The assent was mine, his mother's, and his godparents', given on his behalf; if he wants to, he may reaffirm it at his own confirmation. For now, however, he is oblivious to our assent and that is as it should be. He still dwells in the world before this one, and his self is subsumed in creation's "You." He is the first in his line for five hundred years to be baptized in the church of his oldest known forebears, and in him their great divorce is for a moment healed. Unlike his New England ancestors and their successors down to me, he is not troubled by whether he believes or by whether his belief is real and true in the eyes of men or God. He apprehends the world in its Franciscan "thisness," and his life takes its measure not on fact but on faith. He is two years old. He know nothing. He believes everything.

*          *          *

It is not that way with me. Scarcely four weeks after Easter, my doubt is at times a nagging itch. I do not doubt the things the church teaches and which I affirmed at Easter. They seem plausible enough, mysteries though they are. Rather, I doubt my assent to them, my continuing ability to hold them as I feel I ought to, to believe them aright. The church understands this: Its founder, the first pope, St. Peter, was the epitome of doubt. In speaking to Jesus himself, the best he could muster by way of a credo was, "I believe, Lord. Help my unbelief." That is why "religion" is "binding again"; that is why "conversion" is "turning"; they are not only movements but repetitive movements. Conversion and the practice of religion are the taking on of a perpetual labor as quotidian as housework. Faith is never complete, at rest in the same state, or located in the same place, because we are ourselves in motion. We are forever needing to turn and be turned toward it; to discover and be discovered by it.

Because I am a Catholic, the locus and center of my faith is the eucharist, the mass. To my formerly Protestant sensibility, the most outrageous dogma Catholicism propounds (besides, perhaps, what Protestants like to call "Mariolatry") is the real presence of Christ in the consecrated bread and wine at communion: that these elements are not merely symbols of Him in a commemoration of something He did two millennia ago, but *are* Him, become Him in a sacrifice identical with the Last Supper itself. In the Catholic sacramental world of signs, the mass is the ne plus ultra. So if I do not believe in that, the core of my faith is at stake. And, having been a Catholic for hardly a month, I was not sure, halfway through the mass, that I did believe it.

We had said the Sanctus, the great prayer that inaugurates the consecration, and at its end the congregation knelt for the consecration itself. As Father Ryan began to pray over the bread and wine, a feeling of dread began to overtake me, a fear that when those elements became God, I still would doubt that they were God. I was in a race with my disbelief, my lack of conviction, as the eucharistic prayer drew toward its climax. I felt harried and distracted, and that sense was not being ameliorated by the children in the pew behind me. They were talking—probably not loudly to anyone's ears but mine—and moving, apparently drawing or coloring in order to occupy themselves through the mass. I couldn't get a look at them, because they stayed mostly on the floor, hidden behind the wall of the pew back.

But that was neither here nor there. The children continued to draw and to talk, but the moment was upon me. Father Ryan raised the bread and then the wine—"*This* is my body," "*This* is my blood" —and the bells signifying the consecration rang, and the wafer hung in the air before me like a bone-white moon; and what, what, if anything did I believe?

I did not know. I had stopped breathing in the last few seconds and now I felt a little stunned, as though I had seen something very sudden and appalling and was still taking it in. And I began to think again and to wonder if I had any faith; or if, after all these years— from my first conversion and baptism thirty-five years before, through all my enthusiasms and agnosticisms—I had any business here at all.

The congregation had begun to rise, and I began to lift myself from my knees, scarcely aware of the people around me, sealed in the vacuum of my dread and fear. Then I heard a voice behind me, over the wall of the pew, but clear and bright as the tone of a tuning fork shimmering at my ear. It said, "*This* is for you," and after a pause it said it again, as if I might not have been listening: "*This* is for *you*."

I stopped breathing again, and then let my breath go and turned around. One of the children behind me had risen from the floor and was handing her mother the drawing she had evidently just completed. Her mother thanked her and remarked how pretty it was.

I knew it was only a coincidence, but I took this as a sign, as anything might be a sign, rightly seen, since "Deus est in omnibus rebus, et intime." You can make as much of it, or as little, as you like; only its being—its givenness occurring alongside one's own givenness—is of consequence. But I took it as sustenance, as Augustine took up the book and read. For almost two years, I had pursued altering the religious commitments not just of my own lifetime but of twenty generations, and throughout that journey I wondered whether I was right or *had* any right to do it. And a child's voice heard over a wall told me that, Of course, I did. That has been enough, most of the time, to keep me coming back to the mass; to go on putting my unbelief before the presence of God, my dogged faithlessness—my belief in nothing rather than something—before his Being. Sometimes I see what a small thing becoming bread and wine in the Eucharist must be for Him—a mere substantial sleight-of-hand—and what a great and, to us, unimaginable thing, is his becoming us, taking on our life, right down to our disbelief in Him taking it on—love so great it will nullify its own being in order that we may be.

*       *       *

Later, before I began to write this book, I went through my grandfather's things. I read his letters from the front during World War I, browsed in his scrapbooks, and reframed portraits of him, my grandmother, my mother, and uncles and aunts as children and as adults younger than I was now. I shelved his books: Sinclair Lewis, Conrad, Perry at the Pole, and a first edition of *The Beautiful and the Damned* by his childhood friend F. Scott Fitzgerald. Among these things were also his various genealogies of our family, a chronological list of Griggs ancestors going back to 1550 or so, which he updated every few years to include the latest grandchildren.

I also found a single picture of myself taken when I was about ten, about the time of my cousin's encounter with the wasps. I am standing on our dock on the lake, the house in the forest behind me on the shore, and I am holding a small fish—a perch, I think—still hooked and on the line, and I suppose I must have caught it. I do not look very pleased. The fish, after all, is wet, slippery, strangely legless and furless, and dead, or about to be dead. I am doing this to please my grandfather; no doubt he is doing it to please me. I wish now, now that I am nearly as old as he was when he took the photograph, that we had understood each other better.

That, for me, is the work of memory, and of this book—which, too, is a kind of devotion, the labor of binding back the self to its roots in blood and time, of keeping faith and taking meaning from the past that gave us life. You see, I worry about the past as I worry about death and the value of my existence, and in particular about the ongoing reality of the past and the persons who inhabited it. I worry, as I worry that there is no God, that their passing and the loss of the time in which they lived is proof that everything is annihilated, that nothing has a point, an end beyond merely ending.

Augustine said of finding his faith, "Ecce quantum spatiatus sum in memoria mea quaerens te domine et non te inveni extra eam"—"Behold, Lord, how I wandered in my memory seeking you, and I did not find you outside of it." This is how it is for me, wandering in the lives of my forebears as I have done here. I find in the incident and happenstance of the past the ground, the backlight, that illumines the present; the context, the frame, the picture window that makes the present moment mean and locates it in a larger reality that is the "you" to the present's "I." It is, finally, the love that wills that I, too, learn to love. That is the grace of memory.

My own life and history took me far away from my grandfather. For most of my life, I felt that his stance in relation to the world was passive, based on received wisdom, conformity, and tradition, whereas mine was active. I had gone on a quest to discover myself and the world, and I was sure I had found, if not ultimate truth, then something closer to it than did my grandfather, who was chained to the past. I had instead pursued transcendence—connecting myself, so I thought, to everything that *is* as opposed to *was*. I cut myself off not just from the world as it had been when I was small, but from the past entirely; from my grandfather's world, the world from which the blood that ran in my veins welled up. I did all this in pursuit of a world of my own making, in fulfillment of desire, which is, I suppose, another way of saying fulfillment of ache and emptiness with ache and emptiness.

My grandfather's way was to wait, to stare out across the lake and snap pictures of the sunsets. When his house burned down, I said to myself, "Well, what can you expect from this world?" But he simply built another house and went back to his picture-taking. Just as it had before, this seemed to please him immensely, as though everything he needed had already come to him or would come to him if he waited for it; if he merely attended to the fact of it, the ship that was for him would appear on the horizon and bear him away.

\*      \*      \*

The notion that our selves end at and with ourselves—that both in time and space who we are is constituted by what happens in our present orbit at the present time—seems extraordinarily limited, but is perhaps the logical outgrowth of our belief in the primacy of the individual. But it seems inarguable that we are at least in part the sum of our parts, and that some of those parts bear investigation. We place perhaps too much faith in the centrality of childhood, which is itself the time when we were most caught up in and dependent on faith. Childhood fascinates because it seems to be the moment of our creation, before which we did not exist. If, it seems logical, we could comprehend the moment and circumstances of our creation, we would truly understand ourselves; we would be, as individuals, in possession of the story of our origins rather than the myth the medievals had to settle for. Of course, the story never reveals itself in the way that we would like, and we are left with something less ample, less satisfying than myth. It is the same with nature, where we sense both our origin and our transcendence. I suppose this is why there is so much first-person writing about both childhood and about nature, and why these books often seem so much alike in their yearning, their sense of loss, their vague epiphanies. We are lost in our childhoods, in our aboriginal groves and forests.

That, at least, is how it was for me for much of the last thirty years, from the day my cousin met the wasps until a few years ago. I was trying to make a story for myself for much of that time, or at least a myth with some resonance, a net with which I could sift out the crucial facts of my life. Beside other tales, other myths, that myth—the story of my development, of my identity—looks a little tawdry, like something not quite worth the effort. It is a tale without a "you," in which relation and "beknowing" are confined to the psychological and epistemological self, its triumphs and afflictions.

Although this is a book about faith and religion, its point is not to promote conversion as the solution to my or anyone else's perceived problems. The use of religion as a vehicle for self-improvement strikes me, in fact, as antithetical—if unwittingly so—to the genuine labor of faith, for faith is not a solution but itself a problem, an encounter that offers no fix or cure or certitude but seeks a means to live with mystery. It seeks, in our time, to comprehend "the discovery we have made that we exist" not as an inexorable tragedy that leads to self-annihilation by unquenchable desire and labyrinthine solipsism, but as a sign of something more: that our being and our discovery of it are an analogy to God's being and self-regard and expression, which is to say, his love. Self-consciousness is a sign that God, too, dwells in us "et intime." It is both an affliction and the greatest gift of all. Religion is the hard and lifelong labor of using it well. Doubt does not negate faith, but affirms its difficulty, its arduousness, the toll of ache and fatigue it takes on the heart and the mind. Faith is not much different from work or love, from which life also grants us no rest.

Sometimes, we look up from that work, pausing to catch our breath in this labor which we can never see complete and which we therefore perdure in by faith, posing love and being against death and nothingness; and through the spaces between the fingers that mop our brows and clear the dust from our eyes, we glimpse the world before this one, the tale it told when we were all very young: how creation is the utterance of its creator, how it hums and shimmers with signs of Him. The highest end of our lives is to attend to those signs, those rustlings in the trees that are intimations of his being, his love. We cannot know when or where or how they will come. We can only wait; and so it is that we live in the past, among and with the dead; without them we are lost. So we wait in the overgrown boneyard that is our home, amidst the ashes of our grandfathers' houses. Yet they do come, though it is futile to wish for them; we can scarcely see them, they are more than we know how to desire.

*September 15, 1998*
*Feast of the Mater Dolorosa*
*Seattle*

# A NOTE ON SOURCES

This book makes no claim to be a scholarly work, although I have taken great care to ensure it is historically accurate. The conclusions drawn are, for better or worse, my own, but I also owe a great debt to the following scholars, whose work I have relied upon and been influenced by. I recommend them to readers interested in pursuing these subjects further, and I trust I have not distorted their work here.

On the Middle Ages and the English Reformation: Patrick Collinson, Eamon Duffy, Etienne Gilson, Christopher Haigh, Jacques Le Goff, Diarmaid MacCulloch, Steven Ozment, J. J. Scarisbrick, and R. W. Southern.

On Puritanism and New England culture: David Cressy, Andrew Delbanco, Stephen Foster, David D. Hall, Edmund S. Morgan, and especially the late Perry Miller.

On the Transcendentalists and the nineteenth century: Charles Capper, Peter Gay, Perry Miller, Hershel Parker, and Robert Richardson. I also found Robert Hudspeth's multivolume edition of Margaret Fuller's letters indispensable.

On theology: Richard P. McBrien's *Catholicism* is an excellent summation of Roman Catholic theology and doctrine. My own theological education has been greatly enriched by the work of Karl Rahner and Hans Urs von Balthasar, insofar as I have been able to comprehend their admittedly complex thought. Edward T. Oakes's *Pattern of Redemption* is an excellent overview of the latter.

# ACKNOWLEDGMENTS

This is a book built on research, and my debt to the following institutions is inestimable: the Beinecke Library at Yale University; the Houghton Library at Harvard University; the New York Public Library; the Seattle Public Library; and the University of Washington Library.

I also want to thank the following people for their support and forbearance both in the writing of this book and in my own journey of faith: Marianne Cote; Sallie Gouverneur; Colleen Mohyde; Father Michael Ryan; Britton Steele; Sister Frances Wink; and George Witte. Finally, this book, like all my work, owes its existence to the love and understanding of my family: my children, Tessa and Andrew, and my wife, Caroline, who is to me both grace and reason for faith.